STUDENT GUIDE AND REVIEW MANUAL

John K. Harris

COST ACCOUNTING
A Managerial Emphasis

Second Canadian Edition

Charles T. Horngren
George Foster
Srikant M. Datar
Howard D. Teall

Prentice Hall Canada Inc.
Scarborough, Ontario

Prentice-Hall, Inc., Upper Saddle River, New Jersey
Prentice-Hall International (UK) Limited, London
Prentice-Hall of Australia, Pty. Limited, Sydney
Prentice-Hall Hispanoamericana, S.A., Mexico City
Prentice-Hall of India Private Limited, New Delhi
Prentice-Hall of Japan, Inc., Tokyo
Simon & Schuster Southeast Asia Private Limited, Singapore
Editora Prentice-Hall do Brasil, Ltda., Rio de Janeiro

ISBN 0-13-040128-5

Vice-President and Editorial Director: Patrick Ferrier
Senior Developmental Editor: Lesley Mann
Production Editor: Nicole Mellow
Production Coordinator: Deborah Starks

Original U.S. edition published by Prentice-Hall, Inc., Upper Saddle River, New Jersey, © 2000, 1997

1 2 3 4 5   04 03 02 01 00

Printed and bound in Canada.

Visit the Prentice Hall Canada Web site! Send us your comments, browse our catalogues, and more. **www.phcanada.com**. Or reach us through e-mail at **collegeinfo_pubcanada@prenhall.com**.

Contents

Introduction

This Student Guide and Review Manual is a self-study aid to accompany the 2nd Canadian edition of *Cost Accounting: A Managerial Emphasis*, by Horngren, Foster, Datar, and Teall. It is intended to assist you in two ways: (1) by reinforcing and clarifying your understanding of the textbook material and (2) by helping you to review for exams quickly and effectively. I designed the Student Guide to provide maximum benefit from your study time.

Each Student Guide chapter has the following sections:

- **Chapter Overview** is a one-paragraph description of the textbook chapter.
- **Chapter Highlights** is a comprehensive summary of the chapter presented in an easy-to-read paragraph style, with the textbook "Terms to Learn" in bold type.
- **Featured Exercise** covers key points in the textbook assignment material.
- **Review Questions and Exercises** consist of completion statements, true-false and multiple choice questions, and short exercises. They challenge you to apply the concepts in the chapter. Most chapters include at least five questions/exercises from the Certified Public Accountant (CPA) and Certified Management Accountant (CMA) exams.
- **Answers to Review Questions and Exercises** allow you to check your work. In addition to the basic answers, this section provides concise explanations for each of the false statements and the multiple-choice answers, and easy-to-follow solutions to the exercises.

How to Use the Student Guide

I recommend a five-step approach for using the Student Guide with the textbook:

1. Study the chapter in the textbook and solve the Problem for Self-Study included there.
2. Read the Chapter Overview and Chapter Highlights sections in the Student Guide. Because the Chapter Highlights refer to only *the most essential textbook exhibits and examples* (an average of three per chapter), the Student Guide can almost be used in a stand-alone way at this stage of your study.
3. Prepare your solution to the Featured Exercise in the Student Guide and compare it to the solution provided there.
4. Answer the Review Questions and Exercises in the Student Guide and compare your answers with those provided at the end of the chapter. *(Check Figures for the exercises are at the end of the Student Guide.)*
   - Resist the temptation to look at the answers before preparing your own! This approach keeps you from developing a false sense of confidence about your knowledge of the material.
   - When your answers to an exercise do not agree with the Check Figures, first try reworking the exercise before you look at the solution.
5. Solve the homework problems assigned by your professor.

You can review for exams quickly and effectively with the Student Guide. Concentrate on the Featured Exercises as well as the Review Questions and Exercises that you found most difficult.

As you study cost accounting, keep in mind that there is no substitute for hard work and a desire to learn. These qualities are key to your success.

Acknowledgments

For ideas and assistance, I am indebted to the textbook authors, Jim Payne and Karen Cravens of the University of Tulsa, Dean Graber of Northeastern State University, Richard Metcalf of the University of Arizona, numerous students (especially Sheryl Powers of the University of Tulsa), Craig Palmateer of Mark IV Automotive, and Annie Todd of Prentice Hall. I thank Mary Nelson for her expertise in preparing the camera-ready copy. I also thank the American Institute of Certified Public Accountants and the Institute of Certified Management Accountants for permission to use their professional examination questions.

John K. Harris

CHAPTER 1

The Accountant's Role in the Organization

> If you have not already read the Introduction, p. vii, do so now. It describes the purposes and contents of the Student Guide and recommends a five-step approach for using the Student Guide with the textbook.

Chapter Overview

Welcome to the study of cost accounting. This introductory chapter emphasizes the intertwining roles of managers and accountants in planning and controlling the operations of organizations. Unlike the remainder of the textbook, this chapter has no "number crunching". Its main purpose is to provide a framework for understanding cost accounting.

Chapter Highlights

1. Accounting systems provide information for five major purposes: (a) formulating overall strategies and long-range plans, (b) resource allocation such as product and customer emphasis and pricing, (c) cost planning and cost control of operations and activities, (d) performance measurement and evaluation of people, and (e) meeting external regulatory and legal reporting requirements. Purposes (a) through (d) are **management accounting**. Purpose (e) is **financial accounting**.

- *Management accounting* measures and reports financial and nonfinancial information that helps managers make decisions to fulfill the goals of an organization. Management accounting (a) emphasizes the future, (b) aims to influence the behaviour of managers and other employees, and (c) is not particularly constrained by generally accepted accounting principles (GAAP).
- *Financial accounting* measures and records business transactions and provides financial statements—the balance sheet, income statement, and statement of cash flows—that are based on GAAP.

2. **Cost accounting** provides information for both management accounting and financial accounting. Cost accounting measures and reports financial and nonfinancial information related to the acquisition and consumption of resources by an organization. Cost accounting includes those parts of management accounting and financial accounting where cost information is collected or analyzed.

3. **Cost management** involves the activities of managers in short-run and long-run planning and control of costs. For example, rearranging the production-floor layout might reduce manufacturing costs, or additional product design costs might be incurred in an effort to increase revenues and profits.

4. The **value chain** is the sequence of six business functions in which usefulness (value to the customer) is added to the products or services of an organization. These business functions are **research and development (R&D); design of products, services, or processes; production; marketing; distribution; and customer service.** Managers in each of these parts of the value chain are customers of management accounting information. Rather than proceeding sequentially through the value chain, though, organizations can realize important gains when various parts of the value chain work together. For example, additional spending on R&D and product design might be more than offset by lower costs of production and customer service.

5. Management accounting facilitates **planning** and **control**. Planning is deciding on organization goals, predicting results under various alternative ways of achieving those

goals, and then deciding how to attain the designated goals. Control includes both actions that implement the planning decisions and performance evaluation of the related personnel and operations. Control in one accounting period is linked to planning for the next period by means of **feedback**. Managers use feedback to examine past performance and systematically explore alternative ways of making better-informed decisions in the future.

6. A well-conceived plan includes enough flexibility so that managers can seize opportunities unforeseen at the time the plan is formulated. In no case should control mean that managers cling to a preexisting plan when unfolding events indicate that action not encompassed by the original plan offers better results for the organization.

7. Budgeting is essential for planning and control. A **budget** is the quantitative expression of a proposed plan of action and is an aid to coordination and implementation of the plan. A key input used in developing budgets is the financial and nonfinancial information that has been routinely recorded in the management accounting system.

8. Three important guidelines help management accountants provide the most value in performing their problem solving, scorekeeping, and attention-directing roles:

a. *Employ the* **cost-benefit approach.** This approach helps managers choose among alternative accounting systems. As an example, consider budgeting systems as economic goods. The *expected costs* of a proposed budgeting system (such as personnel, software, and training) should be compared with its *expected benefits*, which are the collective decisions of managers that will better attain the organization's goals. In particular, measurement of the expected benefits is seldom easy.

b. *Give full recognition to technical and behavioural considerations.* A management accounting system should have two simul-taneous missions for providing information: (i) to help managers make wise economic decisions (the technical mission) and (ii) to help motivate managers and other employees to strive for the organization's goals (the behavioural mission). Managers and accountants need to understand that planning and control are primarily human activities; the emphasis needs to be on how to help individuals do their jobs better.

c. *Use different costs for different purposes.* To illustrate this guideline, consider the question of how much cost a manufacturing company will assign to each finished unit of one of its products. For the purpose of preparing financial statements under GAAP, only the manufacturing costs are assigned to the product. For the purpose of determining a long-run selling price, however, costs from all parts of the value chain (not just production) are assigned to the product.

9. Most organizations distinguish between **line management** and **staff management**. Line management is directly responsible for attaining the goals of the organization. Staff management provides advice and assistance to line management. When organizations rely on teams for attaining their goals, the traditional distinction between line and staff management becomes less clear-cut.

10. The **chief financial officer (CFO)**, a staff management function, is responsible for overseeing the financial operations of the organization, which typically include controllership, treasury, risk management, taxes, and internal audit. The **controller**, also a staff management function, is the financial executive primarily responsible for both management accounting and financial accounting. In performing the problem-solving and attention-directing roles, the controller "controls" by exerting an influence that helps managers make better-informed decisions.

11. Management accountants perform three important roles: **problem solving, scorekeeping, and attention directing**. Problem solving uses comparative analysis to identify the best

alternatives in relation to the organization's goals. Scorekeeping entails accumulating data and reporting reliable results to all levels of management. Attention directing helps managers focus on opportunities that can add value to the organization.

12. Accountants consistently rank high in public opinion surveys on the ethics exhibited by members of different professions. Professional accounting organizations such as the **Society of Management Accountants of Canada (SMAC)**, the largest association of management accountants in Canada, play an important role in promoting high ethical standards. For example, the SMAC has issued a Code of Professional Ethics. EXHIBIT 1-5, text p. 12, gives the SMAC's guidance on ethical issues.

13. The design and operation of management accounting systems are shaped by five evolving management themes: *customer satisfaction is priority one, key success factors (cost, quality, time, innovation), total value-chain analysis, continuous improvement,* and *dual external/internal focus.* Collectively, these five themes (and new ones that may evolve in the future) direct the organization toward attracting and retaining profitable customers who are satisfied.

Featured Exercise

Exon Tackle Company manufactures a wide range of fishing equipment and supplies for the retail market. In the current fiscal year, Exon incurred the costs described below. For each of these costs, indicate the applicable part of the value chain by putting the identifying number in the space provided.

Value Chain of Business Functions

1. Research and development
2. Design of products, services, or processes
3. Production
4. Marketing
5. Distribution
6. Customer service

___ a. Cost of repairing reels that malfunctioned during the warranty period.
___ b. Cost of hooks used in making lures.
___ c. Salary of a mechanical engineer working on the basic concept for the next generation of ultra-light fishing rods.
___ d. Cost of overnight delivery of rods and reels to winter boat shows.
___ e. Cost of running advertisements in fishing magazines.
___ f. Cost of printing operating instructions to be packaged with a new model of trolling motor.

Solution (on next page)

Solution

a. 6 c. 1 e. 4
b. 3 d. 5 f. 3

Review Questions and Exercises

This section is designed to help determine how well you have mastered the textbook material. Try to answer all of these questions and exercises without using your textbook or the Chapter Highlights in the Student Guide. *In answering the Review Questions and Exercises, be sure to follow Step 4 of the study approach recommended in the Introduction, p. vii.*

Completion Statements

Fill in the blank(s) to complete each statement.

1. _____ measures and reports financial and nonfinancial information related to the acquisition and consumption of resources by an organization.

2. _____ involves the activities of managers in short-run and long-run planning and control of costs.

3. Deciding on organization goals, predicting results under various alternative ways of achieving these goals, and then deciding how to attain the designated goals is called _____.

4. A _____ is a quantitative expression of a proposed plan of action and is an aid to coordination and implementation of the plan.

5. Name the six business functions in the value chain in their sequential order: _____

_____

_____

_____

6. The _____ approach helps managers choose among alternative accounting systems.

True-False

Indicate whether each statement is true (T) or false (F).

____ 1. Management accounting is not particularly constrained by generally accepted accounting principles.

____ 2. Cost accounting provides information for management accounting but not for financial accounting.

____ 3. Control is defined as the process of setting maximum limits on expenditures.

____ 4. Managers use feedback to examine past performance and systematically explore alternative ways of making better-informed decisions in the future.

____ 5. The scorekeeping role of management accountants uses comparative analysis to identify the best alternatives in relation to the organization's goals.

____ 6. Managers should proceed sequentially through the value chain of business functions.

____ 7. The CFO, a line management function, has the responsibility for overseeing the financial operations of the organization.

Multiple Choice

Select the best answer to each question.

___ 1. Control includes:
a. deciding on organization goals.
b. implementing the planning decisions.
c. deciding how to attain the desired results.
d. preparing budgets.

___ 2. The primary responsibility of the controller is:
a. risk management.
b. overseeing the financial operations of the organization.
c. management accounting and financial accounting.
d. obtaining short-term and long-term financing.

___ 3. Maintaining records on traffic tickets issued by the city of Toronto is performing what management accounting role?
a. Scorekeeping
b. Attention directing
c. Problem solving
d. Internal auditing

___ 4. One of the management themes shaping the design and operation of management accounting systems is key success factors. Which of the following *is not* a key success factor?
a. Time
b. Value-chain and supply-chain analysis
c. Cost
d. Innovation

Exercises

1. Define *management accounting* and *financial accounting*. Then specify three major distinctions between these terms.

_____

_____

_____

_____

_____

_____

_____

_____

_____

_____

2. For each of the following activities, identify what role is being performed by the management accountant.

PS: Problem solving
SK: Scorekeeping
AD: Attention directing

____ a. Interpreting a monthly report that compares actual and budgeted fuel consumption for each major building at a large university.

____ b. Recording the cost of a sewer project on the books of the construction company.

____ c. Analyzing the costs and benefits to a school district that is considering the purchase of new school buses.

____ d. Preparing the monthly statement for a customer.

3. For each of the following actions by companies, identify the applicable management theme.

CS: Customer satisfaction is priority one
KSF: Key success factors (cost, quality, time, innovation)
TVC: Total value-chain analysis
CI: Continuous improvement
DF: Dual external/internal focus

____ a. Company W periodically reports a representative sample of its major competitors' selling prices in addition to its own selling prices.

____ b. Company X monitors the number and nature of customer complaints on a customer-by-customer basis.

____ c. Company Y reports how long it takes a new product to be introduced to the market after the initial concept for the product is approved by management.

____ d. Company Z reduces the budgeted labour cost of a product by 1% each month when evaluating the performance of a plant manager.

Answers to Chapter 1 Review Questions and Exercises

Completion Statements

1. Cost accounting
2. Cost management
3. planning
4. budget
5. research and development (R&D); design of products, services, or processes; production; marketing; distribution; customer service
6. cost-benefit

True-False

1. T
2. F   Cost accounting provides information for *both* management accounting and financial accounting. Cost accounting involves those parts of management accounting and financial accounting where cost information is collected and analyzed.
3. F   Control has two aspects: (i) actions that implement the planning decisions and (ii) performance evaluation of the related personnel and operations.
4. T
5. F   The statement describes the *problem-solving role* of management accountants, not the *scorekeeping role*. The scorekeeping role entails accumulating data and reporting reliable results to all levels of management.

6. F Rather than proceeding sequentially through the value chain, organizations can realize important gains when various parts of the value chain work together. For example, additional spending on R&D and product design might be more than offset by lower costs of production and customer service.

7. F The CFO is a *staff management* function, not a *line management* function. The CFO has the responsibility for overseeing the financial operations of the organization, which typically include controllership, treasury, risk management, taxes, and internal audit. Staff management provides advice and assistance to line management. Line management is directly responsible for attaining the goals of the organization.

Multiple Choice

1. b Control includes both actions that implement the planning decisions and performance evaluation of the related personnel and operations. Answers (a), (c) and (d) are aspects of planning.

2. c The controller is the financial executive primarily responsible for both management accounting and financial accounting.

3. a The scorekeeping role is accumulating data and reporting reliable results to all levels of management.

4. b There are four key success factors: cost, quality, time, and innovation. Value-chain and supply-chain analysis is another management theme shaping the design and operation of management accounting systems.

Exercise 1

Management accounting measures and reports financial and nonfinancial information that helps managers make decisions to fulfill the goals of an organization. Financial accounting measures and records business transactions and provides financial statements that are based on generally accepted accounting principles (GAAP). Three distinctions between management accounting and financial accounting are:

a. Management accounting focuses on internal reporting to managers, whereas financial accounting focuses on external reporting to investors government authorities, and other outside parties.

b. Management accounting places emphasis on the future (budgeting) and on influencing the behaviour of managers and other employees. Financial accounting places emphasis on reporting transactions that have occurred.

c. Management accounting is not nearly as constrained by GAAP as is financial accounting. As a result, management accounting is more wide-ranging. It more extensively embraces such topics as developing and implementing strategies, planning and control, and collecting and using nonfinancial information.

Exercise 2

a. AD   b. SK   c. PS   d. SK

Exercise 3

a. DF   b. CS   c. KSF   d. CI

An Introduction to Cost Terms and Purposes

Chapter Overview

This chapter introduces the basic terminology of cost accounting. Communication among managers is greatly facilitated by having a common understanding of the meaning of cost terms and concepts. The chapter also illustrates a major theme of the textbook: using different costs for different purposes.

Chapter Highlights

1. Accountants define **cost** as a resource sacrificed or forgone to achieve a specific purpose. For example, it might *cost* $3,000 per month to rent a building. To guide their decisions, managers often want to know how much a particular thing costs. This "thing" is called a **cost object**, anything for which a separate measurement of costs is desired. In the following questions, the cost object is in italics: What selling price should be charged for a *product*? Which *machine* is the least expensive to operate?

2. Costing systems account for costs in two basic stages. The first stage is **cost accumulation**, the collection of cost data in some organized way by means of an accounting system. The second stage is **cost assignment**, a general term that encompasses both (a) tracing accumulated costs to a cost object and (b) allocating accumulated costs to a cost object.

3. A key question in cost assignment is whether costs have a direct or an indirect relationship to a particular cost object.

- The **direct costs of a cost object** are the costs that relate to the particular cost object and can be *traced* to it in an economically feasible (cost-effective) way. The term **cost tracing** describes the assignment of direct costs to the particular cost object.

- The **indirect costs of a cost object** are the costs that relate to the particular cost object but cannot be traced to it in an economically feasible way. The term *cost allocation* describes the assignment of indirect costs to the particular cost object.

Several factors affect the classification of a cost as direct or indirect: the materiality of the cost in question, available information-gathering technology, design of operations, and contractual arrangements.

4. Consider this question: Is a company president's salary a direct cost or an indirect cost? The answer is that *it depends on the choice of the cost object*. For example, if the cost object is the company as a whole, the salary is a direct cost because it can be *traced* to the cost object. But if the cost object is one of the company's departments, the salary is an indirect cost because it can be *allocated* (but not traced) to the cost object.

5. Two basic types of cost-behaviour patterns are found in accounting systems.

- A **variable cost** changes *in total* in proportion to changes in the related level of total activity or volume. A variable cost does not change *on a per unit basis* when the related level of total activity or volume changes.

- A **fixed cost** remains unchanged *in total* for a given time period despite wide changes in the related level of total activity or volume. A fixed cost increases/decreases *on a per unit basis* when the related level of total activity or volume decreases/increases.

Costs are variable or fixed *with respect to a specific cost object* and *for a given time pe-*

riod. **A relevant range** is the span of activity or volume in which a specific relationship between the level of activity or volume and the cost in question is valid.

6. A **cost driver** is a factor (such as the level of activity or volume) that causes costs to increase or decrease (over a given time period). In other words, a cause-and-effect relationship exists between a change in the level of activity or volume and a change in the level of the total costs of that cost object.

- The cost driver of variable costs is the level of activity or volume whose change causes these costs to change proportionately. For example, the number of trucks assembled is a cost driver of the cost of steering wheels for the trucks.
- Fixed costs have no cost driver in the short run but may have a cost driver in the long run. For example, the equipment and staff costs of testing a product typically are fixed in the short run with respect to changes in the volume of production. In the long run, however, the company will increase or decrease these costs to the levels needed to support future production levels.

7. Accounting systems typically report both *total costs* and **unit costs** (also called **average costs**). A unit cost is computed by dividing some amount of total costs by the related number of units. Unit costs are often used in financial reports. For many decisions, however, *managers should think in terms of total costs rather than unit costs* because fixed costs per unit change when the related level of total volume changes. Unit costs, therefore, should be interpreted with caution if they include a fixed-cost component. The university social club example, text pp. 34-35 illustrates this important point.

8. Companies in the manufacturing, merchandising, and service sectors of the economy are frequently referred to in the study of cost accounting.

- **Manufacturing-sector companies** purchase materials and components and convert them into finished goods. These companies typically have three types of inventory: **direct materials inventory, work-in-process inventory,** and **finished goods inventory.**
- **Merchandise-sector companies** purchase and then sell tangible products without changing their basic form. These companies have one type of inventory called *merchandise inventory*.
- **Service-sector companies** provide services or intangible products—for example, legal advice or an audit. These companies do not have an inventory of items for sale.

9. For companies with inventories, generally accepted accounting principles distinguish between **inventoriable costs** and **period costs.**

- Inventoriable costs are all of the costs of a product that are regarded as an asset when they are incurred and become cost of goods sold when the product is sold. *For manufacturing companies, all of the manufacturing costs are inventoriable costs.* For merchandising companies, inventoriable costs are the costs of purchasing merchandise. Because service companies have no inventories, they have no inventoriable costs.
- Period costs are all of the costs in the income statement other than cost of goods sold. Period costs are expenses of the period in which they are incurred.

10. Three terms are widely used in describing manufacturing costs. In the following definitions, "cost object" refers to work in process or finished goods.

- **Direct material costs** are the acquisition costs of all materials that eventually become part of the cost object and that can be traced to it in an economically feasible way.
- **Direct manufacturing labour costs** include the compensation of all manufacturing la-bor that can be traced to the cost object in an economically feasible way.

- **Indirect manufacturing costs** (also called **manufacturing overhead costs** or **factory overhead costs**) are all of the manufacturing costs that are part of the cost object but that cannot be traced to it in an economically feasible way. Examples include power, indirect materials, indirect manufacturing labour, plant insurance, plant amortization, and compensation of plant managers.

11. In the income statement of a manufacturing company, cost of goods sold is computed as follows (figures assumed):

Beginning finished goods	$ 51,000
Add cost of goods manufactured	800,000
Cost of goods available for sale	851,000
Deduct ending finished goods	57,000
Cost of goods sold	$794,000

The line item, **cost of goods manufactured**, refers to the cost of all goods completed during the accounting period. Cost of goods manufactured is often computed in a supporting schedule to the income statement (figures assumed).

Beginning direct materials	$ 6,000
Add purchases of direct materials	110,000
Direct materials available for use	116,000
Deduct ending direct materials	5,000
Direct materials used	111,000
Add direct manufacturing labour	42,000
Add indirect manufacturing costs	80,000
Manufacturing costs incurred during the period	233,000
Add beginning work in process	12,000
Total manufacturing cost to account for	245,000
Deduct ending work in process	17,000
Cost of goods manufactured	$228,000

12. Two terms used in manufacturing costing systems are **prime costs** and **conversion costs**.

- Prime costs are all of the direct manufacturing costs. Under the three-part classification of manufacturing costs in paragraph 10, prime costs are equal to direct material costs plus direct manufacturing labour costs. In cases where other direct manufacturing cost categories are used, they too are prime costs. For example, power costs could be categorized as a direct cost if the power is metred in specific areas of a plant that are dedicated to the manufacturing of separate products.

- Conversion costs are all of the manufacturing costs other than direct material costs; they are incurred *to transform direct materials into finished goods*. Under the three-part classification of manufacturing costs, conversion costs are equal to direct manufacturing labour costs plus indirect manufacturing costs. Consider this question: Could a company's conversion costs be equal to its indirect manufacturing costs? The answer is *yes* only if the company does not classify any manufacturing cost other than materials as a direct cost. For example, in a highly automated plant, it may not be cost effective to trace labour costs directly to products.

13. All manufacturing labour compensation, except for direct labour and managers' salaries, is usually classified as indirect labour costs—a major component of manufacturing overhead. Two main categories of indirect labour in manufacturing and service companies are **overtime premium** and **idle time**. Overtime premium consists of wages paid to all of the workers (both direct labour and indirect labour) in *excess* of their straight-time wage rates. Overtime premium is classified as overhead when the overtime is attributable to the heavy overall volume of work. If a particular job, such as a rush order, is the sole reason for the overtime, the overtime premium is classified as a direct cost of that job. Idle time consists of wages paid to all of the workers (both direct and indirect labour) for unproductive time caused by such things as lack of orders, machine breakdowns, material shortages, and poor scheduling.

14. Some manufacturing companies classify payroll fringe benefit costs of direct labour as overhead cost, whereas others classify them as direct labour cost. The latter approach is preferable because these payroll fringe benefit

costs are a fundamental aspect of acquiring the labour services. To prevent disputes about cost items such as payroll fringe benefits, training, overtime premium, idle time, vacation pay, and sick leave, contracts and laws should be as specific as feasible regarding definitions and measurements. The example, text p. 45, shows that the classification of payroll fringe benefits can be important for income tax purposes.

15. An important theme of the textbook is *using different costs for direct purposes*. For example, managers can assign different costs to a product depending on their purpose. A **product cost** is the sum of the costs assigned to a product for a specific purpose, such as (a) preparing financial statements for external reporting under generally accepted accounting principles (GAAP), (b) contracting with government agencies, or (c) pricing and product-emphasis decisions. A product cost includes only inventoriable costs in the financial statements based on GAAP. A product cost includes a broader set of costs for reimbursement under a government contract, or a still broader set of costs for pricing and product-emphasis decisions.

Featured Exercises

1. Whitaker Company's relevant range is between 8,000 units and 16,000 units. If 10,000 units are produced, variable costs are $200,000 and fixed costs are $450,000, Assuming production increases to 15,000 units, compute (a) total variable costs, (b) variable costs per unit, and (c) fixed costs per unit.

Solution

a. Variable costs per unit = $200,000 ÷ 10,000 = $20
    Total variable costs = $20 × 15,000 = $300,000
b. Variable costs per unit = $300,000 ÷ 15,000 = $20
c. Fixed costs per unit = $450,000 ÷ 15,000 = $30

---

2. The following data pertain to Thorpe Company's operations for January of the current year:

Inventories	Beginning	Ending
Direct materials	$18,000	$15,000
Work in process	9,000	6,000
Finished goods	27,000	36,000

Additional cost information for January is direct materials purchased $42,000, direct manufacturing labour $30,000, manufacturing overhead $40,000.

Compute cost of goods manufactured for January.

Solution

Direct material used, ($18,000 + $42,000) − $15,000	$ 45,000
Direct manufacturing labour	30,000
Manufacturing overhead	40,000
Manufacturing costs incurred during the period	115,000
Add beginning work-in-process inventory	9,000
Total manufacturing costs to account for	124,000
Deduct ending work-in-process inventory	6,000
Cost of goods manufactured	$118,000

Review Questions and Exercises

Completion Statements

Fill in the blank(s) to complete each statement.

1. If a manager wants to determine how much it cost to operate the Shipping Department last month, the Shipping Department is the _____ _____.

2. For a given cost object, _____ costs are traced to it and _____ costs are allocated to it.

3. The span of activity or volume in which a specific relationship between the level of activity or volume and the cost in question is valid is called a _____.

4. A _____ is a factor, such as the level of activity or volume, that causes costs to change (over a given time period).

5. All of the costs of a product that are regarded as an asset when they are incurred and become cost of goods sold when the product is sold are called _____ costs.

6. _____ costs are all of the costs in the income statement other than cost of goods sold.

7. Indirect manufacturing costs are also known as_____ costs.

8. _____ costs are incurred to transform direct materials into finished goods.

9. Different costs are assigned to products for different purposes. Three of these purposes are:

_____

_____

_____ .

True-False

Indicate whether each statement is true (T) or false (F).

____ 1. A cost object is a target level of costs to be achieved.

____ 2. Cost accumulation is a general term that encompasses both tracing costs to a cost object and allocating costs to a cost object.

____ 3. A given cost item can be a direct cost of one cost object and an indirect cost of another cost object.

____ 4. When graphed on a per unit basis, both variable costs and fixed costs are linear within the relevant range.

____ 5. For a manufacturer of soft drinks, television advertising and amortization on bottle-capping machines are period costs.

____ 6. In the income statement of a manufacturing company, cost of goods manufactured refers to the goods brought to completion, whether they were started before or during the current accounting period.

____ 7. The concept of inventoriable costs is applicable to manufacturing companies and merchandising companies but not to service companies.

____ 8. Manufacturing costs incurred during the accounting period minus the decrease in work-in-process inventory during the period is equal to cost of goods manufactured.

____ 9. If a manufacturing plant becomes highly automated, the traditional three-part classification of manufacturing costs might not be used.

____ 10. It is preferable to classify payroll fringe benefit costs of direct manufacturing labour as a manufacturing overhead cost.

____ 11. For long-run pricing and product-emphasis decisions, a product's cost includes a set of costs much broader than inventoriable costs.

Multiple Choice

Select the best answer to each question. Space is provided for computations after the quantitative questions.

____ 1. (CMA adapted) A fixed cost that would be considered a direct cost is:
a. a controller's salary if the cost object is a unit of product.
b. the cost of renting a warehouse to store inventory if the cost object is the Purchasing Department.
c. an order clerk's salary if the cost object is the Purchasing Department.
d. the cost of electricity if the cost object is the Internal Audit Department.

____ 2. Booth Company has total fixed costs of $64,000 if 8,000 units are produced. The relevant range is 8,000 units to 16,000 units. If 10,000 units are produced, fixed costs are:
a. $80,000 in total.
b. $8 per unit.
c. $48,000 in total.
d. $6.40 per unit.

____ 3. In general, the costs that can be most reliably predicted are:
a. fixed costs per unit.
b. total costs per unit.
c. total variable costs.
d. variable costs per unit.

4. Oxley Company has total variable costs of $120,000 if 15,000 units are produced. The relevant range is 10,000 units to 20,000 units. If 12,000 units are produced, variable costs are:
   a. $10 per unit.
   b. $120,000 in total.
   c. $8 per unit.
   d. $90,000 in total.

5. (CPA adapted) The monthly cost of renting a manufacturing plant is:
   a. a prime cost and an inventoriable cost.
   b. a prime cost and a period cost.
   c. a conversion cost and an inventoriable cost.
   d. a conversion cost and a period cost.

6. (CPA adapted) Anthony Company has budgeted its cost of goods sold at $4,000,000, including fixed costs of $800,000. The variable cost of goods sold is expected to be 75% of revenues. Budgeted revenues are:
   a. $4,266,667.
   b. $4,800,000.
   c. $5,333,333.
   d. $6,400,000.

7. (CPA) For the year 1999, the gross margin of Dumas Company is $96,000; the cost of goods manufactured is $340,000; the beginning inventories of work in process and finished goods are $28,000 and $45,000, respectively; and the ending inventories of work in process and finished goods are $38,000 and $52,000, respectively. The revenues of Dumas Company for 1999 are:
   a. $419,000.
   b. $429,000.
   c. $434,000.
   d. $436,000.

8. Using the traditional three-part classification of manufacturing costs, prime costs and conversion costs have the common component of:
   a. direct material costs.
   b. direct manufacturing labour costs.
   c. variable manufacturing overhead costs.
   d. fixed manufacturing overhead costs.

9. An assembly worker at a manufacturing company earns $12 per hour for straight time and $18 per hour for time over 40 hours per week. In a given week, the assembler worked 47 hours. The overtime premium for the week is:
   a. $6.
   b. $42.
   c. $84.
   d. $126.

Exercises

Check Figures for the Exercises are on p. 323. The solutions themselves are on pp. 19-20.

1. (CMA adapted) Backus Company estimated its unit costs of producing and selling 12,000 units per month as follows:

Direct materials used	$32
Direct manufacturing labour	20
Variable manufacturing overhead	15
Fixed manufacturing overhead	6
Variable nonmanufacturing costs	3
Fixed nonmanufacturing costs	4
Total costs	$80

The cost driver for manufacturing costs is units produced. The cost driver for nonmanufacturing costs is units sold. The relevant range is 7,000 units to 14,000 units.

a. Compute fixed manufacturing overhead per unit for monthly production of 10,000 units.
b. Compute total manufacturing and nonmanufacturing costs for a month if 9,000 units are produced and 8,000 units are sold.

2. Yardley Corp. incurred the following manufacturing costs in 2000:

Variable manufacturing costs:	
Direct materials	$ 600,000
Direct manufacturing labour	500,000
Manufacturing overhead	40,000
Fixed manufacturing overhead	600,000
Total manufacturing costs	$1,740,000

In 2000, the unit cost at production levels of 40,000 units and 60,000 units are $37.80 and $32.80, respectively. The relevant range is 35,000 units to 70,000 units.

Compute the number of units produced in 2000.

3. (CPA) The following information is from the records of McMechen & Sons for 2000:

	Inventories	
	Ending	Beginning
Finished goods	$95,000	$110,000
Work in process	80,000	70,000
Direct materials	95,000	90,000

Costs Incurred During the Period	
Total manufacturing costs	$584,000
Manufacturing overhead	167,000
Direct materials used	193,000

a. Compute direct materials purchased.
b. Compute direct manufacturing labour costs.
c. Compute cost of goods sold.

Answers to Chapter 2 Review Questions and Exercises

Completion Statements

1. cost object
2. direct, indirect
3. relevant range
4. cost driver
5. inventoriable
6. Period
7. manufacturing overhead (factory overhead)
8. Conversion
9. preparing financial statements, contracting with government agencies, pricing and product-emphasis decisions

True-False

1. F A cost object is anything for which a separate measurement of costs is desired. Some examples of cost objects are products, customers, projects, and departments.
2. F The statement defines *cost assignment*, not *cost accumulation*. Cost accumulation is the collection of cost data in some organized way by means of an accounting system.
3. T
4. F Variable costs per unit remain the same within the relevant range. Fixed costs per unit increase/decrease (though not in a straight line) if the related level of total activity or volume decreases/increases. When graphed on a *total basis*, both variable costs and fixed costs are straight lines (linear) within the relevant range.
5. F Nonmanufacturing costs are period costs, and manufacturing costs are inventoriable costs. Therefore, television advertising is a period cost, and amortization on the bottle-capping machines is an inventoriable cost.
6. T
7. T
8. F If work-in-process inventory decreases during the accounting period (that is, the ending inventory is less than the beginning inventory), cost of goods manufactured exceeds manufacturing costs incurred for the period. Cost of goods manufactured, therefore, is equal to manufacturing costs incurred during the period *plus* the decrease in work-in-process inventory. Exhibit 2-9, Panel B, text p. 40, shows the opposite case where work-in-process inventory increases during the period.
9. T
10. F It is preferable to classify payroll fringe benefit costs of direct manufacturing labour as a direct manufacturing labour cost because payroll fringe benefit costs are a fundamental aspect of acquiring the labour services.
11. T

Multiple Choice

1. c Answers (a), (b), and (d) refer to indirect costs of their respective cost objects.
2. d $64,000 \div 10,000 = 6.40 per unit
3. d In general, variable costs *per unit* and fixed costs *in total* can be most reliably predicted because a forecast of the level of total activity or volume is not required.
4. c $120,000 \div 15,000 = 8 per unit, which is also the variable costs per unit when 12,000 units are produced.

5. c Plant rent is part of manufacturing overhead costs. As a result, it is a conversion cost and an inventoriable cost.

6. a The variable portion of budgeted cost of goods sold is $4,000,000 - $800,000 = $3,200,000. Because this amount is 75% of revenues, budgeted revenues are $3,200,000 ÷ .75 = $4,266,667.

7. b

Beginning finished goods	$ 45,000
Cost of goods manufactured	340,000
Cost of goods available for sale	385,000
Ending finished goods	52,000
Cost of goods sold	$333,000
Revenues	$ R
Cost of goods sold	333,000
Gross margin	$ 96,000

$$R - \$333,000 = \$96,000$$
$$R = \$96,000 + \$333,000 = \$429,000$$

Note that the beginning and ending work-in-process inventories are not explicitly included in these computations because the cost of goods manufactured, $340,000, includes the change in work-in-process inventory.

8. b Under the traditional three-part classification of manufacturing costs:
Prime costs = Direct material costs + Direct manufacturing labour costs
Conversion costs = Direct manufacturing labour costs + Manufacturing overhead costs

9. b Overtime premium = $(47 - 40)(\$18 - \$12) = 7 \times \$6 = \$42$

Exercise 1

a. Fixed manufacturing overhead = $12,000 \times \$6 = \$72,000$
Fixed manufacturing overhead per unit = $\$72,000 ÷ 10,000 = \$7.20$

b. Variable manufacturing costs

9,000 × ($32 + $20 + $15)	$603,000
Fixed manufacturing costs, 12,000 × $6	72,000
Variable nonmanufacturing costs, 8,000 × $3	24,000
Fixed nonmanufacturing costs, 12,000 × $4	48,000
Total costs	$747,000

Exercise 2

Variable costs per unit:
$\$37.80 - (\$600,000 ÷ 40,000) = \$37.80 - \$15.00 = \$22.80$
or
$\$32.80 - (\$600,000 ÷ 60,000) = \$32.80 - \$10.00 = \$22.80$
Units produced = $(\$600,000 + \$500,000 + \$40,000) ÷ \$22.80$
$= \$1,140,000 ÷ \$22.80 = 50,000$ units

Exercise 3

a. Direct materials costs:

Beginning inventory	$ 90,000
Add purchases	P
Available for use	?
Deduct ending inventory	95,000
Direct materials used	$193,000

$$\$90,000 + P - \$95,000 = \$193,000$$
$$P = \$193,000 - \$90,000 + \$95,000 = \$198,000$$

b.

Direct materials used	$193,000
Direct manufacturing labour costs	L
Manufacturing overhead costs	167,000
Manufacturing costs incurred during the period	$584,000

$$\$193,000 + L + \$167,000 = \$584,000$$
$$L = \$584,000 - \$193,000 - \$167,000 = \$224,000$$

c. Two steps are used to obtain the answer. First, compute cost of goods manufactured:

Manufacturing costs incurred during the period	$584,000
Add beginning work in process	70,000
Manufacturing costs to account for	654,000
Deduct ending work in process	80,000
Cost of goods manufactured	$574,000

Second, compute cost of goods sold:

Beginning finished goods	$110,000
Add cost of goods manufactured	574,000
Cost of goods available for sale	684,000
Deduct ending finished goods	95,000
Cost of goods sold	$589,000

CHAPTER 3

Cost-Volume-Profit Analysis

Chapter Overview

This chapter explains a planning tool called **cost-volume-profit (CVP) analysis**. CVP analysis examines the behaviour of total revenues, total costs, and operating income (profit) in response to changes in the level of output, selling price, variable costs per unit, and fixed costs. The reliability of the results that CVP analysis can provide depends on the reasonableness of the underlying assumptions. The Appendix to the chapter gives additional insights about CVP analysis by illustrating decision models and the concept of uncertainty.

Chapter Highlights

1. CVP analysis makes several assumptions including:

a. Changes in the level of revenues and costs occur only because of changes in the number of product (or service) units produced and sold (that is, the number of output units is the only driver of revenues and costs).

b. Total costs can be divided into a fixed component and a component that is variable with respect to the level of output.

c. When graphed, the behaviour of total revenues and total costs is linear (a straight line) in relation to output units within the relevant range.

d. The analysis either covers a single product or assumes that a given sales mix of products remains constant as the level of total units sold changes.

2. Despite the fact that CVP assumptions considerably simplify real-world problems, many companies have found CVP relationships to be helpful in strategic and long-run planning decisions as well as decisions about pricing and product emphasis. Managers, however, must always assess whether these CVP relationships generate sufficiently accurate predictions of how total revenues and total costs behave. If decisions can be significantly improved, managers should choose a more complex approach that, for example, uses multiple cost drivers and nonlinear cost functions.

3. Because managers want to avoid operating losses, CVP is often used to calculate the **breakeven point**. The breakeven point is the quantity of output at which total revenues equal total costs. There is neither a profit nor a loss at the breakeven point. To illustrate, assume a company sells 2,000 units of its only product for $50 per unit, variable costs are $20 per unit, and fixed costs are $60,000 per month. Given these conditions, the company is operating at the breakeven point:

Revenues, 2,000 × $50	$100,000
Deduct:	
Variable costs, 2,000 × $20	40,000
Fixed costs	60,000
Operating income	$ -0-

The breakeven point can be expressed two ways: *2,000 units* and *$100,000 of revenues*.

4. Under CVP analysis, the income statement above is reformatted to show a key line item, **contribution margin**:

Revenues, 2,000 × $50	$100,000
Variable costs, 2,000 × $20	40,000
Contribution margin	60,000
Fixed costs	60,000
Operating income	$ -0-

This format, called the **contribution income statement**, is used extensively in this chapter and throughout the textbook.

21

5. Contribution margin can be expressed three ways: *in total, on a per unit basis,* and *as a percentage of revenues*. In our example, total contribution margin is $60,000. **Contribution margin per unit** is the difference between selling price and variable cost per unit: $50 − $20 = $30. Contribution margin per unit is also equal to contribution margin divided by the number of units sold: $60,000 ÷ 2,000 = $30. **Contribution margin percentage** (also called **contribution margin ratio**) is contribution margin per unit divided by selling price: $30 ÷ $50 = 60%; it is also equal to contribution margin divided by revenues: $60,000 ÷ $100,000 = 60%. This contribution margin percentage means that 60 cents in contribution margin is gained for each $1 of revenues.

6. In our example, compute the breakeven point (BEP) in units and in revenues as follows:

$$\text{BEP units} = \frac{\text{Total fixed costs}}{\text{Contribution margin per unit}}$$

$$\text{BEP units} = \frac{\$60,000}{\$30} = 2,000 \text{ units}$$

$$\text{BEP revenues} = \frac{\text{Total fixed costs}}{\text{Contribution margin percentage}}$$

$$\text{BEP revenues} = \frac{\$60,000}{0.60} = \$100,000$$

While the breakeven point is often of interest to managers, CVP analysis considers a broader question: How much sales in units or in dollars are needed to achieve a specified *target operating income*? The answer is easily obtained by adding target operating income to total fixed costs in the formulas above. Assume target operating income (TOI) is $15,000:

$$\text{Unit sales to achieve TOI} = \frac{\$60,000 + \$15,000}{\$30} = 2,500 \text{ units}$$

$$\text{Revenues to achieve TOI} = \frac{\$60,000 + \$15,000}{0.60} = \$125,000$$

7. Because profit-seeking organizations are subject to income taxes, their CVP analyses must include this factor. For example, if a company earns $50,000 before income taxes and the tax rate is 40%, then:

Operating income	$50,000
Deduct incomes taxes (40%)	20,000
Net income	**$30,000**

To state a target net income figure in terms of operating income, divide target net income by 1 − tax rate: $30,000 ÷ (1 − .40) = $50,000. The income-tax factor does not change the breakeven point because no income taxes arise if operating income is $0.

8. Single-number "best estimates" of input data in CVP analysis are subject to varying degrees of **uncertainty**, the possibility that an actual amount will deviate from an expected amount. One approach to deal with uncertainty is to use *sensitivity analysis* (discussed in paragraphs 9 through 11). Another approach is to compute *expected values* using probability distributions (discussed in paragraph 17).

9. **Sensitivity analysis** is a "what if" technique that managers use to examine how a result will change if the original predicted data are not achieved or if an underlying assumption changes. In the context of CVP analysis, sensitivity analysis examines how operating income (or the breakeven point) changes if the predicted data for selling price, variable costs per unit, fixed costs, or units sold are not achieved. The sensitivity to various possible outcomes broadens managers' perspectives as to what might actually occur *before* they make cost commitments. The widespread use of electronic spreadsheets enables managers to conduct CVP-based sensitivity analyses in a systematic and efficient way.

10. An aspect of sensitivity analysis is the **margin of safety**, the amount of budgeted revenues over and above the breakeven revenues. The margin of safety answers the "what-if" question: If budgeted revenues are above breakeven and decline, how far can they fall below the budget before the breakeven point is reached?

11. CVP-based sensitivity analysis highlights the risks and returns that an existing cost structure holds for an organization. This insight may lead managers to consider alternative cost structures. For example, compensating a salesperson on the basis of a sales commission (a variable cost) rather than a salary (a fixed cost) decreases the company's downside risk if demand is low but decreases its return if demand is high. The risk-return tradeoff across alternative cost structures is usefully summarized in a measure called **operating leverage**. Operating leverage describes the effects that fixed costs have on changes in operating income as changes occur in units sold and hence in contribution margin. Organizations with a high proportion of fixed costs in their cost structures have high operating leverage. Consequently, small changes in units sold cause large changes in operating income. *At any given level of units sold*:

$$\frac{\text{Degree of operating}}{\text{leverage}} = \frac{\text{Contribution margin}}{\text{Operating income}}$$

Knowing the degree of operating leverage helps managers to quickly calculate the effect of changes in units sold on operating income.

12. The time horizon being considered for a decision affects the classification of costs as variable or fixed. The shorter the time horizon, the greater the proportion of total costs that are fixed. For example, virtually all the costs for an airline flight are fixed one hour before takeoff. When the time horizon is lengthened to one year and then five years, more and more costs become variable. In the long-run all costs are variable.

13. **Sales mix** (also called **revenue mix**) is the relative combination of quantities of products (or services) that constitutes total unit sales. If the sales mix changes and the overall unit sales target is still achieved, however, the effect on the breakeven point and operating income depends on how the original proportions of lower or higher contribution margin products have shifted. Other things being equal, for any given total quantity of units sold, the breakeven point decreases and oper-

ating income increases if the sales mix shifts toward products with higher contribution margins.

14. Recall from paragraph 1d that, in multiple product situations, CVP analysis assumes a given sales mix of products remains constant as the level of total units sold changes. In this case, the breakeven point is some number of units of each product, depending on the sales mix. To illustrate, assume a company sells two products, A and B. The sales mix is 4 units of A and 3 units of B. The contribution margins per unit are $80 for A and $40 for B. Fixed costs are $308,000 per month. To compute the breakeven point:

Let $4X$ = No. of units of A to break even
Then $3X$ = No. of units of B to break even

$$\text{BEP in X units} = \frac{\$308,000}{4(\$80) + 3(\$40)}$$

$$\text{BEP in X units} = \frac{\$308,000}{\$440} = 700 \text{ units}$$

A units to break even = $4 \times 700 = 2,800$ units
B units to break even = $3 \times 700 = 2,100$ units

Proof: Contribution margin

A: 2,800 × $80	$224,000
B: 2,100 × $40	84,000
Total	308,000
Fixed costs	308,000
Operating income	$ -0-

15. CVP analysis can be applied to service organizations and nonprofit organizations. The key is measuring their output. Unlike manufacturing and merchandising companies that measure their output in units of product, the measure of output differs from one service industry (or nonprofit organization) to another. For example, airlines measure output in passenger-kilometres and hotels/motels use room-nights occupied. Government welfare agencies measure output in number of clients served and universities use student credit-hours.

16. Recall from paragraph 1a that CVP analysis assumes that the number of output units is the only revenue and cost driver. By relaxing this assumption, CVP analysis can be adapted to *the more general case of multiple cost drivers* but the simple formulas in paragraph 6 can no longer be used. Moreover, *there is no unique breakeven point*. The

example, text p. 77 has two cost drivers—the number of software packages sold and the number of customers. One breakeven point is selling 26 packages to 8 customers. Another breakeven point is selling 27 packages to 16 customers.

17. *Contribution margin*, a key concept in this chapter, contrasts with *gross margin* discussed in Chapter 2. Gross margin is an important line item in the conventional income statements of merchandising and manufacturing companies. Gross margin is total revenues minus cost of goods sold, whereas contribution margin is total revenues minus total variable costs (throughout the value chain). Gross margin and contribution margin will be different amounts (except in the highly unlikely case that cost of goods sold and variable costs are equal). For example, a manufacturing company deducts fixed manufacturing costs from revenues in computing gross margin (but not contribution margin); it deducts sales commissions from revenues in computing contribution margin (but not gross margin).

18. The Appendix to this chapter uses a *probability distribution* to incorporate uncertainty into a *decision model*. This approach provides additional insights about CVP analysis. A decision model, a formal method for making a choice, usually includes five steps: (a) identify a *choice criterion* such as maximize income, (b) identify the set of alternative actions (choices) available to the manager, (c) identify the set of *events* (possible occurrences) that can occur, (d) assign a *probability* to each of the specified events, and (e) identify the set of possible *outcomes* (the economic result of each action-event combination). Uncertainty is present in a decision model because for each alternative action there are two or more possible events, each with a probability of occurrence. The correct decision is to choose the action with the best **expected value**. Expected value is the weighted average of the outcomes, with the probability of each outcome serving as the weight. Although the expected value criterion helps managers make *good decisions*, it does not prevent *bad outcomes* from occurring.

Featured Exercise

In its budget for next month, Gretzky Company has revenues of $500,000, variable costs of $350,000, and fixed costs of $135,000.

a. Compute contribution margin percentage.
b. Compute total revenues needed to break even.
c. Compute total revenues needed to achieve a target operating income of $45,000.
d. Compute total revenues needed to achieve a target net income of $48,000, assuming the income tax rate is 40%.

Solution

a. Contribution margin percentage = ($500,000 − $350,000) ÷ $500,000
    = $150,000 ÷ $500,000 = 30%
    Note that variable costs as a percentage of revenues = $350,000 ÷ $500,000 = 70%

b. Breakeven point = $135,000 ÷ 0.30 = $450,000
    Proof:

Revenues	$450,000
Variable costs, $450,000 × 0.70	315,000
Contribution margin	135,000
Fixed costs	135,000
Operating income	$ -0-

c. Let X = Total revenues needed to achieve target operating income of $45,000

$$X = \frac{\$135,000 + \$45,000}{0.30} = \frac{\$180,000}{0.30} = \$600,000$$

d. Two steps are used to obtain the answer. First, compute operating income when net income is $48,000:

$$\frac{\$48,000}{1 - 0.40} = \frac{\$48,000}{0.60} = \$80,000$$

Second, compute total revenues needed to achieve a target operating income of $80,000 (that is, a target net income of $48,000), which is denoted by Y:

$$Y = \frac{\$135,000 + \$80,000}{0.30} = \frac{\$215,000}{0.30} = \$716,667$$

Review Questions and Exercises

Completion Statements

Fill in the blank(s) to complete each statement.

1. _____ is equal to selling price minus variable cost per unit.

2. The financial report that highlights the contribution margin as a line item is called the _____.

3. The possibility that an actual amount will deviate from an expected amount is called _____.

4. _____ is a "what if" technique that, when used in the context of CVP analysis, examines how a result such as operating income changes if the original predicted data are not achieved or if an underlying assumption changes.

5. The relative combination of quantities of products or services that constitute total revenues is called the _____.

6. _____ describes the effects that fixed costs have on changes in operating income as changes occur in units sold and hence in contribution margin.

7. (Appendix) In a decision model, the correct decision is to choose the action with the best _____, which is the weighted average of the outcomes with the probability of each outcome serving as the weight.

Indicate whether each statement is true (T) or false (F).

___ 1. Generally, the breakeven point in revenues can be easily determined by simply summing all the costs in the company's contribution income statement.

___ 2. At the breakeven point, total fixed costs always equals contribution margin.

___ 3. The amount of budgeted revenues over and above breakeven revenues is called the margin of forecasting error.

___ 4. An increase in the income tax rate increases the breakeven point.

___ 5. Trading off fixed costs in a company's cost structure for higher variable costs per unit decreases downside risk if demand is low and decreases return if demand is high.

___ 6. At any given level of units sold, the degree of operating leverage is equal to contribution margin divided by operating income.

___ 7. If the budget appropriation for a non-profit drug rehabilitation centre is reduced by 15% and the cost-volume relationships remain the same, the client service level decreases by 15%.

___ 8. The longer the time horizon in a decision situation, the lower the percentage of total costs that are variable.

___ 9. Cost of goods sold in manufacturing companies is a variable cost.

___ 10. (Appendix) The probability distribution for the mutually exclusive and collectively exhaustive set of events in a decision model sums to 1.00.

___ 11. (Appendix) Even if a manager makes a good decision, a bad outcome may still occur.

Multiple Choice

Select the best answer to each question. Space is provided for computations after the quantitative questions.

___ 1. (CPA) CVP analysis *does not* assume that:

a. selling prices remain constant.
b. there is a single revenue and cost driver.
c. total fixed costs vary inversely with units of output.
d. total costs are linear within the relevant range.

___ 2. Given for Winn Company in 1999: revenues $530,000, manufacturing costs $220,000 (one-half fixed), and marketing and administrative costs $270,000 (two-thirds variable). The contribution margin is:
a. $40,000.
b. $240,000.
c. $310,000.
d. $330,000.

___ 3. Using the data in question 2 and ignoring inventories, the gross margin for Winn Company is:
a. $40,000.
b. $240,000.
c. $310,000.
d. $330,000.

___ 4. (CPA) Koby Company has revenues of $200,000, variable costs of $150,000, fixed costs of $60,000, and an operating loss of $10,000. By how much would Koby need to increase its revenues in order to achieve a target operating income of 10% of revenues?
a. $200,000
b. $231,000
c. $251,000
d. $400,000

5. (CPA) The following information pertains to Nova Co.'s CVP relationships:

Breakeven point in units   1,000
Variable costs per unit $500
Total fixed costs $150,000

How much will be contributed to operating income by the 1,001st unit sold?

a. $650
b. $500
c. $150
d. $0

6. (CPA) During 1999, Thor Lab supplied hospitals with a comprehensive diagnostic kit for $120. At a volume of 80,000 kits, Thor had fixed costs of $1,000,000 and an operating income of $200,000. Due to an adverse legal decision, Thor's liability insurance in 2000 will increase by $1,200,000. Assuming the volume and other costs are unchanged, what should the selling price be in 2000 if Thor is to earn the same operating income of $200,000?

a. $120
b. $135
c. $150
d. $240

7. In the fiscal year just completed, Varsity Shop reports net income of $24,000 on revenues of $300,000. The variable costs as a percentage of revenues are 70%. The income tax rate is 40%. What is the amount of fixed costs?

a. $30,000
b. $50,000
c. $66,000
d. $170,000

8. The amount of total costs probably will not vary significantly in decision situations where:
a. the time span is quite short and the change in units of output is quite large.
b. the time span is quite long and the change in units of output is quite large.
c. the time span is quite long and the change in units of output is quite small.
d. the time span is quite short and the change in units of output is quite small.

9. (CPA) Product Cott has revenues of $200,000, a contribution margin of 20%, and a margin of safety of $80,000. What are Cott's fixed costs?
a. $16,000
b. $24,000
c. $80,000
d. $96,000

10. For a multiple-product company, a shift in sales mix from products with high contribution-margin percentages toward products with low contribution-margin percentages causes the breakeven point to be:
a. lower.
b. higher.
c. unchanged.
d. different but undeterminable.

11. (Appendix, CMA) The College Honor Society sells large pretzels at the home football games. The following information is available:

Unit Sales	Probability
2,000 pretzels	.10
3,000 pretzels	.15
4,000 pretzels	.20
5,000 pretzels	.35
6,000 pretzels	.20

The pretzels are sold for $2.00 each, and the cost per pretzel is $0.60. Any unsold pretzels are discarded because they will be stale before the next home game. If 4,000 pretzels are on hand for a game but only 3,000 of them are sold, the operating income is:

a. $5,600.
b. $4,200.
c. $3,600.
d. $900.
e. none of the above.

Exercises

Check Figures for the Exercises are on p. 323. The solutions themselves are on pp. 31-32.

1. (CMA) The income statement for Davann Co. presented below shows the operating results for the fiscal year just ended. Davann had sales of 1,800 tonnes of product during that year. The manufacturing capacity of Davann's facilities is 3,000 tonnes of product.

Revenues		$900,000
Variable costs:		
Manufacturing	$315,000	
Nonmanufacturing	180,000	495,000
Contribution margin		405,000
Fixed costs:		
Manufacturing	90,000	
Nonmanufacturing	157,500	247,500
Operating income		157,500
Income taxes (40%)		63,000
Net income		$ 94,500

a. If the sales volume is estimated to be 2,100 tonnes for next year, and if the selling price and cost-behaviour patterns remain the same next year, how much net income does Davann expect to earn next year?

b. Assume Davann estimates the selling price per tonne will decline 10% next year, variable costs will increase by $40 per tonne, and total fixed costs will not change. Compute how many tonnes must be sold next year to earn net income of $94,500.

2. Valdosta Manufacturing Co. produces and sells two products:

	T	U
Selling price	$25	$16
Variable costs per unit	20	13

Total fixed costs are $40,500.

Compute the breakeven point in units assuming the sales mix is five units of U for each unit of T.

3. (CPA) Dallas Corporation wishes to market a new product at a selling price of $1.50 per unit. Fixed costs for this product are $100,000 for less than 500,000 units of output and $150,000 for 500,000 or more units of output. The contribution-margin percentage is 20%.

Compute how many units of this product must be sold to earn a target operating income of $100,000.

4. (Appendix, CMA) The ARC Radio Company is trying to decide whether to introduce a new product, a wrist "radiowatch" designed for shortwave reception of the exact time as broadcast by the National Bureau of Standards. The "radiowatch" would be priced at $60, which is exactly twice the variable costs per unit to manufacture and sell it. The fixed costs to introduce the radiowatch are $240,000 per year. The following probability distribution estimates the demand for the product:

Annual Demand	Probability
6,000 units	.20
8,000 units	.20
10,000 units	.20
12,000 units	.20
14,000 units	.10
16,000 units	.10

a. Compute the expected value of demand for the radiowatch.
b. Compute the probability that the introduction of the radiowatch *will not increase* the company's operating income.

Answers to Chapter 3 Review Questions and Exercises

Completion Statements

1. Contribution margin per unit (Unit contribution margin)
2. contribution income statement
3. uncertainty
4. Sensitivity analysis
5. sales mix (revenue mix)
6. Operating leverage
7. expected value

True-False

1. F   The breakeven point in revenues is computed by dividing total fixed costs by the contribution-margin percentage. The computation described in the statement gives breakeven revenues *only if* the company happened to be operating at the breakeven point.
2. T
3. F   The amount of budgeted revenues over and above breakeven revenues is called the *margin of safety*.
4. F   The breakeven point is unaffected by income taxes because operating income at the breakeven point is $0 and hence no income taxes arise.
5. T
6. T
7. F   If the budget appropriation for a nonprofit drug rehabilitation centre is reduced by 15% and the cost-volume relationships remain the same, the client service level decreases by more than 15% because of the existence of fixed costs. For example, the illustration, text pp. 75-76, has a 21.4% decrease in the service level when the budget appropriation is reduced by 15%.
8. F   The longer the time horizon in a decision situation, the lower the percentage of total costs that are fixed and the higher the percentage of total costs that are variable. In the long run, all costs are variable.
9. F   Cost of goods sold in manufacturing companies includes both variable and fixed manufacturing costs.
10. T
11. T

Multiple Choice

1. c   One of the assumptions in CVP analysis is total fixed costs remain the same within the relevant range.
2. b   Contribution margin = $530,000 − $220,000(1/2) − $270,000(2/3)
   = $530,000 − $110,000 − $180,000 = $240,000
3. c   Gross margin = $530,000 − $220,000 = $310,000
4. a   Let R = Revenues needed to earn a target operating income of 10% of sales revenues
$$R - (\$150,000 \div \$200,000)R - \$60,000 = 0.10R$$
$$R - 0.75R - 0.10R = \$60,000$$
$$0.15R = \$60,000$$
$$R = \$60,000 \div 0.15 = \$400,000$$

Because current revenues are $200,000, an increase in revenues of $200,000 is needed to earn a target operating income of 10% of revenues.

5. c Total costs at breakeven = (1,000 × $500) + $150,000 = $650,000
   Selling price = $650,000 ÷ 1,000 units = $650
   Contribution margin per unit = $650 − $500 = $150

6. b The selling price in 2000 to earn the same operating income of $200,000 is the selling price in 1999, $120, increased by the amount of the higher liability insurance in 2000, $1,200,000, spread over the 80,000-unit sales volume:
   Selling price in 2000 = $120 + ($1,200,000 ÷ 80,000) = $120 + $15 = $135

7. b Three steps are used to obtain the answer. First, compute contribution margin. The contribution margin percentage = 100% − the variable costs percentage of 70% = 30%. Contribution margin = $300,000 × 0.30 = $90,000. Second, compute operating income:

$$\frac{\$24,000}{1 - 0.40} = \frac{\$24,000}{0.60} = \$40,000$$

   Third, the difference between contribution margin and operating income is fixed costs: $90,000 − $40,000 = $50,000

8. d An example of this decision situation is deciding whether to add a passenger to an airline flight that has empty seats and will depart in one hour. Variable costs for the passenger are negligible. Virtually all the costs in this decision situation are fixed.

9. b The margin of safety answers the what-if question: If budgeted revenues are above the breakeven point and decline, how far can they fall below the budget before the breakeven point is reached?
   Breakeven point = $200,000 − $80,000 = $120,000
   Variable costs = $120,000 × (1 − 0.20)
                  = $120,000 × 0.80 = $96,000
   Fixed costs = $120,000 − $96,000 = $24,000
   Proof: $24,000 ÷ 0.20 = $120,000

10. b A shift in the sales mix from high contribution-margin percentage products toward low ones decreases the overall contribution-margin percentage of the sales mix. This change increases the breakeven point.

11. c 3,000($2.00) − 4,000($0.60) = $6,000 − $2,400 = $3,600

Exercise 1

a. Three steps are used to obtain the answer. First, compute selling price: $900,000 ÷ 1,800 = $500. Second, compute variable costs per unit: $495,000 ÷ 1,800 = $275. Third, prepare a contribution income statement at the 2,100-tonne level of output:

Revenues, 2,100 × $500	$1,050,000
Variable costs, 2,100 × $275	577,500
Contribution margin	472,500
Fixed costs	247,500
Operating income	225,000
Income taxes (40%)	90,000
Net income	$ 135,000

b. Let Q = Number of tonnes to break even next year

$$\$500Q(1 - 0.10) - (\$275Q + \$40Q) - \$247,500 = \frac{\$94,500}{1 - 0.40}$$

$$\$450Q - \$315Q = \$247,500 + \$157,500$$
$$\$135Q = \$405,000$$
$$Q = 3,000 \text{ tons}$$

Exercise 2

> Let T = Number of units of T to be sold to break even
> Then 5T = Number of units of U to be sold to break even
> $25T + $16(5T) − $20T − $13(5T) − $40,500 = $0
> $25T + $80T − $20T − $65T = $40,500
> $20T = $40,500; T = 2,025 units; 5T = 2,025 × 5 = 10,125 units
> *Proof:* $25(2,025) + $16(10,125) − $20(2,025) − $13(10,125) − $40,500 = $0
> $50,625 + $162,000 − $40,500 − $131,625 − $40,500 = $0
> $0 = $0

Exercise 3

Two steps are used to obtain the answer. First, determine if fixed costs will be $100,000 or $150,000. If fixed costs are $100,000, the *maximum* operating income is attained at 499,999 units:

Revenues, 499,999 × $1.50	$749,998.50
Variable costs, 80% of revenues	599,998.80
Contribution margin, 20% of revenues	149,999.70
Fixed costs	100,000.00
Operating income	$ 49,999.70

Because this operating income is below the target of $100,000, the level of output needs to be greater than 499,999 units and hence fixed costs will be $150,000. Second, compute the required level of output:

> Let Q = Number of units to be sold to earn a target operating income of $100,000
> $1.50Q − (1 − 0.20)($1.50)Q − $150,000 = $100,000
> $1.50Q − $1.20Q = $100,000 + $150,000
> $0.30Q = $250,000
> Q = 833,333.33, rounded to 833,334 units

Exercise 4

a.

> 6,000 × .20 = 1,200
> 8,000 × .20 = 1,600
> 10,000 × .20 = 2,000
> 12,000 × .20 = 2,400
> 14,000 × .10 = 1,400
> 16,000 × .10 = 1,600
> Expected value of
> demand in units   10,200

b. If the number of units sold each year is equal to or less than the breakeven point, the radiowatch will not increase the company's operating income. At the breakeven point,

> Revenues − Variable costs − Fixed costs = $0
> Let Q = Number of units to be sold to break even
> $60Q − ($60 ÷ 2)Q − $240,000 = $0
> 60Q − $30Q = $240,000
> $30Q = $240,000
> Q = $240,000 ÷ $30 = 8,000 units

Because the company's operating income will not increase if 8,000 units or 6,000 units are sold, the probability of *either* of these events occurring is equal to the sum of their individual probabilities: 0.20 + 0.20 = 0.40.

CHAPTER 4

Job Costing

Chapter Overview

This chapter begins by describing costing systems in general, and then explains how job-costing systems can be used to determine the cost of products or services. Managers use job-costing information for various purposes including pricing, product-mix, and cost management decisions and (in the case of manufacturing companies) inventory valuation. The major illustration in the chapter demonstrates, on a transaction-by-transaction basis, the flow of manufacturing costs through the accounts in the general and subsidiary ledgers.

Chapter Highlights

1. The following points together with paragraph 2 below apply to costing systems in general:

a. The cost-benefit approach is essential in designing and choosing costing systems. Managers should install a more sophisticated system only if they believe that the additional benefits will exceed the additional costs.

b. Costing systems should be tailored to the underlying operations, not vice versa. Any significant change in operations is likely to justify a corresponding change in the costing system.

c. Costing systems are only one source of information for managers' decisions. Other sources include personal observation and nonfinancial performance measures.

2. The building blocks of costing systems are *cost object, direct costs of a cost object, indirect costs of a cost object* (terms introduced in Chapter 2), **cost pool**, and **cost-allocation base** (terms introduced in this chapter). Products, services, and customers are often used as cost objects in costing systems. For example, if product X is the chosen cost object, the direct costs will be *traced* to X and the indirect costs will be *allocated* to X. In order to allocate indirect costs to product X, (a) individual cost items are grouped into one or more *cost pools* and (b) a *cost-allocation base* is chosen for each cost pool to logically link it to product X. Overview diagrams present the building blocks of costing systems in a systematic way. EXHIBIT 4-2, text p. 104, shows an overview diagram for a manufacturing company's job-costing system.

3. There are two basic types of costing systems used to assign costs to products or services: a **job-costing system** and a **process-costing system.**

- In a job-costing system, the cost object is an individual unit (or batch) of a *distinct* product or service, called a **job.** The product or service is often custom-made, such as a construction job or an advertising campaign, and direct and indirect costs are assigned to each job.
- In a process-costing system, the cost object is masses of *identical or similar* units of a product or service. Examples are barrels of oil refined or bank deposits processed. Each period the total costs of producing this type of product or service are divided by the total number of units produced to obtain the average cost per unit.

4. Job-costing systems use a seven-step procedure to assign costs to individual jobs.

Step 1: Identify the job that is the chosen cost object.

Step 2: Identify the direct costs of the job.

Step 3: Select the cost-allocation base(s) to use in allocating indirect costs to the job.

Step 4: Identify the indirect costs associated with each cost-allocation base.

Step 5: Compute the rate per unit of each cost-allocation base used to allocate indirect costs to the job.

Step 6: Compute the indirect costs allocated to the job.

Step 7: Compute the total cost of the job by adding the direct and indirect costs assigned to it.

To illustrate this procedure, assume a custom-made machine is the chosen cost object. After performing Steps 2 through 6 (explained below), the results for Step 7 are as follows:

Direct material costs	$ 7,000
Direct manufacturing labour costs	2,500
Indirect manufacturing costs	8,800
Total manufacturing costs of machine	$18,300

Details about performing Steps 2 through 6:

- For each direct cost traced to the job, the actual quantity used was multiplied by the actual cost rate. To illustrate, assume 700 litres of direct materials were used at an actual cost of $10 per litre: $700 \times \$10 = \$7,000$.
- Machine-hours was selected as the only cost-allocation base for allocating indirect manufacturing costs (manufacturing overhead) to the job.
- All $220,000 of the company's indirect manufacturing costs were grouped in a single cost pool and allocated based on a total of 20,000 machine-hours. The **indirect-cost rate** = $220,000 \div 20,000 = \$11$ per machine-hour.
- Eight hundred machine-hours were used to produce the custom-made machine, so indirect manufacturing costs of $8,800 (800 $\times$ $11) are allocated to the job.

5. In the example above, the indirect-cost rate is computed as follows:

$$\frac{\$220,000}{20,000 \text{ machine-hours}} = \$11 \text{ per machine-hour}$$

In developing such rates, most companies use a time period of one year. There are two important reasons for this practice. First, *the numerator reason:* the time period corresponding with the $220,000 must be long enough to lessen or eliminate the influence of seasonal patterns and erratic items such as repairs. Second, *the denominator reason*: the time period must be long enough to spread the monthly fixed costs in the $220,000 over fluctuating levels of monthly volume.

6. **Actual costing** and **normal costing** are two methods for determining the cost of a job.

- Under actual costing, direct costs are traced to the job by multiplying the actual direct-cost rate(s) times the actual quantity of the direct cost input(s), and indirect costs are allocated to the job by multiplying the actual indirect cost rate(s) times the actual quantity of the cost-allocation base(s). Actual costing is seldom used, however, because it requires waiting until all of the indirect costs are known at year-end before allocating them to jobs.
- Normal costing differs from actual costing in only one respect: a **budgeted indirect-cost rate(s)** is computed at the beginning of the year and used to allocate indirect costs to jobs as work on them progresses during the year.

The example above is actual costing if the $11 indirect-cost rate is an *actual rate*; it is normal costing if the $11 is a *budgeted rate*.

7. In our example, the focus is on a *product* (a custom-made machine) as the main cost object. Managers also focus on a second main cost object: *responsibility centres*, which are parts, segments, or subunits of an organization whose managers are accountable for specified sets of activities. The most commonly encountered responsibility centre is a department. Identifying department costs helps managers to control costs for which they are responsible and enables senior management to evaluate the performance of subordinates. Job-costing systems assign costs first to responsibility centres and then to jobs.

8. Managers and accountants gather information that goes into their costing systems via **source documents**, which are the original records that support journal entries in an accounting system. Three key source documents in job-costing systems are a **job cost record** (also called a **job cost sheet**), a **materials requisition record**, and a **labour time record**. A job cost record is used to record all the costs assigned to a specific job. A materials requisition record charges job cost records and departments for the cost of direct materials used on specific jobs. A labour time record charges job cost records and departments for the cost of labour time used on specific jobs. In many costing systems, the source documents exist only in the form of computer records.

9. For manufacturing companies using job costing, eight summary transactions explain how manufacturing costs flow through the accounts in the general and subsidiary ledgers. These transactions arise from purchasing materials and converting them into finished goods. Each general-ledger account with the word *Control* in its title is supported by a subsidiary ledger. For example, the subsidiary ledger for Materials Control contains details on the quantity and unit cost of each type of material in inventory. The job cost record for each unfinished job is the subsidiary ledger for Work-in-Process Control. The first eight transactions and related journal entries in the normal costing example, beginning text p. 112, are as follows:

(1) Purchases of direct and indirect materials on credit in February, $89,000.

Materials Control	89,000	
Accounts Payable Control		89,000

(2) Materials requisition records for February, $81,000 direct materials and $4,000 indirect materials. (Indirect materials are part of manufacturing overhead, hereafter abbreviated MOH).

Work-in-Process Control	81,000	
MOH Control	4,000	
Materials Control		85,000

(3) Total manufacturing payroll incurred in February, $39,000 direct labour and $15,000 indirect labour.

Work-in-Process Control	39,000	
MOH Control	15,000	
Wages Payable Control		54,000

(4) Paid total manufacturing payroll incurred in February, $54,000.

Wages Payable Control	54,000	
Cash Control		54,000

(5) Additional MOH incurred in February, $44,000 for engineering and supervisory salaries, $11,000 for utilities and repairs, $18,000 for amortization, and $2,000 for insurance.

MOH Control	75,000	
Salaries Payable Control		44,000
Accounts Payable Control		11,000
Accum. Dep. Control		18,000
Prepaid Insurance Control		2,000

(6) MOH allocated to all jobs worked on during February, $80,000 (2,000 actual direct manufacturing labour-hours × $40 budgeted rate).

Work-in-Process Control	80,000	
MOH Allocated		80,000

(7) Transfer to finished goods the individual jobs completed during February, total cost $188,800.

Finished Goods Control	188,800	
Work-in-Process Control		188,800

(8) Cost of goods sold in February, $180,000.

Cost of Goods Sold	180,000	
Finished Goods Control		180,000

In addition to the eight summary transactions for manufacturing costs, journal entries also are made to record revenues and nonmanufacturing costs.

10. In the journal entries above, the actual MOH incurred during February is $94,000 ($4,000 in entry 2 + $15,000 in entry 3 + $75,000 in entry 5). Entry 6 shows $80,000

of MOH allocated to jobs during February. The difference of $14,000 ($94,000 − $80,000) is **underallocated** (also called **underapplied** or **underabsorbed**) MOH. That is, in this example the amount of MOH allocated is *less than* the amount of MOH incurred. Had the allocated amount been *greater than* the amount incurred, MOH would be **overallocated (overapplied** or **overabsorbed)**.

11. The balances of MOH Control and MOH Allocated are carried forward each month. At year-end, under- or overallocated MOH must be disposed of using one of the three approaches described below. To illustrate, assume the year-end balances are MOH Control $1,215,000 and MOH Allocated $1,080,000, which means MOH is underallocated by $135,000. Each approach results in a journal entry to close MOH Control and MOH Allocated.

a. Write-off to Cost of Goods Sold:

Cost of Goods Sold 135,000
MOH Allocated 1,080,000
 MOH Control   1,215,000

This is the simplest approach and is widely used. Because inventory balances of job-costing companies are usually relatively small, this approach is unlikely to cause significant distortions in the financial statements.

b. **Proration**, which spreads under- or overallocated MOH among Work-in-Process Control, Finished Goods Control, and Cost of Goods Sold:

Work-in-Process Control X
Finished Goods Control Y
Cost of Goods Sold Z
MOH Allocated 1,080,000
 MOH Control   1,215,000

The amounts X, Y, and Z depend on whether proration is based on (i) the total amount of overhead allocated (before proration) in the ending balances of these three accounts or (ii) the total ending balances (before proration) of these accounts. Method (i) is more accurate but (ii) is simpler to use. The example, text pp. 118-119, shows computations for these two methods.

c. Adjusted allocation rate:

Same journal entry as in proration method (i).

This approach not only adjusts the general-ledger balances of Work-in-Process Control, Finished Goods Control, and Cost of Goods Sold, but also adjusts the job cost record of every job worked on during the year. Procedurally, all of the adjustments are based on the difference between the actual overhead rate determined at year-end and the budgeted overhead rate used for normal costing during the year.

12. Under generally accepted accounting principles, only manufacturing costs are inventoriable costs; nonmanufacturing costs are period costs. Despite this difference, companies often assign nonmanufacturing costs to individual jobs (just as they do manufacturing costs) for pricing, product-mix, and cost management decisions.

13. Although this chapter focuses on manufacturing, job costing is also useful in service-sector organizations such as accounting firms, law firms, advertising agencies, and auto repair shops. For example, in an accounting firm, each audit is a job. The costs of the audit are accumulated in a job cost record using the seven-step procedure described in paragraph 4. Some service and manufacturing companies use a variation of normal costing in which *both* direct costs and indirect costs are charged to jobs by means of budgeted rates.

Featured Exercise

Madison Company has overallocated manufacturing overhead (MOH) of $45,000 for the year ended December 31, 1999. Before disposing of the overallocated MOH, selected year-end balances from Madison's general ledger are as follows:

MOH Control	$435,000
MOH Allocated	480,000
Work-in-Process Control	24,000
Finished Goods Control	56,000
Cost of Goods Sold	720,000

At year-end, the company prorates under- or overallocated MOH to the last three accounts listed above based on their total ending balances (before proration).

a. Compute the amount of overallocated MOH to be prorated to each of the three accounts and compute their balances after proration.
b. Prepare a journal entry to record the proration.

Solution

a.

	Account Balance (Before Proration) (1)		Proration of $45,000 Overallocated MOH (2)	Account Balance (After Proration) (3) = (1) − (2)
Work in process	$ 24,000	3%	0.03 × $45,000 =$ 1,350	$ 22,650
Finished goods	56,000	7%	0.07 × $45,000 = 3,150	52,850
Cost of goods sold	720,000	90%	0.90 × $45,000 = 40,500	679,500
	$800,000	100%	$45,000	$755,000

The prorated amounts of overallocated MOH are *deducted from* the account balances before proration because too much MOH was allocated to the accounts during the year.

b. The journal entry to record this proration is:

MOH Allocated	480,000	
Work-in-Process Control		1,350
Finished Goods		3,150
Cost of Goods Sold		40,500
MOH Control		435,000

Review Questions and Exercises

Completion Statements

Fill in the blank(s) to complete each statement.

1. A _____ is a grouping of individual cost items.
2. A _____ is a factor that is the common denominator for systematically linking an indirect cost or group of indirect costs to a cost object.
3. In a _____ system, the cost object is an individual unit (or batch) of a distinct product or service, whereas the cost object is masses of identical or similar units of a product or service in a _____ _____ system.
4. Under _____ costing, a manufacturing company debits Work-in-Process Control with the budgeted overhead rate(s) times the actual quantity used of the cost-allocation base(s).

5. In a job-costing system, the source document used to record all costs assigned to a specific job is called a _____.
6. The supporting detail for a general-ledger control account is called a _____ _____.

True-False

Indicate whether each statement is true (T) or false (F).

___ 1. A canning company would use a job-costing system.
___ 2. One reason that budgeted overhead rates are developed annually rather than monthly is to overcome the volatility in unit costs caused by seasonal fluctuations in the level of the cost-allocation base.
___ 3. Overallocated overhead arises when the balance of Manufacturing Overhead Control is less than the balance of Manufacturing Overhead Allocated.

4. In general, the amount of under- or overallocated overhead is greater at year-end than at any month-end during the year.

5. If a company uses normal costing and the actual level of production is substantially less than the budgeted level, overhead will most likely be overallocated.

6. In using the proration approach to dispose of under- or overallocated overhead, it is conceptually superior to prorate based on the total amount of allocated overhead (before proration) in the ending balances of Work in Process Control, Finished Goods Control, and Cost of Goods Sold rather than to prorate based on the total ending balances of these accounts (before proration).

7. Assume a manufacturing company has underallocated overhead at year-end. The year's operating income will be lower if the underallocated overhead is prorated to the appropriate accounts rather than written off to Cost of Goods Sold.

Multiple Choice

Select the best answer to each question. Space is provided for computations after the quantitative questions.

1. A budgeted rate for allocating manufacturing overhead costs to products is preferred to an actual rate if the objective is:
a. timeliness but not accuracy.
b. accuracy but not timeliness.
c. both accuracy and timeliness.
d. neither timeliness nor accuracy.

2. (CPA adapted) Avery Co. uses a budgeted manufacturing overhead rate based on machine-hours. For the month of October, Avery's budgeted overhead was $300,000 based on a budgeted allocation base of 10,000 machine-hours. Actual overhead incurred amounted to $325,000 and 11,000 actual machine-hours were used. How much was the

under- or overallocated overhead?
a. $30,000 overallocated
b. $30,000 underallocated
c. $5,000 overallocated
d. $5,000 underallocated

3. Shadwick Company used a budgeted manufacturing overhead rate of $0.175 per machine-hour during the current year. Two machine-hours were budgeted per unit produced. For the current year, actual manufacturing overhead incurred was $350,000 and overhead was overallocated by $10,500. How many units were produced in the current year?
a. 970,000
b. 1,030,000
c. 1,940,000
d. 2,060,000

4. (CPA) In a job-costing system, issuing indirect materials to production increases which account?
a. Materials Control
b. Work-in-Process Control
c. Manufacturing Overhead Control
d. Manufacturing Overhead Allocated

5. (CPA) In a job-costing system, the dollar amount of the journal entry transferring inventory from Work-in-Process Control to Finished Goods Control is the sum of the costs debited to all jobs:
a. started in production during the period.
b. in production during the period.
c. completed and sold during the period.
d. completed during the period.

6. Under generally accepted accounting principles, the appropriate approach for disposing of under- or overallocated manufacturing overhead at year-end:

    a. is to write it off to Cost of Goods Sold.

    b. is to prorate it to Work-in-Process Control, Finished Goods Control, and Cost of Goods Sold.

    c. is to adjust the overhead rate and use this rate to adjust the balances of Work-in-Process Control, Finished Goods Control, and Cost of Goods Sold as well as the job cost record of every job worked on during the year.

    d. depends on the significance of the amount.

7. (CPA) Worley Company has overallocated overhead of $45,000 for the year ended December 31, 1999. Before disposing of the overallocated overhead, selected December 31, 1999, balances from Worley's accounting records are as follows:

Revenues	$1,200,000
Cost of Goods Sold	720,000
Inventories:	
Materials Control	36,000
Work-in-Process Control	54,000
Finished Goods Control	90,000

Under Worley's accounting system, under- or overallocated overhead is prorated to applicable inventories and Cost of Goods Sold based on their year-end balances (before proration). In its 1999 income statement, Worley should report Cost of Goods Sold of:

    a. $682,500.

    b. $684,000.

    c. $756,000.

    d. $757,500.

Exercises

1. (CMA adapted) Sanger Company provides the following information:

Department 203 Costs Incurred for Current Year

Identified With Specific Jobs	Materials	Labour	Other	Total
Job 1376	$ 1,000	$ 7,000		$ 8,000
Job 1377	26,000	53,000		79,000
Job 1378	12,000	9,000		21,000
Job 1379	4,000	1,000		5,000
Not Identified With Specific Jobs				
Indirect materials and supplies	15,000			15,000
Indirect manufacturing		53,000		53,000
Employee fringe benefits			$23,000	23,000
Amortization			12,000	12,000
Supervision		20,000		20,000
Total	$58,000	$143,000	$35,000	$236,000

Department 203 Budgeted Overhead Rate for Current Year

Budgeted overhead:

Variable

Indirect materials and supplies	$ 16,000
Indirect manufacturing labour	56,000
Employee fringe benefits	24,000

Fixed

Amortization	12,000
Supervision	20,000
Total	$128,000

Budgeted direct manufacturing labour costs	$80,000
Budgeted manufacturing overhead rate	
$128,000 ÷ $80,000	160%

Department 203 Work in Process at Beginning of Current Year

Job. No.	Direct Materials	Direct Labour	Overhead	Total
1376	$17,500	$22,000	$33,000	$72,500

Assume Job 1376 was the only job completed during the current year. It was sold upon completion.

a. Compute under- or overallocated overhead for Department 203 for the current year.
b. Compute cost of goods sold.
c. Compute the cost of work-in-process inventory at the end of the current year.
d. Ignoring your answer in part (a), assume overhead is underallocated by $14,000 in Department 203. If underallocated overhead is prorated to Cost of Goods Sold and applicable inventories based on the current year's total amount of allocated overhead (before proration) in the ending balances of these accounts, compute the amount of underallocated overhead that should be debited to Work-in-Process Control at year-end.

2. Rigdon Company uses a job-costing system. The following accounts are from Rigdon's general ledger:

AP:	Accounts Payable Control
AD:	Accumulated Amortization Control
C:	Cash Control
COGS:	Costs of Goods Sold
FG:	Finished Goods Control
MOHA:	Manufacturing Overhead Allocated
MOHC:	Manufacturing Overhead Control
M:	Materials Control
WP:	Wages Payable Control
WIP:	Work-in-Process Control

Enter the identifying letters in the debit and credit columns to record each transaction.

		Debit(s)	Credit(s)
a.	Indirect materials requisitioned	____	____
b.	Amortization on manufacturing equipment	____	____
c.	Manufacturing overhead allocated to jobs	____	____
d.	Direct manufacturing labour costs	____	____
e.	Completion of jobs	____	____
f.	Dispose of an immaterial amount of underallocated overhead	____	____

3. (CPA) Worrell Corporation uses a job-costing system. The following debits (credits) appeared in the general-ledger account Work-in-Process Control for the month of March, 1999:

March 1, balance	$ 12,000
March 31, direct materials	40,000
March 31, direct manufacturing labour	30,000
March 31, manufacturing overhead allocated	27,000
March 31, transferred to finished goods	(100,000)

Worrell allocates overhead to jobs at a budgeted rate of 90% of direct manufacturing labour costs. Job 232, the only job still in process at the end of March 1999, has $2,250 of manufacturing overhead allocated to it.

Compute the amount of direct materials debited to Job 232.

Answers to Chapter 4 Review Questions and Exercises

Completion Statements

1. cost pool
2. cost-allocation base
3. job-costing, process-costing
4. normal
5. job cost record
6. subsidiary ledger

True-False

1. F A canning company, being a producer of masses of identical or similar units of products, would use a process-costing system.
2. T
3. T
4. F In general, the amount of under- or overallocated overhead is *less* at year-end than at any month-end during the year because the full effect of seasonal influences are recorded by year-end.
5. F If the actual level of production is substantially less than the budgeted level, overhead will most likely be underallocated because the fixed portion of overhead allocated is substantially less than the fixed portion of actual overhead incurred.
6. T
7. F When a manufacturing company disposes of underallocated overhead at year-end, the Cost of Goods Sold account increases regardless of the approach used. Cost of Goods Sold, however, *increases less* under proration than under write-off. Operating income is *higher*, therefore, if underallocated overhead is prorated to Work-in-Process Control, Finished Goods Control, and Cost of Goods Sold rather than written off to Cost of Goods Sold.

Multiple Choice

1. a A budgeted overhead rate is more timely but an actual overhead rate is more accurate.
2. c Budgeted overhead rate = $300,000 ÷ 10,000 hours = $30 per machine-hour

Actual overhead incurred	$325,000
Overhead allocated, 11,000 × $30	330,000
Overallocated overhead	$ 5,000

3. b Three steps are used to obtain the answer. First, compute overhead allocated: $350,000 + $10,500 = $360,500. Second, compute the budgeted overhead rate *per unit of output*: $0.175 per machine-hour × 2 machine-hours per unit = $0.35 per unit. Third, compute the production in units: $360,500 ÷ $0.35 = 1,030,000 units.
4. c The cost of indirect materials used increases Manufacturing Overhead Control and decreases Materials Control.
5. d The journal entry described is triggered by the completion of jobs.
6. d Under GAAP, write off under- or overallocated manufacturing overhead to Cost of Goods Sold if the amount is insignificant (immaterial). If the amount is material, use the approach described in either answer (b) or (c).
7. a Two steps are used to obtain the answer. First, compute the share of the overallocated overhead to be allocated to Cost of Goods Sold: $720,000 ÷ ($54,000 + $90,000 + $720,000) = $720,000 ÷ $864,000 = 5/6. Second, *decrease* Cost of Goods Sold by its share of the overallocated overhead: $720,000 − 5/6($45,000) = $682,500.

Exercise 1

a. Actual overhead for the current year:

Indirect materials and supplies	$ 15,000
Indirect manufacturing labour	53,000
Employee fringe benefits	23,000
Amortization	12,000
Supervision	20,000
Total	$123,000

Actual direct manufacturing labour costs for the current year:

Job 1376	$ 7,000
Job 1377	53,000
Job 1378	9,000
Job 1379	1,000
Total	$70,000

Actual overhead incurred	$123,000
Overhead allocated, $70,000 × 160%	112,000
Underallocated overhead	$ 11,000

b. Cost of goods sold = $72,500 + $1,000 + $7,000 + ($7,000 × 160%) = $91,700
Note that, for use in part (d) below, overhead allocated to cost of goods sold during the current year = $7,000 × 160% = $11,200.

c.

	Job 1377	Job 1378	Job 1379	Total
Direct materials	$ 26,000	$12,000	$4,000	$ 42,000
Direct manufacturing labour	53,000	9,000	1,000	63,000
Overhead allocated				
(Direct manuf. labour costs × 160%)	84,800	14,400	1,600	100,800
Work in process at year-end	$163,800	$35,400	$6,600	$205,800

d. Overhead allocated during the current year:

Portion to cost of goods sold (from part b)	$ 11,200
Portion to work in process (from part c)	100,800
Total overhead allocated	$112,000

Let X = Underallocated overhead debited to ending Work-in-Process Control:

$$X = (\$100,800 \div \$112,000) \times \$14,000$$
$$X = 0.90 \times \$14,000 = \$12,600$$

Exercise 2

	Debit(s)	Credit(s)
a.	MOHC	M
b.	MOHC	AD
c.	WIP	MOHA
d.	WIP	WP
e.	FG	WIP
f.	MOHA, COGS	MOHC

Exercise 3

Three steps are used to obtain the answer. First, compute the March 31 balance of Work-in-Process Control: $12,000 + $40,000 + $30,000 + $27,000 − $100,000 = $9,000. This balance is also the balance of Job 232 because it is the only unfinished job. Second, compute the direct manufacturing labour (DML) debited to Job 232:

$$0.90DML = \$2,250$$
$$DML = \$2,250 \div 0.90 = \$2,500$$

Third, compute the amount of direct materials debited to Job 232:

$$\$9,000 - \$2,250 - \$2,500 = \$4,250$$

CHAPTER 5

Activity-Based Costing and Activity-Based Management

Chapter Overview

This chapter explains why and how companies refine the basic job-costing system introduced in Chapter 4. To refine their costing systems, many companies around the world have implemented activity-based costing (ABC). ABC helps managers make better pricing and product-mix decisions, and also assists them in cost management.

Chapter Highlights

1. The colorful term **peanut-butter costing** (also called **cost smoothing**) describes a costing approach that uses broad averages to assign (spread) the cost of resources uniformly to products, services, or customers, even though these individual cost objects use those resources in a nonuniform way. Peanut-butter costing leads to under- or overcosting of products (services or customers). **Product undercosting/product overcosting** occurs if a product consumes a relatively high/low level of resources but is reported to have a relatively low/high total cost. **Product-cost cross-subsidization** means at least one undercosted/overcosted product causes at least one other product to be overcosted/undercosted in the organization.

2. In the example, beginning text p. 139, Plastim Corporation's existing costing system traces direct costs to products S3 and CL5 and allocates indirect costs to them by using a single indirect-cost rate, similar to the system described in Chapter 4. Under this system, S3 costs $58.75 per unit and CL5 costs $97.00 per unit. These costs, however, are counter-intuitive because they indicate that Plastim is uncompetitive on S3 where it believes it has strong capabilities, and is very profitable on CL5 where it is much less confident of its capabilities. In this situation, the key question

is: How might Plastism's costing system be refined?

3. A **refined costing system** provides better measurement of the nonuniformity in the use of an organization's resources by cost objects. Increased competition and advances in information technology have accelerated these refinements. Three guidelines for refining a costing system are:

a. *Direct-cost tracing*. Classify as many of the total costs as direct costs as is economically feasible. This guideline reduces the amount of costs classified as indirect, thereby improving cost accuracy.

b. *Indirect-cost pools*. Expand the number of indirect-cost pools until each pool is homogeneous. In a *homogeneous cost pool*, all of the costs have the same or a similar cause-and-effect (or benefits-received) relationship with the cost-allocation base.

c. *Cost-allocation bases*. Identify the preferred cost-allocation base for each indirect-cost pool. This chapter emphasizes the cause-and-effect criterion in choosing allocation bases.

4. One of the best tools for refining a costing system is **activity-based costing (ABC)**. ABC refines costing systems by focusing on individual activities as the fundamental cost objects. An **activity** is an event, task, or unit of work with a specified purpose (for example, setting up machines for production runs). ABC calculates the costs of these individual activities and assigns costs to cost objects such as products or services on the basis of the activities undertaken to produce each product or service.

5. A key step in implementing ABC is to identify activities that help explain why an organization incurs its particular costs. In the

Plastim example, a cross-functional team identifies seven activities for ABC—design, molding machine setups, manufacturing operations, mold cleaning and maintenance, shipment setup, distribution, and administration. The costs of the mold cleaning and maintenance activity can be traced directly to S3 and CL5, whereas the costs of the other six activities are indirect costs of the products. Because ABC provides a greater level of detail in understanding how Plastim uses its resources, the costs of products S3 and CL5 are more accurate.

6. An important feature of ABC is how it highlights the different levels of activities in a **cost hierarchy**. A cost hierarchy categorizes costs related to products or services into different cost pools on the basis of different types of cost drivers (or cost-allocation bases) or different degrees of difficulty in determining cause-and-effect (or benefits-received) relationships. ABC commonly uses a cost hierarchy that classifies the costs of products or services into four categories:

a. **Output-unit-level costs** are resources used for activities performed on each individual unit of a product or service. In the Plastim example, costs of the manufacturing-operations activity to support the molding machines (such as energy, machine depreciation, and repair) are output unit-level costs. That is, the costs of this activity increase with each additional unit of output produced (or machine-hour used).

b. **Batch-level costs** are resources used for activities that are related to a group of units of a product or service, rather than to each individual unit of the product or service. In the Plastim example, setup costs for a production run are batch-level costs.

c. **Product-sustaining costs** (or **service-sustaining costs**) are resources used for activities undertaken to support an individual product (or service). In the Plastim example, design costs for a specific product are product-sustaining costs.

d. **Facility-sustaining costs** are resources used for activities that cannot be traced to an individual product or service but sup-port the organization as a whole. In the Plastim example, administration costs (such as rent and building security) are facility-sustaining costs.

EXHIBIT 5-2, text p. 148, summarizes the calculations of Plastism's activity-cost rates for the six indirect-cost pools in its ABC system; column 2 of the exhibit shows the product cost hierarchy category for each activity.

7. Compare Plastim's cost per unit for products S3 and CL5:

	S3	CL5
Single indirect-cost rate system	$58.75	$ 97.00
ABC system	49.98	132.07
Difference	$ 8.77	$(35.07)

Because the ABC system provides more accurate costs, this comparison shows the single indirect-cost rate system overcosts S3 by $8.77 and undercosts CL5 by $35.07. The ABC information makes it clear that selling S3 at a price of, say, $53 per unit will be marginally profitable.

8. **Activity-based management (ABM)** describes management decisions that use ABC information to satisfy customers and improve profits. ABM includes pricing and product-mix decisions, cost reduction and process improvement decisions, and product design decisions. For example, the table, text p. 152, shows how Plastim used process and efficiency improvements to reduce the distribution cost of S3 by $0.75 per unit and CL5 by $1.50 per unit.

9. In many companies, costing systems evolve from using a single indirect-cost rate to using separate indirect-cost rates for each department. Department costing approximates ABC in a department if the department has a single activity or a single cost-allocation base for different activities, or if individual products use the activities of the department in the same proportions. In companies where none of these conditions are met, department costing can be refined using ABC.

10. The conditions under which ABC provides the most benefits include (a) when the existing costing system identifies all or most costs as output-unit-level costs (that is, few, if any, costs are described as batch-level, product-sustaining, or facility-sustaining costs), (b) when an organization has products that make diverse demands on resources because of differences in volume, batch size, and complexity, (c) when an organization is showing small profits on products it is well suited to make and sell, and is showing large profits on products for which it is less suited, (d) when complex products appear to be very profitable and simple products appear to be unprofitable, and (e) when operations management has significant disagreements with the accounting staff concerning the costs of making and selling products and services.

11. Managers choose the level of detail in their costing systems by comparing the expected costs of the system with the expected benefits of using the information to make better decisions. In ABC, the main costs are the measurements necessary to implement the system and to keep activity-cost rates updated regularly. Improvements in information technology and related declines in measurement costs have enabled ABC to be practical in many organizations. As these trends continue, ABC should be better able to pass the cost-benefit test.

12. Although ABC originated in the manufacturing sector, it has many applications in the service and merchandising sectors. In fact, the Plastim example illustrates the application of ABC to a service function (design) and a merchandising function (distribution). Many companies in the banking, insurance, airline, railroad, hospital, accounting, and consulting industries have implemented ABC in an effort to identify profitable product mixes, improve efficiency, and satisfy customers. Similarly, many retail and wholesale companies are working with ABC.

Featured Exercise

A. H. Church, Inc., manufactures a variety of wooden toys for young children. The company uses ABC. The manufacturing activities and related data are as follows:

Activity Area	Cost Driver Used as Cost-Allocation Base	Indirect Costs per Unit of Cost-Allocation Base
Materials handling	Board feet of lumber	$ 0.10
Forming and sanding	Direct manuf. labour-hours	10.00
Painting	Number of painted sets	0.30
Inspection	Number of finished sets	0.04
Packaging	Number of finished sets	0.20

Two types of wooden blocks were manufactured in September, alphabet cubes and numeric shapes. Quantities and per-set data are as follows:

	Alphabet Cubes	Numeric Shapes
Number of sets produced	12,000	2,000
Direct material costs per set	$1.20	$2.00
Board feet of lumber per set	1.50	2.00
Direct manufacturing labour-hours per set	0.05	0.10
Number of sets painted	12,000	none

Compute the manufacturing costs per set for each product.

Solution

	Alphabet Cubes	Numeric Shapes
Direct material costs,		
12,000 × $1.20; 2,000 × $2.00	$14,400	$4,000
Indirect costs:		
Materials handling,		
12,000 × 1.5 × $0.10; 2,000 × 2.0 × $0.10	1,800	400
Forming and sanding,		
12,000 × 0.05 × $10; 2,000 × 0.10 × $10	6,000	2,000
Painting, 12,000 × $0.30	3,600	
Inspection, 12,000 × $0.04; 2,000 × $0.04	480	80
Packaging, 12,000 × $0.20; 2,000 × $0.20	2,400	400
Total manufacturing costs	$28,680	$6,880
Divide by number of sets produced	÷12,000	÷2,000
Manufacturing cost per set	$ 2.39	$ 3.44

Review Questions and Exercises

Completion Statements

Fill in the blank(s) to complete each statement.

1. _____ occurs when a product consumes a relatively high level of resources but is reported to have a relatively low total cost.

2. A _____ provides better measurement of the nonuniformity in the use of an organization's resources by cost objects such as products and services.

3. Three guidelines for refining a costing system are: (a) classify as many of the total costs as _____ costs as is economically feasible, (b) expand the number of indirect-cost pools until each pool is _____, and (c) identify the preferred _____ _____ for each indirect-cost pool.

4. A _____ categorizes costs related to products or services into different cost pools on the basis of different types of cost drivers (or cost-allocation bases) or different degrees of difficulty in determining cause-and-effect (or benefits-received) relationships.

5. _____ uses ABC information to make decisions concerning pricing, product-mix, cost reduction, process improvement, and product design.

True-False

Indicate whether each statement is true (T) or false (F).

___ 1. A main factor driving refinement of costing systems is increasing competition in the marketplace.

___ 2. One of the guidelines for refining costing systems is to use the concept of a homogeneous cost pool for determining how many indirect-cost pools to form.

___ 3. ABC focuses on activities as the fundamental cost object and assigns the costs of products or services to those activities.

___ 4. In ABC, the costs of activities are always indirect costs of products.

___ 5. ABC seeks to identify all costs used by products regardless of whether the costs are variable or fixed in the short run.

___ 6. Output-unit-level costs are resources used for activities undertaken to support an individual product or service.

___ 7. ABC systems can be particularly beneficial if a non-ABC system shows that complex products are very profitable and simple products are unprofitable.

8. A major reason why low-volume products are often overcosted is the batch-level costs and product-sustaining costs of those products are allocated as if they were output unit-level costs of all products.

Multiple Choice

Select the best answer to each question. Space is provided for computations after the quantitative questions.

1. If a costing system uses a single cost-allocation base:
   a. products that use relatively more of this base in comparison with the resources they actually consume tend to be undercosted.
   b. products that use relatively less of this base in comparison with the resources they actually consume tend to be overcosted.
   c. products that use relatively more of this base in comparison with the resources they actually consume tend to be overcosted.
   d. products that use none of this base tend to be overcosted.

2. (CPA) What is the usual effect on the number of cost pools and cost-allocation bases if activity-based costing replaces a traditional costing system?

	Cost pools	Cost-allocation bases
a.	No effect	No effect
b.	Increase	No effect
c.	No effect	Increase
d.	Increase	Increase

3. Which of the following *is not* a characteristic of ABC?
   a. Operating personnel play a key role in identifying the individual activities.
   b. It is usually difficult to find a good cause-and-effect relationship between a cost-allocation base and facility-sustaining costs.
   c. There are many homogenous indirect-cost pools.
   d. Cost-allocation bases of indirect-cost pools are usually financial in nature.

4. Procurement costs, which include the costs of placing orders for materials and paying suppliers, are classified as:
   a. an output-unit-level cost.
   b. a batch-level cost.
   c. a product-sustaining cost.
   d. a facility-sustaining cost.

5. (CMA) Zeta Company is preparing its annual profit plan. As part of its analysis of the profitability of individual products, the controller estimates the amount of manufacturing overhead that should be allocated to the individual product lines from the information given below.

	Wall Mirrors	Specialty Windows
Units produced	25	25
Material moves per product line	5	15
Direct manufacturing labour-hours per unit	200	200

   Budgeted material-handling costs are $50,000.

   Under a costing system that allocates manufacturing overhead on the basis of direct manufacturing labour-hours, the material-handling costs allocated to one wall mirror are:
   a. $1,000.
   b. $500.
   c. $2,000.
   d. $5,000.
   e. $0.

6. Using the data in question 6, the material-handling costs allocated to one wall mirror under ABC are:
   a. $1,000.
   b. $500.
   c. $1,500.
   d. $2,500.
   e. $0.

____ 7. ABC tends to pass the cost-benefit test
for companies with:
a. operations that are relatively simple.
b. many products that use different
amounts of resources.

c. many products that use about the
same amount of resources.
d. few products that use about the same
amount of resources.

Exercises

1. (CMA adapted) New-Rage Cosmetics uses ABC. The following data describe New Rage's
indirect costs of producing 200 cases of Satin Sheen makeup:

Activity	Activity-Cost Rate	Quantity of Activity Used
Incoming material inspection	$11.50 per type of material	12 types of material
Production setup	$30 per setup-hour	16 setup-hours
In-process inspection	$3 per case	200 cases
Product certification	$24 per order	4 orders
Distribution	$1 per kilogram	2,000 kilograms
General administration	$8 per direct manufacturing labour-hour	50 direct manufacturing labour-hours

The direct costs of the 200 cases of Satin Sheen makeup total $8,200.

Compute the cost per case of Satin Sheen makeup.

2. Four managers of Torchlight Company had dinner together. Details of their restaurant bill are as follows:

Diner	Entree	Dessert	Drinks	Total
Jason	$17	$8	$19	$ 44
Kent	24	3	10	37
Lynne	15	4	6	25
Marci	31	6	5	42
				$148

Jason put the entire bill on his credit card. A few days later, he billed each of the other diners for the average cost per diner.

a. Compute the amount by which Jason's billing approach undercosts or overcosts each of the diners. Assume the four diners shared the gratuity at the restaurant by paying cash.
b. What is the fundamental difference between costing the diners in this exercise and costing products in a manufacturing company?

3. Jay & Associates, a CPA firm, has many audit clients. The following information is available for two of Jay's recent audits:

	Fuentes Footwear	Detrick Properties
Direct professional labour-hours		
Partner time used	30 hours	75 hours
Staff time used	150 hours	105 hours
Travel time	0.5 hours	3.0 hours
Phone calls and faxes (estimated hours, detailed records are not kept)	Under 20	Over 100

The existing costing system uses (i) a single direct cost category, direct professional labour-hours (DPLH), costed at $120 per DPLH and (ii) a single indirect-cost rate of $80 per DPLH.

a. Without making computations, which audit do you think actually costs Jay more? Explain.
b. Compute the costs assigned to each audit under the existing costing system.
c. Explain what is wrong with the existing costing system.
d. What is a likely outcome of using the existing costing system?
e. In general, how could the existing costing system be improved?

4. Wescott Foods manufactures many different types of breakfast cereal at its St. Louis plant. The following costs are incurred to produce 28,000,000 boxes of cereal in 1999:

- New-product developments costs—cost of adding new cereals to those already being produced. In 1999, "Wheat Flakes" was added at a cost of $5,684,000.
- Material-handling costs—costs of handling grain, sugar, packaging materials, and the like ($6,628,000). The cost driver is hours of material-handling time, which is highly correlated with hours of production time.
- Material-purchase costs—costs of materials acquired from suppliers ($8,852,000). These costs are directly traced to individual products and are variable with respect to the number of boxes produced.
- Manufacturing labour costs—costs directly traced to (i) individual products on a per-box basis ($7,263,000), or (ii) setups for products when the production line switches from one type of cereal to another ($2,385,000).
- Energy costs—costs of heat, light, and power ($1,029,000). The cost driver is hours of production time.
- Plant administration costs—costs such as salaries, amortization, insurance, and building security ($6,295,000).

The number of boxes of cereal produced is highly correlated with hours of production time.

a. Classify each of Wescott's manufacturing costs as output-unit-level, batch-level, product-sustaining, or facility-sustaining.
b. Compute the manufacturing output-unit-level cost per box.
c. Compute the total manufacturing cost per box.
d. For what purpose might Wescott use the information in part (b)? In part (c)?

Answers to Chapter 5 Review Questions and Exercises

Completion Statements

1. Product undercosting
2. refined costing system
3. direct, homogeneous, cost-allocation base
4. cost hierarchy
5. Activity-based management (ABM)

True-False

1. T
2. T
3. F   The last part of the statement is reversed. ABC assigns the costs of activities to products or services.
4. F   In ABC, the costs of activities are often indirect costs of products but can be direct costs of products. For example, Panel A of Exhibit 5-3, text p. 149, shows that the mold cleaning and maintenance activity is a direct cost of products S3 and CL5, whereas the other six activities are indirect costs of these products.
5. T
6. F   The statement describes *product-sustaining costs* rather than *output-unit-level costs*. Output-unit-level costs are resources used for activities performed on each individual unit of product or service (for example, energy costs to run a molding machine).
7. T
8. F   The statement describes a major reason why low-volume products are often *undercosted*.

Multiple Choice

1. c   If a costing system uses a single cost-allocation base, products that use relatively more/less of that base in comparison to the resources they actually consume will be overcosted/under-costed. The reason is all indirect costs are allocated via the base. The costing system described in the question results in peanut-butter costing (cost smoothing).
2. d   ABC uses more cost pools, each with its own cost-allocation base. For example, compare the traditional costing system in Panel A of Exhibit 5-1, text p. 141, with the ABC system in Panel A of Exhibit 5-3, text p. 149.
3. d.   In ABC, the cost-allocation bases of indirect-cost pools are usually nonfinancial variables. Some examples are setup-hours, number of shipments, and cubic feet of packages shipped.
4. b   Procurement costs are a batch-level cost because they are related to the number of orders placed rather than the quantity or value of materials purchased.
5. a   Two steps are used to obtain the answer. First, compute the budgeted materials-handling cost rate per direct manufacturing labour-hour (DMLH):

$$\frac{\$50,000}{(25 \times 200) + (25 \times 200)} = \frac{\$50,000}{5,000 + 5,000} = \frac{\$50,000}{10,000} = \$5 \text{ per DMLH}$$

Second, compute the material-handling costs allocated to one wall mirror:
200 DMLH $\times$ \$5 = \$1,000
6. b   Two steps are used to obtain the answer. First, compute the budgeted material-handling cost rate per material move: \$50,000 $\div$ (5 + 15) = \$50,000 $\div$ 20 = \$2,500 per move. Second, compute the material-handling costs allocated to one wall mirror:
(\$2,500 $\times$ 5 moves) $\div$ 25 units = \$12,500 $\div$ 25 = \$500

7. b ABC tends to pass the costs-benefit test for companies meeting one or more of the conditions listed in paragraph 10 of the Chapter Highlights.

Exercise 1

Direct costs	$ 8,200
Indirect costs:	
Incoming material inspection, 12 × $11.50	138
Production setup, 16 × $30	480
In-process inspection, 200 × $3	600
Product certification, 4 × $24	96
Distribution, 2,000 × $1	2,000
General administration, 50 × $8	400
Total costs	$11,914

Cost per case = $11,914 ÷ 200 = $59.57

Exercise 2

a. Average cost per diner = $148 ÷ 4 = $37
   Jason: $44 − $37 = $7 undercosted
   Kent: $37 − $37 = $0 (accurately costed)
   Lynne: $25 − $37 = $12 overcosted
   Marci: $42 − $37 = $5 undercosted
b. The fundamental difference is that each cost in the restaurant bill is a *direct cost* that can be traced to one of the diners, whereas many manufacturing costs are *indirect costs* that must be allocated to products. An indirect cost would arise in the dining example if two or more of the diners shared an item such as an appetizer or bottle of wine.

Exercise 3

a. The audit of Detrick Properties actually costs Jay more because, although both audits use 180 DPLH, a much higher proportion of *partner hours* is used for Detrick: 75/180 versus 30/180. Also, Detrick uses much more of the travel and communication resources.
b. Fuentes audit = (180 × $120) + (180 × $80) = $21,600 + $14,400 = $36,000
   Detrick audit = (180 × $120) + (180 × $80) = $21,600 + $14,400 = $36,000
c. With only one direct-cost category and only one indirect-cost pool, the existing costing system does not accurately measure the cost of resources used by each audit. The Fuentes audit is overcosted because it used a lower proportion of the more expensive partner hours as well as relatively less travel and communication. For the opposite reasons, the Detrick audit is undercosted.
d. By misstating the cost of the audits, Jay could easily lose Fuentes as a client. A competing CPA firm with a better costing system is likely to make a lower bid for the Fuentes audit.
e. The costing system could be refined by following three guidelines: (1) classify as many of the total costs as direct costs of audits as is economically feasible, (2) expand the number of indirect-cost pools until each pool is homogeneous, and (3) identify the preferred cost-allocation base for each indirect-cost pool.

Exercise 4

a. New-product development costs are product-sustaining costs.
   Material-handling costs are output-unit-level costs.
   Material-purchase costs are output-unit-level costs.
   Manufacturing labour costs directly traced to individual products are output-unit-level costs.
   Manufacturing labour costs traced directly to production setups are batch-level costs.
   Energy costs are output-unit-level costs.
   Plant administration costs are facility-sustaining costs.

b.
Material-handling costs	$ 6,628,000
Material-purchase costs	8,852,000
Direct manufacturing labour costs	7,263,000
Energy costs	1,029,000
Total output-unit-level costs	$23,772,000

$$\text{Output-unit-level costs per box} = \frac{\$23,772,000}{28,000,000} = \$0.849 \text{ per box}$$

c.
Output-unit-level costs (from part b)	$23,772,000
Batch-level costs	
Production setup costs	2,385,000
Product-sustaining costs	
New-product development costs	5,684,000
Facility-sustaining costs	
Plant administration costs	6,295,000
Total manufacturing costs	$38,136,000

$$\text{Total manufacturing costs per box} = \frac{\$38,136,000}{28,000,000} = \$1.362 \text{ per box}$$

d. Wescott could use the manufacturing output-unit-level cost per box for developing budgets at different levels of output and for evaluating the performance of managers. Total manufacturing cost per box is the inventoriable cost for reporting under generally accepted accounting principles. (Note that some value-chain costs not included in this exercise—such as marketing, distribution, and customer service—are not inventoriable costs, but they could be classified in the cost hierarchy in part a.)

Master Budget and Responsibility Accounting

Chapter Overview

This chapter explains the key role budgets play in the planning and control of operations. The chapter has a dual focus: (1) how to prepare the operating budget part of the master budget and (2) how managers use responsibility accounting to facilitate planning and control. The Appendix to the chapter illustrates how to prepare the cash budget.

Chapter Highlights

1. A *budget* is a quantitative expression of a proposed plan of action by management for a future time period and is an aid to the coordination and implementation of the plan. A budget can cover both financial and nonfinancial aspects of the plan and acts as a blueprint for the organization in the upcoming period. If administered wisely, budgets compel planning, provide performance criteria, and promote coordination and communication within the organization.

2. Well-managed organizations usually have the following budgeting cycle:

a. Planning the performance of the organization as a whole and its subunits.
b. Providing a set of specific expectations against which actual results can be compared.
c. Investigating deviations from plans and, if necessary, taking corrective action.
d. Planning again, in light of feedback and changed conditions.

3. Budgeting is most useful when done as an integral part of the organization's **strategy**. Strategy describes how an organization matches its own capabilities with the opportunities in the marketplace in order to accomplish its overall objectives. Strategic analysis underlies both short-run and long-run planning. In turn, these plans lead to the formulation of budgets.

4. Management at all levels of the organization should understand and support the budgets and the management control system. Top management support is critical for obtaining active line-management participation in formulating and administering budgets. Budgets should not be administered rigidly because changing conditions may call for changes in plans.

5. The most frequently used budget period is one year. The annual budget is often subdivided by months for the first quarter and by quarters for the remainder of the year. Organizations are increasingly using **rolling budgets**. A rolling budget is always available for a specified future time period by adding a month, quarter, or year in the future as the month, quarter, or year just ended is deleted.

6. Pressures often exist within organizations for budgeted revenues to be overestimates and/or budgeted costs to be underestimates of the expected amounts. For example, some organizations set high budgets for revenues and/or low budgets for costs in an attempt to motivate managers and other employees to put forth extra effort and achieve better performance. In other cases, budgets may require below-average effort to be attained. **Budgetary slack** arises if managers underestimate budgeted revenues (or overestimate budgeted costs) to make budgeted targets more easily achievable. Budgetary slack provides managers with a hedge against unexpected adverse circumstances. A major challenge in budget-

ing is providing managers with incentives to make honest budget forecasts.

7. The **master budget** is a comprehensive expression of management's operating and financial plans for a future time period (usually a year) that is summarized in a set of budgeted financial statements. The two main parts of the master budget are the **operating budget** and the **financial budget**. The operating budget includes the budgeted income statement and its supporting budget schedules. The financial budget consists of the capital expenditures budget, cash budget (discussed in paragraph 17 below), budgeted balance sheet, and budgeted statement of cash flows. EXHIBIT 6-2, text p. 183, provides an overview of the master budget.

8. Nine steps are used to develop the operating budget for a manufacturing company:

Step 1: Prepare the revenues budget.
Step 2: Prepare the production budget (in units).
Step 3: Prepare the direct materials usage budget and direct materials purchases budget.
Step 4: Prepare the direct manufacturing labour budget.
Step 5: Prepare the manufacturing overhead budget.
Step 6: Prepare the ending inventories budget (direct materials and finished goods).
Step 7: Prepare the cost of goods sold budget.
Step 8: Prepare the nonmanufacturing costs budget.
Step 9: Prepare the budgeted income statement.

In performing Step 1, the usual starting point is to base revenues on expected demand. Occasionally, factors other than demand limit budgeted revenues. For example, if demand exceeds available production capacity, the revenues budget is based on the maximum number of units that could be produced. Steps 2 and 3 are illustrated below using assumed amounts. Step 2 uses the following schedule:

	Product Units
Budgeted sales	104,000
Add target ending inventory	6,000
Total requirements	110,000
Deduct beginning inventory	10,000
Budgeted production	100,000

Step 3 uses the following schedule for each type of direct material:

	Material A (in litres)
Budgeted production usage (100,000 units above × 2.5 litres per unit)	250,000
Add target ending inventory	11,000
Total requirements	261,000
Deduct beginning inventory	12,500
Budgeted purchases	248,500

9. Software packages are readily available that reduce the computational burden and time required to prepare budgets. These packages do the calculations for **financial planning models**, which are mathematical representations of the interrelationships among operating activities, financial activities, and other factors that affect the master budget. These models enable managers to prepare the first draft of the master budget, and conduct "what if" (sensitivity) analysis of the effects on this budget of changes in the original predicted data or in the underlying assumptions. Sensitivity analysis is especially valuable for examining the effects of interrelated changes to parametres in the master budget; EXHIBIT 6-4, text p. 192, illustrates this point.

10. A key issue facing organizations today is continuous improvement, which the Japanese call *kaizen*. **Kaizen budgeting** explicitly incorporates continuous improvement *during the budget period* into the budget numbers. Budgeted costs are based on future improvements that are yet to be implemented rather than on current practices and methods. Unless a company using kaizen budgeting meets its continuous improvement targets, actual costs will exceed budgeted costs.

11. Most budgeting models use a limited number of cost drivers that are predominantly output-based, such as units produced or units sold. Due, in part, to the growing use of activity-based costing, there is now interest in incorporating a broader set of cost drivers into budgets. **Activity-based budgeting (ABB)** focuses on the budgeted costs of activities necessary to produce and sell products and services. ABB entails formulating budgets for each activity area. An activity-based budget is prepared by multiplying budgeted usage of the cost driver for each activity times the respective budgeted cost rate, and then summing the budgeted costs of the activities. The more detailed information available from ABB gives managers additional insight into ways they can better manage future costs.

12. Budgeting is much more than the mechanical tool implied in paragraphs 8 through 11. Human factors play a crucial part in budgeting. Each manager, regardless of his or her level within the organization, is in charge of a **responsibility centre.** A responsibility centre is a part, subunit, or segment of an organization, whose manager is accountable for a specified set of activities. The higher the manager's level, the broader the responsibility centre he or she manages and, generally, the greater the number of his or her subordinates. Four major types of responsibility centres are:

Type	Manager Is Accountable For
Cost centre	Costs only
Revenue centre	Revenues only
Profit centre	Revenues and costs
Investment centre	Investments, revenues, and costs

13. **Responsibility accounting** is a system that measures the plans (by budgets) and actions (by actual results) of each responsibility centre. The *performance report* for each responsibility centre shows by line item the actual result, the budgeted amount, and the *variance* (the difference between the actual result and the budgeted amount). Performance reports for higher levels of management combine lower-level reports but limit the level of detail; as a result, performance reports for higher-level managers include more total dollars but less detail than lower-level reports.

14. Managers and accountants tend to "play the blame game"—using variances in performance reports for responsibility centres to pinpoint fault for operating problems. When variances occur, the initial focus should be on which manager to *ask,* not which manager to *blame.* Variances should be used to raise questions and direct attention to the managers who are expected to have essential knowledge and information. Fixing the blame for a variance occurs only if the manager's performance is judged to be unsatisfactory.

15. **Controllability** is the degree of influence that a specific manager has over costs, revenues, or other items in question. A **controllable cost** is any cost that is primarily subject to the influence of a given responsibility centre manager for a given time period. A responsibility accounting system either excludes all uncontrollable costs from a manager's performance report or segregates them from the controllable costs in that report.

16. Managers should not overemphasize controllability. Responsibility accounting is more far-reaching. It focuses on knowledge and information, not just control. The key question is: Which person knows the most about the specific item in question regardless of his or her ability to exert personal control? For example, a purchasing manager may be held accountable for total purchase costs, not because she can affect market prices, but because of her ability to predict uncontrollable prices and explain uncontrollable price changes.

17. The Appendix to this chapter illustrates how to prepare the **cash budget,** a key component of the financial budget. The cash budget is a schedule of expected cash receipts and disbursements. (Note that amortization is excluded from this budget because it does not require a current period cash disbursement.) The cash budget helps prevent unexpected cash deficiencies or idle cash, thereby keeping the cash balance in line with needs. Like other

budgets, the quality of the cash budget is enhanced by conducting sensitivity analysis of the effects on this budget of changes in the original predicted data or in the underlying assumptions. EXHIBIT 6-8, text p. 200, shows a cash budget by quarters that includes the cash flows associated with obtaining and repaying a bank loan.

Featured Exercises

1. Cobb Company budgets sales of Product A at 200,000 units for October 2000. Production of one unit of this product requires three kilograms of Material Y and two litres of Material Z. Actual beginning inventories and budgeted ending inventories for the month are as follows:

	October 1	October 31
Product A	25,000 units	8,000 units
Material Y	23,000 kilograms	19,000 kilograms
Material Z	16,000 litres	21,000 litres

Compute the number of litres of Material Z the company needs to purchase during October 2000.

Solution

Two steps are used to obtain the answer. First, compute the budgeted production of Product A in units:

Budgeted sales	200,000
Add target ending inventory	8,000
Total requirements	208,000
Deduct beginning inventory	25,000
Budgeted production in units	183,000

Second, compute budgeted purchases of Material Z in litres:

Budgeted production usage, 183,000 × 2	366,000
Add target ending inventory	21,000
Total requirements	387,000
Deduct beginning inventory	16,000
Budgeted purchases in litres	371,000

----

2. (Relates to the Chapter Appendix) Information pertaining to Noskey Corporation's sales revenues is as follows:

	November 1999 (Actual)	December 1999 (Budget)	January 2000 (Budget)
Cash sales	$ 80,000	$100,000	$ 60,000
Credit sales	240,000	360,000	180,000
Total sales	$320,000	$460,000	$240,000

Management estimates that 5% of credit sales are uncollectible. Of the credit sales that are collectible, 60% are collected in the month of sale and the remainder in the month following sale. Purchases of inventory are equal to next month's sales, and gross margin is 30%. All purchases of inventory are on credit; 25% are paid in the month of purchase, and the remainder are paid in the month following purchase.

a. Compute budgeted cash receipts for January 2000.
b. Compute budgeted cash disbursements for purchases for December 1999.

Solution

a. Budgeted cash receipts for January 2000:
   From credit sales in December
   $360,000 (1−0.05)(1−0.60) $136,800
   From credit sales in January
   $180,000 (1−0.05)(0.60)   102,600
   From cash sales in January   60,000
   Total $299,400

b. Budgeted cash disbursements for purchases for December 1999:
   From purchases in November
   $460,000 (1−0.30)(1−0.25) $241,500
   From purchases in December
   $240,000 (1−0.30)(0.25)   42,000
   Total $283,500

Review Questions and Exercises

Completion Statements

Fill in the blank(s) to complete each statement.

1. _____ describes how an organization matches its own capabilities with the opportunities in the marketplace in order to accomplish its overall objectives.
2. A _____ budget is always available for a specified future time period by adding a month, quarter, or year in the future as the month, quarter, or year just ended is deleted.
3. The practice of underestimating budgeted revenues or overestimating budgeted costs in order to make budgeted targets more easily achievable creates what is called _____

    _____.
4. The master budget consists of two main parts: _____
    and _____.
5. _____ are computer-based mathematical representations of the interrelationships among operating activities, financial activities, and other factors that affect the master budget.
6. _____ budgeting explicitly incorporates continuous improvement during the budget period into the budgeted numbers.
7. A subunit (segment) of an organization whose manager is accountable for a specified set of activities is called a _____

    _____.
8. Any cost that is primarily subject to the influence of a given responsibility centre manager for a given time period is called a _____ cost.
9. _____ is a system that measures the plans (by budgets) and actions (by actual results) of each responsibility centre.

True-False

Indicate whether each statement is true (T) or false (F).

____ 1. The preferable basis for evaluating the results of a cost centre for the current month is the centre's actual results for the same month in the preceding year.
____ 2. The financial budget part of the master budget consists of the capital budget, cash budget, operating budget, and budgeted balance sheet.
____ 3. The usual constraint on the budgeted level of operations is the organization's ability to produce products and services.
____ 4. From the sales staff's standpoint, budgetary slack hedges against unexpected adverse circumstances.
____ 5. The more detailed information used in activity-based budgeting gives managers additional insight into ways to better manage future costs.
____ 6. The organization structure that results if operations are divided into increasingly smaller areas of responsibility at increasingly lower levels is shaped like a pyramid with top management at the peak.
____ 7. Variances, the differences between actual results and budgeted amounts, should initially be used to fix the blame on the managers who are responsible for the variances.
____ 8. (Appendix) Amortization is excluded from the cash budget.

Multiple Choice

Select the best answer to each question. Space is provided for computations after the quantitative questions.

___ 1. In formulating the operating budget, the last step is usually the preparation of the:
a. budgeted income statement.
b. budgeted balance sheet.
c. budgeted statement of cash flows.
d. cash budget.

___ 2. (CPA) Mien Co. is budgeting sales of 53,000 units of product Nous for October 2000. The manufacture of one unit of Nous requires 4 kilos of chemical Loire. During October 2000, Mien plans to reduce the inventory of Loire by 50,000 kilos and increase the finished goods inventory of Nous by 6,000 units. There is no work-in-process inventory of Nous. How many kilos of Loire is Mien budgeting to purchase in October 2000?
a. 138,000
b. 162,000
c. 186,000
d. 238,000

___ 3. (CPA adapted) The Zel Company, a wholesaler, budgets $150,000 of credit sales and $20,000 of cash sales for next month. All merchandise is marked up to sell at 125% of its invoice cost. The budgeted cost of goods sold for next month is:
a. $127,500.
b. $132,500.
c. $136,000.
d. $140,000.

___ 4. (CMA adapted) Rokat Corporation manufactures tables that are sold to schools, hotels, and other institutions. Rokat plans to produce 1,800 tables next month. It takes 20 minutes of labour time to assemble a table. How many employees will be required next month for this assembly work? (Fractional employees are acceptable because employees can be hired on a part-time basis. Assume a 40-hour week and a 4-week month.)
a. 1.5 employees
b. 3.75 employees
c. 15 employees
d. 60 employees
e. 600 employees

___ 5. (CPA) When used for evaluating the performance of a production department manager, performance reports in a responsibility accounting system *should not*:
a. be related to the organization structure.
b. include allocated fixed manufacturing overhead.
c. include variances between actual results and budgeted amounts of controllable costs.
d. distinguish between controllable and uncontrollable costs.

___ 6. Performance reports prepared for successively higher management levels in an organization should include:
a. less total dollars and more detail.
b. less total dollars and less detail.
c. more total dollars and less detail.
d. more total dollars and more detail.

___ 7. (Appendix) During the budget period, Bama Manufacturing Company expects to make $219,000 of sales on credit and collect $143,500 of cash from customers. Assume no other cash inflows are expected, total cash payments during the budget period are expected to be $179,000, and an increase of $10,000 is desired in the cash balance. How much cash needs to be borrowed during the budget period?

    a. $45,500
    b. $44,500
    c. $24,500
    d. $23,500

___ 8. (Appendix, CPA) Steven Corporation began operations in 2000. Steven provides the following information:

Total merchandise purchases for the year	$350,000
Merchandise inventory at December 31, 2000	70,000
Collections from customers	200,000

All merchandise is marked up to sell at 40% above cost. Assuming all sales are on credit and all receivables are collectible, the balance in accounts receivable on December 31, 2000 is:

    a. $50,000.
    b. $192,000.
    c. $250,000.
    d. $290,000.

Exercises

1. (CMA) Berol Company plans to sell 200,000 units of finished product in July 2000 and anticipates a growth rate in unit sales of 5% per month. The target monthly ending inventory in units of finished goods is 80% of the next month's budgeted sales. There are 150,000 finished units in inventory on June 30, 2000. Each unit of finished goods requires four kilograms of direct materials at a cost of $1.20 per kilogram. There are 800,000 kilograms of direct materials in inventory on June 30, 2000.

    a. Compute the budgeted production of finished units for the quarter ending September 30, 2000.
    b. Compute the budgeted cost of direct material purchases for the quarter ending September 30, 2000, assuming direct materials inventory at the end of the quarter is to equal 25% of the usage during that quarter.

2. Minton Company had the following actual results for 1999.

Revenues (1,000,000 units)	$20,000,000
Cost of goods sold	14,000,000
Gross margin	6,000,000
Operating costs (includes straight- line amortization of $900,000)	4,200,000
Operating income	$ 1,800,000

The selling price for 2000 is expected to increase by 3%, and sales volume in units is expected to increase by 5%. Minton uses kaizen budgeting. Under the kaizen approach in 2000, cost of goods sold per unit is expected to decrease by 4%, and total operating costs (excluding amortization) are expected to decline by 6%.

Prepare the budgeted income statement for 2000.

3. (Appendix, CMA adapted) Super Connect manufactures products for computer networks. Information regarding Super Connect's operations include the following:
- Revenues are budgeted at $520,000 for December 2000 and $500,000 for January 2001.
- 80% of the network components are purchased in the month prior to the month of sale, and 20% are purchased in the month of sale. Purchased components comprise 40% of cost of goods sold.
- Payment for the components is made in the month following purchase.
- Cost of goods sold is 80% of revenues.

Compute the budgeted balance of accounts payable on December 31, 2000.

Completion Statements

1. Strategy
2. rolling
3. budgetary slack
4. operating budget, financial budget
5. Financial planning models
6. Kaizen
7. responsibility centre
8. controllable
9. Responsibility accounting

True-False

1. F   The preferable basis for evaluating the actual results of a cost centre for the current month is the centre's budget for the current month. Past performance is generally not a good basis for evaluating current performance because (i) past performance may have been at a low level and/or (ii) current operating conditions may differ significantly from those in the past.

2. F   The financial budget part of the master budget consists of the capital budget, cash budget, budgeted balance sheet, and budgeted statement of cash flows. The operating budget is the other main part of the master budget.

3. F   The usual constraint on the budgeted level of operations is the organization's ability to *sell* products and services (that is, sales are limited by demand). Occasionally, factors other than demand limit sales. For example, if demand exceeds available production capacity, the revenues budget is based on the maximum number of units that can be produced.

4. T
5. T
6. T

7. F   When a variance occurs, the initial focus should be on which manager to *ask*, not which manager to *blame*. A variance should be used to raise questions and to direct attention to the manager who is expected to have the essential knowledge and information. Fixing the blame for a variance occurs only if the manager's performance is judged to be unsatisfactory.

8. T

Multiple Choice

1. a   As shown in Exhibit 6-2, p. 183, preparing the budgeted income statement is the last step in developing the operating budget. The cash budget, budgeted balance sheet, and budgeted statement of cash flows are components of the financial budget.

2. c   Two steps are used to obtain the answer. First, compute the budgeted production in units:

	Units
Budgeted sales	53,000
Add budgeted increase in finished goods inventory	6,000
Budgeted production	59,000

Second, compute budgeted purchases in kilos:

	Kilos
Budgeted production requirement, $59,000 \times 4$	236,000
Deduct budgeted decrease in chemicals inventory	50,000
Budgeted purchases	186,000

Note that in the example, text pp. 187-188, both beginning and ending inventories are given for finished goods and direct materials. In this question, however, only the *changes* in inventories are given.

3. c   Let X = Budgeted cost of goods sold for next month
1.25X = $170,000
        X = $170,000 ÷ 1.25 = $136,000

4. b   It takes 20 minutes or 1/3 hour of labour time to assemble a table.
Assembly-hours for next month = 1,800 tables × 1/3 = 600 hours
Hours worked by a full-time employee per month = 40 hours × 4 weeks = 160 hours
Employees required for next month = 600 ÷ 160 = 3.75 employees

5. b   Allocated fixed manufacturing overhead is generally not controllable by a production department manager. A responsibility accounting system either excludes all noncontrollable costs from the production department manager's performance report or segregates those costs from the controllable costs in that report. The latter approach could change the manager's behaviour in a direction that top management desires. For example, if fixed manufacturing overhead is allocated on the basis of direct manufacturing labour-hours, the manager will be motivated to use less labour-hours.

6. c   Performance reports prepared for successively higher levels of management combine lower-level reports but limit the amount of detail. As a result, performance reports for higher-level managers include more total dollars but less detail than lower-level reports.

7. a
Cash receipts from customers		$143,500
Deduct:		
Cash payments	$179,000	
Desired increase in cash balance	10,000	189,000
Cash deficiency (the borrowing required)		$ 45,500

8. b   Cost of goods sold = $350,000 − $70,000 = $280,000
Revenues = $280,000 × 1.40 = $392,000
Accounts receivable balance on December 31, 2000 = $392,000 − $200,000 = $192,000

Exercise 1

a. Production requirement in units of finished goods = Budgeted sales + Target ending finished goods inventory − Beginning finished goods inventory

Budgeted sales: July = 200,000; August = 200,000(1.05) = 210,000; September = 210,000(1.05) = 220,500; October = 220,500(1.05) = 231,525

Budgeted production of finished units
for the quarter ending September 30, 2000:

July	200,000 + 210,000(0.80) − 150,000	218,000
August	210,000 + 220,500(0.80) − 210,000(0.80)	218,400
September	220,500 + 231,525(0.80) − 220,500(0.80)	229,320
Total		665,720

b.

$$\text{Purchases in kilograms} = \text{Production requirement in kilograms} + \text{Target ending materials inventory} - \text{Beginning materials inventory}$$

Budgeted purchases in kilograms = 665,720(4) + 665,720(4)(0.25) − 800,000
Budgeted purchases in kilograms = 2,662,880 + 665,720 − 800,000 = 2,528,600
Budgeted cost of direct material purchases = 2,528,600 × $1.20 = $3,034,320

Exercise 2

Selling price in 1999 = $20,000,000 ÷ 1,000,000 = $20 per unit
Cost of goods sold in 1999 = $14,000,000 ÷ 1,000,000 = $14 per unit

Budgeted income statement for 2000:

Revenues, 1,000,000(1.05) × $20(1.03)	$21,630,000
Cost of goods sold, 1,000,000(1.05) × $14(1 − 0.04)	14,112,000
Gross margin	7,518,000
Operating costs	
($4,200,000 − $900,000)(1 − 0.06) + $900,000	4,002,000
Operating income	$ 3,516,000

Exercise 3

Budgeted balance of accounts payable on December 31, 2000:

From December purchases related to December sales	
$520,000 × 0.80 × 0.40 × 0.20	$ 33,280
From December purchases related to January sales	
$500,000 × 0.80 × 0.40 × 0.80	128,000
Total	$161,280

Flexible Budgets, Variances, and Management Control: I

Chapter Overview

This chapter and the next explain the key role of flexible budgets and variances in the planning and control of operations. The chapter focuses on: (1) how to prepare flexible budgets and compute variances for operating income and for direct costs and (2) the insight managers gain regarding why the actual results differ from budgeted amounts. The chapter features a *columnar solution format* that is a helpful and intuitive approach to compute variances.

Chapter Highlights

1. A *variance* is the difference between an actual result and a budgeted amount. Organizations differ widely in how they compute and label their budgeted amounts. Some organizations rely mainly on past results in developing budgeted amounts while others rely heavily on detailed engineering studies.

2. Variances assist managers in their planning and control decisions. *Management by exception* is the practice of concentrating on areas not operating as anticipated (such as a cost overrun on a defense project) and giving less attention to areas operating as anticipated. Managers consider the magnitude of variances in deciding how to allocate their energies. Areas with sizable variances receive more of their attention on an ongoing basis than do areas with minimal variances. Variances also are often used in performance evaluation. For example, production-line managers may have a quarterly efficiency incentive linked to achieving a budgeted cost amount.

3. Variances can be computed using amounts from a **static budget** or a **flexible budget**.

- A static budget is based on the level of output *planned at the start of the budget period*. When variances are computed from a static budget at the end of the period, no adjustment is made to the budgeted revenue or cost amounts, regardless of the level of output actually achieved in the budget period.
- A flexible budget is developed using budgeted revenue or cost amounts based on the level of output *actually achieved in the budget period*. A flexible budget enables managers to compute a more informative set of variances than does a static budget.

4. Assuming output units is the only revenue and cost driver, four data items are needed to prepare the static budget of operating income: (a) budgeted selling price, (b) budgeted variable costs per output unit, (c) budgeted quantity of output units, and (d) budgeted fixed costs. The same data items are used to prepare the flexible budget of operating income, except the *actual* quantity of out-put units is used instead of the *budgeted* quantity of output units.

5. Variances are labelled as favourable or unfavourable. A **favourable variance** (denoted F in the textbook and Student Guide) *increases* operating income relative to the budgeted amount. An **unfavourable variance** (denoted U) *decreases* operating income relative to the budgeted amount.

6. Both static budgets and flexible budgets can differ in the level of detail they report. Typically, organizations present budgets with broad summary figures that can be broken down into increasingly more detailed figures via computer software programs. The increasing level of detail pertains to both the number of line items presented in the income statement

and the number of variances computed. The term "level" followed by a number denotes the amount of detail shown by a variance analysis. Level 0 reports the least detail, Level 1 provides more detail, and so on. Level 0 and Level 1 analyses use static budgets only. Level 2 and higher analyses use flexible budgets.

7. A **static-budget variance** is the difference between an actual result and a budgeted amount in the static budget. Under Level 0 analysis, the static-budget variance of operating income is computed by subtracting the static-budget amount of operating income from actual operating income. With the additional detail of Level 1 analysis, static-budget variances are computed for revenues, variable costs, contribution margin, fixed costs, and operating income. EXHIBIT 7-1, text p. 223, shows the computation of these Level 0 and Level 1 variances.

8. Level 2 analysis provides more insight into the causes of variances by incorporating a flexible budget in the computation of variances. Level 2 analysis divides the static-budget variance into the **flexible-budget variance** and the **sales-volume variance**. A flexible-budget variance is the difference between an actual result and a flexible-budget amount based on the level of output actually achieved in the budget period. A sales-volume variance is the difference between a flexible-budget amount and a static-budget amount. Both flexible budgets and static budgets use budgeted amounts for selling price, variable costs per output unit, and fixed costs. As a result, sales-volume variances arise solely because the actual quantity of output differs from the budgeted quantity of output.

9. Flexible-budget variances and sales-volume variances are computed for revenues, variable costs, contribution margin, fixed costs, and operating income. The flexible-budget variance of revenues, often called the **selling-price variance**, is favourable/unfavourable if the actual selling price of a product or service is greater/less than the budgeted selling price. EXHIBIT 7-3, text p. 225, shows the computation of these Level 2 variances presented in a columnar solution format.

10. Level 3 analysis divides the flexible-budget variance for direct material costs or direct manufacturing labour costs into the **price variance** and the **efficiency variance**. Price variances are sometimes called **rate variances**, especially when those variances are for direct labour. Efficiency variances are sometimes called **usage variances**. The formulas for computing the price and efficiency variances are in the box below. The price variance is favourable/unfavourable if the actual price of the input is less/greater than its budgeted price. The efficiency variance is favourable/unfavourable if the actual quantity of input used is less/greater than the budgeted quantity of input that should have been used based on the level of output actually achieved in the budget period. EXHIBIT 7-4, text p. 231, shows the computation of these Level 3 variances presented in a columnar solution format.

11. In computing price and efficiency variances, the budgeted input prices and budgeted input quantities are often based on standards. A **standard** is a carefully predetermined price, cost, or quantity. For example, engineering studies can determine standard quantities of direct materials and direct manufacturing labour-hours per unit of output. To illustrate, assume an engineering study

$$\begin{array}{ccc} \text{Price} \\ \text{variance} \end{array} = \left(\begin{array}{c} \text{Actual price} \\ \text{of input} \end{array} - \begin{array}{c} \text{Budgeted price} \\ \text{of input} \end{array} \right) \times \begin{array}{c} \text{Actual quantity} \\ \text{of input} \end{array}$$

$$\begin{array}{ccc} \text{Efficiency} \\ \text{variance} \end{array} = \left(\begin{array}{c} \text{Actual} \\ \text{quantity of} \\ \text{input used} \end{array} - \begin{array}{c} \text{Budgeted quantity} \\ \text{of input allowed} \\ \text{for actual output} \end{array} \right) \times \begin{array}{c} \text{Budgeted price} \\ \text{of input} \end{array}$$

determines 0.80 direct manufacturing labour-hours (DMLH) is the standard time allowed to produce a unit of output. The standard wage rate is $20 per DMLH. The **standard cost** per unit of output is $16 (0.80 × $20). Assuming 10,000 units of output are produced in April, the flexible budget for direct manufacturing labour costs for April is $160,000 (10,000 × $16). In this example, the 0.80 DMLH per unit of output is a **standard input**. Generally a standard input amount is most useful if it (a) excludes past inefficiencies and (b) takes into account the changes expected to occur in the budget period.

12. Managers consider many possible causes for price variances and efficiency variances. Here are some examples.

- A favourable materials-price variance occurs if the purchasing manager negotiated more skillfully with suppliers than is expected.
- An unfavourable labour-price variance is caused by an unexpected increase in wage rates for highly skilled workers.
- An unfavourable materials-efficiency variance results from inadequate training of the labour force.
- A favourable labour-efficiency variance occurs because budgeted time standards for highly skilled workers are set too low.

13. The most important task in variance analysis is to identify the causes of variances and use this knowledge to promote continuous improvement. Often the causes of variances are interrelated. For example, an unfavourable materials-efficiency variance is likely to be related to a favourable materials-price variance if a purchasing manager buys lower-priced, lower-quality materials. It is always best to consider possible interdependencies among variances rather than to interpret them in isolation of each other. In some cases, the causes of variances are in different parts of the organization's value chain or in other organizations in the supply chain. For example, an unfavourable labour-efficiency variance could be caused by the marketing manager obtaining a large number of rush orders that disrupts the normal flow of production. If rush orders caused the variance, top management could establish a policy limiting the number of rush orders or could increase the selling price for these orders.

14. Managers use variance analysis in performance evaluation. **Effectiveness and efficiency** are two common attributes of performance. Effectiveness is the degree to which a predetermined objective or target is met. Efficiency is the relative amount of inputs used to achieve a given level of output. *Performance can be both effective and efficient, but either condition can occur without the other.* For example, assume a company's static budget calls for production and sales of 12,000 units. If the company produces and sells 15,000 units, performance is effective. Given the 25% increase in output, performance is inefficient, however, if the usage of direct materials and direct manufacturing labour inputs exceeds the static-budget amounts by more than 25%.

15. Managers must decide when to investigate variances. They often use rules of thumb such as "investigate all variances exceeding $5,000 or 5% of budgeted cost, whichever is lower". This approach recognizes the budget represents a *range of possible acceptable outcomes* rather than a single acceptable outcome. Variances within this range are due to chance and hence do not require investigation.

16. **A continuous improvement budgeted cost** is progressively reduced over succeeding time periods. For example, budgeted direct material costs of a product could be reduced by 1% per month. Products in the initial months of production usually have higher budgeted improvement rates than those that have been manufactured for several years. Continuous improvement budgeted costs highlight to managers and other employees the importance of constantly seeking ways to reduce costs.

17. Companies use both financial and nonfinancial performance measures. Managers exercise control on the shop floor by observing workers and by focusing on nonfinancial measures, such as the number of square metres of cloth used to produce 1,000 jackets or the percentage of jackets started and completed without requiring rework. Financial measures summarize the economic impact of diverse physical activities in a way managers readily understand. Moreover, managers are often evaluated based on actual results compared to budgets expressed in financial terms.

18. When standard costs are recorded in the general-ledger accounts, journal entries are made for direct materials (DM) and direct manufacturing labour (DML). In these entries, *unfavourable variances are debits* because they decrease operating income relative to the budgeted amount; *favourable variances are credits*. The journal entries in the example, text p. 237, are:

Materials Control	750,000	
DM Price Variance	25,000	
Accounts Payable Control		775,000
Work-in-Process Control	600,000	
DM Efficiency Variance	66,000	
Materials Control		666,000
Work-in-Process Control	160,000	
DML Price Variance	18,000	
DML Efficiency Variance	20,000	
Wages Payable Control		198,000

- Materials Control is debited (actual quantity purchased × standard price) and then credited (actual quantity used × standard price). Accounts Payable Control is credited for actual quantity purchased × actual price.
- Work-in-Process Control is debited for standard input (DM and DML respectively) allowed for actual output produced × standard price. Wages Payable Control is credited for actual hours worked × actual wage rate.

19. The Levels 1, 2, and 3 framework of variance analysis can be extended to activity-based costs to gain insight into why actual activity costs differ from those in the static budget or flexible budget. Interpreting a cost variance for an activity area requires an understanding of the cost hierarchy used in activity-based costing (that is, knowing whether the cost is an output-unit-level cost, batch-level cost, product-sustaining cost, or facility-sustaining cost). The Kitchen Inc. example, beginning text p. 238, explains how to compute and interpret variances for material-handling labour, a batch-level cost.

20. The term **benchmarking** refers to the continuous process of measuring products, services, and activities against the best levels of performance. These best levels of performance are often found in competing organizations, or in other organizations having similar processes. For example, an airline could use benchmarking to compare itself to the best performance in the industry across various operating measures. Obtaining comparable numbers is a challenging aspect of any benchmarking effort. Moreover, understanding why cost or revenue differences exist across companies can be a challenging task.

Featured Exercises

1. Vermillion Company's actual results and static budget for June 2000 are as follows:

	Actual Results	Static Budget
Units sold	12,000	10,000
Revenues	$132,000	$100,000
Variable costs	70,800	60,000
Contribution margin	61,200	40,000
Fixed costs	32,000	30,000
Operating income	$ 29,200	$ 10,000

a. Explain why actual operating income exceeds static-budget operating income by $19,200.
b. Compute the flexible-budget operating income.
c. Compute the total static-budget variance (that is, static-budget variance of operating income) and indicate whether it is favourable or unfavourable.
d. Compute the total flexible-budget variance and indicate whether it is favourable or unfavourable.
e. Compute the total sales-volume variance and indicate whether it is favourable or unfavourable.
f. Compute the selling-price variance and indicate whether it is favourable or unfavourable.

Solution

(F denotes favourable variances and U denotes unfavourable variances.)

a. Actual contribution margin per unit = $61,200 ÷ 12,000 units = $5.10
   Static-budget contribution margin per unit = $40,000 ÷ 10,000 units = $4.00

Higher-than-expected contribution margin for the static-budget level of units sold, 10,000 × ($5.10 − $4.00)	$11,000
Higher-than-expected contribution margin from selling 12,000 units rather than 10,000 units in the static budget, 2,000 × $5.10	10,200
Higher-than-expected fixed costs, $32,000 − $30,000	(2,000)
Actual operating income exceeds static-budget operating income	$19,200

b. Budgeted selling price = $100,000 ÷ 10,000 units = $10
   Budgeted variable costs per unit = $60,000 ÷ 10,000 units = $6

	Flexible Budget
Units sold	12,000
Revenues, 12,000 × $10	$120,000
Variable costs, 12,000 × $6	72,000
Contribution margin	48,000
Fixed costs	30,000
Operating income	$ 18,000

c. Total static-budget variance = $29,200 − $10,000 = $19,200 F
d. Total flexible-budget variance = $29,200 − $18,000 (from answer b) = $11,200 F
e. Total sales-volume variance = $18,000 − $10,000 = $8,000 F
f. Selling-price variance = $132,000 − $120,000 (from answer b) = $12,000 F

----

2. Randall Company's data for direct manufacturing labour for last month are as follows:

Actual hours worked	20,000
Standard hours allowed for actual output	21,000
Price variance – unfavourable	$3,000
Payroll liability	$126,000

Compute the efficiency variance for direct manufacturing labour.

Solution

Three steps are used to obtain the answer. First, compute the dollar amount for actual hours worked times the standard wage rate (denoted by X)

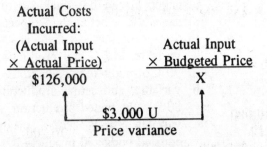

Actual Costs
Incurred:
(Actual Input × Actual Price)
$126,000

Actual Input × Budgeted Price
X

$3,000 U
Price variance

$$X = \$126,000 - \$3,000 = \$123,000$$

The price variance is *subtracted* from the actual payroll because it is unfavourable.

Second, compute the standard wage rate: $\$123,000 \div 20,000 = \$6.15$ per hour

Third, compute the efficiency variance:

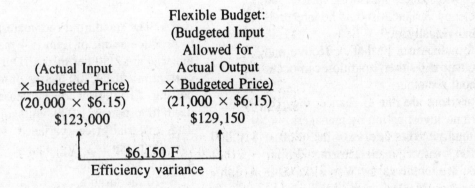

(Actual Input × Budgeted Price)
(20,000 × $6.15)
$123,000

Flexible Budget:
(Budgeted Input
Allowed for
Actual Output
× Budgeted Price)
(21,000 × $6.15)
$129,150

$6,150 F
Efficiency variance

Review Questions and Exercises

Completion Statements

Fill in the blank(s) to complete each statement.

1. A variance is the difference between an _____ and a _____.

2. _____ is the practice of concentrating on areas not operating as anticipated and giving less attention to areas operating as anticipated.

3. A _____ is developed using budgeted revenue or cost amounts based on the level of output actually achieved in the budget period.

4. Price variances are sometimes called _____ variances (especially when these variances are for direct labour), and efficiency variances are sometimes called _____ variances.

5. A _____ is a carefully predetermined price, cost, or quantity.

6. The relative amount of inputs used to achieve a given level of output is the measure of _____.

7. A budgeted cost that is progressively reduced over succeeding time periods is called a _____ budgeted cost.

8. The continuous process of measuring products, services, or activities against the best levels of performance that can be found either inside or outside the organization is called _____.

True-False

Indicate whether each statement is true (T) or false (F).

___ 1. Favourable variances for both revenue items and cost items mean that "good" performance has been achieved.

___ 2. In computing the flexible-budget variance of operating income, fixed costs can be ignored.

___ 3. To facilitate control, materials-price variances are usually based on actual quantities of inputs used.

___ 4. Generally, the same manager has primary responsibility for the materials-price variance and the materials-efficiency variance.

___ 5. Managers usually have more control over efficiency variances than price variances.

___ 6. As performance measures, price and efficiency variances should be interpreted individually.

___ 7. Performance can be both effective and efficient, but either condition can occur without the other.

___ 8. If variances are due to chance, they require no investigation by managers.

___ 9. If standard costs are used in journal entries, direct manufacturing labour costs are credited to Wages Payable Control at standard costs.

___ 10. In a standard-costing system, unfavourable variances should always be recorded as debits in journal entries.

___ 11. Interpreting a cost variance for an activity area requires an understanding of the cost hierarchy used in activity-based costing.

___ 12. The best levels of performance used in benchmarking are generally found within the organization that is using this technique.

Multiple Choice

Select the best answer to each question. Space is provided for computations after the quantitative questions.

___ 1. (CPA adapted) The static budget for a given cost during a given accounting period was $80,000. The actual cost for the period was $72,000. Assuming this cost is controllable by the production manager, it can be concluded that the manager did a better-than-expected job in controlling the cost if the cost is:
a. variable, and actual production was 90% of budgeted production.
b. variable, and actual production was 80% of budgeted production.
c. variable, and actual production equaled budgeted production.
d. fixed, and actual production equaled budgeted production.

___ 2. (CPA) The standard direct-material cost to produce a unit of Lem is 4 metres of material at $2.50 per metre. During the current month, 4,200 metres of material costing $10,080 were purchased and used to produce 1,000 units of Lem. The material-price variance for the current month is:
a. $400 favourable.
b. $420 favourable.
c. $ 80 unfavourable.
d. $480 unfavourable.

3. (CPA) Information on Rex Co.'s direct materials for the current month is as follows:

Actual quantity of direct
  materials purchased
  and used   30,000 lbs.
Actual cost of direct
  materials $84,000
Unfavourable direct materials-
  efficiency variance $3,000
Standard quantity of direct
  materials allowed for
  July production   29,000 lbs.

For July, Rex's direct materials-price variance is:
a. $2,800 favourable.
b. $2,800 unfavourable.
c. $6,000 unfavourable.
d. $6,000 favourable.

4. (CMA) ChemKing uses a standard-costing system in the manufacturing of its only product. The 35,000 units of direct materials in inventory were purchased for $105,000, and two units of direct materials are required to produce one unit of finished product. In May, the company produced 12,000 finished units. The standard cost allowed for direct materials is $60,000, and there is an unfavourable efficiency variance of $2,500. ChemKing's standard price for one unit of direct materials is:
a. $2.00.
b. $2.50.
c. $3.00.
d. $5.00.
e. $6.00.

5. Using the data in question 4, the units of direct materials used to produce May's output total:

a. 12,000 units.
b. 12,500 units.
c. 23,000 units.
d. 24,000 units.
e. 25,000 units.

6. (CMA adapted) In evaluating the performance within a company, a materials-efficiency variance can be caused by all of the following *except* the:
a. quantity of actual output produced.
b. performance of the workers using the materials.
c. quality of the materials.
d. skill level of the workers using the materials.

7. (CPA) Lab Corp. uses a standard-costing system. Direct manufacturing labour information for Product CER for the month of October is as follows:

Standard price $6.00 per hour
Actual price $6.10 per hour
Standard hours
  allowed for actual
  output produced   1,500 hours
Direct manufacturing
  labour efficiency
  variance—unfavourable $600

How many actual hours were worked?
a. 1,400
b. 1,402
c. 1,598
d. 1,600

8. If material-price variances are recognized in the general-ledger accounts at the time materials are purchased, the inventory of materials is carried on the books at:
a. actual quantities at actual prices.
b. standard quantities at standard prices.
c. actual quantities at standard prices.
d. standard quantities at actual prices.

Exercises

1. Cyrus Medicinal Products, Inc. uses a standard-costing system and provides the following data concerning one of its products for April, 2000:

Units of output produced	300 units
Standard kilograms of materials allowed per unit of output	10 kilograms
Standard materials price per kilogram	$2.00
Actual materials purchase price per kilogram	$1.80
Actual quantity of materials purchased	4,000 kilograms
Actual quantity of materials used in production	3,500 kilograms
Direct manufacturing labour payroll	$6,050
Direct manufacturing-labour-price variance	$550 favourable
Direct manufacturing-labour-efficiency variance	$600 unfavourable

a. Compute the direct materials variances in the columnar solution format below, assuming the price variance is isolated when materials are purchased. Use F for favourable variances and U for unfavourable variances.

Actual Costs Incurred: Actual Input × Actual Price	Actual Input × Budgeted Price	Flexible Budget: (Budgeted Input Allowed for Actual Output × Budgeted Price)

```
      |_____$_____↑      |_____$_____↑
        Materials-price variance        Materials-efficiency variance
```

b. Prepare journal entries to record the direct materials variances and direct manufacturing labour variances.

General Journal	Debit	Credit

2. (CMA adapted) Dash Company uses a standard-costing system. The standard costs for the direct costs of manufacturing its only product are as follows:

Direct materials	
8 kilograms @ $5.00 per kilogram	$40.00
Direct Manufacturing labour	
3 hours @ $16.40 per hour	49.20

The following operating data are for November:

Actual output	6,300 units
Budgeted output	6,000 units
Purchases of materials	50,000 kilograms
Actual direct manufacturing labour (DML) costs	$300,760
Actual hours of DML	18,250 hours
Materials-efficiency variance	$1,500 unfavourable
Materials-price variance	$750 favourable

Compute the following for November:
a. DML price variance
b. DML efficiency variance
c. Actual kilograms of materials used in the production process
d. Actual price per kilogram of materials, assuming the materials-price variance is isolated at the time of purchase
e. Total amount of materials cost transferred to finished goods
f. Total amount of DML cost transferred to finished goods

Answers to Chapter 7 Review Questions and Exercises

Completion Statements

1. actual result, budgeted amount
2. Management by exception
3. flexible budget
4. rate, usage
5. standard
6. efficiency
7. continuous improvement
8. benchmarking

True-False

1. F Favourable variances for both revenue items and cost items increase operating income relative to the budgeted amount. Favourable variances, however, *do not necessarily* mean "good" performance has been achieved. For example, a favourable materials-price variance is not good if the materials are of such poor quality that they increase scrap, rework, and customer-service costs by more than the amount of the price variance.
2. T
3. F To facilitate control, materials-price variances are usually based on actual quantities of inputs *purchased* rather than *used*. This approach isolates the price variance at the earlier time.
4. F A purchasing manager is responsible for acquisition of materials, whereas a production manager is responsible for usage of materials.
5. T
6. F As performance measures, price and efficiency variances should not be interpreted individually because their causes can be interrelated. For example, an unfavourable materials-efficiency variance can be related to a favourable materials-price variance if a purchasing manager buys lower-priced, lower-quality materials. It is best to always consider possible interdependencies among variances rather than interpreting variances in isolation from each other.
7. T
8. T
9. F When standard costs are used in journal entries, direct manufacturing labour costs are debited to Work-in-Process Control at standard costs and are credited to Wages Payable Control at actual costs. Any difference between the actual costs and standard costs is recorded as a price variance and/or an efficiency variance.
10. T
11. T
12. F The best levels of performance used in benchmarking are often found in competing organizations or in other organizations having similar processes.

Multiple Choice

1. c The production manager's performance is properly evaluated by means of the flexible-budget variance. A performance report for each of the four answers is as follows:

	Actual Cost Incurred	Flexible Budget Based on Actual Output Produced	Flexible-Budget Variance
a.	$72,000	$72,000 (90% of $80,000)	$ -0-
b.	$72,000	$64,000 (80% of $80,000)	$8,000 U
c.	$72,000	$80,000 (100% of $80,000)	$8,000 F
d.	$72,000	$80,000 (100% of $80,000)	$8,000 F

While answers (c) and (d) give the same favourable variance of $8,000, the latter is misleading. Incurring less than the amount budgeted for a fixed cost (such as an employee training program) could result from failure to carry out a plan as budgeted or a poor estimate of the amount of the cost to be incurred. Answer (a) refers to a situation where the manager did exactly *as well as* expected in controlling cost.

2. b

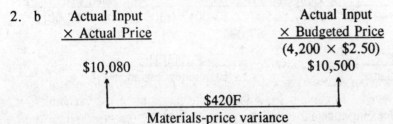

Actual Input × Actual Price	Actual Input × Budgeted Price
	(4,200 × $2.50)
$10,080	$10,500

$420F
Materials-price variance

3. d Standard cost per lb. = $3,000 ÷ (30,000 − 29,000) = $3,000 ÷ 1,000 = $3
   Direct materials-price variance = $84,000 − (30,000 × $3)
   $\qquad\qquad\qquad\qquad\qquad = \$84,000 - \$90,000 = -\$6,000,$ or $6,000 F

4. b Standard price of direct materials per finished unit = $60,000 ÷ 12,000 = $5
   Each finished unit requires two units of direct materials. As a result, the standard price per unit of direct materials = $5 ÷ 2 = $2.50. Note that the actual purchase price of direct materials is $3.00 per unit ($105,000 ÷ 35,000).

5. e Standard cost of materials allowed for
   actual output produced $\qquad\qquad\qquad\qquad\qquad$ $60,000
   Add unfavourable materials-efficiency variance $\qquad$ 2,500
   Actual quantity used × Standard price $\qquad\qquad$ $62,500
   Units of direct materials used = $62,500 ÷ $2.50 = 25,000 units

6. a The quantity of actual output produced is used in computing the materials-efficiency variance but it is not a *cause* of this variance.

7. d Let X = Actual hours worked

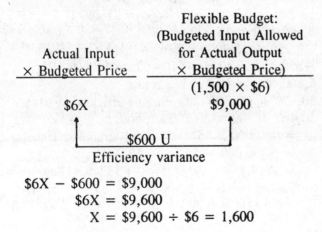

Actual Input × Budgeted Price	Flexible Budget: (Budgeted Input Allowed for Actual Output × Budgeted Price)
	(1,500 × $6)
$6X	$9,000

$600 U
Efficiency variance

$6X − $600 = $9,000
$\qquad$ $6X = $9,600
$\qquad\quad$ X = $9,600 ÷ $6 = 1,600

8. c When materials are purchased, Materials Control is debited for the actual quantities purchased at standard prices. When materials are issued to production, Materials Control is credited for the actual quantities used at standard prices. The balance of Materials Control, therefore, is carried on the books at actual quantities at standard prices.

Exercise 1

a.

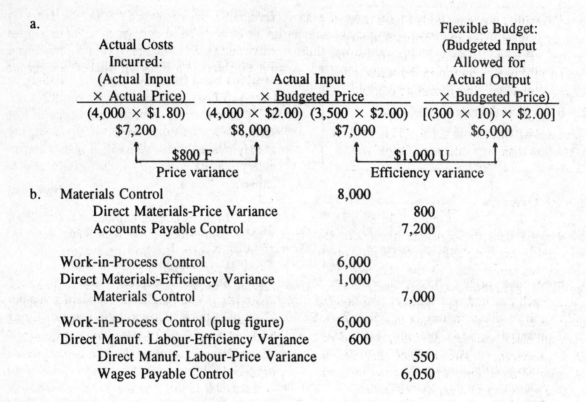

	Actual Costs Incurred: (Actual Input × Actual Price)		Actual Input × Budgeted Price	Flexible Budget: (Budgeted Input Allowed for Actual Output × Budgeted Price)
	(4,000 × $1.80)	(4,000 × $2.00)	(3,500 × $2.00)	[(300 × 10) × $2.00]
	$7,200	$8,000	$7,000	$6,000

$800 F
Price variance

$1,000 U
Efficiency variance

b.
Materials Control	8,000	
Direct Materials-Price Variance		800
Accounts Payable Control		7,200

Work-in-Process Control	6,000	
Direct Materials-Efficiency Variance	1,000	
Materials Control		7,000

Work-in-Process Control (plug figure)	6,000	
Direct Manuf. Labour-Efficiency Variance	600	
Direct Manuf. Labour-Price Variance		550
Wages Payable Control		6,050

Exercise 2

a. Actual DML wage rate = $300,760 ÷ 18,250 = $16.48 per hour
DML price variance = 18,250 × ($16.48 − $16.40)
  = 18,250 × ($0.08) = $1,460, or $1,460 U

b. Standard DML allowed = 6,300 × 3 = 18,900 hours
DML efficiency variance = (18,250 − 18,900) × $16.40
  = −650 × $16.40 = −$10,660, or $10,660 F

c. Standard materials allowed = 6,300 × 8 = 50,400 kilograms
Actual materials used = 50,400 + ($1,500 unfavourable efficiency variance ÷ $5)
  = 50,400 + 300 = 50,700 kilograms

d. Actual purchase price of materials = [(50,000 × $5) − $750 favourable variance] ÷ 50,000
  = ($250,000 − $750) ÷ 50,000
  = $249,250 ÷ 50,000 = $4.985 per kilogram

e. Total materials cost transferred to finished goods = 6,300 × 8 × $5 = $252,000

f. Total DML cost transferred to finished goods = 6,300 × 3 × $16.40 = $309,960

Flexible Budgets, Variances and Management Control: II

In writing this Student Guide I have tried to add significant value to your learning experience. How am I doing? Please use the Student Comment button in the website for *Cost Accounting*, 2nd Canadian edition:

www.prenticehall.ca/horngren

to complete the online form. This activity takes less than five minutes. Thank you.

Chapter Overview

This chapter uses the concepts introduced in Chapter 7 to explain the key role flexible budgets and variances play in the planning and control of indirect (overhead) costs. The chapter focuses on (1) how to compute variances for variable and fixed manufacturing overhead costs and (2) the interpretation of these variances.   The chapter features a *columnar solution format* that is a helpful and intuitive approach to compute variances.

Chapter Highlights

1.   Effective planning of variable overhead costs involves two challenges: (a) undertake only   essential   variable   overhead   activities—those activities that add value for customers using the related product or service and (b) perform the essential variable overhead activities efficiently. For example, because a clothing manufacturer's customers perceive sewing to be an essential activity, maintenance activities for the sewing machines (included in variable overhead costs) are also essential activities. Such maintenance should be done in a cost-effective way.

2.   Effective planning of fixed overhead costs involves three challenges: (a) undertake only essential fixed overhead activities, (b) perform the essential fixed overhead activities

efficiently, and (c) choose the appropriate level of capacity that will benefit the company over an extended time period. Consider a clothing manufacturer that leases sewing machines, each of which has a fixed cost per year. Failure to lease sufficient machine capacity results in not being able to meet demand (and hence in lost sales).   On the other hand, if the company greatly overestimates demand, it incurs unnecessary leasing costs on the underutilized machines.

3.   In the example, beginning text p. 260, Webb Company uses **standard costing**. Standard costing is a costing method that (a) traces direct costs to a cost object by multiplying the standard price(s) or rate(s) times the standard   inputs   allowed   for   actual   output produced and (b) allocates indirect costs on the basis of the standard indirect rate(s) times the standard inputs allowed for the actual output produced. (Chapter 7 described (a) while (b) is described in this chapter.) Once standards have been set, the costs of using standard costing can be low relative to actual costing or normal costing.

4.   The *budgeted variable overhead (VOH) rate* plays a key role in VOH variance analysis. To compute this rate, divide the budgeted VOH costs by the budgeted quantity of the cost-allocation base. It is preferable to use the cause-and-effect criterion for selecting the cost-allocation base. A manufacturing company can express the VOH overhead rate on an *input basis* or *output basis*. In the Webb Company example, the budgeted VOH rate on an input basis is $30 per machine-hour. Because 0.40 machine-hours are budgeted per output unit, the budgeted VOH rate per output unit is $12 ($30 × 0.40).

5.   There are three VOH cost variances. The **VOH flexible-budget variance**, a Level 2

variance, divides into two Level 3 variances: the **VOH spending variance** and the **VOH efficiency variance.**

- The VOH flexible-budget variance is the difference between the actual VOH costs incurred and VOH costs in the flexible budget. This variance is favourable/unfavourable if the actual VOH costs incurred are less/greater than the flexible-budget VOH costs. The amount of the VOH flexible-budget variance is the same as the amount of under- or overallocated VOH. If the VOH flexible-budget is favourable/unfavourable, VOH is overallocated/underallocated.
- The formula for the VOH spending variance is in Panel A of the box on the next page. The variance is favourable/unfavourable if the actual VOH rate is less/greater than the budgeted VOH rate.
- The formula for the VOH efficiency variance is also in Panel A of the box. This variance is favourable/unfavourable if the actual units of the VOH cost-allocation base used for actual output are less/greater than the budgeted units of this base allowed for actual output.

Panel B of the box shows the computation of the three VOH variances presented in a columnar solution format.

6. Interpreting the VOH efficiency is straightforward, but the VOH spending variance is difficult to interpret.

- First consider the computation of the VOH efficiency variance in Panel B. This variance is unfavourable simply because *more* machine-hours were used (4,500) than were allowed in the flexible budget to produce the actual output of 10,000 jackets (0.40 × 10,000 = 4,000). Possible causes for using the additional 500 machine-hours include: (a) workers were less skillful in the use of machines than expected and (b) the machines were not maintained in good working condition. Cause (a) has implications for the employee-hiring practices and training procedures. Cause (b) has

implications for scheduling and/or performing plant maintenance.

- Now consider the computation of the VOH spending variance in Panel B. This variance is favourable because the actual VOH rate per machine-hour ($29) is *less than* the budgeted VOH rate per machine-hour ($30). To understand this variance, consider the question: Why is the actual rate less than the budgeted rate? The answer is, relative to the flexible budget, the percentage increase in the actual quantity of machine-hours used [(4,500 − 4,000) ÷ 4,000 = 12.5%] is *more than* the percentage increase in the actual VOH costs incurred [($130,500 − $120,000) ÷ $120,000 = 8.75%]. Because actual VOH costs incurred increased relatively *less than* machine-hours, the actual VOH rate per machine-hour is *less than* the budgeted rate. Two main reasons could explain why actual VOH costs incurred increased less than machine-hours in the example: (a) the actual prices of individual items included in VOH, such as the purchase price of energy, indirect materials, and/or indirect manufacturing labour, are *less than* the budgeted prices and (b) relative to the flexible budget, the percentage increase in the actual quantity used of individual VOH items (such as kilowatt-hours of energy usage) is *less than* the percentage increase in machine-hours.

7. Consider another example on interpreting the VOH efficiency and spending variances. Assume energy is the only item of VOH and machine-hours is the cost-allocation base. Assume also actual machine-hours used to produce the actual output equals budgeted machine-hours and the actual price of energy equals the budgeted price. *In this case there is no VOH efficiency variance but there might be a VOH spending variance.* The company has been efficient with respect to the number of machine-hours used to produce the actual output. It could have used too much energy, however, not because of excessive machine-hours but because energy was wasted. The

The amounts in this box are from the Webb Company example, text p. 260.

Panel A: Formulas for VOH Variances

$$\begin{matrix} \text{VOH} \\ \text{spending} \\ \text{variance} \end{matrix} = \left(\begin{matrix} \text{Actual VOH} \\ \text{cost per unit of} \\ \text{cost-allocation base} \end{matrix} - \begin{matrix} \text{Budgeted VOH} \\ \text{cost per unit of} \\ \text{cost-allocation base} \end{matrix} \right) \times \begin{matrix} \text{Actual quantity of} \\ \text{VOH cost-allocation base} \\ \text{allowed for actual output} \end{matrix}$$

$$= (\$29 - \$30) \times 4,500$$
$$= -\$1 \times 4,500 = -\$4,500, \text{ or } \$4,500 \text{ F}$$

$$\begin{matrix} \text{VOH} \\ \text{efficiency} \\ \text{variance} \end{matrix} = \left(\begin{matrix} \text{Actual units of VOH} \\ \text{cost-allocation base} \\ \text{used for actual output} \end{matrix} - \begin{matrix} \text{Budgeted units of VOH} \\ \text{cost-allocation base} \\ \text{allowed for actual output} \end{matrix} \right) \times \begin{matrix} \text{Budgted} \\ \text{VOH} \\ \text{rate} \end{matrix}$$

$$= [4,500 - (0.40 \times 10,000)] \times \$30$$
$$= (4,500 - 4,000) \times \$30$$
$$= 500 \times \$30 = \$15,0000, \text{ or } \$15,000 \text{ U}$$

Panel B: VOH Variance Analysis in Columnar Format

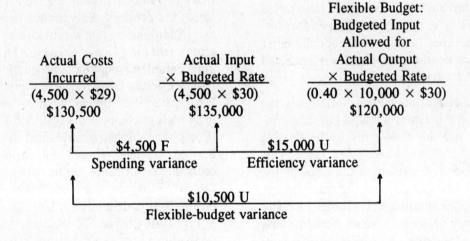

Actual Costs Incurred	Actual Input × Budgeted Rate	Flexible Budget: Budgeted Input Allowed for Actual Output × Budgeted Rate
(4,500 × $29)	(4,500 × $30)	(0.40 × 10,000 × $30)
$130,500	$135,000	$120,000

$4,500 F $15,000 U
Spending variance   Efficiency variance

$10,500 U
Flexible-budget variance

cost of this higher energy usage is measured by the spending variance.

8. Fixed overhead (FOH) costs are, by definition, a lump-sum that remains unchanged in total for a given time period despite wide changes in the related level of total activity or volume. To compute the *budgeted FOH rate*, divide budgeted FOH costs by the **denominator level** of the cost-allocation base. Manufacturing companies commonly call the denominator level the **production-denominator level**. Using amounts in the Webb Company example, text p. 259, the budgeted fixed overhead costs are $3,312,000 per year and the production-denominator level is 57,600 machine-hours. The budgeted fixed overhead rate = $3,312,000 ÷ 57,600 = $57.50 *per machine-hour*. Because 0.40 machine-hours are budgeted per output unit, the budgeted fixed overhead *per output unit* is $23 ($57.50 × 0.40).

9. There are two FOH costs variances: the **FOH flexible-budget variance** (also called *FOH spending variance*) and the **production-volume variance**. Other terms for the latter variance are **denominator-level variance** and **output-level variance**.

- The FOH flexible-budget variance is the difference between actual FOH costs incurred and the FOH costs in the flexible budget. Within the relevant range, this flexible-budget amount is the same as the amount of FOH costs in the static budget (that is, no adjustment is required for any difference between actual output and budgeted output). The FOH flexible-budget variance is favourable/unfavourable if actual FOH costs incurred are less/greater than the flexible-budget amount. In the Webb Company example, investigation revealed the unfavourable FOH flexible-budget variance of $9,000 is attributable to an unexpected increase in equipment leasing costs. Management concluded, however, that the higher lease rates are an industrywide phenomenon.
- The production-volume variance is the difference between budgeted FOH and the FOH allocated on the basis of the budgeted quantity of the FOH cost-allocation base allowed for the actual output produced. The variance is favourable/unfavourable if budgeted FOH is less/greater than the FOH allocated. To calculate FOH allocated, multiply the budgeted FOH rate by the budgeted quantity of the FOH allocation base allowed for actual output produced.
- The algebraic sum of the FOH flexible-budget variance and the production-volume variance is equal to the amount of under- or overallocated FOH. If this algebraic sum is favourable/unfavourable, FOH is overallocated/underallocated.

EXHIBIT 8-3, Panel B, text p. 267, shows the computation of the FOH variances presented in a columnar solution format.

10. Assume a manager in the Webb Company example is interpreting the unfavourable production-volume variance of $46,000. Although this variance means the budgeted FOH is $46,000 greater than the FOH allocated, the cause of the variance is not apparent. Additional insight is provided by knowing the underlying relationship: an unfavourable/favourable production-volume variance arises whenever actual production is less/greater than the production-denominator level used to compute the budgeted FOH rate. (Computing this rate is explained in paragraph 8.) Management should not attribute much economic significance to this variance for two reasons. First, the plant capacity may exceed the production-denominator level (as explained in Part II of Chapter 9). Second, the production-volume variance focuses only on costs; it does not take into account any reduction in the selling price necessary to spur customer demand that would in turn make use of idle capacity.

11. There are four ways to analyze overhead variances. One way, *4-variance analysis,* describes the full detail of overhead variances. The four variances are VOH spending, FOH flexible budget (spending), VOH efficiency, and production volume. The example, bottom text p. 267, shows the 4-variance analysis,

used in the context of activity-based costing, for batch-level setup overhead costs. *3-variance analysis* combines the VOH and FOH spending variances. The three variances are total overhead spending, VOH efficiency, and production volume. *2-variance analysis* combines the spending and efficiency variances. The two variances are total overhead flexible budget and production volume. Finally, *1-variance analysis* combines the total overhead flexible-budget and production-volume variances into a single variance, the *total overhead variance* (which is the amount of under- or overallocated total overhead). The total overhead variance is favourable/unfavourable if the actual overhead incurred is less/greater than the total overhead allocated to the actual output produced. The amount of the total overhead variance is the same as the amount of under- or overallocated total overhead. If the total overhead variance is favourable/unfavourable, total overhead is overallocated/underallocated.

12. Variable and fixed manufacturing overhead (MOH) costs are used for two main purposes of cost accounting: (a) planning and control and (b) inventory costing under generally accepted accounting principles (GAAP). In the case of variable MOH costs, the budgeted rate serves both purposes. For a given level of production, therefore, the flexible-budget amount of variable MOH is the same as the amount of variable MOH allocated as an inventoriable cost under GAAP. In the case of fixed MOH costs, the budgeted amount for planning and control remains the same within the relevant range. The amount of fixed MOH allocated as an inventoriable cost under GAAP, however, behaves *as if* it were a variable cost; this amount is equal to the fixed overhead rate per unit of output multiplied by the quantity of actual output produced.

13. The separate analysis of variable and fixed MOH costs requires the use of separate MOH Control accounts and separate MOH Allocated accounts in the general ledger. Variable and fixed MOH are each recorded by means of the same set of three summary jour-

nal entries. Entry 1 records the actual variable (fixed) MOH incurred.

(1) Variable (Fixed) MOH Control   X
    Accounts Payable and
    other accounts   X

Entry 2 records the variable (fixed) MOH allocated as an inventoriable cost under GAAP.

(2) Work-in-Process Control   Y
    Variable (Fixed) MOH
    Allocated   Y

Entry 3 closes the variable (fixed) MOH accounts from the preceding entries and records the variable (fixed) overhead variances.

(3) Variable (Fixed) MOH
    Allocated   Y
    Variable (Fixed) MOH
    Unfavourable Variances   U
        Variable (Fixed) MOH Control   X
        Variable (Fixed) MOH
        Favourable Variances   F

14. The overhead variances described in this chapter are examples of financial performance measures. Managers also find nonfinancial measures provide useful information. In fact, many overhead variances initially appear as nonfinancial measures. For example, the difference between actual and budgeted energy usage per machine-hour often is reported on the shop floor daily or even hourly. Expressing a nonfinancial variance in financial terms informs managers of its relative importance.

15. In some cases, managers find it useful to use the variance analysis framework described in this chapter for overhead costs in *nonmanufacturing* areas. For example, in industries where distribution costs are high, using standard costs to compute variable distribution overhead spending and efficiency variances may be cost effective. Moreover, variance analysis of fixed distribution overhead costs or other nonmanufacturing costs can be useful in capacity planning and utilization decisions.

Featured Exercise

Franklin Company provides the following information about its manufacturing operations for the period just ended:

Actual machine-hours used	22,000
Budgeted total overhead	$900,000
Actual variable overhead incurred	$352,000
Actual fixed overhead incurred	$575,000

Budgeted production is 200,000 units of output and actual production is 198,000 units of output. One-tenth of a machine-hour is budgeted per unit of output. The budgeted fixed overhead rate is $30 per machine-hour. The company uses 4-variance analysis for overhead.

a. Using the columnar solution format below, compute the variable overhead spending and efficiency variances.
b. Using the columnar solution format below, compute the fixed overhead flexible-budget (spending) and production-volume variances.
c. Is total overhead under- or overallocated? By what amount?

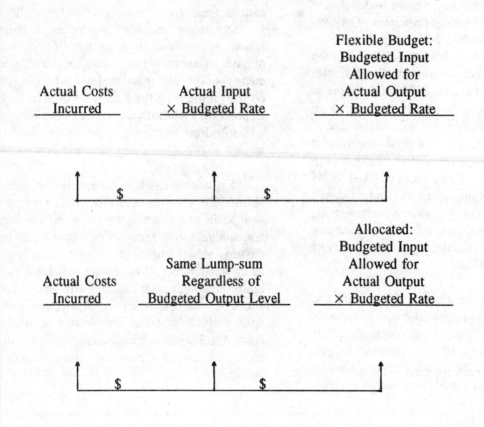

Solution

a. Three steps are used to compute the variable overhead variances. First, compute the budgeted variable overhead.

Budgeted total overhead	$900,000
Deduct budgeted fixed overhead, 200,000 × (0.10 × $30)	600,000
Budgeted variable overhead	$300,000

Second, compute the budgeted variable overhead rate per machine-hour.

$$\text{Budgeted variable overhead rate} = \frac{\$300,000}{200,000 \times 0.10} = \$15 \text{ per machine-hour}$$

Third, compute the variances.

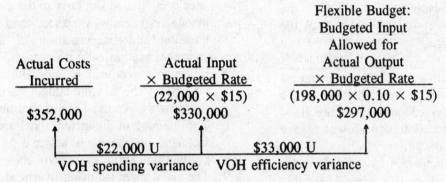

b. The budgeted fixed overhead, $600,000, is computed in part (a).

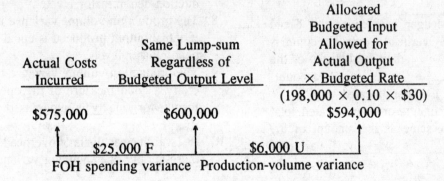

c. Variable overhead allocated is $297,000, the flexible-budget amount from column 3 in part (a). Fixed overhead allocated is $594,000 from column 3 in part (b).

	Variable	Fixed	Total
Actual overhead incurred	$352,000	$575,000	$927,000
Allocated overhead	297,000	594,000	891,000
Underallocated (overallocated)	$ 55,000	$(19,000)	$ 36,000

Note that, because total overhead is underallocated by $36,000, the total overhead variance is $36,000 U.

Review Questions and Exercises

Completion Statements

Fill in the blank(s) to complete each statement.

1. The variable overhead flexible-budget variance divides into which two variances? _____ and _____

2. To compute the budgeted variable overhead rate for a manufacturing company, divide budgeted variable overhead costs by the budgeted quantity of the _____ _____ .

3. To compute the budgeted fixed overhead rate for a manufacturing company, divide budgeted fixed overhead costs by the _____ of the cost-allocation base.

4. The _____ variance is the difference between budgeted FOH and the fixed overhead allocated on the basis of the budgeted quantity of the fixed overhead cost-allocation base allowed for the actual output produced.

5. Manufacturing companies treat fixed manufacturing overhead *as if* it were a variable cost for which purpose of cost accounting? _____

6. If the general-ledger balance of the Fixed Manufacturing Overhead Control account is _____ than the balance of the _____ account, fixed overhead is underallocated.

7. The amount of under- or overallocated total overhead is the same as the amount of the _____ variance.

True-False

____ 1. Budgeted overhead rates can be expressed as an amount per unit of output or per unit of input.

____ 2. There is no fundamental difference between the budgeted variable-overhead rate per unit of input and the budgeted price of individual direct materials.

____ 3. The variable-overhead spending variance is unfavourable if the actual variable overhead rate per unit of input (the cost-allocation base) is greater than the budgeted variable overhead rate per unit of input.

____ 4. The variable overhead efficiency variance is computed similarly to the direct-labour efficiency variance, and the meaning and interpretation of these variances are basically the same.

____ 5. If variable overhead is underallocated, this means the flexible-budget variance for variable overhead is unfavourable.

____ 6. The amount of budgeted fixed manufacturing overhead is affected by the production-denominator level chosen.

____ 7. The fixed manufacturing overhead cost per unit is inversely related to the production-denominator level.

____ 8. The production-volume variance is zero if actual output produced is equal to the denominator level.

____ 9. The production-volume variance is generally a good measure of the operating income forgone by having unused capacity.

____ 10. In 2-variance analysis of overhead costs, there is only one spending variance.

Multiple Choice

Select the best answer to each question. Space is provided for computations after the quantitative questions.

___ 1. (CPA) Information on Fire Company's overhead costs is as follows:

Actual variable overhead	$73,000
Actual fixed overhead	$17,000
Budgeted hours allowed for actual output produced	32,000
Budgeted variable overhead rate per machine-hour	$2.50
Budgeted fixed overhead rate per machine-hour	$0.50

The total overhead variance is:
a. $1,000 unfavourable.
b. $6,000 favourable.
c. $6,000 unfavourable.
d. $7,000 favourable.

___ 2. (CPA adapted) Geyer Company uses standard costing. For the month of April 2000, total overhead is budgeted at $80,000 based on using 20,000 machine-hours. At standard, each finished unit of output requires 2 machine-hours. The following data are available for April 2000:

Actual units of output produced	9,500
Machine-hours used	19,500
Total overhead incurred	$79,500

What amount should Geyer credit to the Manufacturing Overhead Allocated account for April 2000?
a. $76,000
b. $78,000
c. $79,500
d. $80,000

___ 3. The following information is for Pappillon Corporation's variable manufacturing overhead costs last month: favourable flexible-budget variance of $3,000, unfavourable efficiency variance of $2,500. The spending variance is:
a. $500 favourable.
b. $5,500 unfavourable.
c. $5,500 favourable.
d. none of the above.

___ 4. (CPA) Fawcett Company prepared the following information for 1999:

	Budgeted Capacity	Maximum Capacity
Percent of capacity	80%	100%
Machine-hours	32,000	40,000
Variable manufacturing overhead	$64,000	$80,000
Fixed manufacturing overhead	$160,000	$160,000

Fawcett operated at 90% of maximum capacity during 1999. Actual manufacturing overhead for 1999 is $252,000. Fawcett uses the 2-variance analysis of manufacturing overhead. The flexible-budget variance for the year is:
a. $36,000 unfavourable.
b. $0.
c. $18,000 unfavourable.
d. $20,000 unfavourable.

___ 5. (CMA) Edney Company uses standard costing. The standard cost of its product is as follows:

Direct materials	$14.50
Direct manufacturing labour	16.00
Manufacturing overhead	
2 machine-hours @ $11	22.00
Total standard cost	$52.50

The manufacturing overhead rate is based on a denominator level of 600,000 machine-hours. Edney planned to produce 25,000 units each month during 1999. The budgeted manufacturing overhead for 1999 is as follows:

Variable	$3,600,000
Fixed	3,000,000
Total	$6,600,000

During November of 1999, Edney Company produced 26,000 units. Edney used 53,500 machine-hours in November. Actual manufacturing overhead for the month is $315,000 variable and $260,000 fixed. The total manufacturing overhead allocated during November is $572,000. The variable overhead spending variance for November is:
a. $9,000 unfavourable.
b. $4,000 unfavourable.
c. $11,350 unfavourable.
d. $9,000 favourable.
e. $6,000 favourable.

___ 6. Using the data in question 5, the variable overhead efficiency variance for November is:
a. $3,000 unfavourable.
b. $9,000 unfavourable.
c. $1,000 favourable.
d. $12,000 unfavourable.
e. $0.

___ 7. Using the data in question 5, the fixed overhead flexible-budget (spending) variance for November is:
a. $10,000 favourable.
b. $10,000 unfavourable.
c. $6,000 favourable.
d. $4,000 unfavourable.
e. $0.

___ 8. Using the data in question 5, the production-volume variance for November is:
a. $10,000 favourable.
b. $10,000 unfavourable.
c. $3,000 unfavourable.
d. $22,000 favourable.
e. $0.

___ 9. Considering questions 5 through 8, Edney Company is using which type of overhead variance analysis?
a. 1-variance analysis
b. 2-variance analysis
c. 3-variance analysis
d. 4-variance analysis

Exercises

1. Regal Company provides the following information on its manufacturing operations for April:

Production in output units	400
Budgeted variable overhead per output unit	$3
Actual machine-hours used	700
Actual variable overhead incurred	$1,350
Budgeted machine-hours allowed per output unit	1.50

a. Compute the budgeted variable overhead rate per machine-hour.
b. Compute the budgeted machine-hours allowed for actual output produced.
c. Using the columnar solution format below, compute the variable overhead flexible-budget, spending, and efficiency variances. Use F for favourable variances and U for unfavourable variances.

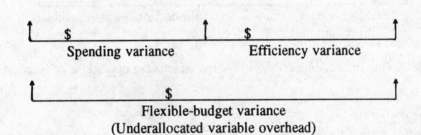

d. Prepare the journal entries to record variable overhead incurred, variable overhead allocated, and the variable overhead spending and efficiency variances.

General Journal	Debit	Credit

2. The following information pertains to the manufacturing operations of Payton Corporation:

Budgeted fixed overhead	$1,800
Actual fixed overhead incurred	$1,750
Denominator level in machine-hours	300
Budgeted machine-hours allowed for actual output produced	280

   a. Compute the budgeted fixed overhead rate per machine-hour.
   b. Using the columnar solution format below, compute the fixed overhead flexible-budget (spending) and production-volume variances. Use F for favourable variances and U for unfavourable variances.

Actual Costs Incurred	Same Lump-Sum Regardless of Budgeted Output Level	Allocated: Budgeted Input Allowed for Actual Output × Budgeted Rate

$\quad$ $ $\qquad$ $

Flexible-budget variance   Production-volume variance
(Spending variance)

3. (CPA) The following information relates to the manufacturing operations of Herman Company for March:

Actual total overhead incurred	$178,500
Flexible-budget formula based on machine-hours (MH)	$110,000 + $0.50 per MH
Budgeted total overhead rate per MH	$1.50 per MH
Total overhead spending variance	$8,000 unfavourable
Production-volume variance	$5,000 favourable

Herman uses the 3-variance analysis of overhead costs.

   a. Compute the actual machine-hours used in March.
   b. Compute the budgeted machine-hours allowed for actual output produced in March.

Completion Statements

1. variable overhead spending variance, variable overhead efficiency variance
2. cost-allocation base
3. production-denominator level (denominator level)
4. production-volume (denominator-level or output-level)
5. Inventory costing purpose
6. greater, Fixed Manufacturing Overhead Allocated
7. total overhead

True-False

1. T
2. F   The budgeted variable-overhead rate includes the cost of *many diverse* overhead items, whereas each type of direct material has its own individual budgeted price.
3. T
4. F   The variable overhead efficiency variance and the direct-labour efficiency variance are computed in a similar manner (for example, compare Exhibit 8-2, text p. 262, and Exhibit 7-4, text p. 231). The meaning and interpretation of these variances, however, is fundamentally different. Consider the case when both of the variances are unfavourable. An unfavourable direct-labour efficiency variance arises from inefficient use of direct labour-hours. In contrast, an unfavourable variable overhead efficiency variance means the cost-allocation base was used inefficiently. The example, text p. 263, lists five possible causes of the unfavourable variable overhead efficiency variance.
5. T
6. F   Budgeted fixed overhead is a lump-sum amount that does not change within the relevant range. The choice of the production-denominator level has no effect on the amount of budgeted fixed manufacturing overhead.
7. T
8. T
9. F   Two reasons explain why the production-volume variance *is not* a good measure of the operating income forgone by having unused capacity. First, the plant capacity may exceed the production-denominator level. Second, a reduction in the selling price may be necessary to spur customer demand that would in turn make use of idle capacity.
10. F   In 2-variance analysis of overhead costs, there is no spending variance. The two variances are the total overhead flexible-budget variance and the production-volume variance.

Multiple Choice

1. b   Total overhead variance = Total overhead incurred − Total overhead allocated
Total overhead variance = ($73,000 + $17,000) − 32,000($2.50 + $0.50)
Total overhead variance = $90,000 − $96,000 = − $6,000, or $6,000 F

2. a   Budgeted total overhead rate = $80,000 ÷ 20,000 = $4 per machine-hour
Budgeted hours allowed for actual output produced = 9,500 × 2 = 19,000 machine-hours
Manufacturing overhead allocated = 19,000 × $4 = $76,000

3. c   Flexible-budget variance = Spending variance + Efficiency variance
$3,000 F = Spending variance + $2,500 U
Spending variance = $3,000 F − ($2,500 U)
= $3,000 F + $2,500 F = $5,500 F

$$\textit{Proof:} \quad \begin{array}{lr} \text{Spending variance} & \$5,500 \text{ F} \\ \text{Efficiency variance} & \underline{2,500} \text{ U} \\ \text{Flexible-budget variance} & \underline{\$3,000} \text{ F} \end{array}$$

4. d Budgeted variable overhead rate = $\$64,000 \div 32,000 = \$2$ per machine-hour

(or $\$80,000 \div 40,000 = \$2$ per machine-hour)

$$\begin{aligned} \text{Flexible-budget variance} &= \$252,000 - [\$160,000 + (40,000 \times 0.90)(\$2)] \\ &= \$252,000 - (\$160,000 + \$72,000) \\ &= \$252,000 - \$232,000 = \$20,000, \text{ or } \$20,000 \text{ U} \end{aligned}$$

5. e Budgeted variable overhead rate = $\$3,600,000 \div (25,000 \times 12 \text{ months})$

= $\$3,600,000 \div 600,000 = \$6$ per machine-hour

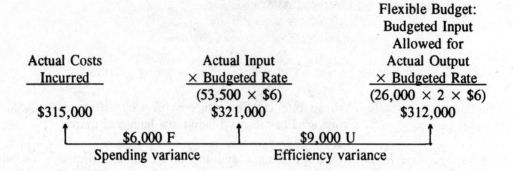

6. b See the preceding answer. The efficiency variance is $9,000 U.

7. b Budgeted fixed overhead rate = $\$3,000,000 \div 600,000 = \$5$ per machine-hour

Actual Costs Incurred		Same Lump-Sum Regardless of Budgeted Output Level ($3,000,000 ÷ 12 months)		Allocated: Budgeted Input Allowed for Actual Output × Budgeted Rate (26,000 × 2 × $5)
$260,000		$250,000		$260,000

    $10,000 U $10,000 F

   Spending variance   Production-volume variance

8. a See the preceding answer. The production-volume variance is $10,000 F.

9. d Edney Company uses 4-variance analysis because four overhead variances are isolated:

Variable overhead spending variance	$ 6,000 F
Variable overhead efficiency variance	9,000 U
Fixed overhead spending variance	10,000 U
Production-volume variance	10,000 F
Total overhead variance (underallocated total overhead)	$ 3,000 U

Exercise 1

a. Budgeted variable overhead rate = $\$3 \div 1.50 = \$2$ per machine-hour
b. Budgeted machine-hours allowed for actual output produced = $400 \times 1.50 = 600$ hours

c.

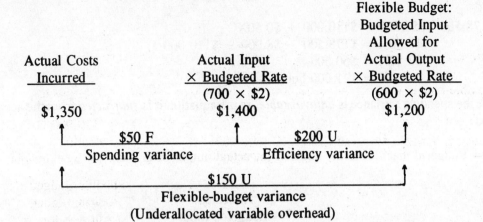

Actual Costs Incurred — $1,350

Actual Input × Budgeted Rate (700 × $2) — $1,400

Flexible Budget: Budgeted Input Allowed for Actual Output × Budgeted Rate (600 × $2) — $1,200

$50 F Spending variance

$200 U Efficiency variance

$150 U Flexible-budget variance (Underallocated variable overhead)

d.   In the following journal entries, MOH denotes manufacturing overhead:

Variable MOH Control	1,350	
Accounts Payable Control and other accounts		1,350
Work-in-Process Control	1,200	
Variable MOH Allocated		1,200
Variable MOH Allocated	1,200	
Variable MOH Efficiency Variance	200	
Variable MOH Control		1,350
Variable MOH Spending Variance		50

Exercise 2

a. Budgeted fixed overhead rate = $1,800 ÷ 300 = $6 per machine-hour

b.

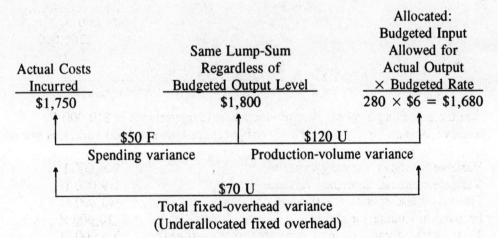

Actual Costs Incurred — $1,750

Same Lump-Sum Regardless of Budgeted Output Level — $1,800

Allocated: Budgeted Input Allowed for Actual Output × Budgeted Rate — 280 × $6 = $1,680

$50 F Spending variance

$120 U Production-volume variance

$70 U Total fixed-overhead variance (Underallocated fixed overhead)

Exercise 3

a.   Let X = Actual machine-hours used:

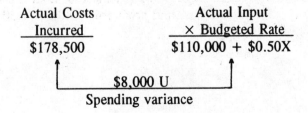

Actual Costs Incurred — $178,500

Actual Input × Budgeted Rate — $110,000 + $0.50X

$8,000 U Spending variance

$$\$178{,}500 - \$8{,}000 = \$110{,}000 + \$0.50X$$
$$\$0.50X = \$178{,}500 - \$8{,}000 - \$110{,}000$$
$$\$0.50X = \$60{,}500$$
$$X = 121{,}000 \text{ hours}$$

Because the spending variance is *unfavourable,* in the equation it is *subtracted* from the actual costs incurred.

b. Let Y = Budgeted machine-hours allowed for actual output produced:

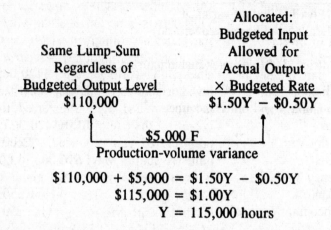

Same Lump-Sum Regardless of Budgeted Output Level	Allocated: Budgeted Input Allowed for Actual Output × Budgeted Rate
$110,000	$1.50Y − $0.50Y

$5,000 F
Production-volume variance

$$\$110{,}000 + \$5{,}000 = \$1.50Y - \$0.50Y$$
$$\$115{,}000 = \$1.00Y$$
$$Y = 115{,}000 \text{ hours}$$

Because the production-volume variance is *favourable*, in the equation it is *added* to the flexible-budget amount.

Income Effects of Alternative Inventory Costing Methods

Chapter Overview

This chapter examines how the operating income of manufacturing companies is affected by cost accounting choices related to inventories. There are two basic choices, each of which is explained in a separate part of the chapter: (I) inventory costing methods for manufacturing companies and (II) denominator-level capacity concepts.

Chapter Highlights

Part I

1. *Inventoriable costs* for manufacturing companies include the manufacturing costs of a product that are regarded as an asset when they are incurred. Inventoriable costs become cost of goods sold when the product is sold.

2. **Variable costing** and **absorption costing** are the two most commonly used methods of costing inventories in manufacturing companies.

- Variable costing treats *only variable manufacturing costs* as inventoriable costs; all fixed manufacturing costs are costs of the period in which they are incurred.
- Absorption costing treats *all variable and fixed manufacturing costs* as inventoriable costs.

Under both methods, the respective amount of inventoriable costs becomes cost of goods sold when the products are sold.

3. Variable costing and absorption costing differ in how they account for fixed manufacturing costs. To illustrate, assume a company beginning its operations in May 2000, budgets and incurs $120,000 of fixed manufacturing costs for the month in producing 8,000 units.

Assume also the denominator level is 8,000 units per month, and sales in May are 6,000 units. Under variable costing, the fixed cost of $120,000 is a period cost in May's income statement; accordingly, variable costing never has a production-volume variance. Under absorption costing, the $120,000 is an inventoriable cost—initially recorded as work in process and then transferred to finished goods—at the rate of $15 ($120,000 ÷ 8,000) per finished unit produced. Because 6,000 units are sold in May, $90,000 (6,000 × $15) is transferred from finished goods to cost of goods sold; the fixed manufacturing cost component of the ending balance of finished goods is $30,000 ($120,000 − $90,000, or 2,000 units unsold × $15). When these 2,000 units are sold, the $30,000 is transferred to cost of goods sold. In other words, the $120,000 gets written off in the income statement under either variable costing or absorption costing, but the timing differs if there is any inventory at the end of the period.

4. Absorption costing (but not variable costing) is a generally accepted accounting principle for external reporting purposes. Absorption costing recognizes both variable and fixed manufacturing costs are necessary to produce finished goods. The role of variable costing is to help companies avoid undesirable buildups of inventory (explained in paragraphs 8 and 9 below).

5. Variable costing uses the contribution income statement to highlight the distinction between variable costs and fixed costs. Absorption costing uses the conventional income statement (that shows gross margin) to emphasize the distinction between manufacturing costs and nonmanufacturing costs. EXHIBIT 9-1, text p. 292, presents income statements for variable costing and absorption costing.

6. Although variable costing is sometimes called **direct costing**, this term is inappropriate for two reasons. First, variable costing includes all variable manufacturing costs—both direct and indirect—as inventoriable costs. Second, variable costing does not include all direct costs as inventoriable costs. Only direct variable manufacturing costs are included. Direct fixed manufacturing costs and direct nonmanufacturing costs are excluded from inventoriable costs.

7. In general, choosing between variable costing and absorption costing affects period-to-period operating income *whenever the inventory level changes*. The reason is absorption costing transfers fixed manufacturing costs into inventory if inventory increases or out of inventory if it decreases. Assuming the amount of budgeted fixed manufacturing cost per unit is constant from period to period and the production-volume variance is written off as a period cost,

ACOI > VCOI if the inventory level increases
ACOI = VCOI if the inventory level remains the same
ACOI < VCOI if the inventory level decreases

where:

ACOI = Absorption-costing operating income
VCOI = Variable-costing operating income

For many accounting periods combined, total ACOI tends to equal total VCOI because units produced will be approximately the same as units sold (that is, the inventory level will be virtually unchanged).

8. The period-to-period change in VCOI is *driven solely by the change in the unit level of sales*, assuming a constant contribution margin per unit and constant fixed manufacturing costs. As a result, managers cannot increase VCOI by producing more units. The clear-cut relationship between units sold and VCOI helps managers gear the production schedule to the expected level of customer demand. On the other hand, the period-to-period change in ACOI is *driven by the change in the unit level of sales and by the change in the unit level of production*. Consequently, managers can increase ACOI in the short-run simply by increasing production (called "producing for inventory"). Such decisions are manipulative if the expected level of customer demand does not justify increased production.

9. Criticism of absorption costing increasingly emphasizes its potentially undesirable incentive for managers to produce for inventory in the short-run. One way of avoiding such excessive inventories is to evaluate the managers' performance based on VCOI instead of ACOI, since production does not affect VCOI. An alternative is to base the evaluation on ACOI along with nonfinancial performance measures, such as the period-to-period tracking of the unit level of inventory in relation to the unit level of sales.

10. A relatively new inventory costing method, **throughput costing** (also called **super-variable costing**), considers *only variable direct material costs* to be inventoriable costs; all other costs are costs of the period in which they are incurred. Because a smaller amount of cost is inventoried under throughput costing, its operating income is less/greater than ACOI and VCOI if units produced is greater/less than units sold. An important subtotal in the throughput-costing income statement is *throughput contribution*, which is revenues minus variable direct material costs of the goods sold. EXHIBIT 9-5, text p. 301, presents the income statement for throughput costing.

Part II

11. The denominator level chosen for allocating fixed manufacturing costs under absorption costing can greatly impact the amount of inventoriable costs, the magnitude of the favourable/unfavourable production-volume variance, and the amount of ACOI. A manufacturing company can use any one of four denominator levels: **theoretical capacity**, **practical capacity**, **normal capacity utilization**, and **master-budget capacity utilization**. Both theoretical capacity and practical capacity

measure the denominator level in terms of what a manufacturing plant can *supply,* whereas normal capacity utilization and master-budget capacity utilization measure the denominator level in terms of *demand* for the output of the plant. In many cases, demand is considerably less than the potential supply.

12. Theoretical capacity is the denominator level based on producing at full efficiency all of the time. This capacity is theoretical in the sense it does not allow for such things as plant maintenance and machine breakdowns. Practical capacity is the denominator level that reduces theoretical capacity by the amount of unavoidable operating interruptions such as scheduled maintenance time and shutdowns for holidays.

13. Normal capacity utilization is the denominator level based on the level of capacity utilization that satisfies average customer demand over a time period (say, two or three years) that includes seasonal, cyclical, and trend factors. Master-budget capacity utilization is the denominator level based on the expected level of capacity utilization for the budget year. A key reason for choosing master-budget capacity utilization instead of normal capacity utilization is the difficulty of forecasting normal capacity utilization in industries with long-run cyclical patterns.

14. The higher/lower the denominator level chosen, the lower/higher the fixed manufacturing costs allocated per unit of output as an inventoriable cost, and the lower/higher ACOI will be. For example, using the highest denominator level (theoretical capacity) results in the lowest inventory costs and the lowest ACOI. That is, the smallest amount of fixed manufacturing costs is allocated to inventory when theoretical capacity is the denominator level. EXHIBIT 9-7, text p. 306, compares the income statement effects of using the four alternative denominator levels.

15. Managers face uncertainty about the demand for their products and need to consider this factor in their capacity planning decisions. For example, practical capacity is often larger than demand in the current period, in part to provide the capacity to meet possible surges in demand. Even if surges do not occur in a given period, it is erroneous to conclude that all of the unused capacity in that period is wasted resources. The gain from being able to meet sudden demand surges may well require having unused capacity in other periods.

16. If there are large differences between practical capacity and master-budget capacity utilization, some companies classify all or part of this difference as *planned unused capacity.* The reason relates to using responsibility accounting for performance evaluation. Top management decides on the amount of practical capacity by focusing on demand over, say, the next five years. In contrast, marketing managers—middle management—make pricing decisions by focusing on the potential customer base in the current year. If the accounting system tracks separately the costs of planned unused capacity, marketing managers can focus on the controllable costs they are responsible for in the current period. That is, their controllable costs will not be commingled with the costs of planned unused capacity.

Featured Exercise

(Relates to Part I of the Chapter) The following information is for Carthage Manufacturing Company's first year of operations:

Revenues	$1,400,000
Manufacturing costs	
Variable	$272,000
Fixed	$630,000
Operating costs	
Variable	$140,000
Fixed	$198,000
Units manufactured	68,000
Units sold	60,000
Work in process, ending inventory	None

For simplicity, this exercise assumes actual costs are equal to budgeted costs.

Assume the company uses variable costing:
a. Compute the cost of ending finished goods inventory.
b. Compute operating income.

Assume the company uses absorption costing and the denominator level is 70,000 units:
c. Compute the cost of ending finished goods inventory.
d. Compute the production-volume variance.
e. Compute operating income.

Solution

a. Variable manufacturing costs per unit = $272,000 ÷ 68,000 = $4
    Finished goods, ending inventory = (68,000 − 60,000) × $4 = $32,000
b. Variable-costing income statement:

Revenues		$1,400,000
Variable costs		
Variable cost of good sold		
60,000 × $4	$240,000	
Variable operating costs	140,000	
Total variable costs		380,000
Contribution margin		1,020,000
Fixed costs		
Fixed manufacturing costs	630,000	
Fixed operating costs	198,000	
Total fixed costs		828,000
Operating Income		$ 192,000

c. Variable manufacturing costs per unit,

from part (a)	$ 4
Fixed manufacturing costs per unit	
for the denominator level	
$630,000 ÷ 70,000	9
Total manufacturing costs per unit	$13

Finished goods, ending inventory = (68,000 − 60,000) × $13 = $104,000

d. Production-volume variance = (68,000 − 70,000) × $9 = $18,000 U
   This variance is unfavourable because the actual production is *less than* the denominator level.

   Note that the production-volume variance exists only under absorption costing; all fixed manufacturing costs are written off as period costs under variable costing.

e. Absorption-costing income statement:

Revenues		$1,400,000
Cost of goods sold		
Before considering variances,		
60,000 × $13	$780,000	
Add unfavourable production-		
volume variance	18,000	
After adjusting for variances		798,000
Gross margin		602,000
Operating costs		
Variable costs	140,000	
Fixed costs	198,000	
Total operating costs		338,000
Operating income		$ 264,000

Note that absorption-costing operating income is greater than variable-costing operating income by $72,000 ($264,000 − $192,000). This difference arises because production exceeds sales, and each unit of the inventory increase is assigned $9 of fixed manufacturing costs under absorption costing: (68,000 − 60,000) × $9 = $72,000.

Review Questions and Exercises

Completion Statements

Fill in the blank(s) to complete each statement.

Part I

1. Variable costing divides costs into which two classifications in the income statement? _____ and _____

2. Variable-costing operating income is greater than absorption-costing operating income for an accounting period if the inventory level _____ during the period.

3. Absorption-costing operating income decreases for a given period if either units sold or _____ decrease (with the other one held constant, or if both of these quantities decrease).

4. Only variable direct material costs are inventoriable costs under _____ costing (also called _____ costing).

Part II

5. _____ is the denominator level based on the level of capacity utilization that satisfies average customer demand over a time period (say, two or three years) that includes seasonal, cyclical, and trend factors.

True-False

Indicate whether each statement is true (T) or false (F).

Part I

___ 1. The fundamental difference between absorption costing and variable costing is absorption costing treats fixed manufacturing costs as inventoriable costs, whereas variable costing treats fixed manufacturing costs as period costs.

___ 2. A company's gross margin is the same under absorption costing, variable costing, and throughput costing.

___ 3. There is no production-volume variance under variable costing.

___ 4. Assume a single-product company holds its selling price constant and its fixed and variable costs follow their cost-behaviour patterns. If the company uses absorption costing, its operating income could not decrease if more units are sold in the current period compared to last period.

___ 5. Variable costing motivates managers to produce more units than are needed to meet demand.

Part II

___ 6. Choosing a denominator-level concept is only applicable to absorption costing.

___ 7. The use of practical capacity rather than master-budget capacity utilization generally results in higher operating income, assuming all variances are written off to cost of goods sold at the end of the accounting period.

___ 8. If normal capacity utilization is used to compute the budgeted fixed manufacturing overhead rate, inventoriable cost per unit tends to fluctuate because of year-to-year differences in the utilization of capacity.

Multiple Choice

Select the best answer to each question. Space is provided for computations after the quantitative questions.

Part I

___ 1. During its first year of operations, Vintage Co. made 4,000 units of a product and sold 3,000 units for $600,000. There is no ending work in process. Total costs were $600,000: $250,000 of direct materials and direct manufacturing labour, $200,000 of indirect manufacturing costs (50% fixed), and $150,000 of nonmanufacturing costs (100% variable). The cost of the 1,000 units of ending finished goods inventory under variable costing is:

a. $112,500.
b. $125,000.
c. $87,500.
d. none of the above.

____ 2. Using the data in question 1, the cost of the ending finished goods inventory under absorption costing is:
   a. $112,500.
   b. $150,000.
   c. $25,000.
   d. none of the above.

____ 3. Using the data in question 1, the contribution margin is:
   a. $337,500.
   b. $187,500.
   c. $100,000.
   d. none of the above.

____ 4. Using the data in question 1, the gross margin is:
   a. $100,000.
   b. $150,000.
   c. $262,500.
   d. none of the above.

____ 5. (CPA adapted) Indiana Corporation began its operations on January 1, 1999, and produces a single product that sells for $9.00 per unit. Production is 100,000 units and 90,000 units are sold in 1999. There is no work-in-process inventory at December 31, 1999. Manufacturing, marketing, and administrative costs for 1999 are as follows:

	Total Fixed Costs	Variable Costs Per unit
Direct materials		$1.75
Direct manufacturing labour		1.25
Indirect manufacturing costs	$100,000	.50
Nonmanufacturing costs	70,000	.60

The cost driver for manufacturing costs is units produced, and the cost driver for nonmanufacturing costs is units sold. Indiana's operating income for 1999 using variable costing is:
   a. $181,000.
   b. $271,000.
   c. $281,000.
   d. $371,000.

____ 6. (CPA adapted) Variable-costing operating income is higher than absorption-costing operating income:
   a. if the amount of fixed manufacturing overhead in beginning inventory is greater than the amount in ending inventory.
   b. if the amount of fixed manufacturing overhead in beginning inventory equals the amount in ending inventory.
   c. if the amount of fixed manufacturing overhead in beginning inventory is less than the amount in ending inventory.
   d. under no circumstances.

7. (CPA adapted) Edmond Company has operating income of $50,000 for 1999 under variable costing. Beginning and ending inventories of finished goods for 1999 are 13,000 units and 18,000 units, respectively. There is no work-in-process inventory at the beginning or end of 1999. If the fixed overhead is $2.00 per unit of output in 1998 and 1999, operating income for 1999 under absorption costing is:
   a. $40,000.
   b. $50,000.
   c. $60,000.
   d. $70,000.

capacity, is used as the denominator level. Using normal capacity utilization based on DMLH, the total overhead rate in the flexible budget is:
   a. $6.00.
   b. $6.50.
   c. $7.50.
   d. $8.13.

Part II

8. (CPA) The budgeted variable manufacturing overhead rate under the denominator-level concepts of normal capacity utilization, practical capacity, and master-budget capacity utilization is:
   a. the same except for normal capacity utilization.
   b. the same except for practical capacity.
   c. the same except for master-budget capacity utilization.
   d. the same for all three denominator-level concepts.

9. (CPA adapted) Dean Company is preparing a flexible budget for the coming year and the following practical capacity estimates for Department M are available:

	At practical capacity
Direct manufacturing labour-hours (DMLH)	60,000
Variable manufacturing overhead	$150,000
Fixed manufacturing overhead	$240,000

Assume Department M's normal capacity utilization, which is 80% of practical

Exercises

Part I

1. (CMA adapted) Denham Company began operations on January 3, 1999. Standard costs were established soon thereafter. The budgeted fixed manufacturing overhead rate is based on a denominator level of 160,000 units. During 1999, Denham produced only 140,000 units of output and sold 100,000 units at a selling price of $180 per unit. Variable costs total $7,000,000, of which 60% are for manufacturing. Fixed costs total $11,200,000, of which 50% are for manufacturing. Denham has no materials or work-in-process inventories at December 31, 1999. Actual input prices per unit of output and actual input quantities per unit of output are equal to the standard amounts.

   a. Compute the cost of finished goods inventory at December 31, 1999 under variable costing.

   b. Compute the cost of finished goods inventory at December 31, 1999 under absorption costing.

   c. Compute operating income for 1999 under variable costing.

   d. Compute the production-volume variance for 1999 under absorption costing.

   e. Compute operating income for 1999 under absorption costing.

   f. Reconcile by formula the difference between operating income for 1999 under variable costing and absorption costing (that is, the difference between the answers for parts (c) and (e) above).

   g. Assume in the coming year (2000) sales increase by 1,000 units and production increases by 1,000 units (over 1999). Assume selling price, variable costs per unit, total fixed costs, and denominator level remain the same. Without preparing an income statement, compute the increase or decrease in operating income in 2000 under variable costing.

   h. Using the data in part (g), compute the increase or decrease in operating income in 2000 under absorption costing.

Part II

2. Bouchard Company provides the following data for 1999:

Fixed manufacturing costs:	
Budgeted	$720,000
Actual	$740,000
Practical capacity in machine-hours	20,000 hours
Normal capacity utilization in machine-hours	16,000 hours
Master-budget capacity utilization in machine-hours	12,000 hours
Budgeted input allowed for actual output produced	13,000 hours

a. Using master-budget capacity utilization:
   (1) Compute the budgeted fixed-manufacturing overhead rate.
   (2) Compute the fixed manufacturing overhead allocated.
   (3) Is fixed manufacturing under- or overallocated? By what amount?
   (4) Compute the production-volume variance.
b. Compute the production-volume variance using normal capacity utilization.
c. Compute the production-volume variance using practical capacity.

Answers to Chapter 9 Review Questions and Exercises

Completion Statements

1. Variable costs, fixed costs
2. decreases
3. units produced
4. throughput, super-variable
5. Normal capacity utilization

True-False

1. T
2. F   Gross margin is a key line item in the income statement only under absorption costing. A key line item in the variable-costing income statement is contribution margin, and throughput contribution is a key line item in the throughput-costing income statement.
3. T
4. F   Under absorption costing, operating income is driven by *both units sold and units produced.* If the increase in operating income from selling more units in the current period is more than offset by the decrease in operating income from producing fewer units, the net effect is a decrease in operating income for the current period.
5. F   Because variable-costing operating income is not affected by changes in units produced, managers are not motivated to produce more units than are needed to meet demand. Under absorption costing, however, managers can increase operating income in the short-run solely by producing more units.
6. T
7. F   Practical capacity is generally larger than master-budget capacity utilization. Accordingly, practical capacity results in a lower fixed overhead rate and lower operating income because a smaller portion of fixed overhead costs is allocated to inventory.
8. F   The budgeted fixed manufacturing overhead rate is equal to budgeted fixed manufacturing overhead divided by the denominator level. Normal capacity utilization is the denominator level that satisfies average customer demand over a time period (say, two or three years) that includes seasonal, cyclical, and trend factors. Year-to-year differences in utilization of capacity, therefore, do not affect the budgeted manufacturing overhead rate and do not affect inventoriable cost per unit.

Multiple Choice

1. c   Total variable manufacturing costs = \$250,000 + \$200,000(0.50) = \$350,000, which is
$$\$87.50 \ (\$350,000 \div 4,000) \text{ per unit}$$
   Cost of ending finished goods inventory = (4,000 − 3,000) × \$87.50 = \$87,500
2. a   Total manufacturing costs per unit = (\$250,000 + \$200,000) ÷ 4,000 = \$112.50
   Cost of ending finished goods inventory = (4,000 − 3,000) × \$112.50 = \$112,500
3. b   Using amounts from answer 1 above:
   Variable cost of goods sold = \$350,000 − \$87,500 = \$262,500
   Contribution margin = Revenues − (Variable COGS + Variable nonmanufacturing costs)
   Contribution margin = \$600,000 − (\$262,500 + \$150,000) = \$187,500
   Note that ending finished goods inventory of \$87,500 is deducted in these computations because it is carried forward to the next accounting period as an asset.

4. c Cost of goods sold = 3,000 × \$112.50 (from answer 2 above) = \$337,500
        Gross margin = \$600,000 − \$337,500 = \$262,500

5. b \$9.00 − (\$1.75 + \$1.25 + \$0.50 + \$0.60) = \$9.00 − \$4.10 = \$4.90;
      (90,000 × \$4.90) − (\$100,000 + \$70,000) = \$441,000 − \$170,000 = \$271,000

6. a

$$\text{ACOI} - \text{VCOI} = \left(\begin{array}{c} \text{Fixed manufacturing OH} \\ \text{in ending inventory} \\ \text{under absorption costing} \end{array} - \begin{array}{c} \text{Fixed manufacturing OH} \\ \text{in beginning inventory} \\ \text{under absorption costing} \end{array} \right)$$

If the amount of fixed manufacturing OH in beginning inventory is greater than the amount in ending inventory, the right-hand side of the equation is negative. This outcome means VCOI is greater than ACOI.

7. c Substituting amounts from this question into the equation in the preceding answer:
      ACOI − \$50,000 = (18,000 × \$2) − (13,000 × \$2)
              ACOI = \$36,000 − \$26,000 + \$50,000 = \$60,000

8. d The budgeted *variable* manufacturing overhead rate is not affected by the denominator-level concept chosen. Of course, the budgeted *fixed* manufacturing overhead rate is affected by the choice.

9. c The budgeted variable overhead rate remains the same within the relevant range.

$$\text{Budgeted variable overhead rate} = \frac{\$150,000}{60,000 \text{ DMLH}} = \$2.50 \text{ per DMLH}$$

$$\text{Budgeted variable overhead rate} = \frac{(0.80)\$150,000}{(0.80)60,000 \text{ DMLH}} = \frac{\$120,000}{48,000 \text{ DMLH}} = \$2.50 \text{ per DMLH}$$

The budgeted fixed overhead rate is computed by dividing fixed manufacturing overhead by the denominator level:

$$\text{Budgeted fixed overhead rate} = \frac{\$240,000}{(0.80)60,000 \text{ DMLH}} = \frac{\$240,000}{48,000 \text{ DMLH}} = \$5.00 \text{ per DMLH}$$

The budgeted total overhead rate = \$2.50 + \$5.00 = \$7.50 per DMLH

Exercise 1

a. \$7,000,000 × 0.60 = \$4,200,000; \$4,200,000 ÷ 140,000 = \$30;
    (140,000 − 100,000) × \$30 = \$1,200,000

b. \$11,200,000 × 0.50 = \$5,600,000; \$5,600,000 ÷ 160,000 = \$35;
    (140,000 − 100,000) × (\$30 + \$35) = 40,000 × \$65 = \$2,600,000

c. \$7,000,000 × 0.40 = \$2,800,000; \$2,800,000 ÷ 100,000 = \$28;

Revenues, 100,000 × \$180	\$18,000,000
Variable costs, 100,000 × (\$30 + \$28)	5,800,000
Contribution margin	12,200,000
Fixed costs	11,200,000
Operating income	\$ 1,000,000

d. Budgeted fixed manufacturing overhead = \$11,200,000 × 0.50 = \$5,600,000
    Budgeted fixed manufacturing overhead rate = \$5,600,000 ÷ 160,000 = \$35 per unit
    Production-volume variance = (160,000 − 140,000) × \$35 = \$700,000 U

e. Revenues, 100,000 × $180 $18,000,000
    Cost of goods sold
        At standard, 100,000 × ($30 + $35) $6,500,000
        Add unfavourable production-volume
            variance   700,000   7,200,000
        Gross margin   10,800,000
        Nonmanufacturing costs
            Variable, $7,000,000 × 0.40   2,800,000
            Fixed, $11,200,000 × 0.50   5,600,000   8,400,000
    Operating income $ 2,400,000

f. $\quad$ ACOI − VCOI = Change in unit level of inventory × Fixed overhead rate

$\$2,400,000 - \$1,000,000 = (140,000 - 100,000) \times \$35$

$\$1,400,000 = 40,000 \times \$35$

$\$1,400,000 = \$1,400,000$

g. Variable-costing operating income (VCOI) is driven solely by units sold (units produced have no effect):

Effect on VCOI $= 1,000 \times [\$180 - (\$30 + \$28)]$

$\qquad\qquad = 1,000 \times \$122 = \$122,000$ increase

h. Absorption-costing operating income (ACOI) is driven by both units sold and units produced:

Effect on ACOI $= 1,000 \times [\$180 - (\$30 + \$28)] + 1,000(\$35)$

$\qquad\qquad = (1,000 \times \$122) + \$35,000$

$\qquad\qquad = \$122,000 + \$35,000 = \$157,000$ increase

Exercise 2

a. (1) $\$720,000 \div 12,000 = \$60$ per machine-hour
    (2) $13,000 \times \$60 = \$780,000$
    (3) $\$740,000 - \$780,000 = \$40,000$ overallocated
    (4) $\$720,000 - (13,000 \times \$60) = \$720,000 - \$780,000 = \$60,000$ F

b. and c.

	Normal Capacity Utilization	Practical Capacity
Budgeted fixed manufacturing overhead rate $720,000 ÷ 16,000; $720,000 ÷ 20,000	$45	$36
Fixed manufacturing overhead allocated 13,000 × $45; 13,000 × $36	$585,000	$468,000
Production-volume variance ($720,000 − $585,000); ($720,000 − $468,000)	$135,000 U	$252,000 U

Determining How Costs Behave

Chapter Overview

This chapter explains how regression analysis and other methods can be used to estimate cost functions. Cost functions help managers make better planning and control decisions. Although most cost functions are assumed to be linear, the learning curve and step costs are important nonlinear cost functions. The Appendix to the chapter provides details on choosing among cost functions developed by regression analysis.

Chapter Highlights

1. A **cost function** is a mathematical expression describing how a cost changes with changes in the level of an activity. Cost functions can be plotted on a graph by measuring the level of an activity on the *x*-axis and the corresponding level of total cost on the *y*-axis.

2. Estimating cost functions often relies on two basic assumptions: (i) changes in the total costs of a cost object are explained by changes in the level of a *single* activity and (ii) cost behaviour is adequately approximated by a **linear cost function**. The graph of a linear cost function is a straight line within the *relevant range*. The relevant range, introduced in Chapter 2, is the span of activity in which the relationship between total cost and the level of activity is valid. *These two assumptions apply to all of the paragraphs below except 15 through 18, and 24.*

3. The equation for a linear cost function is:

$$y = a + bX$$

where:

$y =$ estimated total cost

$a =$ **constant** (or intercept), the component of total cost that, within the relevant range, does not vary with changes in the level of activity

$b =$ **slope coefficient**, the amount by which total cost changes when a one-unit change occurs in the level of activity within the relevant range

$X =$ actual level of activity within the relevant range

Three types of linear cost functions are variable costs, $y = bX$; fixed costs, $y = a$; and **mixed costs** or **semivariable costs**, which have both fixed and variable components, $y = a + bX$. In the equation for a mixed cost, the constant is an estimate of fixed costs *only if the zero level of activity (shutdown) is within the relevant range*.

4. Measuring a past relationship between cost and the level of activity is called **cost estimation**. Managers are interested in cost estimation because it can help them make more accurate **cost predictions** (forecasts) in the future. Cost estimation and cost prediction underlie major cost accounting topics such as CVP analysis and flexible budgets.

5. The most important issue in estimating a cost function is to determine whether or not a *cause-and-effect relationship* exists between an activity and the cost in question. For example, producing more units *causes* more direct materials and more direct manufacturing labour to be used. In contrast, the usage of direct materials and direct manufacturing labour move together (are highly correlated), *but neither causes the other*. Only a true cause-and-effect relationship—one that is logical to the operating manager and the management accountant—establishes *economic plausibility* between the level of an activity and a cost. *In such cases, the activity measure is*

called a cost driver. Economic plausibility is essential for cost estimation.

6. *Four approaches to cost estimation are the industrial engineering method, conference method, account analysis method, and quantitative analysis.* Many organizations use a combination of these approaches.

7. The **industrial engineering method** (also called the **work-measurement method**) estimates cost functions by analyzing the relationship between inputs and outputs in physical terms. To illustrate, assume a time-and-motion study determines 0.20 direct manufacturing labour-hours are required per unit of output. If labour is expected to cost $20 per hour, the estimated cost function is $4 ($20 × 0.20) per unit of output. The industrial engineering method is very time-consuming, but some government contracts mandate its use.

8. The **conference method** estimates cost functions on the basis of analysis and opinions about costs and their drivers gathered from various departments of an organization. Because this method does not require detailed analysis of data, cost functions can be developed quickly. The emphasis on opinions, however, means the accuracy of the estimates depends largely on the care, skill, and knowledge of the individuals providing the inputs.

9. The **account analysis method** estimates cost functions by having individuals thoroughly knowledgeable about the operations classify cost accounts in the ledger as variable, fixed, or mixed with respect to a single activity. Typically, managers use qualitative rather than quantitative analysis in making these cost classifications. The account analysis method is widely used.

10. *Quantitative analysis* uses a formal mathematical method to fit cost functions to past data. There are six steps in estimating a linear cost function by means of quantitative analysis.

Step 1: Choose the **dependent variable**, the particular cost to be predicted.
Step 2: Identify the **independent variable**, the cost driver.
Step 3: Collect data on the dependent variable and the cost driver.
Step 4: Plot the data.
Step 5: Estimate the cost function.
Step 6: Evaluate the cost driver of the estimated cost function.

In performing Step 2, there should be an economically plausible relationship between the cost driver and the cost to be predicted. Collecting data is usually the most difficult step in the analysis. Common problems in data collection include missing data, recording errors, a changing relationship over time between the cost driver and the cost, and distortions caused by inflation. Plotting the data not only depicts the relationship between the cost driver and the cost, but also highlights observations outside the general pattern the analyst should check for errors or unusual events. The two most common forms of quantitative analysis for estimating a cost function are the **high-low method** and **regression analysis**. The four criteria for evaluating the cost driver of the estimated cost function are listed in paragraph 13.

11. The *high-low method* is a very simplified way to estimate cost functions. This method computes the equation for a straight line by using only the highest and lowest observed values of the cost driver within the relevant range and their respective costs. This equation is the estimated cost function; however, there is an obvious danger of relying on the high-low method if the two observations chosen are not a representative high and a representative low.

12. *Regression analysis* is a statistical method that measures the average amount of change in the dependent variable associated with a unit change in one or more independent variables. **Simple regression** analysis estimates the relationship between the dependent variable and *one* independent variable. **Multiple regression** analysis estimates the relation-

ship between the dependent variable and *two or more* independent variables. Regression analysis uses all available data to estimate the cost function. This cost function is much more useful than the one obtained from only two points under the high-low method.

13. Commonly available computer software makes it quick and inexpensive to develop numerous simple and multiple regressions. As a result, the question is: Which regression cost function should be chosen? *Four criteria are used for choosing among cost functions: (i) economic plausibility, (ii) goodness of fit, (iii) significance of the independent variable(s), and (iv) specification analysis.* Economic plausibility was discussed in paragraph 5. The other three criteria are discussed in paragraphs 19 through 24.

14. When using activity-based costing (ABC), operating managers and cost analysts identify key activities, and the cost driver and costs of each activity at the output-unit level, batch level, or product-sustaining level. To estimate cost functions, ABC uses a variety of methods—industrial engineering, conference, and regression. Generally, ABC emphasizes long-run relationships between the cost drivers and their corresponding costs. The long-run focus means more costs are variable, which strengthens cause-and-effect relationships.

15. In practice, cost functions are not always linear. The graph of a **nonlinear cost function** is not a straight line within the relevant range. A **step cost function** is one type of nonlinear cost function: this cost remains the same over various ranges of the level of activity, but the cost increases by discrete amounts (that is, in steps) as the level of activity changes from one range to the next. If the steps are narrow, this is a *step variable-cost function*. If the steps are wide, this is a *step fixed-cost function*.

16. **Learning curves** are another type of nonlinear cost function. A learning curve shows how labour-hours (or labour costs) per unit decrease as units of production increase

due to workers learning and becoming better at their jobs. Managers use learning curves to predict how labour-hours (or labour costs) will change as more units are produced. The **experience curve** extends the learning curve beyond manufacturing to other business functions in the value chain. The experience curve is a cost function that shows how the costs per unit in various parts of the value chain decline as units produced and sold increase.

17. Two models of the learning curve are the **cumulative average-time learning model** and the **incremental unit-time learning model**. In the cumulative average-time learning model, the cumulative average time per unit decreases by a constant percentage each time the cumulative quantity of units produced doubles. In the incremental unit-time learning model, the incremental unit time (the time required to produce the last unit) decreases by a constant percentage each time the cumulative quantity of units produced doubles. The preferable model to use is the one that more accurately approximates cost behaviour; this choice can only be made on a case-by-case basis. EXHIBITS 10-12 and 10-14 text, p. 337 and p. 338, show the detailed computations under the two models of the learning curve.

18. The lower costs brought about by the learning curve (and experience curve) can have a major influence on decisions. For example, a company can set a low selling price on its product in order to generate high demand. As the company's production increases to meet this growing demand, cost per unit declines. The company "rides the product down the learning curve" as it establishes a higher market share and earns more operating income per unit. Another example is that a company can incorporate learning-curve effects into budgets and standards to provide a better means of evaluating performance.

19. The Appendix to this chapter provides details on choosing among cost functions developed by regression analysis. Specifically, the Appendix discusses three of the four criteria identified in paragraph 13—goodness of fit,

significance of the independent variables(s), and specification analysis.

20. *Goodness of fit* indicates the strength of the relationship between the cost driver and the cost. The closer the regression line estimates of cost are to actual cost amounts, the better the goodness of fit. A statistical measure of goodness of fit is the **coefficient of determination** (r^2), which is the percentage of variation in the dependent variable (the cost) explained by the independent variable (the cost driver). If the estimated costs exactly equal the actual costs, $r^2 = 1$. Generally, an r^2 of .30 or higher passes the goodness-of-fit test. This test is meaningful, however, only if economic plausibility has been established between the cost driver and the cost. *A high r^2 between two variables does not imply or prove that a cause-and-effect relationship exists; it merely indicates that these variables move together.*

21. *Significance of the independent variable* focuses on a key question: Is the slope of the regression line, the estimated value b, statistically significant (that is, statistically different than zero)? The answer depends on the t-value of the slope coefficient, which is equal to b divided by the **standard error of the estimated coefficient**. The standard error measures how much of the estimated value b is likely to be affected by random factors. If the t-value of this slope coefficient is greater than 2.00, a statistically significant relationship exists between the independent variable (the cost driver) and the dependent variable (the cost).

22. When simple regression is used, **specification analysis** tests four assumptions: (i) linearity within the relevant range, (ii) constant variance of residuals, (iii) independence of residuals, and (iv) normality of residuals. A **residual** is the vertical difference in a graph between the actual cost and estimated cost for a given observation of the cost driver.

a. The assumption of *linearity within the relevant range* can be tested by studying the data in a scatter diagram. This assumption holds in EXHIBIT 10-6, p. 331. (A scatter diagram can be prepared in the case of simple regression but not for multiple regression).

b. *Constant variance of residuals* can also be tested by studying the data in a scatter diagram. For this assumption to hold, there must be a uniform scatter (dispersion) of the data points around the regression line. This assumption holds in Panel A of EXHIBIT 10-18, p. 347, but does not hold in Panel B.

c. *Independence of residuals* can be tested by studying a plot of the residuals. For this assumption to hold, the residual for an observation must not be related to the residual for any other observation. Residuals are not independent if, considered sequentially, they have a systematic pattern. This condition is *serial correlation* (also called *autocorrelation)*. Serial correlation does not exist in Panel A of EXHIBIT 10-19, p. 347, but does exist in Panel B. Serial correlation can be measured by the Durbin-Watson statistic. For samples of 10 to 20 observations, this statistic falling in the 1.10 to 2.90 range indicates the residuals are independent.

d. The assumption of *normality of residuals* can be tested by studying the frequency distribution of a plot of the residuals.

23. EXHIBIT 10-17, p. 346, presents a convenient format for summarizing the regression results. EXHIBIT 10-21, p. 349, presents a comprehensive comparison of two cost functions using the four criteria.

24. In multiple regression, specification analysis must also test the assumption that there is no **multicollinearity**. Multicollinearity exists whenever two or more independent variables are highly correlated with each other. For the no-multicollinearity assumption to hold, the coefficient of correlation (r) between any pair of independent variables cannot exceed .70.

Featured Exercise

Kenton Corporation predicts its monthly energy costs by using simple regression analysis. The cost driver is degree-days, which is the absolute difference between 65 degrees and the average daily temperature. The regression results are as follows:

Constant	$2,000
Slope coefficient	$3
Standard error of the estimated coefficient	$1
Coefficient of determination	.73
Durbin-Watson statistic	1.82

a. Specify the regression equation.
b. How much is the increase in predicted energy costs from one additional degree-day?
c. Compute the predicted energy costs if there are 320 degree-days in a particular month.
d. Is the constant in the regression equation an acceptable estimate of the fixed cost of energy? Explain.
e. (Appendix) Comment on goodness of fit.
f. (Appendix) Compute the t-value of the slope coefficient.
g. (Appendix) Comment on the significance of the slope coefficient.
h. (Appendix) Comment on the independence of residuals, assuming 18 monthly observations were used in the regression analysis.

Solution

a. $y = \$2,000 + \$3X$
b. $\$3$, the slope coefficient
c. $y = \$2,000 + \$3(320) = \$2,000 + \$960 = \$2,960$
d. No, the constant is not an acceptable estimate of the fixed cost of energy, unless the zero level of the cost driver is within the relevant range (which is not logical in this case). The constant here, therefore, is a component of the regression equation that provides the best available linear approximation of how the dependent variable behaves within the relevant range.
e. This regression meets the goodness-of-fit test because the r^2 of .73 satisfies the requirement of $r^2 \geq .30$.
f. $\$3 \div \$1 = 3.00$
g. The slope coefficient is significantly different than zero because the t-value is greater than 2.00, as computed in part (f). An alternative approach is to determine the confidence interval for b: $\$3 \pm (2.00 \times \$1)$, or a range of $\$1$ to $\$5$. That is, there is less than a 5% chance that the true value of the degree-days coefficient of $\$3$ falls outside this range; therefore, the likelihood that $b = \$0$ is remote.
h. The residuals are independent (that is, serial correlation is not a problem) because the Durbin-Watson statistic lies in the acceptable range of 1.10 to 2.90 for sample sizes of 10 to 20 observations.

Review Questions and Exercises

Completion Statements

Fill in the blank(s) to complete each statement.

1. It is often assumed that a cost function is _____ within the relevant range of a single activity.
2. The _____ in an estimated cost function is the component of total cost that, within the relevant range, does not vary with changes in the level of activity.
3. The _____ in an estimated cost function is the amount by which total cost changes when a one-unit change occurs in the level of activity within the relevant range.
4. The most important issue in estimating a cost function is to determine whether or not a _____ relationship exists between an activity and the cost in question.
5. The _____ method estimates cost functions by analyzing the relationship between inputs and outputs in physical terms.

6. A statistical method that measures the average amount of change in the dependent variable associated with a unit change in one or more independent variables is _____ _____.
7. A _____ remains the same over various ranges of the level of activity, but increases by discrete amounts as the level of activity changes from one range to the next.
8. (Appendix) A statistical measure of goodness of fit is the _____, which is the percentage of variation in the dependent variable (the cost) explained by the independent variable (the cost driver).
9. (Appendix) The vertical difference in a graph between the actual cost and the estimated cost for a given observation of the activity or cost driver is called a _____.

True-False

Indicate whether each statement is true (T) or false (F).

___ 1. The main purpose for estimating cost functions is to improve the accuracy of cost predictions.

___ 2. In the equation $y = a + bX$, the constant a is an estimate of fixed costs.

___ 3. To obtain reliable estimated cost functions using the account analysis method, the cost-classification decisions should be made by individuals thoroughly knowledgeable about the operations.

___ 4. Usually, the most difficult step in estimating a cost function based on quantitative analysis is data collection.

___ 5. If the high-low method is used, the constant in the cost function equation is always computed after computing the slope coefficient.

___ 6. The closer the predicted amounts of y in a cost function are to the actual cost amounts, the better the economic plausibility.

___ 7. The main purpose of the learning curve is to assist managers in developing techniques for increasing the speed and efficiency of production.

___ 8. A higher learning-curve percentage indicates a faster pace of learning.

___ 9. (Appendix) If the t-value of the slope coefficient is less than 2.00, the independent variable is not a cost driver.

___ 10. (Appendix) When simple regression is used, specification analysis tests the assumption regarding the reliability of data collection procedures.

___ 11. (Appendix) In simple regression, a scatter diagram is useful to check for constant variance of residuals.

___ 12. (Appendix) Multicollinearity exists whenever residuals, considered sequentially, have a systematic pattern.

Multiple Choice

Select the best answer to each question. Space is provided for computations after the quantitative questions.

___ 1. (CPA) Jackson, Inc., is preparing a flexible budget for the coming year and requires the cost of steam used in its plant to be divided into its fixed and variable elements. The following data on the cost of steam used and direct manufacturing labour-hours (DMLH) worked are available for the last six months:

Month	Cost of Steam	DMLH
July	$ 15,850	3,000
August	13,400	2,050
September	16,370	2,900
October	19,800	3,650
November	17,600	2,670
December	18,500	2,650
Total	$101,520	16,920

Assuming Jackson uses the high-low method, the estimated variable cost of steam per DMLH is:
a. $4.00.
b. $5.42.
c. $5.82.
d. $6.00.

___ 2. Using the data in question 1 and assuming Jackson uses the high-low method, the estimated amount of the constant is:
a. $6,400.
b. $0.
c. $5,200.
d. none of the above.

___ 3. In a step cost function where the steps are narrow, the cost behaviour approaches the pattern of a:
a. fixed cost.
b. variable cost.
c. mixed cost.
d. semivariable cost.

4. (CPA) Adams Corporation developed the following flexible budget for annual indirect manufacturing labour cost:

$$\frac{\text{Total}}{\text{cost}} = \$4,800 + \$0.50\,(\text{Machine-hours})$$

The operating budget for the current month is based on 20,000 machine-hours. Indirect manufacturing labour cost included in the monthly flexible budget is:
a. $14,800.
b. $10,000.
c. $14,400.
d. $10,400.

__ 5. (CPA) Quo Co. rented a building to Hava Fast Food. Each month Quo receives a fixed rental amount plus a variable rental amount based on Hava's revenues for that month. As revenues increase so does the variable rental amount, but at a reduced rate. Which of the following curves reflects the monthly rentals under the agreement?

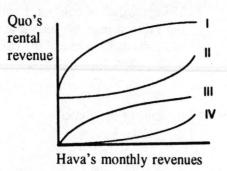

Quo's rental revenue

I
II
III
IV

Hava's monthly revenues

a. I
b. II
c. III
d. IV

__ 6. (CMA) Ace Manufacturing Corporation found the production of a certain product is subject to an 80% learning curve. The product is produced in lots of 100 units and 8 labour-hours are required for the first lot. Assuming Ace uses the cumulative average-time learning model, the total time required to produce 400 units is:
a. 32 hours.
b. 20.48 hours.
c. 25.6 hours.
d. 19.52 hours.
e. none of the above.

__ 7. Using the data in question 6 and assuming Ace uses the cumulative average-time learning model, the incremental time required to produce the second lot of 100 units is:
a. 0.0640 hours per unit.
b. 12.80 hours.
c. 0.0480 hours per unit.
d. 0.1120 hours per unit.
e. none of the above.

__ 8. (Appendix) Serial correlation is measured by:
a. the standard error of the slope coefficient.
b. the coefficient of determination.
c. the t-value of the slope coefficient.
d. the Durbin-Watson statistic.

Exercises

1. Barnes Company estimated the cost function for its maintenance cost. The cost function has a variable component and a step fixed component that increases by $10,000 for each additional 20,000 units of output between 40,000 and 80,000 units of output. Total maintenance cost would be $130,000 at 40,000 units of output and $180,000 at 60,000 units of output.

   What is the variable cost per unit of output in this cost function?

2. Addison Construction Company has begun paving roads for the Illinois highway system. Each paving project is similar. Recently, the company completed its first paving project in 20,000 hours. Direct labour is paid $20 per hour. The company needs to predict its direct labour cost for purposes of making a competitive bid on a contract for three additional paving projects. Addison's experience indicates that a 90% learning curve is appropriate for these projects.

   Using the cumulative average-time learning model:
   a. Compute the predicted direct labour cost for the contract of three additional paving projects.
   b. Disregard the 90% learning curve in part (a). Assume 36,448 direct labour-hours are needed for these three paving projects. Compute the learning-curve percentage.
   Using the incremental unit-time learning model:
   c. Compute the predicted direct labour cost for the contract of three additional paving projects, assuming a 90% learning curve.

3. (Appendix) Steve Kovzan was given the task of developing a cost function for predicting indirect manufacturing costs (manufacturing overhead) for the Kansas City personal computer plant of Electronic Horizons. The plant is highly automated. The following information has been collected:

Month	Indirect Manufacturing Costs	Machine-Hours	Direct Manufacturing Labour-Hours (DMLH)
January	$2,530	2,730	324
February	1,900	1,810	210
March	4,710	3,403	347
April	1,270	2,200	331
May	4,380	3,411	272
June	4,020	2,586	202
July	3,730	3,364	342
August	3,070	2,411	247
September	4,980	3,964	347
October	3,310	2,897	328
November	1,270	2,207	293
December	3,510	2,864	307

Kovzan estimates two cost functions using regression analysis:

Regression Model A: Indirect manufacturing costs = f(Machine-hours)

Variable	Coefficient	Standard Error	t-Value
Constant	−1,707.70	912.94	−1.87
Independent variable:			
Machine-hours	1.75	0.32	5.47

$r^2 = .75$; Standard error of residuals = 657.44; Durbin-Watson statistic = 2.59

Regression Model B: Indirect manufacturing costs = f(Direct manufacturing labour-hours)

Variable	Coefficient	Standard Error	t-Value
Constant	1,914.10	2,264.60	0.85
Independent variable:			
DMLH	4.43	7.55	0.59

$r^2 = .03$; Standard error of residuals = 1,300.77; Durbin-Watson statistic = 2.45

Which cost function should Kovzan use for predicting indirect manufacturing costs? Present your answer in the following format, as used in Exhibit 10-21, text p. 349.

Criterion	Regression Model A (Machine-hours)	Regression Model B (Direct manufacturing labour-hours)
1.		
2.		
3.		
4.		
a.		
b.		
c.		
d.		

State your conclusion:

Completion Statements

1. linear
2. constant (intercept)
3. slope coefficient
4. cause-and-effect
5. industrial engineering (work measurement)
6. regression analysis
7. step cost function
8. coefficient of determination (r^2)
9. residual

True-False

1. T
2. F The constant a is an estimate of fixed cost only if the zero level of activity (shutdown) is within the relevant range.
3. T
4. T
5. T
6. F The statement refers to *goodness of fit*, not *economic plausibility*. Only a true cause-and-effect relationship—one that is logical to the operating manager and the management accountant—establishes economic plausibility between the level of an activity and a cost. In such cases, the activity measure is called a cost driver.
7. F Managers use learning curves to predict how labour-hours (or labour costs) change as more units are produced. Such predictions have a major influence on decisions about setting selling prices, budgets, and standards.
8. F A higher learning-curve percentage indicates a *slower* pace of learning. To illustrate, assume a company uses the cumulative average-time learning model with an 80% learning curve. If the first unit requires 10 labour-hours, the second unit requires 8 (10 × 0.80) labour-hours. The total time for the first 2 units = 10 + 8 = 18 labour-hours. Under a 90% learning curve, the total time for the first 2 units = 10 + 10(0.90) = 19 labour-hours.
9. T
10. F If simple regression is used, specification analysis tests four assumptions: linearity within the relevant range, constant variance of residuals, independence of residuals, and normality of residuals.
11. T
12. F The statement describes *serial correlation* (also called *autocorrelation*), not *multicollinearity*. Multicollinearity exists in multiple regression whenever two or more independent variables are highly correlated with each other. Multicollinearity is not a problem if the coefficient of correlation (r) between any pair of independent variables does not exceed .70.

Multiple Choice

1. a The highest and lowest observations of DMLH are 3,650 and 2,050 respectively:
   ($19,800 − $13,400) ÷ (3,650 − 2,050) = $6,400 ÷ 1,600 = $4 per hour
2. c At the high point, $19,800 − 3,650($4) = $5,200
   At the low point, $13,400 − 2,050($4) = $5,200

3. b The steps in a step variable-cost function are not as wide as those in a step fixed-cost function (compare Panels B and C in Exhibit 10-9, text p. 335). Where the steps in a step-variable cost function are very narrow, the cost behaviour approaches the pattern of a variable cost.

4. d The key point in the question is that the flexible-budget equation is for a *year*, whereas the flexible budget is for a *month*: $4,800 \div 12 = $400; $400 + 20,000($0.50) = $10,400

5. a The monthly rentals under this agreement are increasing at a decreasing rate as the cost driver increases.

6. b

Cumulative Number of Units	Cumulative Average Hours Per Unit		Cumulative Total Hours	
100	$8.0 \div 100$	$= 0.0800$	$100 \times 0.0800 =$	8.00
200	$0.0800 \times 80\%$	$= 0.0640$	$200 \times 0.0640 =$	12.80
400	$0.0640 \times 80\%$	$= 0.0512$	$400 \times 0.0512 =$	20.48

7. c Using amounts from the computations in the preceding answer, $12.80 - 8.00 = 4.80$ hours; $4.80 \div$ the second lot of 100 units $= 0.0480$ hours per unit.

8. d Serial correlation is measured by the Durbin-Watson statistic. This statistic falling in the 1.10 to 2.90 range for samples of 10 to 20 observations suggests that the residuals are independent.

Exercise 1

Increase in total cost $= $180,000 - $130,000 = $50,000$ (of which $10,000 is fixed cost)
Increase in variable cost $= $50,000 - $10,000 = $40,000$
Variable cost per unit $= $40,000 \div (60,000 - 40,000) = $40,000 \div 20,000 = 2

Proof:
At 60,000 units, fixed cost $= $180,000 - (60,000 \times $2) = $60,000$
At 40,000 units, fixed cost $= $130,000 - (40,000 \times $2) = \underline{50,000}$
Increase (that is, the step) in fixed cost $\underline{\underline{$10,000}}$

Exercise 2

a.

Cumulative Number of Projects	Cumulative Average Hours Per Project	Cumulative Total Hours
1	20,000	20,000
2	18,000 (20,000 × 0.9)	36,000
4	16,200 (18,000 × 0.9)	64,800

Predicted direct labour cost for the contract of three additional projects:
$(64,800 - 20,000) \times $20 = $896,000$

b. Total hours to complete the first four projects $= 36,448 + 20,000 = 56,448$; cumulative average hours per project $= 56,448 \div 4 = 14,112$; Let X = Learning curve percentage; $14,112 = 20,000(X)(X)$; $X^2 = 14,112 \div 20,000$; $X^2 = .7056$; $X = 0.84$, or 84%

c.

Cumulative Number of Projects	Individual Project Hours for Xth Project	Cumulative Total Hours
1	20,000	20,000
2	18,000(20,000 × 0.9)	38,000
3	16,924*	54,924
4	16,200(18,000 × 0.9)	71,124

* This amount is computed by using logarithms (see the bottom section of Exhibit 10-14, text p. 338).

Predicted direct labour cost for the contract of three additional projects:
$(71,124 - 20,000) \times $20 = $1,022,480$

Exercise 3

Plots of the scatter diagram for each regression model are as follows:

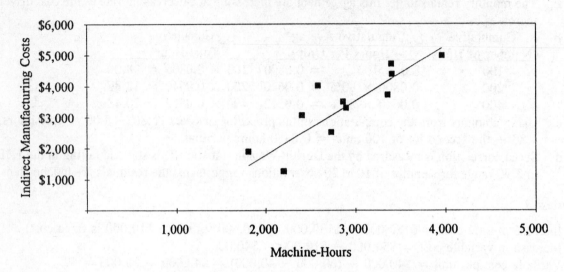

Electronic Horizons - Regression Model A

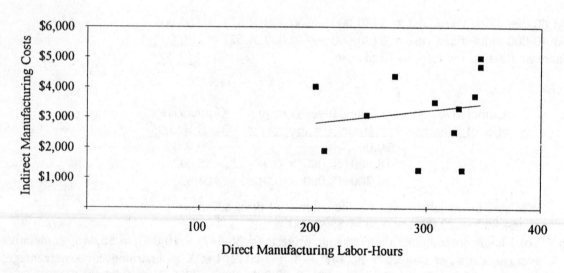

Electronic Horizons - Regression Model B

A comparison of the cost functions is on the next page.

Criterion	Regression Model A (Machine-hours)	Regression Model B (Direct manufacturing labour-hours)
1. Economic plausibility	Positive relationship between indirect manufacturing costs and machine-hours is economically plausible in a highly automated plant.	Positive relationship between indirect manufacturing costs and DMLH is economically plausible, but less so than machine-hours on a month-by-month basis.
2. Goodness of fit	$r^2 = .75$ Excellent goodness of fit.	$r^2 = .03$ Very poor goodness of fit.
3. Significance of independent variable	t-value for machine-hours of 5.47 is significant.	t-value for DMLH of 0.59 is not significant.
4. Specification analysis		
a. Linearity within the relevant range	Appears reasonable from a plot of the data, but inferences drawn from only 12 observations are not reliable.	Appears questionable from a plot of the data, but inferences drawn from only 12 observations are not reliable.
b. Constant variance of residuals	Appears reasonable from the plot of the data, but inferences drawn from only 12 observations are not reliable.	Appears questionable from the plot of the data, but inferences drawn from only 12 observations are not reliable.
c. Independence of residuals	Durbin-Watson statistic = 2.59, thus the assumption of independence is not rejected.	Durbin-Watson statistic = 2.45, thus the assumption of independence is not rejected.
d. Normality of residuals	Database is too small to make reliable inferences.	Database is too small to make reliable inferences.

Conclusion: The cost function using machine-hours as the cost driver is clearly preferred. It is important to realize that the cost analyst often must make a choice among "imperfect" cost functions. That is, the data of any particular cost function will not perfectly meet all of the criteria for choosing among regressions. In this exercise for example, the cost function using machine-hours as the cost driver is imperfect because the database of 12 observations is too small to make reliable inferences about linearity within the relevant range, constant variance of residuals, and normality of residuals.

Decision Making and Relevant Information

Chapter Overview

This chapter focuses on several types of management decisions: accepting or rejecting a one-time-only special order, insourcing or outsourcing (making or buying) a product or service, choosing a product mix, keeping or dropping a customer or business segment, and keeping or replacing equipment. Management accountants help managers make these decisions by clearly distinguishing relevant revenues and costs from irrelevant ones. The Appendix to the chapter describes linear programming, an optimization technique for making product-mix decisions where multiple constraints exist.

Chapter Highlights

1. Managers use a **decision model** to choose among alternative courses of action. A decision model is a formal method for making a choice, frequently involving both quantitative and qualitative analyses. Management accountants assist managers by presenting and analyzing relevant data to guide their decisions.

2. In the decision process, managers proceed through a sequence of five steps: (a) obtain information, (b) make predictions about future revenues and costs, (c) choose an alternative, (d) implement the decision, and (e) evaluate performance to provide feedback. The feedback, in turn, might affect any of the first four steps in making future decisions.

3. The most important decision-making concepts in this chapter are **relevant costs** and **relevant revenues**. Relevant costs (revenues) must meet two criteria: *(a) they must be expected future amounts and (b) they must differ between two of the alternatives being considered.* Only future costs (revenues) can be relevant to decisions because there is no

way to alter what happened in the past. While historical costs are always irrelevant to decisions, they can be a useful basis to predict future costs. *There are two common pitfalls in relevant-cost analysis: (a) assuming all variable costs are relevant and (b) assuming all fixed costs are irrelevant.*

4. To determine the change in total operating income between two alternatives, compare the total future operating income (the "all data" approach) or compute the difference in future operating income (the "relevant data" approach). While both approaches provide the same result, the latter one has the advantage of focusing the manager's attention only on relevant items. EXHIBIT 11-2, text p. 371, illustrates the two approaches.

5. Due consideration must be given to both **quantitative factors** and **qualitative factors** in management decisions. Quantitative factors are outcomes measured in numerical (financial or nonfinancial) terms. Qualitative factors are outcomes that cannot be measured numerically (for example, employee morale). Cost analysis generally emphasizes quantitative factors that can be expressed in financial terms. Just because qualitative factors and quantitative nonfinancial factors cannot be measured easily in financial terms, however, does not make them unimportant. Managers must at times give more weight to these factors.

6. If a company has idle production capacity, it may be advisable to accept a *one-time-only special order* at a price below the normal selling price. The phrase "one time only" highlights the point that a special order has no long-run implications. A one-time-only special order should be accepted if its additional revenues exceed its additional costs. EXHIBIT 11-4, text p. 373, shows the analysis

of a one-time-only special order: additional revenues are $55,000, additional costs are $37,500, and additional operating income is $17,500.

7. In a one-time-only special order decision (as in all decisions involving relevant costs), *total costs should be used rather than unit costs*. Reliance on unit-cost numbers that include a fixed cost component can mislead managers about the effect that increasing output has on operating income. Unit costs also are misleading if any variable costs are irrelevant; for example, variable marketing costs often remain the same whether a one-time-only special order is accepted or rejected.

8. Organizations must decide between **insourcing** and **outsourcing** various products or services. Insourcing is the process of producing goods or performing services within the organization rather than purchasing the same goods or services from outside suppliers, which is outsourcing. For example, a company might decide to insource a component part for one of its products and outsource payroll processing. Decisions on insourcing or outsourcing are also called **make-or-buy decisions**. The main quantitative factor in these decisions is cost. The most important qualitative factors are quality and dependability of suppliers. In some cases, despite the cost and other advantages of insourcing, companies outsource in order to focus on their own core competencies.

9. Two commonly used terms in decision making are **incremental cost** and **differential cost**. An incremental cost is the additional cost incurred for an activity. A differential cost is the difference in cost between two alternatives. To illustrate, consider the following make-or-buy decision:

	Make	Buy
Total relevant costs	$130,000	$119,000
Difference in favour of buying	$11,000	

The incremental cost of making is $130,000. The incremental cost of buying is $119,000. The differential cost (in favour of buying) is $11,000. Two parallel terms, *incremental revenue* and *differential revenue*, are defined in a like manner. Incremental revenue is the additional revenue from an activity. Differential revenue is the difference in revenue between two alternatives.

10. Whenever a manufacturing company is deciding between making or buying a component part, technically the buy alternative should be stated as *how best to use the available production facilities*. The facilities that would have been used to manufacture the part in question could be idle, used for other production purposes, or rented out. Fixed costs are relevant to the analysis if they are avoidable when buying from an outside supplier. EXHIBIT 11-6, text p. 377, shows the analysis of a make-or-buy decision.

11. Deciding to use a resource in one particular way causes a manager to give up the opportunity to use the resource in alternative ways. The lost opportunity is a cost that the manager must take into account in making a decision. **Opportunity cost** is the contribution to income that is forgone (rejected) by not using a limited resource in its next-best alternative use. For example, a company uses some of its production capacity to make a product that increases operating income by $20,000 rather than renting out the space for $16,000, the next-best alternative. The company's opportunity cost of making the product is $16,000. Opportunity costs are not included in financial accounting records because these records are limited to transactions involving alternatives actually selected; when alternatives are rejected, they do not qualify as transactions.

12. If a multiple-product plant is operating at capacity, managers must often make **product-mix decisions**—which products to manufacture and in what quantities. These decisions have a short-run focus because the level of capacity can be expanded in the long run. The

proper criterion that maximizes operating income when operating at capacity is to obtain *the highest contribution margin per unit of the resource (factor) that limits the production or sale of products*. To illustrate, assume the demand for one of a company's products, Product A, uses all the production capacity. A's contribution margin per unit is $100 and the limiting factor is machine-hours. Four machine-hours are required to make a unit of A, so its contribution margin per machine-hour is $25 ($100 ÷ 4). If the contribution margin per machine-hour of each of the company's other products is less than $25, short-run operating income is maximized by manufacturing only Product A. If a company has a variety of products and faces more than one limiting factor, the most profitable product mix can be determined by using linear programming (discussed in paragraph 16).

13. In addition to making choices among individual products, managers must often make decisions about adding or dropping a product line, a customer, or a business segment. The key question in each decision is: What are the relevant revenues and relevant costs? Relevant costs can be driven by one or more cost drivers. In making these decisions, managers should ignore allocated overhead costs and focus instead on how total overhead costs differ among the alternatives.

14. Another important type of decision is *keeping or replacing equipment*. These decisions focus on relevant costs over the useful life of the equipment; for simplicity in this chapter, the time value of money and income taxes are ignored. The **book value** (original cost minus accumulated amortization) of existing ("old") equipment is irrelevant to these decisions because it is a past cost (also called is a **sunk cost**). The book value of the old equipment is written off in the income statement either at the time of replacement or as

amortization each year if the equipment is kept. The disposal price of old equipment and the acquisition cost of replacement ("new") equipment are relevant because they are future amounts that differ between the keep and replace alternatives.

15. On the surface, keeping or replacing equipment seems like a straightforward decision: the manager analyzes the relevant costs and chooses the lower-cost alternative. In reality, however, the manager tends to favour the alternative that makes his or her short-run performance look better. To illustrate, assume (a) relevant costs are lower for replacing an old machine, (b) a significant loss on disposal of the old machine would be reported in the income statement for the year of replacement, and (c) the manager's annual performance bonus is based on each year's operating income. (Of course, there is no loss on disposal if the old machine is kept for its entire useful life.) Under these conditions, the manager's temptation to keep the old machine is overwhelming. Resolving this conflict between the decision model and performance evaluation is frequently a baffling problem in practice. The practical difficulty is that accounting systems rarely track each decision separately. Performance evaluation focuses on responsibility centres for a specific time period, not on individual items of equipment for their entire useful lives.

16. The Appendix to this chapter describes **linear programming (LP)**, an optimization technique used to maximize the total contribution margin of a mix of products, given multiple constraints. In cases involving two products and a few constraints, the trial-and-error or graphic approach can be used to formulate and solve LP problems. While these approaches provide insight about LP, computer software packages are used to solve most real-world LP problems.

Featured Exercises

1. Sedona Corporation has an annual plant capacity of 2,800,000 units of output. Its regular operations for the year are budgeted as follows:

Revenues, 2,000,000 units at $38 each	$76,000,000
Manufacturing costs	
Variable	$25 per unit
Fixed	$18,000,000
Marketing and administrative costs	
Variable (sales commissions)	$6 per unit
Fixed	$2,000,000

Sedona has been contacted about supplying a one-time-only special order of 60,000 units at a selling price of $32 each, subject to half the usual sales commission per unit.

Assuming this special order will have no effect on regular sales, should Sedona accept the order? Show your computations.

Solution

Yes, accept this special order because operating income increases $240,000.

Incremental revenues, 60,000 × $32		$1,920,000
Incremental costs (all variable in this case):		
Manufacturing, 60,000 × $25	$1,500,000	
Sales commission, 60,000 × $3	180,000	1,680,000
Incremental operating income		$ 240,000

2. Cardinal Company needs 20,000 units of Part K28 to use in its production cycle. The following information is available:

Costs to Cardinal to make Part K28:

Direct materials	$ 4
Direct manufacturing labour	16
Variable overhead allocated	8
Fixed overhead allocated	10
Total costs	$38

If Cardinal buys the part from Oriole instead of making it, the released facilities will be idle. Sixty percent of the fixed overhead allocated will continue if the part is bought from Oriole.

Should Cardinal make or buy Part K28? Show your computations.

Solution

Relevant Items	Make	Buy
Outside purchase of part, 20,000 × $36		$720,000
Direct materials, 20,000 × $4	$ 80,000	
Direct manufacturing labour, 20,000 × $16	320,000	
Variable overhead, 20,000 × $8	160,000	
Fixed overhead, 20,000 × $10(1−0.60)	80,000	
Total relevant costs	$640,000	$720,000
Difference in favour of making	$80,000	

Fixed overhead that cannot be avoided = 20,000 × ($10 × 0.60) = $120,000. This amount is irrelevant to the decision because it is the same under both alternatives.

Review Questions and Exercises

Completion Statements

Fill in the blank(s) to complete each statement

1. A _____ is a formal method for making a choice, frequently involving both quantitative and qualitative analysis.
2. In a one-time-only special order decision, the relevant costs are the _____ costs that _____ between the "accept" and "reject" alternatives.
3. In management decisions, outcomes that cannot be measured numerically are called _____.
4. Producing goods or performing services within the organization rather than purchasing the same goods or services from outside suppliers is called _____.
5. _____ is the contribution to income that is forgone (rejected) by not using a limited resource in its next-best alternative use.
6. In equipment replacement decisions, an item that is always irrelevant is the _____ _____.
7. (Appendix) _____ is an optimization technique used to maximize the total contribution margin of a mix of products, given multiple constraints.

True-False

Indicate whether each statement is true (T) or false (F).

___ 1. In general, all variable costs are relevant to decisions, and all fixed costs are irrelevant to decisions.
___ 2. Historical costs are always irrelevant to decisions but they can be helpful in predicting future costs.
___ 3. A car rental company is comparing two makes of cars to add to its fleet. Kilometres per litre of fuel consumption is a qualitative factor in this decision.
___ 4. Assuming sufficient idle production capacity is available, a one-time-only

special order should not be accepted at a selling price below the total manufacturing costs per unit.
___ 5. Opportunity costs do not entail cash receipts or disbursements.
___ 6. Incremental cost and differential cost have the same meaning.
___ 7. In deciding among three alternatives for the sale of units held in finished goods inventory, the manager should regard historical cost of the inventory as irrelevant, whether or not the inventory is obsolete.
___ 8. If there is an inconsistency between the decision model and performance evaluation in a decision to keep or replace some old equipment, the manager's choice tends to be influenced more by the decision model.
___ 9. (Appendix) The LP model is not applicable to situations where there are more than three constraints.
___ 10. (Appendix) The area of feasible solutions in an LP graphic solution shows the boundaries of those combinations of the two products that satisfy all constraints.

Multiple Choice

Select the best answer to each question. Space is provided for computations after the quantitative questions.

___ 1. (CPA) Light Company has 2,000 obsolete light fixtures that were manufactured at a cost of $30,000. If the fixtures are reworked for $10,000, they can be sold for $18,000. Alternatively, the fixtures can be sold for $3,000 to a jobber. Assuming the fixtures are reworked and sold, the opportunity cost is:
a. $3,000.
b. $5,000.
c. $10,000.
d. $30,000.

2. (CPA) The manufacturing capacity of Jordan Company's facilities is 30,000 units of a product per year. A summary of operating results for the year ended December 31, 1998 is as follows:

Revenues,	
18,000 units × $100	$1,800,000
Variable costs	990,000
Contribution margin	810,000
Fixed costs	495,000
Operating income	$ 315,000

A foreign distributor has offered to buy 15,000 units at $90 per unit during 1999. Assume all of Jordan's costs will have the same behaviour patterns in 1999 as in 1998. If Jordan accepts this offer and rejects 3,000 units of business from regular customers so as not to exceed its capacity, total operating income for 1999 is:

a. $855,000.
b. $840,000.
c. $705,000.
d. $390,000.

3. (CPA) Gata Co. plans to discontinue a division with a $48,000 contribution margin, and allocated fixed costs of $96,000, of which $42,000 cannot be eliminated. What is the effect on Gata's operating income of discontinuing this division?

a. Increase of $48,000
b. Decrease of $48,000
c. Increase of $6,000
d. Decrease of $6,000

4. Which one of the following items is relevant to an equipment replacement decision?

a. Original cost of the old equipment
b. Disposal price of the old equipment
c. Gain or loss on the disposal of the old equipment
d. Book value of the old equipment

5. (CPA) Maxwell Company has an opportunity to acquire a new machine to replace one of its old machines. The new machine costs $90,000 and has an estimated useful life of five years, with a zero terminal disposal price. Variable operating costs are $100,000 per year. The old machine has a book value of $50,000 and a remaining life of five years. Its disposal price now is $5,000 but would be zero after five years. Variable operating costs are $125,000 per year. Considering the five years in total, but ignoring the time value of money and income taxes, what is the difference in operating income by replacing the old machine?

a. $10,000 decrease
b. $15,000 decrease
c. $35,000 increase
d. $40,000 increase

6. (Appendix, CMA adapted) Pleasant Valley Company makes two products, ceramic vases (V) and ceramic bowls (B). Each vase requires two kilograms of direct materials and three hours of direct manufacturing labour. Each bowl requires two kilograms of direct materials and one hour of direct manufacturing labour. During the next production week, 100 kilograms of direct materials and 60 hours of direct manufacturing labour are available to make vases and bowls. Each kilogram of direct material costs $4 and each hour of direct manufacturing labour costs $10. All manufacturing overhead is fixed and is estimated to be $200 per week for this production process. Pleasant Valley sells vases for $50 each and bowls for $35 each. The objective function for total contribution margin is:

a. $50V + $35B.
b. $12V + $17B.
c. $38V + $18B.
d. $12V + $17B − $200.

7. Using the data in question 6, one of the constraints is:
a. 2V + 2B ≤ 60.
b. 2V + 2B ≤ $400.
c. 3V + B ≤ 60.
d. V + 3B ≤ 100.
e. $8V + $8B ≤ 600.

Exercises

1. Edgewood Corporation has 1,440 machine-hours of plant capacity available during a particular period for manufacturing two products with the following characteristics:

	T	L
Selling price	$42	$75
Variable costs per unit	$20	$25
Units that can be manufactured per machine-hour	8	3
Demand in units	13,500	6,000

Compute the number of available machine-hours that should be used to manufacture each product.

2. (CMA) Richardson Motors uses ten units of Part T305 each month in the production of large diesel engines. The cost to manufacture one unit of T305 is as follows:

Direct materials	$ 2,000
Materials handling	
(20% of direct material costs)	400
Direct manufacturing labour	16,000
Manufacturing overhead	
(150% of direct manufacturing labour)	24,000
Total manufacturing costs	$42,400

Materials handling, a separate cost category that is not included in manufacturing overhead, represents those direct variable costs of the Receiving Department that are allocated to direct materials and purchased components on the basis of their cost. Richardson's annual manufacturing overhead budget is one-third variable and two-thirds fixed. Simpson Castings, one of Richardson's reliable vendors, offers to supply T305 at a unit price of $30,000. Assume Richardson Motors could rent out all its idle production capacity for $50,000 per month.

Compute how much Richardson's monthly cost of T305 increases/decreases if the company purchases the ten units from Simpson Castings.

3. (CPA) Bradshaw Manufacturing Company is reviewing the profitability of the company's four products and the potential of several proposals for improving the profitability of the product mix. An income statement and other data follow:

	Total	Product W	Product X	Product Y	Product Z
Revenues	$62,600	$10,000	$18,000	$12,600	$22,000
Cost of goods sold	44,274	4,750	7,056	13,968	18,500
Gross margin	18,326	5,250	10,944	(1,368)	3,500
Operating costs	12,012	1,990	2,976	2,826	4,220
Operating income	$ 6,314	$ 3,260	$ 7,968	$(4,194)	$ (720)
Units sold		1,000	1,200	1,800	2,000
Selling price		$ 10.00	$ 15.00	$ 7.00	$ 11.00
Variable cost of goods sold per unit		$ 2.50	$ 3.00	$ 6.50	$ 6.00
Variable operating costs per unit		$ 1.17	$ 1.25	$ 1.00	$ 1.20

Each of the following proposals is to be considered independently. Consider only the product changes stated in each proposal; the production and sales levels of the other products remain the same.

a. Compute the effect on operating income if Y is dropped.
b. Compute the total effect on operating income if Y is dropped and a resulting loss of customers causes a decrease of 200 units in the production and sales of X.
c. Assume the part of the plant in which W is manufactured can easily be adapted to the production of Z, but changes in quantities produced necessitate changes in selling prices. Compute the total effect on operating income if production of W is reduced to 500 units (to be sold at $12 each) and production of Z is increased to 2,500 units (to be sold at $10.50 each).

4. (Appendix, CPA) Williamson Manufacturing intends to produce two products, X and Y. Product X requires 6 hours of time on Machine 1 and 12 hours of time on Machine 2. Product Y requires 4 hours of time on Machine 1 and no time on Machine 2. Both machines are available for 24 hours.

Assuming the objective function of the total contribution margin is $2X + $1Y, what is the optimal product mix?

Answers to Chapter 11 Review Questions and Exercises

Completion Statements

1. decision model
2. expected future, differ
3. qualitative factors
4. insourcing
5. Opportunity cost
6. book value of the existing ("old") equipment
7. linear programming (LP)

True-False

1. F   Only *expected future costs (whether variable or fixed)* that *differ* between the alternatives under consideration are relevant to a decision.
2. T
3. F   Kilometres per litre of fuel consumption is a quantitative factor because it is an outcome measured in numerical terms. An example of a qualitative factor in the decision is the expected comfort of the cars.
4. F   In the example, beginning text p. 372, total manufacturing costs are $12 per unit. At a selling price of $11 per unit, accepting the one-time-only special order *adds* $17,500 of operating income.
5. T
6. F   In the solution to the Featured Exercise, p. 135, the incremental cost of the make alternative is $640,000, and the incremental cost of the buy alternative is $720,000. The differential cost (in favour of making) is $80,000.
7. T
8. F   Managers tend to favour the alternative that makes their performance look better. They focus, therefore, on the measure(s) used in performance evaluation.
9. F   The LP model is applicable to situations where any number of constraints exist. If there are only two products and the number of constraints is manageable, the optimal solution can be found by trial and error or graphically. If the LP problem is more complex, computer software packages are used to compute the optimal solution.
10.   T

Multiple Choice

1. **a** The following analysis shows there is a $5,000 advantage of reworking the fixtures:

Relevant Items	Rework and Sell	Sell As Is
Revenue	$18,000	$3,000
Deduct costs	10,000	-0-
Operating income	$ 8,000	$3,000

Difference in favour of reworking ⌐ $5,000 ⌐

The *difference* in operating income between the alternatives, however, *is not* the opportunity cost. Opportunity cost is the contribution to income that is forgone (rejected) by not using a limited resource in its next-best alternative use. If the fixtures (a limited resource) are reworked and sold, the opportunity cost is the rejected alternative of selling them "as is" for $3,000.

2. **c**

Revenues, (15,000 × $100) + (15,000 × $90)	$2,850,000
Variable costs, ($990,000 ÷ 18,000) × 30,000	1,650,000
Contribution margin	1,200,000
Fixed costs	495,000
Operating income	$ 705,000

Note that, although opportunity cost is *not explicitly shown* in this income statement, it is present in this situation because the short-run capacity of 30,000 units is insufficient to accommodate both the regular business of 18,000 units and the special order of 15,000 units (that is, 3,000 units of regular business must be forgone in order to accept the special order). Knowing that the variable costs per unit are $55($990,000 ÷ 18,000), the opportunity cost can be *shown explicitly* in an incremental analysis as follows:

Increase in contribution margin from the special order itself, 15,000 × ($90 − $55)	$525,000
Deduct forgone contribution margin from the regular business, 3,000 × ($100 − $55)	135,000
Increase in operating income from accepting the special order	390,000
Add operating income before considering the special order	315,000
Operating income	$705,000

3. **c**

	Before Discontinuance	After Discontinuance
Contribution to fixed costs	$ 48,000	$ 0
Deduct allocated fixed costs	96,000	42,000
Operating income of division	$(48,000)	$(42,000)
Difference in favour of discontinuing the division		$6,000

4. **b** The disposal price of the old equipment is relevant because it is an expected future cash flow that differs between the keep and replace alternatives. The gain or loss on the disposal of the old equipment is the difference between the irrelevant book value of the old equipment and the relevant disposal price.

5. d

Relevant Items	Keep	Replace
Variable operating costs		
$125,000 × 5; $100,000 × 5	$625,000	$500,000
Cost of new machine		90,000
Disposal price of old machine		(5,000)
Total relevant costs	$625,000	$585,000
Difference in favour of replacing old machine	$40,000	

6. b

	Vase	Bowl
Selling price	$50	$35
Variable costs per unit		
Direct materials		
2 lbs. × $4; 2 lbs. × $4	8	8
Direct manufacturing labour		
3 hrs. × $10; 1 hr. × $10	30	10
Total variable cost per unit	38	18
Contribution margin per unit	$12	$17

7. c Constraint for direct materials: $2V + 2B \leq 100$
Constraint for direct manufacturing labour: $3V + B \leq 60$

Exercise 1

	T	L
Selling price	$ 42	$ 75
Variable costs per unit	20	25
Contribution margin per unit	22	50
Multiply by number of units that can be manufactured per hour	× 8	× 3
Contribution margin per hour of plant capacity	$176	$150

All 1,440 machine-hours should be used to manufacture product T, because T has the higher contribution margin per unit of the limited resource (machine-hours) *and* producing 11,520 (1.440 × 8) units of T does not exceed its demand of 13,500 units.

Exercise 2

Relevant Costs	Make	Buy
Direct materials, $2,000 × 10	$ 20,000	
Materials handling, $20,000 × ($400 ÷ $2,000)	4,000	
Direct manufacturing labour, $16,000 × 10	160,000	
Variable manufacturing overhead		
($24,000 × 1/3) × 10	80,000	
Outside purchase of T305		
$30,000 × 10		$300,000
Rental income		(50,000)
Total relevant costs per month	$264,000	$250,000
Monthly decrease in cost from buying T305	$14,000	

Exercise 3

a. Effect on operating income of dropping Y:

Loss of revenues, 1,800 units × $7	$(12,600)
Savings of variable costs,	
1,800 units × ($6.50 + $1.00)	13,500
Increase in operating income	$ 900

This analysis includes *relevant items only*. The same answer can also be obtained by including *both* relevant and irrelevant items, albeit more time-consuming. Under that presentation (not shown), the company's income statement without Y would show operating income of $7,214, which is $900 more than the present level of $6,314. Note that when the product mix changes, total fixed costs (which are the same with or without Y) are merely allocated (reallocated) to the new mix of products W, X and Z.

b. Effect on operating income of changes in Y and X:

Increase in operating income from	
dropping Y (from part a)	$ 900
Loss of part of X's contribution margin	
200 units × ($15.00 − $3.00 − $1.25)	(2,150)
Increase (decrease) in operating income	$(1,250)

c. Effect on operating income of changes in W and Z:

Loss of present contribution margin	
W: 1,000 units × ($10.00 − $2.50 − $1.17)	$(6,330)
Z : 2,000 units × ($11.00 − $6.00 − $1.20)	(7,600)
Addition of proposed contribution margin	
W: 500 units × ($12.00 − $2.50 − $1.17)	4,165
Z : 2,500 units × ($10.50 − $6.00 − $1.20)	8,250
Increase (decrease) in operating income	$(1,515)

Exercise 4

Constraint for Machine 1: $6X + 4Y \leq 24$
Constraint for Machine 2: $12X \leq 24$

Solving these inequalities as simultaneous equations:

$$12X = 24; \ X = 2$$
$$6(2) + 4Y = 24$$
$$4Y = 24 - 12$$
$$Y = 12 \div 4 = 3$$

Thus, the optimal product mix is 2 units of X and 3 units of Y.

Pricing Decisions, Product Profitability Decisions, and Cost Management

Chapter Overview

This chapter focuses on the important role that cost data play in pricing decisions. These decisions challenge managers because there is no single way of computing a product cost that is suitable for both short-run and long-run time horizons. The relevant-revenue and relevant-cost analysis introduced in Chapter 11 helps managers make pricing decisions.

Chapter Highlights

1. The three major influences on pricing decisions are *customers*, *competitors*, and *costs* ("the three C's"). Customers influence price through their effect on demand. Competitors offer alternative or substitute products that may affect demand and price. Costs influence price through there effect on supply. Knowing how costs behave when the level of one or more cost drivers changes provides insight into the predicted operating income from various price-volume combinations for a product.

2. Surveys of how managers make pricing decisions reveal companies consider customers, competitors, and costs differently. For companies selling similar commodity-type products in highly competitive markets, the market sets the price. In these cases, cost data help managers to decide on the level of output that maximizes operating income. In less competitive markets, products are differentiated and managers have some discretion in setting prices. In these cases, the pricing decision depends on the value that customers place on the product, the prices competitors charge for their products, and the costs of the product.

3. In determining the costs that are relevant for a pricing decision, managers must consider costs in all six business functions of the value chain, from R&D to customer ser-

vice, as well as whether the time horizon is short-run (less than a year) or long-run. A classic short-run pricing decision is a one-time-only special order with no long-run implications. There are two key differences in pricing for the long-run compared to the short-run: (a) costs that are irrelevant for short-run pricing decisions, such as fixed costs that cannot be changed, are generally relevant in the long-run and (b) prices are often set to earn an acceptable return on investment in the long-run while short-run pricing is more opportunistic—in the short run, prices are decreased if demand is weak and increased if demand is strong.

4. Long-run pricing decisions can be market-based or cost-based.

- The *market-based approach to long-run pricing* starts by asking: Given what our customers want and how our competitors will react to what we do, what price should we charge? This approach starts by considering customers and competitors and then looks at costs.

- The *cost-based approach to long-run pricing* starts by asking: What does it cost us to make this product and, hence, what price should we charge to recoup our costs and achieve a desired return on investment? This approach first considers costs and then looks at customers and competitors.

Both approaches consider the three C's; only their *starting points* differ.

5. An important form of the market-based approach is target pricing. A **target price** is the estimated price for a product (or service) that potential customers are willing to pay. This estimate is based on an understanding of customers' perceived value for a product and competitors' responses. The target price forms

the basis for calculating **target cost per unit**. The target cost per unit is the target price minus **target operating income per unit**. Target operating income per unit is the average operating income that a company wants to earn per unit of a product (or service) sold. Target cost per unit is the estimated long-run cost per unit of a product that enables the company to achieve its target operating income per unit by selling at the target price. All future costs, both variable and fixed, are relevant to target cost calculations because the time horizon is long-run. Because target cost per unit is often lower than the existing full cost per unit of the product, target cost really is a target at which the company must aim.

6. There are four steps in developing target prices and target costs:

Step 1: Develop a product that satisfies the needs of potential customers.
Step 2: Choose a target price.
Step 3: Derive a target cost per unit by subtracting the target operating income per unit from the target price.
Step 4: Perform **value engineering** to achieve the target cost.

Value engineering is a systematic evaluation of all aspects of the value-chain business functions, with the objective of reducing costs while satisfying customer needs.

7. Managers find the distinction between value-added and nonvalue-added activities and costs useful in value engineering. A *value-added cost* is a cost that, if eliminated, reduces the value customers obtain from using the product or service. Examples are costs of specific product features and attributes desired by customers such as preloaded software on a personal computer, product reliability, and prompt customer service. A *nonvalue-added cost* is a cost that, if eliminated, does not reduce the value customers obtain from using the product or service. An example is the cost of reworking defective products. Value engineering attempts to achieve greater efficiency in value-added activities in order to reduce value-added costs. Value engineering also seeks to reduce nonvalue-added activities and hence nonvalue-added costs by reducing the use of the cost drivers of nonvalue-added activities.

8. To successfully apply value engineering, **cost incurrence** must be distinguished from **locked-in costs** (also called **designed-in costs**). Cost incurrence is using a resource to meet a specific objective. The accrual basis of accounting records costs when they are incurred. Locked-in costs are those costs that have not yet been incurred but, based on decisions already made, will be incurred in the future. For example, a product's direct material costs are incurred when each unit is manufactured and sold, but these costs are locked-in much earlier—at the time the product is designed. The distinction between when costs are locked-in and when they are incurred is important because locked-in costs are difficult to reduce. EXHIBIT 12-4, text p. 424, shows a typical pattern for a product of wide divergence between the time when costs are locked-in and the time when those costs are incurred.

9. Costs are not always locked-in at the design stage. In some industries, such as legal and consulting, costs are locked-in and incurred as the services are performed. If costs are not locked-in early, cost reduction can be achieved up to the time costs are incurred. In these industries, the key to lowering costs is improved operating efficiency and productivity rather than better design.

10. The cost-based approach to long-run pricing is often called *cost-plus pricing*. Under this approach, a company chooses a cost base it regards as reliable and a markup component to recover its costs and earn a desired return on investment. The basic formula is:

$$\frac{Cost}{base} + \frac{Markup}{component} = \frac{Prospective}{selling\ price}$$

Although several cost bases are usually available for pricing decisions, surveys indicate that most managers use *full costs of the product*—the sum of all the fixed and variable costs of the business functions in the value chain.

Advantages cited for using this cost base include full recovery of all costs of the product, price stability, and simplicity. The markup component is often based on **target rate of return on investment**. To illustrate, assume this rate is 18%, invested capital (total assets) required for the product is $96,000,000, and sales are expected to be 200,000 units per year. The target annual operating income is $17,280,000 (18% × $96,000,000), and the markup component per unit is $86.40 ($17,280,000 ÷ 200,000). Assuming the cost base is $720 per unit, the prospective selling price is $806.40 ($720 + $86.40). In these computations it is important to distinguish between the target rate of return on investment, 18%, and the markup component expressed as a percentage of the cost base, $86.40 ÷ $720 = 12%.

11. The selling prices computed under cost-plus pricing are *prospective* prices. Customer and competitor reactions to the original price may cause it to be reduced. Alternatively, the product may be redesigned to cut costs in an effort to maintain the original price. The eventual design and cost-plus price chosen must balance the conflicting tensions among costs, markup, and customer reactions.

12. The target pricing approach (discussed in paragraphs 5 and 6) reduces the need to go back and forth among prospective cost-plus prices, customer reactions, and design modifications. Instead, target pricing first determines product characteristics and target price on the basis of customer preferences and expected competitor responses. Market considerations and the target price then serve to focus and motivate managers to reduce costs and achieve the target cost per unit and the target operating income per unit.

13. Companies sometimes need to consider how to cost and price a product over its multiyear life cycle. The **product life cycle** spans the time from initial R&D on a product to when customer support is no longer offered for that product—typically a period of several years or more. Using **life-cycle budgeting**, managers estimate the revenues and costs attributable to each product from its initial R&D to its final servicing and support. **Life-cycle costing** tracks and accumulates the individual value-chain costs attributable to each product from its initial R&D to its final customer servicing and support. The term "cradle-to-grave costing" conveys the idea of fully capturing all costs associated with the product. A key benefit of life-cycle costing is that the full set of costs associated with each product becomes visible rather than being buried in the traditional income statement.

14. Life-cycle costs for individual products reinforce the importance of locked-in costs, target costing, and value engineering in pricing decisions and cost management. The earlier in a product's life-cycle that costs are locked-in (before there is much information on the likelihood of the product being successful in the marketplace), the riskier the product in terms of profitability.

15. A different notion of life-cycle costs is **customer life-cycle costs**. Here the focus is on the total costs incurred by a customer to acquire and use a product until it is replaced. Customer life-cycle costs can be an important consideration in pricing decisions. For example, manufacturers of washing machines and air conditioners charge higher prices for models that save electricity and have low maintenance costs.

16. Many pricing decisions are driven by factors other than cost. Two examples are **price discrimination** and **peak-load pricing**.

- Price discrimination is the practice of charging some customers a higher price for the same product or service than is charged to other customers. Airlines use price discrimination because, in contrast to pleasure travelers, business travelers are relatively insensitive to price.

- Peak-load pricing is the practice of charging a higher price for the same product or service when demand approaches physical capacity limits. A main user of peak-load pricing is the electric utility industry; higher rates are charged during the summer months when air conditioning creates peak-load demand for electricity.

17. Another factor affecting pricing decisions is the Competition Act. The purpose of this legislation is to "protect the specific public interest in free competition". The Competition Act prohibits **predatory pricing.** A company engages in predatory pricing if it sells products at unreasonably low prices which either tend to substantially lessen competition or were designed to have that effect.

18. Canadian laws also prohibit **dumping** and **collusive pricing**. Dumping is closely related to predatory pricing. It occurs when a non-Canadian company sells a product in Canada at a price below the market value in the country of its creation, and this action materially injures or threatens to materially injure an industry in Canada. Collusive pricing occurs when companies in an industry conspire in their pricing and output decisions to achieve a price above the competitive price.

19. Companies that have concerns about their conformance to antitrust laws should (a) keep detailed records of variable costs for all value-chain business functions and (b) review all proposed prices below variable costs in advance, with a presumption that claims of predatory intent will occur.

Featured Exercise

E. Berg & Sons build custom-made pleasure boats that range in price from $30,000 to $250,000. For the past 30 years, Ed Berg, Sr., has determined the selling price of each boat by estimating the costs of direct materials, direct manufacturing labour, an allocated portion of total overhead (which includes some nonmanufacturing costs), and adding a 20% markup to the total of these costs. For example, a recent price quotation was determined as follows:

Direct materials	$10,000
Direct manufacturing labour	16,000
Total overhead	4,000
Total estimated costs	30,000
Markup, 20% × $30,000	6,000
Selling price	$36,000

The total overhead figure was determined by budgeting total overhead costs for the year and allocating them at 25% of direct manufacturing labour costs.

If a customer rejects the price and business is slack, Ed Berg, Sr., often reduces his markup to as little as 5% of total estimated costs. The average markup for the year is expected to be 15%.

Ed Berg, Jr., just completed a course on pricing in which contribution margin was emphasized. He feels this approach will help in determining the selling prices of his company's boats.

Total overhead for the year has been budgeted at $600,000 of which $360,000 is fixed and the remainder varies in proportion to direct manufacturing labour costs.

a. Assume the customer in the example rejects the $36,000 quotation and also rejects a $31,500 quotation (5% markup) during a slack period. The customer counters with a $30,000 offer. Compute the minimum selling price Ed Berg, Jr., could quote without decreasing or increasing operating income?

b. What is the main disadvantage of emphasizing contribution margin in pricing decisions?

Solution

a. Two steps are used to obtain the selling price that has no effect on operating income. First, compute the budgeted variable overhead rate (denoted by X):

$$X = \frac{\text{Budgeted variable overhead costs}}{\text{Budgeted direct manufacturing labour costs}}$$

$$X = \frac{\$600,000 - \$360,000}{\$600,000 \div 0.25} = \frac{\$240,000}{\$2,400,000} = 10\%$$

Second, compute the relevant costs of the boat. Only the variable costs are relevant in this case.

Direct materials	$10,000
Direct manufacturing labour	16,000
Variable overhead,	
$16,000 × 10%	1,600
Total relevant costs	$27,600

b. If the boat is sold for $27,600, operating income is not affected. Focusing exclusively on contribution margin in pricing decisions, however, fails to recognize fixed costs. Although fixed costs are often irrelevant in the short-run, they must be recovered in the long-run, along with an acceptable return on investment, for the company to stay in business.

Review Questions and Exercises

Completion Statements

Fill in the blank(s) to complete each statement.

1. The estimated long-run cost per unit of a product or service that enables the company to achieve the target operating income per unit by selling at the target price is called the

_____.

2. _____ is a systematic evaluation of all aspects of the value-chain business functions, with the objective of reducing costs while satisfying customer needs.

3. Costs that have not yet been incurred but, based on decisions already made, will be incurred in the future are called _____ _____ costs.

4. _____ tracks and accumulates the individual value-chain costs attributable to each product from its initial R&D to its final customer servicing and support.

5. The practice of charging some customers a higher price for the same product or service than is charged to other customers is called

_____.

6. The practice of charging a higher price for the same product or service when demand approaches physical capacity limits is called

_____.

7. A company engages in _____

_____ if it deliberately prices below its costs in an effort to drive out competitors and restrict supply; later it raises prices rather than enlarge demand.

True-False

Indicate whether each statement is true (T) or false (F).

____ 1. The three major influences on pricing decisions are customers, competitors, and costs.

2. A company should accept a one-time-only special order if the order's total contribution margin is positive.

___ 3. Value engineering is usually constrained by locked-in costs.

___ 4. The target rate of return on investment for a product is the same as the product's markup as a percentage of its full unit cost.

___ 5. The cost of preparing an owner's manual and including it in each product package is a value-added cost.

___ 6. One reason managers use the full costs of products as the cost base in their pricing decisions is to promote price stability.

___ 7. Life-cycle costing highlights manufacturing costs more than the costs of other business functions in the value chain.

___ 8. When there is price discrimination, pricing is not linked closely to the cost of the product.

___ 9. Under the Competition Act, a manufacturing company cannot price discriminate between two customers if its intent is to lessen or prevent competition.

___ 10. Setting prices above average variable costs is regarded as pricing that is nonpredatory.

___ 11. Collusive pricing occurs when a non-Canadian company sells a product in Canada at a price below the market value in the country of its creation, and this action materially injures or threatens to materially injure an industry in the Canada.

Multiple Choice

Select the best answer to each question. Space is provided for computations after the quantitative questions.

___ 1. In regard to supply and demand, demand is affected by:
   a. customers, competitors, and costs.
   b. customers and competitors.
   c. customers and costs.
   d. competitors and costs.

___ 2. (CPA) Relay Corporation manufactures batons. Relay can manufacture 300,000 batons a year at variable costs of $750,000 and fixed costs of $450,000. Fixed costs will remain the same between 200,000 and 300,000 batons. Based on Relay's predictions, 240,000 batons will be sold at the regular price of $5.00 each. In addition, a one-time-only special order was received for 60,000 batons to be sold at a 40% discount off the regular price. By what amount does operating income increase or decrease as a result of accepting the special order?
   a. $30,000 increase
   b. $60,000 decrease
   c. $36,000 increase
   d. $180,000 increase

___ 3. (CPA) Nile Co.'s cost allocation and product-costing procedures follow activity-based costing principles. Activities related to each product have been identified and classified as being either value-adding or nonvalue-adding. Which of the following activities, used in Nile's production process, is nonvalue-adding?
   a. Design engineering activity
   b. Heat treatment activity
   c. Drill press activity
   d. Materials storage activity

___ 4. For a company manufacturing personal computers, a graph of locked-in costs and incurred costs shows:
   a. locked-in costs rising much faster initially than incurred costs, but dropping to zero after the product is manufactured.
   b. locked-in costs rising much faster initially than incurred costs, but joining the incurred cost line at the completion of the value-chain functions.
   c. the two cost lines running parallel until the end of the production process, where they join.
   d. no differences unless the product is manufactured inefficiently.

5. (CPA) Purvis Company manufactures a product that has a variable cost of $50 per unit. Fixed costs total $1,000,000 and are allocated on the basis of the number of units produced. Selling price is computed by adding a 10% markup to full costs of the product. How much should the selling price per unit be for 100,000 units?
   a. $55
   b. $60
   c. $61
   d. $66

6. (CPA) Diva Co. wants to establish a selling price that will yield a gross margin of 40% on the sales revenue of a product whose cost is $12.00 per unit. The selling price should be:
   a. $16.80.
   b. $19.20.
   c. $20.00.
   d. $30.00.

7. (CPA) Briar Co. signed a government construction contract providing for a formula price of actual cost plus 10% of cost. In addition, Briar was to receive one-half of any savings resulting from the formula price being less than the target price of $2,200,000. Briar's actual costs incurred were $1,920,000. How much should Briar receive from the contract?
   a. $2,060,000
   b. $2,112,000
   c. $2,156,000
   d. $2,200,000

8. Peak-load pricing is:
   a. an illegal form of price discrimination.
   b. a legal form of price discrimination.
   c. illegal, but is not a form of price discrimination.
   d. legal, but is not a form of price discrimination.

Exercises

1. Silverthorne, Inc. is deciding on the price for a new product. The company uses cost-plus pricing based on the target return on investment. The following information is available for the product:

Invested capital	$25 million
Target rate of return on investment	20%
Full costs of the product (per unit) at the output level of 125,000 units	$200
Full costs of the product (per unit) at the output level of 80,000 units	$250

a. Compute the prospective selling price assuming the predicted output level is 125,000 units.
b. Compute markup as a percentage of full costs of the product assuming the predicted output level is 80,000 units.

2. Appletree, Inc., is analyzing the profitability of two of its accounting software packages. Summary data on the packages over their two-year product life cycle are as follows:

Package	Selling Price	Sales in Units
Quick Tax	$250	Year 1, 4,000
		Year 2, 16,000
Fast Audit	$200	Year 1, 10,000
		Year 2, 6,000

The life-cycle revenue and cost information is (in thousands):

	Quick Tax		Fast Audit	
	Year 1	Year 2	Year 1	Year 2
Revenues	$1,000	$4,000	$2,000	$1,200
Costs:				
R&D	1,400	0	480	0
Product design	370	30	160	32
Manufacturing	150	450	286	130
Marketing	280	720	480	416
Distribution	30	120	120	72
Customer service	100	650	440	776

Appletree is particularly concerned with increases in R&D and product design costs for many of its software packages in recent years. Consequently, major efforts have been made to reduce these costs on the Fast Audit package.

a. Prepare a product life-cycle income statement for each software package.
b. Compare the two packages in terms of their profitability and cost structure. State your conclusions.

1. target cost per unit
2. Value engineering
3. locked-in (designed-in)
4. Life-cycle costing
5. price discrimination
6. peak-load pricing
7. predatory pricing

True-False

1. T
2. F A one-time-only special order should be accepted if it increases a company's operating income. A special order increases operating income if its total contribution margin is positive *and* exceeds the relevant fixed costs (if any) related to the order. Of course, if the positive total contribution margin is less than the relevant fixed costs, the special order decreases operating income and should be rejected.
3. F Value engineering attempts to control costs *before* they are locked-in (designed-in), with the objective of reducing costs while satisfying customers needs.
4. F *Target rate of return on investment* and *markup* are not the same. In the example, text p. 427, target return on investment for the product is 18% while the product's markup is 12% of its full cost per unit.
5. T
6. T
7. F Life-cycle costing tracks and accumulates the individual value-chain costs attributable to each product from its initial R&D to its final customer servicing and support. The costs of each value-chain function are highlighted.
8. T
9. T
10. T
11. F The statement refers to *dumping*, not *collusive pricing*. Collusive pricing occurs when companies in an industry conspire in their pricing and output decisions to achieve a price above the competitive price.

Multiple Choice

1. a Customers, competitors, and costs are all important factors in setting prices. The value customers place on the product and the prices competitors charge for competing products affect demand, and the costs of producing and delivering the product influence supply.
2. a For the special order:

Selling price, $5.00(1 − 0.40)	$3.00 per baton
Incremental costs, $750,000 ÷ 300,000	2.50 per baton
Increase in operating income	$0.50 per baton × 60,000 batons = $30,000

3. d A nonvalue-added activity is an activity that, if eliminated, does not reduce the value customers obtain from using a particular product or service. The other answers are examples of value-added activities (that is, activities that, if eliminated, reduce the value customers obtain from using particular products or services).
4. b In this graph, locked-in costs rise much faster than incurred costs during R&D and product design, incurred costs accelerate during production while locked-in costs are nearly flat, and

both costs are equal at the completion of the value-chain functions. Exhibit 12-4, text p. 424, presents this graph.

5. d   Full costs of the product = \$50 + (\$1,000,000 ÷ 100,000) = \$50 + \$10 = \$60
      Selling price = \$60 + \$60(0.10) = \$60 + \$6 = \$66

6. c   Let X = Selling price

$$X - \$12.00 = 0.40X$$
$$0.60X = \$12.00$$
$$X = \$12.00 \div 0.60 = \$20.00$$

    Proof: \$20.00 − \$12.00 = \$8.00; \$8.00 ÷ \$20.00 = 40%

7. c   Two steps are used to obtain the answer. First, determine if the formula price is less than the target price, in which case savings result:

Target price	\$2,200,000
Deduct formula price	
\$1,920,000 + \$1,920,000(0.10)	2,112,000
Savings	\$ 88,000

Second, compute the amount to be received from the contract:

Formula price (from above)	\$2,112,000
Add one-half of savings	
\$88,000 × 50%	44,000
Amount to be received	\$2,156,000

8. b   Peak-load pricing is the practice of charging a higher price for the same product or service when demand approaches physical capacity limits. Peak-load pricing is a legal form of price discrimination used in major industries including telephone, electric utility, hotel, and car rental.

Exercise 1

a. Total target return on investment = \$25,000,000 × 0.20 = \$5,000,000
   Target return on investment per unit = \$5,000,000 ÷ 125,000 = \$40
   Prospective selling price = \$200 + \$40 = \$240

b. Total target return on investment = \$25,000,000 × 0.20 = \$5,000,000
   Target return on investment per unit = \$5,000,000 ÷ 80,000 = \$62.50
   Markup as a percentage of full cost of the product = \$62.50 ÷ \$250 = 25%

Exercise 2

a. and b. (dollars in thousands)	Quick Tax		Fast Audit	
Revenues (two-year totals)	\$5,000		\$3,200	
Costs (two-year totals):		%		%
R&D	1,400	32.5	480	14.1
Product design	400	9.3	192	5.7
Manufacturing	600	14.0	416	12.3
Marketing	1,000	23.3	896	26.4
Distribution	150	3.5	192	5.7
Customer service	750	17.4	1,216	35.8
Total costs	4,300	100.0	3,392	100.0
Operating income	\$ 700		\$ (192)	

Quick Tax is profitable, whereas Fast Audit is unprofitable. The product life-cycle report highlights possible causal relationships among costs classified by business function of the value chain. The relatively much lower R&D and product design costs on Fast Audit might be the reason for this outcome. Quick Tax has 41.8% of its costs in R&D and product design compared to 19.8% for Fast Audit. Also, customer service costs are relatively much higher for Fast Audit (35.8% versus 17.4%), which suggests the customer service problems most likely relate to the lower costs of Fast Audit's R&D and product design.

Strategy, Balanced Scorecard, and Strategic Profitability Analysis

Chapter Overview

This chapter explores the use of management accounting information in the implementation and evaluation of an organization's strategy. The chapter introduces key aspects of strategy, explains the role of the balanced scorecard in implementing strategy, presents an analysis of operating income to evaluate the success of a strategy, and describes the strategic initiatives of productivity improvement, reengineering and downsizing. The Appendix to the chapter explains how to measure productivity.

Chapter Highlights

1. An organization's *strategy* describes how it matches its own capabilities with the opportunities in the marketplace in order to accomplish its overall objectives. In formulating its strategy, an organization must thoroughly understand the industry in which it operates. Industry analysis focuses on five forces: (a) competitors, (b) potential entrants into the market, (c) equivalent products, (d) bargaining power of customers, and (e) bargaining power of input suppliers. The collective effect of these forces shapes an organization's profit potential. In general, profit potential decreases with greater competition, stronger potential entrants, more equivalent products, and more demanding customers and suppliers.

2. Two basic strategies that organizations use are **product differentiation** and **cost leadership**.

- Product differentiation is an organization's ability to offer products or services that are perceived by its customers to be superior and unique relative to those of competitors. Product differentiation increases brand loyalty and the prices that customers are willing to pay.

- Cost leadership is an organization's ability to achieve low costs relative to its competitors through productivity and efficiency improvements, elimination of waste, and tight cost control. For companies that are cost leaders, lower selling prices—rather than unique products or services—provide a competitive advantage.

Of course, successful product differentiation or cost leadership generally increases market share and helps a company to grow.

3. Many organizations use a **balanced scorecard** to manage the implementation of their strategies. The balanced scorecard translates an organization's mission, goals, and strategy into a comprehensive and linked set of performance measures that provides the framework for implementing its strategy. The balanced scorecard gets its name from the attempt to balance financial and nonfinancial measures in evaluating both short-run and long-run performance in a single report. To properly focus managers' attention, a good balanced scorecard includes only the critical performance measures; moreover, it reduces the emphasis managers place on short-run financial performance (such as quarterly earnings), because improvements in nonfinancial performance measures often cause earnings growth in the future.

4. The balanced scorecard measures performance from four key perspectives:

a. The *financial perspective* evaluates the profitability of the organization's strategy. Under the strategy of product differentiation, the financial perspective focuses on how much operating income and return on capital result from charging premium selling prices. Under the strategy of cost leadership, the financial perspective focuses on how much operating income and return on capital result from reducing costs and selling more units of output.

b. The *customer perspective* identifies the targeted market segments and measures the organization's success in these segments. Performance measures for this perspective include market share, number of new customers, and customer satisfaction ratings in the targeted segments.

c. The *internal business process perspective* focuses on internal operations that further the customer perspective (by creating value for customers) and the financial perspective (by increasing shareholder wealth). Performance measures for this perspective include production yield and on-time order delivery rate.

d. The *learning and growth perspective* identifies the capabilities in which the organization must excel in order to achieve superior internal processes that create value for customers and shareholder wealth. Performance measures for this perspective include employee education and skill levels, employee satisfaction ratings, and number of suggestions per employee.

These four perspectives are linked in a cause-and-effect chain, moving backward from (d) to (a). That is, gains in learning and growth lead to improvements in internal business processes, which in turn lead to higher customer satisfaction and market share, and finally result in superior financial performance. In this chain, many nonfinancial measures serve as leading indicators of future financial performance.

5. EXHIBIT 13-1, text p. 457, presents the balanced scorecard for Chipset Inc., a manufacturer of devices used in modems and communication networks. Chipset uses a strategy of cost leadership. For each of the four key perspectives of performance, Chipset's balanced scorecard for 2000 specifies the "objectives", "measures", "initiatives", and "target performance" (the first four columns in the exhibit). Comparing "actual performance"

(the last column in the exhibit) to "target performance" shows that Chipset met most of its targets in the year 2000.

6. In EXHIBIT 13-1, one of Chipset's initiatives under the internal business process perspective is to reengineer its order delivery process. **Reengineering** is the fundamental rethinking and redesign of business processes to achieve improvements in critical measures of performance such as cost, quality, service, speed, and customer satisfaction. Reengineering tends to be more beneficial if it cuts across functional lines in the organization to focus on an entire business process (as in the Chipset example). Successful reengineering efforts involve changing roles and responsibilities, eliminating unnecessary activities and tasks, using information technology, and developing employee skills.

7. As noted above, Chipset uses a strategy of cost leadership. One of its competitors, Visilog, uses a strategy of product differentiation. What are the contents of Visilog's balanced scorecard? Some likely possibilities are:

- The financial perspective measures how much operating income and return on capital result from charging premium selling prices.
- The customer perspective measures the percentage of revenues derived from new products and new customers.
- The internal business process perspective measures the development of advanced manufacturing capabilities to produce custom products.
- The learning and growth perspective measures new product development time.

Of course, Visilog also uses some of the measures in Chipset's balanced scorecard, such as revenue growth, customer satisfaction ratings, on-time delivery rate, and employee satisfaction ratings.

8. Pitfalls to avoid in implementing a balanced scorecard include:

a. Do not assume the cause-and-effect linkages are precise. They are merely hypotheses. With experience, organizations should alter their scorecards to include those nonfinancial objectives and measures that are the best leading indicators of subsequent financial performance. Committing to evolve the scorecard over time avoids the paralysis associated with trying to design the "perfect" scorecard at the outset.

b. Do not seek improvements across all of the measures all of the time. For example, emphasizing quality and on-time performance beyond a point may not be worthwhile. That is, further improvement in these objectives may be inconsistent with profit maximization.

c. Do not use only objective measures in the scorecard. When using subjective measures, though, management must be careful to trade off the benefits of the richer information these measures provide against the costs of their imprecision and the potential for manipulation.

d. Do not fail to consider both costs and benefits of initiatives, such as spending on information technology and R&D, before including these objectives in the scorecard. Otherwise, management may focus the organization on measures that will not result in long-run financial benefits.

e. Do not ignore nonfinancial measures when evaluating managers and other employees. If nonfinancial measures are ignored in evaluations, managers reduce the importance they give to these measures.

9. After an organization implements a strategy, it must evaluate the strategy's success. One aspect of the evaluation is comparing actual performance and target performance for the financial and nonfinancial performance measures in the balanced scorecard. A more detailed aspect of the evaluation is to subdivide the change in operating income from one period to the next into a **growth component**, a **price-recovery** component, and a **productivity component**.

- The *growth component* measures the change in operating income attributable solely to a change in the quantity of output sold from period 1 to period 2. The calculations for the growth component are similar to those for the sales-volume variance introduced in Chapter 7.
- The *price-recovery component* measures the change in operating income attributable solely to the change in output prices relative to the change in input prices from period 1 to period 2. The calculations for the price-recovery component are similar to those for the selling-price variance and input price and spending variances for materials, labour, and overhead introduced in Chapters 7 and 8.
- The *productivity component* measures the reduction in costs attributable to a reduction in the quantity of inputs used in period 2 relative to the quantity of inputs that would have been used in period 1 to produce the period 2 output. The calculations for the productivity component are similar to those for the efficiency variances introduced in Chapters 7 and 8.

A company is considered to be successful in implementing its cost leadership or product differentiation strategy if the amounts of the three components align closely with the strategy.

10. Because subdividing the change in operating income into the growth, price-recovery, and productivity components is similar to variance analysis, a component is labelled favourable (F) if it increases operating income and unfavourable (U) if it decreases operating income. The following table shows the variances—*called revenue effects and cost effects in this context*—measured for each component:

Component	Revenue Effect	Cost Effect
Growth	Yes	Yes
Price recovery	Yes	Yes
Productivity	No	Yes

11. In the Chipset example, text p. 462, operating income is $2,750,000 in 1999 and

$5,250,000 in 2000, an increase of $2,500,000. Based on the formulas, beginning text p. 463, the increase is explained as follows:

Growth component		
Revenue effect	$4,050,000 F	
Cost effect	630,000 U	$3,420,000 F
Price-recovery component		
Revenue effect	2,300,000 U	
Cost effect	720,000 U	3,020,000 U
Productivity component		2,100,000 F
Change in operating income		$2,500,000 F

This analysis indicates Chipset was successful in implementing its cost leadership strategy: productivity contributed $2,100,000 to the increase in operating income and growth contributed $3,420,000. Operating income decreased by $3,020,000 because Chipset was unable to raise selling prices to pass along increases in input prices. Had Chipset been able to differentiate its product, the price-recovery effects would have been less unfavourable or even favourable.

12. The $2,500,000 change in operating income can be analyzed in more detail. For instance, Chipset's growth may have been helped by an increase in industry market size. At least a part of the increase in operating income, therefore, may be attributable to favourable economic conditions in the industry rather than to successfully implementing a strategy. Some of the growth also may have resulted from a management decision to take advantage of the productivity gains by reducing selling price. Using additional information, text p. 466, the $2,500,000 increase in Chipset's operating income can be analyzed in terms of three factors: cost leadership, growth/decline in industry market size, and product differentiation. The box on the next page presents the results of this analysis

13. Because an organization's fixed costs are tied to its capacity, managers must understand and manage **unused capacity** in order to reduce fixed costs. Unused capacity is the additional amount of productive capacity available over and above the productive capacity employed to meet customer demand in the current period. To understand unused capacity, it is important to distinguish between **engineered costs** and **discretionary costs**.

- Engineered costs result from a cause-and-effect relationship between the cost driver, output, and the (direct or indirect) resources used to produce that output. For example, direct material costs are direct engineered costs, and conversion costs are indirect engineered costs. Although some conversion costs are fixed in the short run, over time there is a cause-and-effect relationship between output and manufacturing capacity required (and conversion costs needed).
- Discretionary costs have two important features: (a) they arise from periodic (usually annual) decisions regarding the maximum amount to be incurred, and (b) there is no measurable cause-and-effect relationship between output and resources used. Some examples of discretionary costs are advertising, executive training, and R&D. The most noteworthy aspect of discretionary costs is that managers are seldom confident the "correct" amounts are being incurred.

Identifying unused capacity is easier for engineered costs than for discretionary costs.

14. When an organization has identified its unused capacity, attempts can be made to either eliminate it or use it to grow revenues. In recent years, many organizations have downsized in an attempt to eliminate unused capacity. **Downsizing** (also called **rightsizing**) is an integrated approach to configuring processes, products, and people to match costs to the activities that need to be performed for operating effectively and efficiently in the present and future. Downsizing often means eliminating jobs, which can have an adverse effect on employee morale and the culture of the organization. Downsizing, therefore, must be done in the context of the organiza-

tion's strategy, and by retaining individuals with key management, leadership, and technical skills.

15. The Appendix to this chapter illustrates how to measure **productivity**, which is the relationship between actual inputs used (both quantities and costs) and actual output produced. Measuring productivity improvements over time highlights the specific input-output relationships that contribute to cost leadership. Two measures of productivity are **partial productivity** and **total factor productivity**.

- Partial productivity is a measure that compares the quantity of output produced with the quantity of an individual input used. Although partial productivity is easily understood by operations personnel, it does not allow managers to evaluate the effect of input substitutions on overall productivity.

- Total factor productivity is a measure that considers all inputs simultaneously and also considers the tradeoffs among inputs based on current input prices. A drawback of total factor productivity is operations personnel find it difficult to understand.

Many companies use both partial productivity and total factor productivity to evaluate performance.

The amounts in this box are from the Chipset example, text p. 466.

Analysis of the Change in Chipset's Operating Income (OI) from 1999 to 2000

Cost leadership factors:		
Productivity component (same as in previous analysis)	$2,100,000	F
Strategic decision to reduce selling price	862,500	U
Growth in market share due to productivity component and strategic decision to reduce selling price	1,140,000	F
Change in OI due to cost leadership	$2,377,500 F	
Change in OI due to the growth in industry market size	2,280,000 F	
Product differentiation factors:		
Decrease in selling price beyond the strategic decision to reduce selling price that is accounted for as a cost leadership factor	1,437,500	U
Increase in prices of inputs (same as cost effect of price-recovery component)	720,000	U
Change in OI due to product differentiation	2,157,500 U	
Change in OI	$2,500,000 F	

This analysis shows that, consistent with its cost leadership strategy, Chipset's productivity gains in 2000 are key to the $2,500,000 increase in OI.

Featured Exercise

Castleton Company makes a chemical fertilizer, Turfgro. The market for Turfgro is highly competitive. As a result, managing costs is critical for long-run profitability and growth. Data for Turfgro for 1999 and 2000 are as follows:

		1999	2000
1.	Tonnes of Turfgro produced and sold	10,000	10,400
2.	Selling price per tonne	$300	$315
3.	Direct materials used in tonnes	11,500	12,000
4.	Direct materials cost per tonne	$120	$123
5.	Tonnes of Turfgro manufactured per batch	40	40
6.	Manufacturing capacity in batches	350	345
7.	Conversion costs	$1,050,000	$1,069,500
8.	Conversion costs per batch of capacity (row 7 ÷ row 6)	$3,000	$3,100
9.	Number of advertisements run	1,400	1,395
10.	Advertising costs	$350,000	$351,540
11.	Advertising costs per advertisement run (row 10 ÷ row 9)	$250	$252

Each year's conversion costs depend on production capacity (defined in terms of number of batches of Turfgro that can be produced), not the actual number of batches produced. At the start of each year, management uses its discretion in deciding how many advertisements to run for the year. The number of advertisements run has no direct cause-and-effect relationship with the quantity of Turfgro produced and sold.

a. Is Castleton using a strategy of product differentiation or cost leadership? Explain briefly.
b. Compute the change in operating income from 1999 to 2000.
c. Compute the growth, price-recovery, and productivity components of the change in operating income from 1999 to 2000.

Solution

a. Castleton's strategy is cost leadership. The reason is that the company operates in a highly competitive market—one in which managing costs is critical to its long-run profitability and growth.

b.

	1999	2000
Revenues,		
10,000 × $300; 10,400 × $315	$3,000,000	$3,276,000
Costs:		
Direct material costs,		
11,500 × $120; 12,000 × $123	1,380,000	1,476,000
Conversion costs	1,050,000	1,069,500
Advertising costs	350,000	351,540
Total costs	2,780,000	2,897,040
Operating income	$ 220,000	$ 378,960

Increase in operating income $158,960

c. *Growth Component*

Revenue effect, (10,400 − 10,000) × $300	$120,000 F
Cost effect:	
Direct material costs	
(11,960* − 11,500) × $120	55,200 U
Conversion costs	
(350 − 350) × $3,000	0
Advertising costs	
(1,400 − 1,400) × $250	0
Increase in operating income due to growth component	$ 64,800 F

    *(11,500 ÷ 10,000) × 10,400 = 11,960

Price-Recovery Component

Revenue effect, ($315 − $300) × 10,400	$156,000 F
Cost effect:	
Direct material costs	
11,960* × ($123 − $120)	35,880 U
Conversion costs	
350 × ($3,100 − $3,000)	35,000 U
Advertising costs	
1,400 × ($252 − $250)	2,800 U
Increase in operating income due to price-recovery component	$ 82,320 F

    *Same as computed for growth component

Productivity Component

Direct material costs	
(12,000 − 11,960*) × $123	$ 4,920 U
Conversion costs	
(345 − 350) × $3,100	15,500 F
Advertising costs	
(1,395 − 1,400) × $252	1,260 F
Increase in operating income due to productivity component	$11,840 F

    *Same as computed for growth component

Recap:

Increase in operating income due to growth component	$ 64,800 F
Increase in operating income due to price-recovery component	82,320 F
Increase in operating income due to productivity component	11,840 F
Increase in operating income from 1999 to 2000	$158,960 F

Review Questions and Exercises

Completions Statements

Fill in the blank(s) to complete each statement.

1. An organization's ability to offer products or services that are perceived by its customers to be superior and unique relative to those of its competitors is the strategy called _____ _____.

2. The _____ translates an organization's mission, goals, and strategy into a comprehensive and linked set of performance measures that provides the framework for implementing its strategy.

3. The fundamental rethinking and redesign of business processes to achieve improvements in critical measures of performance such as cost, quality, service, speed, and customer satisfaction is called _____.

4. In subdividing the change in operating income from 1999 to 2000 into components, the _____ component measures the change in operating income attributable solely to a change in the quantity of output sold from 1999 to 2000.

5. _____ costs result from a cause-and-effect relationship between the cost driver, output, and the (direct or indirect) resources used to produce that output.

6. _____ is an integrated approach to configuring processes, products, and people to match costs to the activities that need to be performed for operating effectively and efficiently in the present and future.

7. (Appendix) _____ is a measure that compares the quantity of output produced with the quantity of an individual input used.

8. (Appendix) A measure that considers all inputs simultaneously and also considers the tradeoffs among inputs based on current input prices is called _____ _____.

True-False

Indicate whether each statement is true (T) or false (F).

___ 1. The balanced scorecard has separate columns for objectives, initiatives, performance measures, target performance, and actual performance.

___ 2. The balanced scorecard gets its name from the attempt to balance short-run and long-run financial performance measures in a single report.

___ 3. Under the strategy of product differentiation, the financial perspective of a good balanced scorecard focuses on how much operating income results from charging premium selling prices.

___ 4. The cause-and-effect relationship underlying the balanced scorecard is that gains in learning and growth lead to improvements in internal business processes, which in turn lead to higher customer satisfaction and market share, and finally result in superior financial performance.

___ 5. In a good balanced scorecard, many financial performance measures serve as leading indicators of future nonfinancial performance.

___ 6. Successful reengineering efforts involve changing roles and responsibilities, eliminating unnecessary activities and tasks, using information technology, and developing employee skills.

___ 7. A good balanced scorecard uses only objective financial and nonfinancial performance measures.

___ 8. To analyze the change in a company's operating income from one year to the next, the calculations for the growth component are similar to those for the sales-volume variance.

___ 9. The most noteworthy aspect of engineered costs is that managers are seldom confident that the "correct" amounts are being spent.

___ 10. (Appendix) The lower the inputs for a given quantity of output or the higher the output for a given quantity of inputs, the higher the level of productivity.

___ 11. (Appendix) Fluctuations in input prices affect partial productivity measures.

Multiple Choice

Select the best answer to each question. Space is provided for computations after the quantitative questions.

___ 1. Brand loyalty is associated closely with:
   a. both cost leadership and product differentiation.
   b. cost leadership but not product differentiation.
   c. product differentiation but not cost leadership.
   d. neither cost leadership nor product differentiation.

___ 2. The percentage of manufacturing processes with real-time feedback is a performance measure under which perspective in the balanced scorecard?
   a. Financial perspective
   b. Customer perspective
   c. Internal business process perspective
   d. Learning and growth perspective

___ 3. Reengineering relates to which perspective in the balanced scorecard?
   a. Financial perspective
   b. Customer perspective
   c. Internal business process perspective
   d. Learning and growth perspective

___ 4. In analyzing the change in a company's operating income from one year to the next, which effect(s) is computed for the price-recovery component?

	Revenue Effect	Cost Effect
a.	Yes	Yes
b.	Yes	No
c.	No	Yes
d.	No	No

___ 5. Nesbitt Company analyzed the change in its operating income from 1999 to 2000 into three components as follows:

Growth component	$684,000 favourable
Price-recovery component	604,000 unfavourable
Productivity component	450,000 favourable

If operating income is $1,050,000 in 2000, operating income in 1999 is:
a. $212,000.
b. $520,000.
c. $1,580,000.
d. Cannot be determined from the information given.

___ 6. Drummond Enterprises had an increase in its operating income from 1999 to 2000 of $200,000. Two of the three factors accounting for the increase are:

Change due to cost leadership $498,500 favourable
Change due to product differentiation   454,500 unfavourable

The third factor to complete this analysis is:
a. Change due to a strategic decision to adjust selling price, $156,000 favourable.
b. Change due to a strategic decision to adjust selling price, $156,000 unfavourable.
c. Change due to industry market size, $156,000 favourable.
d. Change due to input prices, $156,000 favourable.

___ 7. (Appendix, CMA) Fabro Inc. produced 1,500 units of Product RX-6 last week. The inputs for this production are as follows:

450 kilograms of Material A at a cost of $1.50 per kilogram
300 kilograms of Material Z at a cost of $2.75 per kilogram
300 labour-hours at a cost of $15.00 per hour

The total factor productivity for Product RX-6 is:
a. 2.00 output units per kilogram.
b. 1.00 output unit per dollar of input costs.
c. 5.00 output units per hour.
d. 0.25 output units per dollar of input costs.
e. 0.33 output units per dollar of input costs.

Exercises

1. The following information is from the Solution to the Featured Exercise, pp. 166-167:

   - Castleton Company's strategy is cost leadership.
   - Increase in operating income due to growth component $ 64,800 F
     Increase in operating income due to price-recovery component   82,320 F
     Increase in operating income due to productivity component   11,840 F
     Increase in operating income from 1999 to 2000 $158,960 F

   During 2000 the unit sales for Castleton's fertilizer product, Turfgro, increased by 4% (from 10,000 tonnes in 1999 to 10,400 tonnes in 2000). A trade association reports the industry market size for this type of fertilizer increased by 3% in 2000. The increase in Turfgro's market share (that is, its unit sales grew by more than the 3% growth in industry market size) and the increase in its selling price are due to customers perceiving this product to be a superior fertilizer.

   a. Compute the change in operating income from 1999 to 2000 that is due to three factors: industry market size, cost leadership, and product differentiation.
   b. How successful has Castleton been in implementing its cost leadership strategy for Turfgro? Explain.

2. (Appendix) Vander Lind Industries makes a chemical product using direct materials and direct manufacturing labour, which are partial substitutes for each other. The company reported the following data for the last two years of operations:

	1999	2000
Output units	8,500	10,200
Direct materials used (in kilograms)	5,700	7,000
Direct materials cost per kilogram	$3.20	$3.00
Direct manufacturing labour-hours used	700	800
Wages per labour-hour	$14	$15
Manufacturing capacity in output units	12,000	11,500
Manufacturing overhead costs	$15,000	$14,950
Manufacturing overhead costs per unit of capacity	$1.25	$1.30

a. Compute the partial productivity ratios for each input for each year, and compute the change in partial productivity for each input from 1999 to 2000.
b. Compute the change in total factor productivity from 1999 to 2000.

Completion Statements

1. product differentiation
2. balanced scorecard
3. reengineering
4. growth
5. Engineered
6. Downsizing (Rightsizing)
7. Partial productivity
8. total factor productivity

True-False

1. T
2. F   The statement does not include an important aspect of the balanced scorecard, *nonfinancial performance measures*. That is, the balanced scorecard gets its name from the attempt to balance financial *and* nonfinancial measures to evaluate both short-run and long-run performance in a single report.
3. T
4. T
5. F   The statement is reversed. That is, as a result of the cause-and-effect relationship described in question 4, many nonfinancial measures serve as leading indicators of future financial performance.
6. T
7. F   One of the pitfalls to avoid in implementing a balanced scorecard is using only objective performance measures. When using subjective measures, though, management must be careful to trade off the benefits of the richer information these measures provide against the costs of their imprecision and the potential for manipulation.
8. T
9. F   The statement describes *discretionary costs*, not *engineered costs*. Discretionary costs have two important features: (a) they arise from periodic (usually annual) decisions regarding the maximum amount to be incurred, and (b) there is no measurable cause-and-effect relationship between output and resources used. Some examples of discretionary costs are advertising, executive training, and R&D. In contrast, engineered costs result from a cause-and-effect relationship between the cost driver, output, and the (direct or indirect) resources used to produce that output. For example, direct material costs are direct engineered costs, and conversion costs are indirect engineered costs.
10. T
11. F   Partial productivity is measured only in terms of physical inputs and outputs; fluctuations in input prices *do not affect* partial productivity measures.

Multiple Choice

1. c   Product differentiation is an organization's ability to offer products or services that are perceived by its customers to be superior and unique relative to those of competitors. Product differentiation, therefore, increases brand loyalty and the prices that customers are willing to pay.

2. d   Exhibit 13-1, text p. 457, shows the percentage of manufacturing processes with real-time feedback is a performance measure under the learning and growth perspective. The related objective is to enhance information system capabilities, and the related initiative is to improve off-line data gathering.

3. c   Exhibit 13-1, text p. 457, shows reengineering the order delivery process is an initiative under the internal business process perspective. The related objective is to meet specified delivery dates, and the related performance measure is the on-time delivery rate.

4. a   Paragraph 10 of the Chapter Highlights shows the price-recovery component computes both the revenue and cost effects.

5. b
Growth component	$684,000	F
Price-recovery component	604,000	U
Productivity component	450,000	F
Change in operating income	$530,000	F

Operating income in 1999 = Operating income in 2000 − $530,000
= $1,050,000 − $530,000 = $520,000

Proof:

Operating income in 1999	$ 520,000
Add increase in operating income	530,000
Operating income in 2000	$1,050,000

6. c
Change due to cost leadership	$498,500	F
Change due to industry market size	156,000	F
Change due to product differentiation	454,500	U
Change in operating income	$200,000	F

If, in fact, a strategic decision were made to change the selling price, its effects are already included in the cost leadership and product differentiation factors. Likewise, these two factors already include the effects of a change in input prices.

7. d   Let TFP = Total factor productivity

$$TFP = \frac{Output\ units}{Cost\ of\ all\ inputs\ used}$$

$$TFP = \frac{1,500}{(450 \times \$1.50) + (300 \times \$2.75) + (300 \times \$15)}$$

$$TFP = \frac{1,500}{\$675 + \$825 + \$4,500} = \frac{1,500}{\$6,000} = 0.25\ output\ units/dollar\ of\ input\ costs$$

Exercise 1

a.   Effect of industry-market-size factor

Of the 400-tonne increase in sales, 300 (3% × 10,000) tonnes is due to the growth in industry market size. The other 100 tonnes is due to the growth in market share.

$64,800 F growth component × (300 ÷ 400) = $48,600 F

Effect of product-differentiation factor
Price-recovery component $82,320 F
Growth in market share due to product differentiation
$64,800 F growth component × (100 ÷ 400)   16,200 F
Total $98,520 F
Effect of cost-leadership factor
Productivity component $11,840 F

Change in operating income from 1999 to 2000 = $48,600 F + $98,520 F + $11,840 F
= $158,960 F

b. The analysis shows that $98,520 of the $158,960 (approximately 62%) is due to customers perceiving Turfgro to be a superior product. As a result, Castleton was able to pass along all input price increases in the form of a higher selling price. The strong product differentiation could be linked to Castleton's effective advertising or the lack of such advertising by its competitors. If, however, Castleton believes the benefits of product differentiation are only temporary—either because it expects competitors to advertise more effectively or because customers will soon realize that Turfgro is not really superior to competitors' products—management should be concerned. The reason is Castleton has achieved little success with its cost leadership strategy ($11,840 F). The company needs to improve productivity both in its use of direct materials and by reducing its manufacturing capacity. Currently, Castleton has manufacturing capacity for 345 batches or 13,800 (345 × 40) tonnes of Turfgro. Unless the company expects to grow its business significantly in the short run, management may want to downsize, reducing its manufacturing capacity from 13,800 tonnes to, say, 12,000 tonnes, or 300 (12,000 ÷ 40) batches.

Exercise 2

a. Inputs that would have been used in 2000 to produce 2000 output, assuming the 1999 input-output relationship continued in 2000, are as follows:

Direct materials   5,700 × (10,200 ÷ 8,500)   = 6,840 kilograms
Direct manufacturing labour   700 × (10,200 ÷ 8,500)   = 840 labour-hours
Manufacturing capacity   Remains the same because
                              adequate capacity is available = 12,000 units

Input	Partial Productivity in 2000	Partial Productivity in 1999	Percentage Change From 1999 to 2000
Direct materials	10,200÷7,000=1.46	10,200÷6,840=1.49	(1.46−1.49)÷1.49=−2.0%
Direct manufacturing labour	10,200÷800=12.75	10,200÷840=12.14	(12.75−12.14)÷12.14= 5.0%
Manufacturing OH	10,200÷11,500=0.89	10,200÷12,000=0.85	(0.89−0.85)÷0.85= 4.7%

b.

$$\text{Total factor productivity for 2000 using 2000 prices} = \frac{10{,}200}{(7{,}000 \times \$3.00) + (800 \times \$15) + (11{,}500 \times \$1.30)}$$

$$= \frac{10{,}200}{\$21{,}000 + \$12{,}000 + \$14{,}950}$$

$$= \frac{10{,}200}{\$47{,}950} = 0.213 \text{ output units per dollar of input costs}$$

$$\text{Benchmark total factor productivity} = \frac{10{,}200}{(6{,}840 \times \$3.00) + (840 \times \$15) + (12{,}000 \times \$1.30)}$$

$$= \frac{10{,}200}{\$20{,}520 + \$12{,}600 + \$15{,}600}$$

$$= \frac{10{,}200}{\$48{,}720} = 0.209 \text{ output units per dollar of input costs}$$

The change in total factor productivity from 1999 to 2000 = $(0.213 - 0.209) \div 0.209 =$ +0.019, or an increase of 1.9%. The fact that total factor productivity increased means that the partial productivity increases in direct manufacturing labour (5.0%) and manufacturing overhead (4.7%) more than offset the partial productivity decrease in direct materials (−2.0%).

Cost Allocation

Chapter Overview

This chapter explains how costs are allocated to several cost objects: divisions, departments, products, and contracts. These allocations are often debatable and seldom clearly right or clearly wrong. The chapter provides insight into the dimensions of the cost-allocation questions, even though the answers might seem contrived.

Chapter Highlights

1. The cornerstone of this chapter is *the four purposes for allocating indirect costs to cost objects:*

a. To provide information for economic decisions
b. To motivate managers and other employees
c. To justify costs or compute reimbursement
d. To measure income and assets for reporting to external parties.

The allocation of a particular cost need not satisfy all four purposes simultaneously because different costs are used for different purposes. The key is to determine which purpose of cost allocation is dominant in the given situation. EXHIBIT 14-1, text p. 487, gives illustrations of each of the four purposes of cost allocation.

2. Four criteria are used to guide cost-allocation decisions: (a) cause and effect, (b) benefits received, (c) fairness or equity, and (d) ability to bear. Managers must first choose the purpose for a particular cost allocation and then select the appropriate criterion to implement the allocation. The chapter emphasizes the superiority of the cause-and-effect and the benefits-received criteria, especially when the purpose of cost allocation is economic decisions or motivation.

3. Companies place great importance on the cost-benefit approach in designing and implementing their cost-allocation systems. The costs of a cost-allocation system—collecting data and educating management about the system—are highly visible, and companies work to reduce them. However, the benefits of a well-designed cost-allocation system—managers being able to make better-informed decisions—are less visible and difficult to measure. Today's information technology moves companies to more detailed cost-allocation systems.

4. The Computer Horizons illustration, text pp. 492-493, explains how product costs can be determined for the company's two products, computers and peripheral equipment. The illustration allocates the corporate costs to the two plants and reallocates them to each division's products. Some examples of corporate costs (and possible allocation bases) are as follows: corporate executive salaries (sales, assets employed) and corporate Personnel Department (number of employees, payroll dollars, number of new hires).

5. A key decision in the Computer Horizons illustration is how many cost pools should be used in allocating corporate costs to the divisions. The concept of homogeneity is important in making this decision. In a **homogeneous cost pool**, all of the costs have the same or a similar cause-and-effect (or benefits-received) relationship with the cost-allocation base. Using homogeneous cost pools results in more accurate costs of a given cost object.

6. Two alternative cost-allocation methods are the **single-rate method** and **dual-rate method.**

• The single-rate method pools all costs being considered into one cost pool and uses a single allocation base for allocating these costs to cost objects. The single-rate method is easy to implement. This method, however, may lead department or division managers to make outsourcing decisions that are in their own best interest but are not in the best interest of the organization as a whole.

- The dual-rate method classifies costs being considered into two cost pools, a variable cost pool and a fixed cost pool. Each pool uses a different cost-allocation base. Because the dual-rate method focuses on cost-behaviour, it guides department or division managers to make decisions that are in their own best interest as well as in the best interest of the organization as a whole.

7. Under either the single-rate or dual-rate method, the choice between using *budgeted cost rates* and *actual cost rates* affects the level of uncertainty user departments (or divisions) face. Budgeted rates let user departments know, in advance, the cost rates they will be charged. User departments are better equipped to determine the amount of the service to request and, if the option exists, whether or not to outsource. Budgeted rates also help motivate the managers of the supplier departments to improve efficiency. In contrast, actual rates are not known until the end of the budget period and do not promote efficiency.

8. Under the dual-rate method, the choice between *budgeted usage* and *actual usage* for allocating fixed costs can affect how managers behave. Budgeted usage lets user departments know, in advance, their allocated costs, which is especially helpful for long-run planning. If fixed costs are allocated on the basis of budgeted long-run usage, however, managers of user departments may be tempted to underestimate their planned usage. If so, a user department that underestimates its planned usage bears a lower percentage of the fixed costs, assuming all other managers do not similarly underestimate their usage. This temptation can be countered by offering incentives to managers whose actual usage does not exceed their

budgeted usage. There are two disadvantages if fixed costs are allocated on the basis of actual usage. First, the amount of fixed costs allocated to a given user department is affected by the usage of the other user departments. Second, the actual fixed costs allocated to user departments are not known until the end of the budget period.

9. Organizations distinguish between **operating departments** and **support departments**. An operating department (also called **a production department** in manufacturing companies) adds value to a product or service. A support department (also called **a service department**) renders the services that maintain other internal departments (operating departments and other support departments) in the organization. Support departments create special cost-allocation problems if they render reciprocal services to each other as well as services to operating departments.

10. Support department costs can be allocated to operating departments by the **direct method**, **step-down method**, or **reciprocal method**.

- The direct method allocates each support department's costs directly to the operating departments. *This method ignores any services rendered by a support department to other support departments.* The direct method is the most widely used method of allocating support department costs. The advantage of this method is its simplicity—there is no need to predict the usage of support department services by other support departments.
- The step-down method (also called the **sequential method**) provides *partial recognition of the services rendered by support departments to other support departments.* This method requires the support departments to be ranked (sequenced) in the order that the step-down allocation is to proceed. Different sequences result in different allocations of support department costs to operating departments. A popular step-down sequence begins with the department that renders the highest percentage of

its total services to other support departments. The sequence continues with the department that renders the next-highest percentage of its total services to other support departments, and so on, ending with the support department that renders the lowest percentage of its total services to other support departments. Once a support department's costs are allocated under the step-down method, it receives no further allocation.

- The reciprocal allocation method allocates costs by *fully recognizing the services rendered among all support departments*. Under this method, support-department costs and support-department reciprocal service relationships are expressed in linear equations (one equation for each support department). Solving these equations simultaneously gives the **complete reciprocated costs** (also called **artificial costs**) of each support department. The complete reciprocated costs of a support department are the department's own costs plus its portion of the costs of the other support departments rendering services to it. Although the reciprocal method is conceptually the most defensible of the three methods, it is not widely used.

The support-department costs allocated to each operating department are included in a cost pool, which is divided by an appropriate allocation base to compute the budgeted overhead rate. These rates are used to allocate overhead to products, contracts, or other cost objects.

11. Another type of cost allocation concerns **common costs**, which are the costs of operating a facility, activity, or like cost object that is shared by two or more users. Two methods for allocating common costs are the **stand-alone method** and the **incremental method**. The stand-alone method allocates costs to each user of a cost object on the basis of its proportion of the total costs that would be incurred if each user were the only user of the cost object. The incremental method ranks the individual users of a cost object and uses this ranking to allocate costs among those users. The first-ranked user of the cost object is called the primary party and is allocated costs equal to its costs as a stand-alone user. Any remaining cost is allocated to the incremental party or parties on the basis of their ranked sequence. Under the incremental method, the primary party typically receives the highest allocation of the common costs.

12. Cost data are important in contracts. Contract disputes arise with some regularity, often in regard to cost allocation. The areas of possible dispute between contracting parties can be reduced by making the "rules of the game" explicit in the contract. These rules include details such as the allowable cost items, the acceptable cost-allocation bases, and whether to use budgeted or actual costs.

13. Some contracts specify how **allowable costs** are to be determined. Allowable costs are costs the contracting parties agree to include as reimbursable costs. For example, only economy-class airfares are allowable in many contracts. Some contracts identify cost categories that are not allowable. For example, expenditures for lobbying activities and alcoholic beverages are not allowable costs in some contracts.

14. There are two main approaches to reimbursing contractors: (a) the contractor is paid a set price without analysis of actual contract cost data (such as in competitive bidding situations) or (b) the contractor is paid after analysis of actual contract cost data (such as reimbursement of allowable costs plus a set fee).

Featured Exercise

The following information is for Secrest Manufacturing Company:

	Support Departments		Operating Departments	
	T	V	1	2
Budgeted manufacturing overhead before allocation of support department costs	$60,000	$80,000	$30,000	$25,000
Proportions of service provided by T	–	30%	50%	20%
Proportions of service provided by V	10%	–	60%	30%

a. Complete the schedule below using the direct method to allocate the costs of the support departments to Departments 1 and 2.

	T	V	1	2	Total
Budgeted manufacturing overhead before allocation of support dept. costs	$60,000	$80,000	$30,000	$25,000	$195,000
Allocation of T					
Allocation of V					
	$ 0	$ 0			
Total budgeted manufacturing overhead of operating departments			$	$	$195,000

b. Complete the schedule below using the step-down method to allocate the costs of the support departments to Departments 1 and 2. Allocate Department T first.

	T	V	1	2	Total
Budgeted manufacturing overhead before allocation of support dept. costs	$60,000	$80,000	$30,000	$25,000	$195,000
Allocation of T					
Allocation of V					
	$ 0	$ 0			
Total budgeted manufacturing overhead of operating departments			$	$	$195,000

c. Complete the schedule below using the reciprocal method to allocate the costs of the support departments to Departments 1 and 2. (Hint: the first step is to formulate and solve two linear equations).

	T	V	1	2	Total
Budgeted manufacturing overhead before allocation of support dept. costs	$60,000	$80,000	$30,000	$25,000	$195,000
Allocation of T					
Allocation of V					
	$ 0	$ 0			
Total budgeted manufacturing overhead of operating departments			$	$	$195,000

Solution

a. Direct method:

	T	V	1	2	Total
Budgeted manufacturing overhead before allocation of support dept. costs	$60,000	$80,000	$ 30,000	$25,000	$195,000
Allocation of T(5/7, 2/7)[1]	(60,000)		42,857	17,143	
Allocation of V(6/9, 3/9)[2]		(80,000)	53,333	26,667	
	$ 0	$ 0			
Total budgeted manufacturing overhead of operating departments			$126,190	$68,810	$195,000

[1]50%/(50%+20%); 20%/(50%+20%)
[2]60%/(60%+30%); 30%/(60%+30%)

b. Step-down method:

	T	V	1	2	Total
Budgeted manufacturing overhead before allocation of support dept. costs	$60,000	$80,000	$ 30,000	$25,000	$195,000
Allocation of T(30%,50%,20%)	(60,000)	18,000	30,000	12,000	
Allocation of V(6/9, 3/9)[1]		(98,000)	65,333	32,667	
	$ 0	$ 0			
Total budgeted manufacturing overhead of operating departments			$125,333	$69,667	$195,000

[1]60%/(60%+30%); 30%/(60%+30%)

c. Reciprocal method:

	T	V	1	2	Total
Budgeted manufacturing overhead before allocation of support dept. cost	$60,000	$ 80,000	$ 30,000	$25,000	$195,000
Allocation of T: (see below)	(70,103)	21,031[1]	35,051[2]	14,021[3]	
Allocation of V: (see below)	10,103[4]	(101,031)	60,619[5]	30,309[6]	
	$ 0	$ 0			
Total budgeted manufacturing overhead of operating departments			$125,670	$69,330	$195,000

T = $60,000 + 0.10V
V = $80,000 + 0.30T

T = $60,000 + 0.10($80,000 + 0.30T)
T = $60,000 + $8,000 + 0.03T
0.97T = $68,000
T = $70,103

V = $80,000 + 0.30($70,103)
V = $80,000 + $21,031 = $101,031

[1]30% × $70,103 = $21,031
[2]50% × $70,103 = $35,051
[3]20% × $70,103 = $14,021
[4]10% × $101,031 = $10,103
[5]60% × $101,031 = $60,619
[6]30% × $101,031 = $30,309

Review Questions and Exercises

Completion Statements

Fill in the blank(s) to complete each statement.

1. In a _____ cost pool, all of the costs have the same or a similar cause-and-effect (or benefits-received) relationship with the cost-allocation base.
2. The _____ method of cost allocation uses a variable cost pool and a fixed cost pool.
3. The _____ method allocates costs of support departments to both operating and support departments, giving partial recognition of services rendered by support departments to other support departments.
4. The _____ method fully incorporates the relationships of interdepartmental services rendered among support departments.
5. The costs of operating a facility, activity, or other cost object that is shared by two or more users are called _____ costs.
6. _____ costs are costs the contracting parties agree to include as reimbursable costs.

True-False

Indicate whether each statement is true (T) or false (F)

___ 1. One of the four purposes of cost allocation is to measure income and assets for reporting to external parties.
___ 2. The fairness criterion is superior to other criteria used for guiding cost-allocation decisions if the purpose of the allocation is either to provide information for economic decisions or to motivate managers and other employees.
___ 3. If the degree of homogeneity is greater among costs, more cost pools are required to explain accurately the differences in how products use the resources of a company.
___ 4. To allocate the fixed costs of a department so that fluctuations of usage in one user department do not affect charges to other user departments, the allocation should be based on actual usage in the current accounting period.
___ 5. For a given support department serving other support departments, its complete reciprocated costs are always larger than its actual costs.
___ 6. A major reason for allocating support department costs to operating departments in a manufacturing plant is to compute budgeted department overhead rates.
___ 7. If two users share a facility such as a mailroom, the primary user prefers the common costs be allocated using the incremental method.
___ 8. Expenditures for lobbying activities are not allowable costs in some contracts.

Multiple Choice

Select the best answer to each question. Space is provided for computations after the quantitative questions.

___ 1. (CPA) Of most relevance in deciding how indirect costs should be allocated to products is the degree of:
   a. avoidability.
   b. causality.
   c. controllability.
   d. linearity.
___ 2. (CMA) Which one of the following companies is most likely to experience suboptimal motivation from its managers due to the cost-allocation method used?
   a. To allocate amortization of forklifts used by workers at its central warehouse, Shahlimar Electronics uses budgeted amounts computed on the basis of the long-run average use of the services rendered by the warehouse to the various subunits.

b. Rainier Industrial does not allow its support departments to pass on their cost overruns to the operating departments.

c. Manhattan Electronics uses the revenues of its divisions to allocate costs associated with the maintenance of its corporate headquarters building.

d. Tashkent Auto's management information system (MIS) operates from corporate headquarters and serves all of its divisions. Tashkent's allocation of the MIS-related costs to its divisions is limited to costs the divisions would incur if they were to outsource their MIS needs.

e. Golkonda Refinery separately allocates variable and fixed costs incurred by its support departments to its operating departments.

___ 3. The most accurate and most widely used method for allocating support department costs is:
a. the direct method.
b. the step-down method.
c. the reciprocal method.
d. none of the above.

___ 4. (CPA adapted) Boa Corp. allocates support department overhead costs to operating departments X and Y by means of the reciprocal allocation method. Information for the current month is as follows:

| | Support Departments | |
	A	B
Overhead costs	$20,000	$10,000

Services provided to departments:

A	–	10%
B	20%	–
X	40%	30%
Y	40%	60%
	100%	100%

The linear equation to be used in the allocation of A's costs is:
a. A = $20,000 + 0.20B.
b. A = $10,000 + 0.10B.
c. A = $10,000 + 0.20B.
d. A = $20,000 + 0.10B.

___ 5. Bixler Manufacturing Company uses the step-down method for allocating its support department costs to operating depart-ments. The overhead costs of support Department A are to be allocated first, followed by the costs of B, and then those of C. The distribution of services is as follows:

Service Supplied By	Support Depts.			Operating Depts.	
	A	B	C	X	Y
A	–	10%	50%	20%	20%
B	40%	–	15%	30%	15%
C	25%	25%	–	20%	30%

The percentage of B's costs that should be allocated to Y is:
a. 15%.
b. 33⅓%.
c. 25%.
d. none of the above.

___ 6. Using the data in question 5, the percentage of C's costs that should be allocated to B under the step-down method is:
a. 0%.
b. 20%.
c. 33⅓%.
d. none of the above.

Exercises

1. Hanover Company's power plant provides electricity for its two operating departments, A and B. The year 2000 budget for the power plant shows:

Budgeted fixed costs	$80,000
Budgeted variable costs per kilowatt hour (kwh)	$0.20

Additional data for 2000:

	Budget (kwh)	Actual (kwh)
Department A	240,000	215,000
Department B	160,000	195,000

Actual power-plant costs: fixed $92,000, variable $88,000

a. Compute the budgeted power-plant costs allocated to A and B using the single-rate method with budgeted usage as the allocation base.

b. Compute the budgeted power-plant costs allocated to A and B using the dual-rate method with actual usage as the allocation base for variable costs and budgeted usage as the allocation base for fixed costs.

c. From the standpoint of Departments A and B, what are the two main benefits of the dual-rate method?

2. (CMA) Cosmo Inc.'s income statement by segments for November 1999 is as follows:

	Total	Mall Store	Town Store
Revenues	$200,000	$80,000	$120,000
Variable costs	116,000	32,000	84,000
Contribution margin	84,000	48,000	36,000
Direct fixed costs	60,000	20,000	40,000
Contribution by store	24,000	28,000	(4,000)
Indirect fixed costs	10,000	4,000	6,000
Operating income	$ 14,000	$24,000	$ (10,000)

Additional information regarding Cosmo's operations is as follows:

- One-fourth of each store's direct fixed costs will continue through December 31, 2000, even if either store is closed.
- Cosmo allocates indirect fixed costs to each store on the basis of revenues. These costs are regarded as unavoidable.
- Management estimates that closing the Town Store would result in a 10% decrease in the Mall Store's sales volume; whereas, closing the Mall Store would not affect the Town Store's sales volume.
- The operating results for November 1999 represent the average for all months.

a. Compute the increase/decrease in Cosmo's monthly operating income for 2000 if the Town Store is closed.
b. Cosmo is considering a promotion campaign at the Town Store that would not affect the Mall Store. Compute the increase/decrease in Cosmo's monthly operating income during 2000, assuming annual promotion costs at the Town Store are increased by $60,000 and its sales volume increases by 10%.
c. One-half of Town Store's revenues are from items sold at variable cost in order to attract customers to the store. Cosmo is considering dropping these items, a move that would reduce the Town Store's direct fixed costs by 15% and result in the loss of 20% of its remaining revenues and variable costs. This change would not affect the Mall Store. Compute the increase/decrease in Cosmo's monthly operating income for 2000, assuming the items sold at variable cost are dropped.

3. Adams Company and Baker Company are in noncompeting lines of business and use a common database for marketing purposes. The variable costs associated with accessing the database are readily identifiable and kept in separate cost pools that are charged to each user. The fixed costs of maintaining the database, however, cannot be identified by user on a cause-and-effect basis. These fixed costs for next year are budgeted at $55,000. If Baker does not use the database, the fixed costs to Adams are $48,000. An outside vendor offers to provide Adams access to a comparable database for a fixed fee of $60,000 per year plus variable costs of accessing the database. The same vendor offers to provide Baker access to that database for a fixed fee of $20,000 per year plus variable costs of accessing the database.

Compute how much of the $55,000 fixed costs of maintaining the database are borne by each user:
a. Under the stand-alone allocation method.
b. Under the incremental allocation method, assuming Adams is regarded as the primary user.

Answers to Chapter 14 Review Questions and Exercises

Completion Statements

1. homogenous
2. dual-rate
3. step-down
4. reciprocal
5. common
6. Allowable

True-False

1. T
2. F The cause-and-effect criterion is superior to other criteria used for guiding cost-allocation decisions if the purpose of the allocation is economic decisions or motivation. If the cause-and-effect criterion is not operational, the benefits-received criterion is often used.
3. F If the degree of homogeneity is greater among costs, *more* cost items have the same or a similar cause-and-effect relationship with the individual allocation bases. *Fewer* cost pools are required, therefore, to explain accurately the differences in how products use the resources of a company.
4. F Exhibit 14-5, text p. 497, shows that using *actual usage* does affect the allocation of fixed costs to departments when fluctuations occur in actual usage. Allocation is not affected by fluctuations in usage, however, if the allocation base is *budgeted usage*.
5. T
6. T
7. F The example, text pp. 503-504, allocates the Montreal employer (the primary user) $1,200 under the incremental method and $600 under the stand-alone method.
8. T

Multiple Choice

1. b   Decisions on cost allocation are often guided by the cause-and-effect criterion. That is, it is desirable that all of the individual activities whose costs are included in a cost pool have the same or a similar cause-and-effect relationship with the cost-allocation base.

2. c   The costs of maintaining the corporate headquarters building are not controllable by the division managers, and hence the company is likely to experience suboptimal motivation from its managers due to the cost-allocation method used.

3. d   The reciprocal method is the most accurate method for allocating support department costs because it fully recognizes the relationships of interdepartmental services rendered among support departments. The direct method is the most widely used method because of its simplicity.

4. d   The equation must include A's own costs *plus its percentage use of B's services*, which is 10%.

5. c   Department A's costs have already been allocated, so its usage of B's services (40%) should be disregarded in answering this question: $0.15 \div (0.15 + 0.30 + 0.15) = 0.15 \div 0.60 = 0.25$, or 25%. Note that the sequence of allocating the costs of the support departments in the question is consistent with the popular step-down sequence based on the percentage of a support department's total services rendered to other support departments.

Order of Allocation	% of a Support Department's Total Services Rendered to Other Support Departments
1st A	10% to B + 50% to C = 60%
2nd B	40% to A + 15% to C = 55%
3rd C	25% to A + 25% to B = 50%

6. a   Once a support department's costs are allocated under the step-down method, it receives on further allocation.

Exercise 1

a.   Total pool of budgeted costs = \$80,000 + (240,000 + 160,000)\$0.20
              = \$80,000 + \$80,000 = \$160,000
     Budgeted cost per kwh = \$160,000 ÷ (240,000 + 160,000)
              = \$160,000 ÷ 400,000 = \$0.40
     Total costs allocated to A = 215,000 × \$0.40 = \$86,000
     Total costs allocated to B = 195,000 × \$0.40 = \$78,000

b.   Fixed cost allocation:
     To A = [240,000 ÷ (240,000 + 160,000)] × \$80,000 = 0.60 × \$80,000 = \$48,000
     To B = [160,000 ÷ (240,000 + 160,000)] × \$80,000 = 0.40 × \$80,000 = \$32,000
     Total cost allocation:
     To A = \$48,000 + (215,000 × \$0.20) = \$48,000 + \$43,000 = \$91,000
     To B = \$32,000 + (195,000 × \$0.20) = \$32,000 + \$39,000 = \$71,000

c.   First, costs allocated to each department are not affected by the kwh usage of the other department. Second, inefficiencies in the power plant are not charged to Departments A and B because both variable and fixed costs are allocated using budgeted rates.

Exercise 2

a. Compare the company's total operating income at present, $14,000, and the amount of operating income from the proposed situation of operating only the Mall Store:

		Proposed Situation
Contribution margin of Mall Store		
$48,000 × 90%		$43,200
Deduct:		
Direct fixed costs of Mall Store	$20,000	
Unavoidable direct fixed costs		
of Town Store, $40,000 × 25%	10,000	
Indirect fixed costs of company		
as a whole	10,000	
Total fixed costs		40,000
Operating income of company		
as a whole		$ 3,200

Closing the Town Store, therefore, decreases operating income for the year by $10,800($14,000 − $3,200).

b. The two items affected in the proposed situation are the Town Store's contribution margin and its promotion costs. Monthly contribution margin increases by $36,000 × 10% = $3,600. *Monthly* promotion costs are $60,000 ÷ 12 = $5,000. Monthly operating income of the Town Store, therefore, decreases by $5,000 − $3,600 = $1,400.

c. Compare the Town Store's contribution at present, −$4,000, and the amount of its contribution with the proposed changes:

		Proposed Situation
Revenues, 0.50 × $120,000 × (1 − 0.20)		$48,000
Deduct:		
Variable costs		
50% of original revenues of $120,000		
are variable that and would be		
avoided; also there will be a 20%		
reduction in the *remainder of*		
the original variable costs,		
($84,000 − $60,000) × (1 − 0.20)	$19,200	
Direct fixed costs,		
$40,000 × (1 − 0.15)	34,000	
Total costs		53,200
Contribution by store		$ (5,200)

The proposed situation, therefore, decreases the Town Store's contribution by $1,200 (from −$4,000 to −$5,200). This $1,200 decrease is also the effect on the company's operating income because indirect fixed costs in total will remain the same, regardless of how they are allocated between the two stores.

Exercise 3

a. Total individual stand-alone costs = $60,000 + $20,000 = $80,000
Allocated to Adams = ($60,000 ÷ $80,000) × $55,000 = $41,250
Allocated to Baker = ($20,000 ÷ $80,000) × $55,000 = $13,750

b. Adams, the primary party, bears $48,000.
Baker, the incremental party, bears $55,000 − $48,000 = $7,000.

CHAPTER 15

Cost Allocation: Joint Products and Byproducts

Chapter Overview

This chapter explains methods of allocating **joint costs** to products; joint costs are the costs of a single production process that yields two or more products simultaneously (for example, the costs of processing raw milk into cream and skim milk). The focus is on allocating joint costs to individual products for the purpose of measuring income and assets for external reporting. For economic decisions, allocating joint costs provides misleading information to managers. These decisions should be guided by the relevant-revenue and relevant-cost analysis introduced in Chapter 11. The chapter concludes with a description of accounting for byproducts.

Chapter Highlights

1. In a joint-production process, the juncture where one or more products become separately identifiable is called the **splitoff point**. **Separable costs** are all of the costs incurred beyond the splitoff point that are assignable to one or more individual products. For example, the joint-production process of milling timber (logs) yields various grades of lumber as well as sawdust and wood chips. The splitoff point is where individual boards are cut from the timber. The costs of planing these boards into finished lumber are separable costs of the finished lumber.

2. A joint-production process can yield **joint products** (or a **main product**) and **byproducts**. A joint product has relatively high sales value (revenue) compared to the other products yielded by the joint-production process. If a joint-production process yields only one product with a relatively high sales value, that product is called a main product. A byproduct has a relatively low sales value compared with the sales value of a joint or main product. A joint product can become a byproduct (or vice versa) if its market price moves sizably in one direction.

3. Four methods of allocating joint costs are the **sales value at splitoff method, physical-measure method, estimated net realizable value (NRV) method,** and **constant gross-margin percentage NRV method.** All of the methods except physical measure base their allocations on market-price data such as revenues. The physical-measure method bases its allocations on weight, volume, or other physical measures. In general, market-price data are a better allocation base than a physical measure.

4. The *sales value at splitoff method* allocates joint costs to joint products based on the relative sales value of the *total production* of these products at the splitoff point. Total production of the accounting period is used because joint costs are incurred for all units produced, not just those sold in the current period. The sales value at splitoff method exemplifies the benefits-received criterion of cost allocation: costs are allocated to products in proportion to their ability to contribute revenues. This method is widely used when market prices for the individual products are available at the splitoff point, even if further processing occurs.

5. The *physical-measure method* allocates joint costs to joint products on the basis of the relative weight, volume, or other physical measure of the *total production* of these products at the splitoff point. The major criticism of this method is that the physical measure used for allocating joint costs may have no relationship to the revenue-generating power of the individual products.

6. The *estimated net realizable value (NRV) method* allocates joint costs to joint products based on the relative estimated NRV (expected final sales value in the ordinary course of business minus the expected separable costs) of the *total production* of these products. Because separable costs are used in its computations, the estimated NRV method does not meet the benefits-received criterion as well as the sales value at splitoff method. It is impossible to use the sales value at splitoff method, however, unless market prices for the individual products are available at the splitoff point.

7. The *constant gross-margin percentage NRV method* allocates joint costs to joint products in such a way that the overall gross-margin percentage is identical for each of the individual products. In its computations, this method uses the expected final sales value of the *total production* during the accounting period. The rationale for the constant gross-margin percentage NRV method is that, given the arbitrary nature of joint-cost allocation under any method, none of the individual products show a loss.

8. All of the methods for allocating joint costs to individual products are subject to criticism. As a result, some companies refrain entirely from this allocation. Instead, they carry their inventories at estimated NRV, which recognizes income on each product when production is completed. Industries that use variations of the no-allocation approach include meatpacking, canning, and mining.

9. In joint-cost situations, managers must often decide whether to sell a joint (or main) product at the splitoff point or process it further. *Because joint costs incurred up to the splitoff point are past (sunk) costs, they are irrelevant to the sell-or-process further decision.* In other words, the sell-or-process further decision should not be influenced either by the total amount of joint costs or by the portion of the joint costs allocated to individual products. *It is profitable to process a product beyond the splitoff point if the incremental revenues resulting from that processing exceed the incremental costs.* Note that the separable costs of a product (defined in paragraph 1) are usually greater than the incremental costs of further processing the product beyond the splitoff point. The reason is separable costs include an allocated amount of fixed manufacturing overhead, but total fixed manufacturing overhead often remains the same whether or not the product is processed further.

10. Joint-production processes may yield not only joint and main products but byproducts as well. The textbook describes Method A and Method B to account for byproducts.

- Method A (the production method) recognizes a byproduct in the financial statements *at the time its production is completed*: debit Byproduct Inventory and credit Work in Process for the estimated net realizable value of the byproduct produced. Crediting Work in Process reduces the joint costs allocated to the joint products (or the main product). When sales of the byproduct occur, debit Cash or Accounts Receivable and credit Byproduct Inventory.
- Method B (the sale method) recognizes a byproduct in the financial statements *at the time it is sold*: debit Cash or Accounts Receivable and credit Byproduct Revenues. No joint costs are allocated to the byproduct and there is no general-ledger account for Byproduct Inventory.

Method A is conceptually superior but Method B is widely used because the dollar amounts of byproducts tend to be immaterial.

Featured Exercise

Cascade Sawmill manufactures two lumber products from a joint milling process. The products are mine support braces (MSB) and commercial building lumber (CBL). A production run results in 60,000 units of MSB and 90,000 units of CBL at the splitoff point. The joint costs are $300,000. MSB and CBL can be sold at splitoff for $1.50 per unit and $4 per unit, respectively.

a. Compute the amount of total joint costs allocated to MSB and CBL using the physical-measure method.
b. Compute the amount of total joint costs allocated to MSB and CBL using the sales value at splitoff method.
c. Assume CBL is not salable at the splitoff point but must be further planed and sized requiring separable costs of $200,000. During this process, 10,000 units are unavoidably spoiled; this spoilage has zero sales value. The good units of CBL can be sold at $10 per unit. The MSB is coated with a tar-like preservative requiring separable costs of $100,000. After further processing, MSB can be sold for $5 per unit. Compute the inventoriable costs per unit of MSB and CBL using the estimated net realizable value method.
d. Assume incremental costs of further processing are 90% of separable costs. Compute the change in operating income that results from further processing of MSB.

Solution

a.

	MSB	CBL	Total
Physical measure of production (units)	60,000	90,000	150,000
Weighting (60,000 ÷ 150,000; 90,000 ÷ 150,000)	0.40	0.60	
Joint costs allocated (0.40 × $300,000; 0.60 × $300,000)	$120,000	$180,000	$300,000

b.

	MSB	CBL	Total
Sales value at splitoff (60,000 × $1.50; 90,000 × $4)	$90,000	$360,000	$450,000
Weighting ($90,000 ÷ $450,000; $360,000 ÷ $450,000)	0.20	0.80	
Joint costs allocated (0.20 × $300,000; 0.80 × $300,000)	$60,000	$240,000	$300,000

c.

	MSB	CBL	Total
Expected final sales value of production 60,000 × $5;[(90,000 − 10,000) × $10]	$300,000	$800,000	$1,100,000
Deduct expected separable costs to complete and sell	100,000	200,000	300,000
Estimated net realizable value at split-off point	$200,000	$600,000	$ 800,000
Weighting ($200,000 ÷ $800,000; $600,000 ÷ $800,000)	0.25	0.75	
Joint costs allocated (0.25 × $300,000; 0.75 × $300,000)	$75,000	$225,000	$300,000
Inventoriable cost per unit ($75,000 + $100,000) ÷ 60,000	$2.92		
($225,000 + $200,000) ÷ (90,000 − 10,000)		$5.31	

d.

Incremental revenues, (60,000 × $5) − (60,000 × $1.50)	$210,000
Deduct incremental costs, $100,000 × 0.90	90,000
Increase in operating income	$120,000

Review Questions and Exercises

Completion Statements

Fill in the blank(s) to complete each statement.

1. The juncture in a joint-production process where one or more products become separately identifiable is called the _____ _____.

2. If a joint-production process yields two or more products but only one of the products has a high sales value, this product is called a _____.

3. All costs incurred beyond the splitoff point that are assignable to one or more individual products are called _____ costs.

4. A _____ has a relatively low sales value compared with the sales value of a joint or main product.

5. The _____ of a product is equal to expected final sales value in the ordinary course of business minus expected separable costs of production and marketing.

6. Of the methods for allocating joint costs to products, which three use market-price data:

_____

_____

_____

_____ .

True-False

Indicate whether each statement is true (T) or false (F).

____ 1. Joint products have relatively high sales value and must be salable at the splitoff point.

____ 2. The amount of the joint costs to be allocated should not be considered in choosing the allocation method.

____ 3. The estimated net realizable value (NRV) method recognizes the revenue-generating power of the individual products and presupposes management decisions on further-processing steps to be undertaken after the splitoff point.

____ 4. The constant gross-margin percentage NRV method is sometimes preferred to set a fair selling price in rate-regulation situations because it avoids the circular reasoning of other methods.

____ 5. The sales value at splitoff method allocates joint costs based on the sales value of total units sold during the accounting period.

____ 6. The main criticism of the physical-measure method is that the physical measure used may have no relationship to the revenue-generating power of the individual products.

____ 7. Allocation of joint costs assists managers in deciding whether joint products should be sold at the splitoff point or processed further.

____ 8. A byproduct is the portion of the production of a main or joint products that has been further processed.

____ 9. In accounting for a byproduct, if no joint costs are allocated to it, there will be no Byproduct Inventory account in the general ledger.

Multiple Choice

Select the best answer to each question. Space is provided for computations after the quantitative questions.

____ 1. (CPA) O'Connor Company manufactures Products J and K from a joint process. For Product J, 4,000 units are produced having a sales value at splitoff of $15,000. If Product J were processed further, the separable costs would be $3,000 and the expected final sales value would be $20,000. For Product K, 2,000 are produced having a sales value at splitoff of $10,000. If Product K were processed further, the separable costs would be $1,000 and the expected final sales value would be $12,000. Using the sales value at splitoff method, the portion of the total joint costs allocated to Product J is $9,000. The total joint costs are:
   a. $14,400.
   b. $15,000.
   c. $18,400.
   d. $19,000.

____ 2. If the constant gross-margin percentage NRV method is used and the overall gross margin of the joint products is 40%, the amount of joint costs allocated to a joint product with an expected final total sales value of $1,800 and separable costs of $400 is:
   a. $1,080.
   b. $780.
   c. $720.
   d. $680.

___ 3. (CPA adapted) Ohio Corporation manufactures liquid chemicals A and B from a joint process. Joint costs are allocated on the basis of sales value at splitoff. It costs $13,680 to process 500 litres of A and 1,000 litres of B up to the splitoff point. The sales value at splitoff is $10 per litre for A and $14 per litre for B. B requires additional processing beyond splitoff at separable costs of $1 per litre before it can be sold. Assuming the 1,000 litres of B are processed further and sold for $18 per litre, Ohio's gross margin on this sale is:

a. $7,920.
b. $7,420.
c. $7,880.
d. $6,920.

___ 4. (CPA) Actual sales values at the splitoff point for joint Products Y and Z are not known. For purposes of allocating joint costs to Products Y and Z, the estimated net realizable value method is used. Assume an increase in the separable costs beyond splitoff for Product Z occurs, while those of Product Y remain constant. If the selling prices of finished Products Y and Z remain constant, the percentage of the total joint costs allocated to Product Y and Product Z:

a. decreases for both products.
b. increases for Y and decreases for Z.
c. decreases for Y and increases for Z.
d. increases for both products.

___ 5. (CMA) Copeland Inc. produces X-547 in a joint-production process. The company is considering whether to sell X-547 at the splitoff point or upgrade the product to become Xylene. The following information is available.

(1) Selling price per kilogram of X-547.
(2) Variable manufacturing costs of the upgrade process.
(3) Avoidable fixed costs of the upgrade process.
(4) Selling price per kilogram of Xylene.
(5) Joint costs to produce X-547.

Which items are relevant to the upgrade decision?

a. 1, 2, 4.
b. 1, 2, 3, 4.
c. 1, 2, 3, 4, 5.
d. 1, 2, 4, 5.
e. 2, 3.

___ 6. (CPA) Crowley Company produces joint Products A and B from a process that also yields a byproduct, Y. The byproduct requires additional processing before it can be sold. The cost assigned to the byproduct is its market value minus additional costs incurred after splitoff. Information concerning a batch produced in the current month at joint costs of $40,000 is as follows:

Product	Units Produced	Market Value	Costs After Splitoff
A	800	$44,000	$4,500
B	700	32,000	3,500
Y	500	4,000	1,000

How much of the joint costs should be allocated to the joint products?

a. $36,000
b. $37,000
c. $39,000
d. $40,000

Exercises

1. The Tri-Ken Corporation incurred $3,000 to produce the following products in a joint production process:

	Product T	Product K
Quantity produced and processed beyond splitoff point	130 units	390 units
Separable costs	$1,000	$1,460
Selling price of a fully processed unit	$40	$10

   a. Compute the amount of joint costs allocated to each product using the physical-measure method.

   b. Based on your allocation of joint costs in part (a), compute the gross margin of Product T, Product K, and both products together, assuming all units are sold.

   c. Compute the amount of joint costs allocated to each product using the estimated NRV method.

   d. Compute the amount of joint costs allocated to each product using the constant gross-margin percentage NRV method.

   e. If the selling prices at splitoff are $34 per unit for Product T and $4 per unit for Product K, is it profitable to further process either or both products? Assume incremental costs are 80% of separable costs. Show your computations.

2. The Cambridge Chemical Company prepared the following data for September 1999:

Total manufacturing costs of a	
joint-production process	$ 75,000
Revenues of main product	100,000
Estimated net realizable value	
of byproduct produced	2,000
Beginning inventories	none

Ending inventory of the main product is 10% of the quantity produced. Ending inventory of the byproduct is 30% of the quantity produced.

Compute the gross margin of the main product, assuming the byproduct is recognized in the financial statements at the time it is sold.

Answers to Chapter 15 Review Questions and Exercises

Completion Statements

1. splitoff point
2. main product
3. separable
4. byproduct
5. net realizable value (NRV)
6. sales value at splitoff method, estimated net realizable value (NRV) method, constant gross-margin percentage NRV method

True-False

1. F   Joint products have relatively high sales value and are not separately identifiable as individual products until the splitoff point. Joint products may or may not be salable at the splitoff point.
2. T
3. T
4. F   The methods using market-price data—sales value at splitoff, estimated NRV, and constant gross-margin percentage NRV—involve circular reasoning for setting prices: using selling prices to allocate joint costs that serve, in turn, as a basis for setting selling prices. Only the physical-measure method avoids this circular reasoning because it does not use market-price data.
5. F   The sales value at splitoff method allocates joint costs based on the sales value of total units *produced* during the accounting period. This method exemplifies the benefits-received criterion of cost allocation: costs are allocated to products in proportion to their ability to contribute revenues.

6. T

7. F The allocation of joint costs is irrelevant to the decision of whether joint or main products should be sold at the splitoff point or further processed because the *total amount* of the joint costs remains the same whether or not further processing occurs. Only revenues and costs that are *incremental beyond the splitoff point* are relevant to the decision.

8. F Byproducts have low sales value compared with the sales value of joint or main products. Byproducts are identified at the splitoff point; they may or may not require further processing.

9. T

Multiple Choice

1. b Total sales value at splitoff of the two products together = $15,000 + $10,000 = $25,000; the portion of joint costs allocated to Product J = $15,000 ÷ $25,000 = 60%; total joint costs = $9,000 ÷ 0.60 = $15,000. Note that it is a coincidence the sales value at splitoff of Product J is the same amount as total joint costs, $15,000. Also note that in using the sales value at splitoff method, ignore information regarding further processing of the products.

2. d
Expected final sales value of total production	$1,800
Deduct gross margin, $1,800 × 0.40	720
Cost of good sold	1,080
Deduct separable costs	400
Joint costs allocated	$ 680

3. d Sales value at splitoff:
A, 500 × $10	$ 5,000
B, 1,000 × $14	14,000
Total sales value at splitoff	$19,000

Cost of Product B (fully processed):
Allocation of joint costs, ($14,000 ÷ $19,000) × $13,680	$10,080
Separable costs, 1,000 × $1	1,000
Cost of goods sold	$11,080
Revenues, 1,000 units of B × $18	$18,000
Cost of goods sold	11,080
Gross margin of B	$ 6,920

4. b An effective way to answer this question is to assume any set of "before change" figures you desire and compute "after change" amounts by incorporating an increase in the separable costs of Product Z. Select any reasonable amount for the increase in separable costs ($2,000 is used in the following computations).

	Before Change	
	Y	Z
Expected final sales value of total production	$9,000	$8,000
Deduct separable costs	3,000	4,000
Estimated net realizable value	$6,000	$4,000
Joint cost allocation percentage:		
$6,000 ÷ ($6,000 + $4,000)	60%	
$4,000 ÷ ($6,000 + $4,000)		40%

	After Change	
	Y	Z
Expected final sales value of total production	$9,000	$8,000
Deduct separable costs	3,000	6,000
Estimated net realizable value	$6,000	$2,000
Joint cost allocation percentage:		
$6,000 ÷ ($6,000 + $2,000)	75%	
$2,000 ÷ ($6,000 + $2,000)		25%

The percentage of total joint costs allocated to Product Y increases (to 75% from 60%) and decreases for Product Z (to 25% from 40%).

5. b The first four items are relevant to the decision because they differ depending on whether X-547 is sold at the splitoff point or upgraded. Item 5 is irrelevant to the decision because it is the same under either alternative.

6. b This question uses Method A (the production method) to account for the byproduct.
Joint costs allocated to the byproduct = $4,000 − $1,000 = $3,000
Joint costs allocated to the joint products = $40,000 − $3,000 = $37,000

Exercise 1

a. Allocation of joint costs:
To T: 130 ÷ (130 + 390) × $3,000 = $750
To K: 390 ÷ (130 + 390) × $3,000 = $2,250

b.

	T	K	Total
Revenues, 130 × $40; 390 × $10	$5,200	$3,900	$9,100
Cost of goods sold			
Joint costs (computed above)	750	2,250	3,000
Separable costs	1,000	1,460	2,460
Cost of goods sold	1,750	3,710	5,460
Gross margin	$3,450	$ 190	$3,640

c.

	T	K	Total
Expected final sales value of total production			
130 × $40; 390 × $10	$5,200	$3,900	$9,100
Deduct separable costs	1,000	1,460	2,460
Estimated net realizable value	$4,200	$2,440	$6,640
Allocation of $3,000 joint costs:			
To T: ($4,200 ÷ $6,640) × $3,000	$1,898		
To K: ($2,440 ÷ $6,640) × $3,000		$1,102	

d.

		Total
Expected final sales value of total production		
(130 × $40) + (390 × $10)		$9,100
Cost of goods sold		
Total joint costs	$3,000	
Total separable costs	2,460	5,460
Gross margin of both products together		$3,640
Gross margin percentage of both products together, $3,640 ÷ $9,100		40%

	T	K	Total
Expected final sales value of total production	$5,200	$3,900	$9,100
Deduct gross margin at 40%	2,080	1,560	3,640
Total manufacturing costs	3,120	2,340	5,460
Deduct separable costs	1,000	1,460	2,460
Joint costs allocated	$2,120	$ 880	$3,000

e.

	T	K
Incremental revenue beyond splitoff ($40 − $34) × 130; ($10 − $4) × 390	$780	$2,340
Incremental costs beyond splitoff, which are 80% of separable costs $1,000 × 0.80; $1,460 × 0.80	800	1,168
Oper. income (loss) from further processing	$(20)	$1,172

Exercise 2

This exercise uses Method B (the sale method) to account for the byproduct.

Revenues		
Main product		$100,000
Byproduct, $2,000 × 0.70		1,400
Total		101,400
Cost of goods sold		
Total manufacturing costs	$75,000	
Deduct ending inventory of main product, $75,000 × 0.10	7,500	67,500
Gross margin		$ 33,900

CHAPTER 16 | Revenues, Sales Variances, and Customer-Profitability Analysis

Chapter Overview

This chapter highlights the importance of having a detailed understanding of revenues in making decisions related to products and customers. The chapter is divided into three major parts: (I) revenue allocation, (II) sales variances applicable to companies selling multiple products or services, and (III) customer-profitability analysis. The Appendix to the chapter shows how the framework explained in Part II can be used to analyze cost variances for substitutable production inputs.

Chapter Highlights

Part I

1. *Revenues* are inflows of assets received in exchange for products or services provided to customers. Just as costs can be allocated to specific products, so can revenues. **Revenue allocation** occurs if revenues are related to a particular *revenue object*, but cannot be traced to it in an economically feasible way. The revenue objects in this chapter are products and customers. Of course, products and customers can also be *cost objects*. For example, in the case where a manager is deciding whether to keep or drop a product, the product is both the revenue object and the cost object.

2. If department or division managers have revenue or profit responsibility for individual products (or services), an important revenue allocation issue arises if **bundled products** are sold. A bundled product is a package of two or more products (or services), sold for a single price, where the individual components of the bundle also may be sold as separate items at their own "stand-alone" prices. The single price for a bundled product is typically less than the sum of the prices of the individual products sold separately.

3. There are two main methods for allocating bundled product revenues to the individual products in the bundle.

- The **stand-alone revenue allocation method** uses individual-product information on the bundled product as the weights for allocating the bundled revenues to the individual products. Four types of weights for the stand-alone method are selling prices, unit costs, physical units, and stand-alone product revenues. Selling prices and stand-alone product revenues better capture the benefits received by customers who purchase a bundled product.

- The **incremental revenue allocation method** ranks the individual products in a bundle according to criteria determined by management, and uses this ranking for allocating the bundled revenues to the individual products. The first-ranked product is termed the primary product in the bundle. The second ranked product is the first incremental product, the third ranked product is the second incremental product, and so on.

Part II

4. If a company sells more than one product or service, several sales variances help managers gain insight into why actual results differ from budgeted amounts. Sales variances, which are usually measured in terms of contribution margin, can be described using the levels-of-detail approach introduced in Chapter 7. Level 1 analysis computes the *static-budget variance*—the difference between actual contribution margin and the static-budget amount of contribution margin. Level 2 analysis divides the static-budget variance into the *flexible-budget variance* and the *sales-volume variance*.

5. Level 3 analysis divides the sales-volume variance into the **sales-mix variance** and the **sales-quantity variance**.

- The sales-mix variance is the difference between the budgeted contribution margin for the actual sales mix and the budgeted contribution margin for the budgeted sales mix. A favourable/unfavourable sales-mix variance arises for an individual product if its actual sales-mix percentage is greater/less than its budgeted sales-mix percentage.

- The sales-quantity variance is the difference between (a) the budgeted contribution margin based on actual units sold of all products at the budgeted mix and (b) static-budget contribution margin, which is based on the budgeted units to be sold of all products at the budgeted mix. A favourable/unfavourable sales-quantity variance arises if the actual units sold of all products is greater/less than the budgeted units to be sold of all products.

EXHIBIT 16-1, text p. 562, shows the computation of the sales-mix and sales-quantity variances using a columnar solution format.

6. The *total* sales-mix variance and *total* sales-quantity variance can be computed by algebraically summing the respective variances for the individual products. A second approach computes these total variances by using the budgeted contribution margin per **composite product unit**, a hypothetical unit with weights based on the mix of individual products. The box on the next page illustrates this approach.

7. Level 4 analysis divides the sales-quantity variance into the **market-share variance** and the **market-size variance**.

- The market-share variance is the difference between actual and budgeted market share multiplied by actual industry market size in units and by budgeted contribution margin per composite unit for the budgeted mix. This variance is favourable/unfavourable if actual market share is greater/less than budgeted market share.

- The market-size variance is the difference between actual and budgeted industry market size in units multiplied by the budgeted market share and by the budgeted contribution margin per composite unit for the budgeted mix. This variance is favourable/unfavourable if actual industry market size is greater/less than budgeted industry market size.

EXHIBIT 16-2, text p. 564, shows the computation of the market-share and market-size variances using a columnar solution format.

8. The Appendix to this chapter explains how, when a company uses multiple types of substitutable materials or labor inputs in producing a finished good, Level 4 analysis divides the efficiency variance into the **mix variance** and the **yield variance**. The mix variance focuses on how different inputs are combined while the yield variance focuses on how much of each input is used. EXHIBIT 16-10, text p. 578, shows the computation of the direct materials mix and yield variances using a columnar solution format.

Part III

9. Companies that prosper have a strong customer focus in their decisions. Accordingly, management accountants are giving increased attention to **customer-profitability analysis**, the reporting and analysis of customer revenues and customer costs. Customer-profitability analysis helps managers in two main ways. First, it frequently shows a small percentage of customers account for a large percentage of the organization's operating income. Sufficient resources need to be devoted to maintaining and expanding relationships with these key contributors to profitability. Second, it identifies low-profitability and loss-category customers. Ways can be explored to make these customers more profitable in the future.

10. Two variables explain revenue differences among customers: the volume of units they purchase and the magnitude of **price discounting**. Price discounting is the reduc-

tion of selling prices below list prices in order to encourage increases in customer purchases. Tracking the amount of price discounts by customer, and by salesperson, can provide valuable information about ways to improve customer profitability.

11. A **customer cost hierarchy** categorizes costs related to customers into different cost pools on the basis of different types of cost drivers (or cost-allocation bases) or different degrees of difficulty in determining cause-and-effect (or benefits- received) relationships. In the Spring Distribution example, text p. 567, there are four categories in the customer cost hierarchy:

a. *Customer specific costs* are resources that are traced or allocated to individual customers. An example is cost of goods sold.

b. *Distribution-channel costs* are resources used for activities that are related to a particular distribution channel. An example is the salary of the manager of the retail distribution channel.

c. *Customer support costs* are resources traced or allocated to customer support but not to individual customers or distribution channels. An example is the cost of a 24-hour hot-line that handles customer complaints.

d. *Corporate-sustaining costs* are resources used for activities that cannot be traced to individual customers or distribution channels. An example is the company president's salary.

Customer-level costs include the costs incurred in the first and third categories of the cost hierarchy. EXHIBIT 16-4, text p. 568, shows a customer-profitability analysis for four of Spring Distribution's customers.

Product	Budgeted Contribution Margin (1)	Actual Sales Mix Percentage (2)	Budgeted Contribution Margin Per Composite Unit For Actual Mix (3)=(1)×(2)	Budgeted Sales Mix Percentage (4)	Budgeted Contribution Margin Per Composite Unit For Budg. Mix (5)=(1)×(4)
X	$3,200	0.10	$ 320	0.05	$ 160
Y	2,400	0.25	600	0.15	360
Z	900	0.65	585	0.80	720
		1.00	$1,505	1.00	$1,240

Sales volume of all three products:

Actual units	24,000
Budgeted units	20,000

Total sales-mix variance = 24,000 × ($1,505 − $1,240) = $6,360,000 F

Total sales-quantity variance = (24,000 − 20,000) × ($1,505 − $1,240) = $1,060,000 F

The sales-mix variance is favourable because the budgeted contribution margin per composite unit is greater for the actual mix ($1,505) than for the budgeted mix ($1,240). The sales-quantity variance is favourable because actual sales volume of all three products (24,000 units) is greater than budgeted sales volume of all three products (20,000 units).

12. The activity-based costing system underlying EXHIBIT 16-4 provides a road-map showing explicitly how costs are reduced if individual customers use less of the cost drivers. For example, the delivery costs assigned to a customer will decrease by combining some orders and making fewer deliveries. Another means of cost reduction is to take actions that lower the costs in the individual activity areas. For example, processing customer orders more efficiently reduces the costs of the order-taking activity.

13. Customer-profitability analysis often focuses on a single accounting period. Short-run profitability is one of several factors that managers consider in deciding how to allocate resources among customers. The other factors to be considered relate to long-run customer profitability; they include the likelihood of customer retention, the potential for customer growth, the increases in overall demand from having well-known customers, and the ability to learn from customers.

Featured Exercise

(Relates to Part II of the Chapter) Stover Company manufactures fine chocolate candies. The following sales information is for its industry and its operations for the year 2000:

	Number of Cases
Budgeted industry volume	550,000
Actual industry volume	560,000
Stover's budgeted volume	88,000
Stover's actual volume	84,000

Stover measures its sales variances in terms of contribution margin. For 2000, budgeted contribution margin per composite unit for the budgeted mix is $300 per case.

a. Compute the market-share variance and market-size variance.
b. Compute the sales-volume variance, assuming the sales-mix variance is $40,000 favourable.

Solution

a.

$$\begin{array}{c} \text{Market-share} \\ \text{variance} \end{array} = \begin{array}{c} \text{Actual} \\ \text{market-size} \\ \text{in units} \end{array} \times \left(\begin{array}{c} \text{Actual} \\ \text{market} \\ \text{share} \end{array} - \begin{array}{c} \text{Budgeted} \\ \text{market} \\ \text{share} \end{array} \right) \times \begin{array}{c} \text{Budgeted} \\ \text{contribution margin} \\ \text{per composite unit} \\ \text{for budgeted mix} \end{array}$$

$$= 560,000(0.15 - 0.16) \times \$300$$
$$= 560,000(-0.01) \times \$300 = -\$1,680,000, \text{ or } \$1,680,000 \text{ U}$$

The market-share variance is unfavorable because actual market share is less than budgeted market share.

$$\begin{array}{c} \text{Market-size} \\ \text{variance} \end{array} = \left(\begin{array}{c} \text{Actual} \\ \text{market size} \\ \text{in units} \end{array} - \begin{array}{c} \text{Budgeted} \\ \text{market size} \\ \text{in units} \end{array} \right) \times \begin{array}{c} \text{Budgeted} \\ \text{market} \\ \text{share} \end{array} \times \begin{array}{c} \text{Budgeted} \\ \text{contribution margin} \\ \text{per composite unit} \\ \text{for budgeted mix} \end{array}$$

$$= (560,000 - 550,000) \times 0.16 \times \$300$$
$$= 10,000 \times 0.16 \times \$300 = \$480,000, \text{ or } \$480,000 \text{ F}$$

The market-size variance is favorable because actual market size is greater than budgeted market size.

b. Two steps are used to obtain the answer. First, compute the sales-quantity variance, which is the algebraic sum of the two variances computed above:

$$\text{Sales-quantity variance} = \$1,680,000 \text{ U} + \$480,000 \text{ F} = \$1,200,000 \text{ U}$$

Second, compute the sales-volume variance, which is the algebraic sum of the sales-mix variance and sales-quantity variance:

$$\text{Sales-volume variance} = \$40,000 \text{ F} + \$1,200,000 \text{ U} = \$1,160,000 \text{ U}$$

Review Questions and Exercises

Completion Statements

Fill in the blank(s) to complete each statement.

Part I

1. A _____ is a package of two or more products, sold for a single price, where the individual components of the package may also be sold as separate items at their own "stand-alone" prices.

2. The _____ revenue allocation method uses individual-product information on the bundled product as the weights for allocating the bundled revenues to the individual products.

Part II

3. The sales-volume variance divides into which two variances? _____ and_____.

4. The sales-quantity variance divides into which two variances? _____ and_____.

5. (Appendix) The direct materials (DM) efficiency variance divides into which two variances? _____ and_____.

Part III

6. Reducing selling prices below list prices in order to encourage increases in customer purchases is called _____.

True-False

Indicate whether each statement is true (T) or false (F).

Part I

___ 1. If a manager is deciding whether to keep or drop a product, the product is both the revenue object and the cost object.

___ 2. The selling price for a bundled product is typically less than the sum of the prices of the individual products sold separately.

___ 3. The stand-alone revenue allocation method ranks the individual products in a bundle according to criteria determined by management, and uses this ranking for allocating the bundled revenues to the individual products.

Part II

___ 4. An unfavourable sales-mix variance arises for an individual product if its actual sales-mix percentage is less than its budgeted sales-mix percentage.

___ 5. The sales-quantity variance can conceal the fact that a company's market share declined even though unit sales of one or more of its products grew.

___ 6. Marketing managers generally find the market-size variance is more controllable than the market-share variance.

___ 7. Reliable industry statistics needed to compute market-share and market-size variances are available in almost all industries.

___ 8. (Appendix) If multiple inputs of direct materials can be combined in varying proportions within certain specified limits, they are called substitutable inputs.

___ 9. (Appendix) An unfavourable direct materials mix variance arises for an individual type of direct material if its actual mix percentage is less than its budgeted mix percentage.

Part III

___ 10. Customer-profitability analysis often shows a small percentage of customers account for a large percentage of the organization's operating income.

___ 11. In the customer cost hierarchy, the delivery cost for a customer order is a customer support cost.

Multiple Choice

Select the best answer to each question. Space is provided for computations after the quantitative questions.

Part I

___ 1. Revenue objects include:

	Customers	Distribution Channels
a.	No	No
b.	No	Yes
c.	Yes	No
d.	Yes	Yes

___ 2. Under the stand-alone method, which weights better capture the benefits received by customers who purchase a bundled product?
a. Selling prices and physical units
b. Selling prices and unit costs
c. Selling prices and stand-alone product revenues
d. Stand-alone product revenues and physical units

Part II

___ 3. The following data are for Eucha Corp. for the first quarter of the current fiscal year:

	Actual Results	Static Budget
Unit sales:		
Product X	15,000	40,000
Product Y	65,000	60,000
Total	80,000	100,000
Contribution margin per unit:		
Product X	$4	$5
Product Y	$3	$2

The sales-mix variance for both products together is:
a. $51,000 unfavourable.
b. $64,000 unfavourable.
c. $115,000 unfavourable.
d. $115,000 favourable.

___ 4. Using the data in question 3, the total sales-quantity variance for Product Y is:
a. $40,000 unfavourable.
b. $40,000 favourable.
c. $24,000 unfavourable.
d. $24,000 favourable.

___ 5. Using the data in question 3, the amount of the budgeted contribution margin per composite unit is:
a. $3.50.
b. $3.20.
c. $2.5625.
d. none of the above.

___ 6. (Appendix) The following data are for Kershaw Company for April 2000:

Budgeted direct labor mix at budgeted prices for actual output produced

3,825 skilled hours at $16 per hour
1,275 unskilled hours at $12 per hour
5,100 total hours

Actual results

4,000 skilled hours at $19 per hour
1,000 unskilled hours at $9 per hour
5,000 total hours

The total direct labor yield variance is:
a. $1,500 favourable.
b. $1,000 unfavourable.
c. $1,000 favourable.
d. $500 favourable.

___ 7. (Appendix) Using the data in question 6, the mix variance for skilled labor is:
a. $1,200 favourable.
b. $4,000 unfavourable.
c. $2,800 unfavourable.
d. $2,800 favourable.

Part III

___ 8. In a customer cost hierarchy, the cost of a sales visit made to a customer is:
   a. a customer output-unit-level cost.
   b. a customer batch-level cost.
   c. a customer-sustaining cost.
   d. a distribution-channel cost.

___ 9. Customer-profitability profiles rank customers based on their:

	Customer-Level Operating Income	Customer Revenues
a.	Yes	Yes
b.	Yes	No
c.	No	Yes
d.	No	No

Exercises

Part I

1. Van Sickle Tours is located in Atlanta. The company sells "mini-vacation" travel packages. A travel package is comprised of air travel, lodging, and a multiple-day scenic bus tour of the local sights. Each of the three revenue components of travel packages is the responsibility of a different manager. One of Van Sickle's most popular travel packages is the three-day, two person "Fall Foliage of Vermont" priced at $849. This package includes:

   • Two round-trip airline tickets (Atlanta to Burlington, Vermont)—separately priced at $330 per person.
   • Three nights' lodging—separately priced at $130 per night for two.
   • Three-day sightseeing bus tour—separately priced at $125 per person.

Allocate the $849 Vermont-package revenue to the three components of the travel package using:
a. The stand-alone revenue allocation method.
b. The incremental revenue allocation method (with the bus tour as the primary product, lodging as the first incremental product, and air travel as the second incremental product).
For both methods, use selling prices as the weights. Round all computations to the nearest dollar.

Part II

2. (CMA) Given the following information for Xerbert Company (in thousands):

	Static Budget for 1999			Actual Results for 1999		
	Xenox	Xeon	Total	Xenox	Xeon	Total
Units sold	150	100	250	130	130	260
Revenues	$900	$1,000	$1,900	$780	$1,235	$2,015
Variable costs	450	750	1,200	390	975	1,365
Contribution margin	$450	$ 250	700	$390	$ 260	650
Fixed costs:						
Manufacturing			200			190
Marketing			153			140
Customer service			95			90
Total fixed costs			448			420
Operating income			$ 252			$ 230

a. Compute the total sales-volume variance.
b. Compute the total sales-mix variance.
c. Compute the total sales-quantity variance.

Part III

3. Cambridge Industries collects information on two customers for 1999:

	Langley Supply	Sweeney, Inc.
Revenues	$1,492,000	$640,000
Cost of goods sold	$1,164,000	$486,000
Number of in-stock orders	14	4
Number of out-of-stock orders	12	24

Cambridge estimates the following activity-based costs:

Cost of processing and delivering an in-stock order	$1,200
Cost of processing and delivering an out-of-stock order	$3,500

An in-stock order is an order for which all the items included are in inventory at the time the order is received.

Compute the customer specific contribution of each customer for 1999 using:
a. 16% of revenues as the allocation rate for customer-related costs.
b. The activity-based costing approach.

Answers to Chapter 16 Review Questions and Exercises

Completion Statements

1. bundled product
2. stand-alone
3. sales-mix variance, sales-quantity variance
4. market-share variance, market-size variance
5. DM mix variance, DM yield variance
6. price discounting

True-False

1. T
2. T
3. F   The statement describes the *incremental revenue allocation method*, not the *stand-alone revenue allocation method*. The stand-alone method uses individual-product information on the bundled product as the weights for allocating bundled revenues to the individual products.
4. T
5. T
6. F   Marketing managers generally find the market-share variance is more controllable than the market-size variance. Pricing and sales promotion decisions are more likely to affect market share than total market size. If market size and the demand for an industry's products are largely influenced by factors such as economic conditions, the market-size variance is less controllable by marketing managers.
7. F   Reliable industry statistics needed to compute market-share and market-size variances are not available in many industries.
8. T
9. F   An unfavourable direct materials mix variance arises for an individual type of direct material if its actual mix percentage is *greater than* its budgeted mix percentage. Note that this question is worded in a parallel manner to question 4. Question 4 is true, however, because it refers to *contribution margin* rather than *input cost*. In other words, in the income statement contribution margin has a *positive* algebraic sign while input cost has a *negative* algebraic sign.
10. T
11. F   In the customer cost hierarchy, the delivery cost for a customer order is a customer specific cost because the cost can be traced or allocated to individual consumers.

Multiple Choice

1. d   A revenue object is anything for which a separate measurement of revenues is desired. Examples of revenue objects are products, customers, divisions, and distribution channels.
2. c   Four types of weights for the stand-alone revenue allocation method are selling prices, stand-alone product revenues, unit costs, and physical units. Selling prices and stand-alone product revenues better capture the benefits received by customers who purchase a bundled product.

3. a

> For illustrative purposes, *formulas* are used to answer questions 3 and 4, and the *columnar solution format* is used to answer questions 6 and 7.

Let SMV-X = Sales-mix variance for Product X
Let SMV-Y = Sales-mix variance for Product Y
Let SMV-T = Total sales-mix variance

SMV-X = 80,000 × [(15,000 ÷ 80,000) − (40,000 ÷ 100,000)] × $5
SMV-X = 80,000 × (0.1875 − 0.40) × $5
SMV-X = 80,000 × (−0.2125) × $5 = −$85,000, or $85,000 U

SMV-Y = 80,000 × [(65,000 ÷ 80,000) − (60,000 ÷ 100,000)] × $2
SMV-Y = 80,000 × (0.8125 − 0.60) × $2
SMV-Y = 80,000 × 0.2125 × $2 = $34,000, or $34,000 F

SMV-T = SMV-X + SMV-Y
SMV-T = $85,000 U + $34,000 F = $51,000 U

Alternative solution:

Budgeted contribution margin per composite unit at actual mix:

$$\frac{(\$15,000 \times \$5) + (\$65,000 \times \$2)}{15,000 + 65,000} = \frac{\$75,000 + \$130,000}{80,000} = \frac{\$205,000}{80,000} = \$2.5625$$

Budgeted contribution margin per composite unit at budgeted mix:

$$\frac{(\$40,000 \times \$5) + (\$60,000 \times \$2)}{40,000 + 60,000} = \frac{\$200,000 + \$120,000}{100,000} = \frac{\$320,000}{100,000} = \$3.20$$

Total sales-mix variance = ($2.5625 − $3.20) × 80,000
= −$0.6375 × 80,000 = −$51,000, or $51,000 U

4. c Let SQV-Y = Sales-quantity variance for Product Y

SQV-Y = (80,000 − 100,000) × (60,000 ÷ 100,000) × $2
SQV-Y = −20,000 × 0.60 × $2 = −$24,000, or $24,000 U

5. b The alternative solution in answer 3 shows the budgeted contribution margin per composite unit is $3.20.

6. a

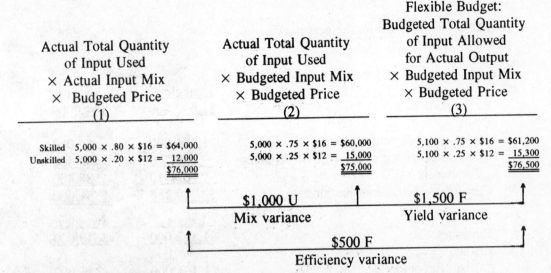

	Actual Total Quantity of Input Used × Actual Input Mix × Budgeted Price (1)	Actual Total Quantity of Input Used × Budgeted Input Mix × Budgeted Price (2)	Flexible Budget: Budgeted Total Quantity of Input Allowed for Actual Output × Budgeted Input Mix × Budgeted Price (3)
Skilled	5,000 × .80 × $16 = $64,000	5,000 × .75 × $16 = $60,000	5,100 × .75 × $16 = $61,200
Unskilled	5,000 × .20 × $12 = 12,000	5,000 × .25 × $12 = 15,000	5,100 × .25 × $12 = 15,300
	$76,000	$75,000	$76,500

$1,000 U
Mix variance

$1,500 F
Yield variance

$500 F
Efficiency variance

Supporting computations:

Actual labor mix:
Skilled = 4,000 ÷ 5,000 = 80%
Unskilled = 1,000 ÷ 5,000 = 20%

Budgeted labor mix:
Skilled = 3,825 ÷ 5,100 = 75%
Unskilled = 1,275 ÷ 5,100 = 25%

7. b Using the amounts for skilled labor in columns 1 and 2 from the preceding answer, the mix variance = $64,000 − $60,000 = $4,000 U

8. c Customer-sustaining costs are incurred for activities undertaken to support an individual customer.

9. a Exhibit 16-6, text p. 570, presents customer-profitability profiles. Panel A ranks customers based on customer-level operating income. Panel B ranks customers based on revenues.

Exercise 1

a. Stand-alone revenues:

Air travel, $330 × 2	$ 660	
Lodging, $130 × 3	390	
Bus tour, $125 × 2	250	
Total	$1,300	

Stand-alone revenue allocation method:
Allocation to air travel = ($660 ÷ $1,300) × $849 = $431
Allocation to lodging = ($390 ÷ $1,300) × $849 = 255
Allocation to bus tour = ($250 ÷ $1,300) × $849 = 163
Total Vermont-package revenue $849

b. Incremental revenue allocation method:

Components Listed in Order of Allocation	Revenue Allocated	Revenue Remaining to Be Allocated to Other Components
Bus tour, $125 × 2	$250	$849 − $250 = $599
Lodging, $130 × 3	390	$599 − $390 = $209
Air travel	209	$209 − $209 = $0
Total Vermont-package revenue	$849	

Exercise 2

See the Solution Exhibit on the next page.

Exercise 3

a.

	Langley	Sweeney
Revenues	$1,492,000	$640,000
Costs:		
Cost of goods sold	1,164,000	486,000
Customer-related costs, 16% of revenues	238,720	102,400
Total costs	1,402,720	588,400
Customer specific contribution	$ 89,280	$ 51,600

b.

	Langley	Sweeney
Revenues	$1,492,000	$640,000
Costs:		
Cost of goods sold	1,164,000	486,000
In-stock costs		
14 × $1,200; 4 × $1,200	16,800	4,800
Out-of-stock costs		
12 × $3,500; 24 × $3,500	42,000	84,000
Total costs	1,222,800	574,800
Customer specific contribution	$ 269,200	$ 65,200

SOLUTION EXHIBIT

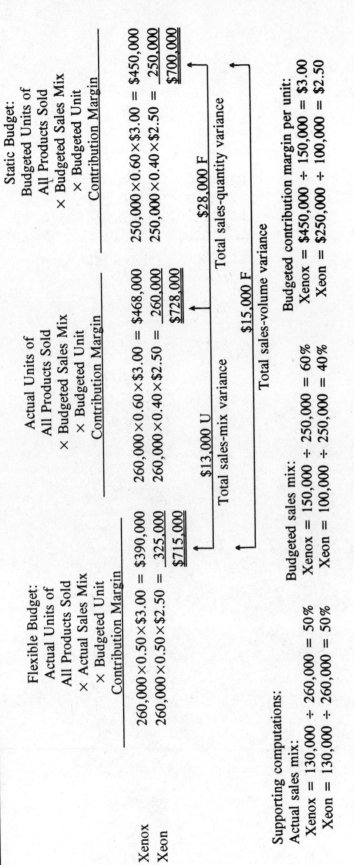

	Flexible Budget: Actual Units of All Products Sold × Actual Sales Mix × Budgeted Unit Contribution Margin	Actual Units of All Products Sold × Budgeted Sales Mix × Budgeted Unit Contribution Margin	Static Budget: Budgeted Units of All Products Sold × Budgeted Sales Mix × Budgeted Unit Contribution Margin
Xenox	260,000×0.50×$3.00 = $390,000	260,000×0.60×$3.00 = $468,000	250,000×0.60×$3.00 = $450,000
Xeon	260,000×0.50×$2.50 = 325,000	260,000×0.40×$2.50 = 260,000	250,000×0.40×$2.50 = 250,000
	$715,000	$728,000	$700,000

$13,000 U
Total sales-mix variance

$28,000 F
Total sales-quantity variance

$15,000 F
Total sales-volume variance

Supporting computations:

Actual sales mix:
Xenox = 130,000 ÷ 260,000 = 50%
Xeon = 130,000 ÷ 260,000 = 50%

Budgeted sales mix:
Xenox = 150,000 ÷ 250,000 = 60%
Xeon = 100,000 ÷ 250,000 = 40%

Budgeted contribution margin per unit:
Xenox = $450,000 ÷ 150,000 = $3.00
Xeon = $250,000 ÷ 100,000 = $2.50

Alternative solution:

Budgeted contribution margin per composite unit at actual mix:

$$\frac{(130{,}000 \times \$3) + (130{,}000 \times \$2.50)}{260{,}000} = \frac{\$390{,}000 + \$325{,}000}{260{,}000} = \frac{\$715{,}000}{260{,}000} = \$2.75$$

Budgeted contribution margin per composite unit at budgeted mix:

$$\frac{(150{,}000 \times \$3) + (100{,}000 \times \$2.50)}{250{,}000} = \frac{\$450{,}000 + \$250{,}000}{250{,}000} = \frac{\$700{,}000}{250{,}000} = \$2.80$$

Total sales-volume variance = (260,000 × $2.75) − (250,000 × $2.80) = $715,000 − $700,000 = $15,000, or $15,000 F

Total sales-mix variance = ($2.75 − $2.80) × 260,000 = −$0.05 × 260,000 = −$13,000, or $13,000 U

Total sales-quantity variance = (260,000 − 250,000) × $2.80 = 10,000 × $2.80 = $28,000, or $28,000 F

CHAPTER 17 — Process Costing

Chapter Overview

This chapter explains how process costing can be used to determine the cost of products or services. In the simplest case, a process has no beginning or ending work-in-process inventory. Considerable complexity is added when a process has beginning and ending work-in-process inventory. This case necessitates selecting an inventory cost-flow method. The chapter illustrates two of these methods: the weighted-average method and the first-in, first-out (FIFO) method. Many detailed exhibits are included in the chapter because *process costing is highly procedural*. The Appendix to the chapter illustrates how operation costing can be used to determine the cost of products.

Chapter Highlights

1. A *process-costing system* determines the cost of a product (or service) by assigning costs to masses of identical or similar units of output. A process-costing system separates costs into cost categories according to the timing of when costs are introduced into the process. Often only two cost classifications, direct materials and conversion costs, are necessary to assign costs to products. *The key feature of process costing is that it averages production costs over all units produced.* Industries using process costing include chemical, pharmaceutical, and semiconductor.

2. The chapter uses three cases to illustrate the costing of the DG-19 component in the Assembly Department of Global Defense Inc. The following table shows the cases differ in regard to whether or not the Assembly Department has work-in-process inventory.

	Beginning Inventory	Ending Inventory
Case 1	No	No
Case 2	No	Yes
Case 3	Yes	Yes

3. Case 1 is simple because there is no work-in-process inventory. That is, all units of DG-19 are started and completed during the accounting period. The unit cost of the 400 units of DG-19 in this case is computed as follows:

Direct material costs	
$32,000 ÷ 400	$ 80
Conversion costs	
$24,000 ÷ 400	60
Assembly Dept. cost per unit	$140

4. Case 2 has some unfinished units of DG-19 at the end of the accounting period but no beginning work-in-process inventory. Whenever there is an ending work-in-process inventory (*with or without beginning work-in-process inventory*), the following five-step approach is an effective way to compute the cost of fully completed and partially completed units.

Step 1: Summarize the flow of physical units of output.
Step 2: Compute output in terms of **equivalent units**.
Step 3: Compute equivalent unit costs.
Step 4: Summarize total costs to account for.
Step 5: Assign total costs to units completed and to units in ending work-in-process inventory.

Steps 1 and 2 deal only with units, whereas Steps 3, 4, and 5 incorporate costs. Step 1 tracks where *physical units* come from and where they go to during the accounting period.

That is, units in beginning inventory + units started = units completed + units in ending inventory. In Step 2, *equivalent units* is a derived amount of output units that takes the quantity of each input (factor of production) in units completed or in work in process, and converts it into the amount of completed output units that could be made with that quantity of input. For DG-19, direct materials are added at the beginning of the process in the Assembly Department, and conversion costs are added evenly during the process. EXHIBIT 17-1, text p. 595, shows the details for Steps 1 and 2 in Case 2.

5. The accuracy of the completion percentages used for partially completed units in equivalent unit computations depends on the care and skill of the estimator and the nature of the process. Estimating the degree of completion is often easier for direct materials than for conversion costs because the quantity of direct materials needed for a completed unit or a partially completed unit can be measured more easily. In contrast, the degree of completion for conversion costs depends on what proportion of the total effort needed to complete a unit or a batch of production has been devoted to the units still in process. This estimate is more difficult to make accurately. Because of the difficulties in estimating the completion percentages for conversion costs, department supervisors and line managers—individuals most familiar with the process—often make these estimates.

6. Steps 3, 4, and 5 together are called the *production cost worksheet*. Step 3 computes equivalent unit costs by dividing the costs in each input cost category by the respective quantity of equivalent units. In Step 4, total costs to account for are equal to the sum of the amounts debited to the department's Work in Process account. Given no beginning inventory, the Assembly Department's debits are for direct materials used and conversion costs incurred during the period. Step 5 assigns total costs to account for from Step 4 to units completed and transferred out of the process and to units remaining in process at the end of the period. EXHIBIT 17-2, text p. 596, shows the details for Steps 3, 4 and 5 in Case 2.

7. Using dollar amounts from EXHIBIT 17-2, summary journal entries for the Assembly Department for February are as follows:

Work in Process–Assembly	32,000	
Materials Control		32,000
Work in Process–Assembly	18,600	
Various accounts		18,600
Work in Process–Testing	24,500	
Work in Process–Assembly		24,500

Given that the Assembly Department had no beginning inventory in February, Work in Process—Assembly has a balance at the end of February of $26,100 ($0 + $32,000 + $18,600 − $24,500).

8. Case 3 adds complexity: there is both beginning and ending work-in-process inventory of DG-19. Under these conditions it is necessary to select an *inventory cost-flow method*. The textbook illustrates two of these methods:

- The **weighted-average process-costing method** computes the equivalent unit cost of work done to date (regardless of the period in which it is done) and assigns this cost to (a) equivalent units completed and transferred out of the process and (b) equivalent units in ending work-in-process inventory.
- The **first-in, first-out (FIFO) process-costing method** (a) assigns the cost of the previous period's equivalent units in beginning work-in-process inventory to the first units completed and transferred out of the process, and (b) assigns the cost of equivalent units worked on during the current period—first to complete beginning inventory, then to start and complete new units, and finally to units in ending work-in-process inventory.

Both methods use the five-step approach presented in paragraph 4.

9. The key difference in computing equivalent units (Step 2) under the two methods is the treatment of work done on the physical units to account for in the process.

- *The weighted-average method combines work done to date regardless of whether it is performed in the previous period or the current period.* Thus, the stage of completion of the current period's beginning work in process *is not* used in computing equivalent units.
- *The FIFO method separates work done on beginning inventory in the previous period from work done in the current period.*

EXHIBIT 17-4, text p. 599, shows the details of Steps 1 and 2 for the weighted-average method. EXHIBIT 17-6, text p. 602, is a parallel presentation for the FIFO method.

10. To compute equivalent unit costs (Step 3), the weighted-average method divides *costs incurred to date in each cost category by the respective amount of work done to date*, whereas the FIFO method divides *costs incurred in the current period in each cost category by the respective amount of work done in the current period*. The assignment of costs (Step 5) is more complicated under FIFO because units completed and transferred out of the process have both a beginning inventory component and a started and completed component, versus a single component for these units under weighted average. The major advantage of FIFO is that it provides managers with information about changes in the costs per unit from one period to the next. This information can be used for evaluating performance in the current period by comparing actual costs and budgeted costs. EXHIBIT 17-5, text p. 600, shows the details of Steps 3, 4, and 5 for the weighted-average method. EXHIBIT 17-7, text p. 603, is a parallel presentation for the FIFO method.

11. The cost of units completed (and hence operating income) can differ materially between the weighted-average and FIFO methods if (a) the direct materials or conversion costs per unit vary significantly from period to period, and (b) the unit level of work in process is large in relation to the total number of units transferred out of the process. Thus, as companies move toward long-term procurement contracts to reduce differences in unit costs from period to period, and reduce inventory levels, the difference in the cost of units completed under the weighted-average and FIFO methods decreases.

12. The *standard-costing method* is often used in process-costing systems. Standards are set for quantities of inputs needed to produce output. Standard costs per input unit can be assigned to these physical quantities to develop standard costs per output unit. The standard-costing method is especially useful for companies that manufacture a *wide variety of similar products*, such as rubber products and textiles. Identifying standard costs for each individual product overcomes the disadvantage of costing all products at a single average actual cost amount.

13. Variances arise under the standard-costing method if the standard costs assigned to products on the basis of work done in the current period do not equal the actual costs incurred in the current period. As described in Chapters 7 and 8, variances can be measured and analyzed in little or much detail for planning and control purposes.

14. In addition to their role in planning and control, standard costs make it easier to use the five-step approach. Steps 1 and 2 are the same under standard costing as under FIFO, but *Step 3 requires no computations because the equivalent unit costs are the standard costs per unit of output*. Step 5 assigns the total standard costs to account for from Step 4 to units completed and transferred out of the process and to units in ending work-in-process inventory. EXHIBIT 17-8, text p. 607, and EXHIBIT 17-9, text p. 608, illustrate the five-step approach for standard costing.

15. Many process-costing systems have two or more departments or processes in the production cycle. In the example, text p. 626, the DG-19 component moves from the Assembly Department to the Testing Department and then to Finished Goods. In the Testing Department, direct materials (crating and other packing materials) are added at the *end* of the process, and conversion costs are added evenly during the process. Because the Testing Department is not the first process in the production cycle, it has an input cost category called **transferred-in costs** or **previous department costs**. Transferred-in costs are the costs incurred in a previous department that are carried forward as the product's cost as it moves to a subsequent department in the production cycle. That is, as units move from one department to the next, their costs are transferred with them. DG-19's cost, therefore, consists of the transferred-in costs as well as the direct materials and conversion costs added in the Testing Department.

16. As in a first-department situation, the five-step approach assigns the costs of a subsequent department to units completed and transferred out, and to units in ending inventory. In computing a subsequent department's equivalent units (Step 2), *transferred-in costs are treated as if they are a separate type of direct material added at the beginning of the process.* Recall that the weighted-average equivalent units are work done to date, whereas the FIFO equivalent units are work done in the current period. EXHIBIT 17-11, text p. 612, and EXHIBIT 17-13, text p. 613, show this contrast in the computation of equivalent units.

17. Steps 3, 4 and 5 are basically the same for a subsequent department as for a first department, except transferred-in costs must be accounted for. These steps under the weighted-average and FIFO methods, as described for a first department in paragraph 10, are applied in a similar manner to a subsequent department. EXHIBIT 17-12, text p. 612, shows the details of Steps 3, 4 and 5 for weighted average. EXHIBIT 17-14, text p. 613, is a parallel presentation for FIFO.

18. Product-costing systems do not always fall neatly into the categories of job costing or process costing. A **hybrid-costing system** blends characteristics from both job-costing systems and process-costing systems. Manufacturers of a relatively wide variety of closely related standardized products tend to use hybrid-costing systems. For example, automobiles are mass produced, but individual units may be customized with a special combination of engine size, transmission, sound system, and so on. Companies develop hybrid-costing systems to meet such situations.

19. The Appendix to this chapter illustrates an **operation-costing system**, which is a hybrid-costing system applied to batches of similar products. Individual batches of products are often a variation of a single design and proceed through a sequence of selected, though not necessarily the same, **operations**. An operation is a standardized method or technique performed repetitively regardless of the distinguishing features of the finished goods. Within each operation, all product units use identical amounts of the operation's resources. Manufacturers of clothing and shoes commonly use operation-costing systems.

Featured Exercise

Rogers Company manufacturers a component, Y-28, in a two-process production cycle, Departments 1 and 2. In Department 2, direct materials are added at the beginning of the process and conversion costs are added evenly during the process. Conversion costs were 60% complete for the 6,000 units in process on May 1, and 75% complete for the 8,000 units in process on May 31. Twelve thousand units were completed and transferred out of Department 2 during May. Department 2's costs for May are as follows:

	Transferred-in Costs	Direct Materials	Conversion Costs
Work in process, May 1	$140,000	$ 28,000	$ 72,000
Costs added in May	280,000	112,000	216,000

a. Using the weighted-average method in Department 2 for May:
   - Summarize the flow of physical units of output.
   - Compute output in terms of equivalent units.
   - Compute equivalent unit costs.
   - Summarize total costs to account for.
   - Assign total costs to units completed and transferred out and to units in ending work-in-process inventory.
   - Prepare the journal entry to record the transfer of completed work to Finished Goods.

b. Using the FIFO method, repeat part (a).

Solution

a.   Weighted-average method:

Flow of Production	Physical Units	Equivalent Units Trans.-in Costs	Direct Materials	Conversion Costs
Work in process, beginning	6,000			
Transferred-in during May	14,000*			
To account for	20,000			
Completed and transferred out during May	12,000	12,000	12,000	12,000
Work in process, ending	8,000			
8,000 × 100%; 100%; 75%		8,000	8,000	6,000
Accounted for	20,000			
Work done to date		20,000	20,000	18,000

*A plug figure: 20,000 units accounted for minus 6,000 units in beginning inventory.

	Total Production Costs	Trans.-in Costs	Direct Materials	Conversion Costs
Work in process, beginning	$240,000	$140,000	$ 28,000	$ 72,000
Costs added in May	608,000	280,000	112,000	216,000
Costs incurred to date		$420,000	$140,000	$288,000
Divide by equivalent units		÷20,000	÷20,000	÷18,000
Equivalent unit costs		$ 21	$ 7	$ 16
Total costs to account for	$848,000			
Assignment of costs:				
Completed and trans. out	$528,000	12,000 × ($21 + $7 + $16)		
Work in process, ending				
Transferred-in costs	168,000	8,000 × $21		
Direct materials	56,000	8,000 × $7		
Conversion costs	96,000	6,000 × $16		
Total work in process	320,000			
Total costs accounted for	$848,000			

The journal entry to record the transfer of completed work is:

Finished Goods	528,000	
Work in process—Dept. 2		528,000

b. FIFO method:

Flow of Production	Physical Units	Equivalent Units		
		Trans.-in Costs	Direct Materials	Conversion Costs
Work in process, beginning	6,000			
Transferred-in during May	14,000*			
To account for	20,000			
Completed and transferred out during May:				
Work in process, beginning	6,000			
$6,000 \times 0\%; 0\%; (100\% - 60\%)$		0	0	2,400
Started and completed	6,000			
$6,000 \times 100\%; 100\%; 100\%$		6,000	6,000	6,000
Work in process, ending	8,000			
$8,000 \times 100\%; 100\%; 75\%$		8,000	8,000	6,000
Accounted for	20,000			
Work done in May		14,000	14,000	14,400

*A plug figure: 20,000 units accounted for minus 6,000 units in beginning inventory.

	Total Production Costs	Trans.-in Costs	Direct Materials	Conversion Costs
Work in process, beginning	$240,000	(costs of work done before May)		
Costs added in May	608,000	$280,000	$112,000	$216,000
Divide by equivalent units		÷14,000	÷14,000	÷14,400
Equivalent unit costs		$ 20	$ 8	$ 15
Total costs to account for	$848,000			

Assignment of costs:

Work in process, beginning	$240,000	
Direct materials added in May	-0-	0 × $8
Conversion costs added in May	36,000	2,400 × $15
Total work in process, beg.	276,000	
Started and completed	258,000	6,000 × ($20 + $8 + $15)
Total completed and trans. out	534,000	
Work in process, ending		
Transferred-in costs	160,000	8,000 × $20
Direct materials	64,000	8,000 × $8
Conversion costs	90,000	6,000 × $15
Total work in process, ending	314,000	
Total costs accounted for	$848,000	

The journal entry to record the transfer of completed work is:

Finished Goods	534,000	
Work in process—Dept. 2		534,000

Review Questions and Exercises

Completion Statements

Fill in the blank(s) to complete each statement.

1. The overall objective of the five-step approach to process costing is to assign the total costs to account for to units _____ _____ and to units _____.

2. _____ is a derived amount of output units that takes the quantity of each input (factor of production) in units completed or in work in process, and converts it into the amount of completed output units that could be made with that quantity of input.

3. The journal entry to transfer completed goods out of Painting, the final processing department in the production cycle, is:
   Debit: _____
   Credit: _____

4. (Appendix) A hybrid-costing system applied to batches of similar products is called an _____ system.

True-False

Indicate whether each statement is true (T) or false (F).

___ 1. A process-costing system separates costs into cost categories according to the timing of when costs are introduced into the process.

___ 2. In any process for a given month, physical units are always equal to or greater than equivalent units.

___ 3. In terms of physical units in a processing department, the sum of units completed and transferred out and units in ending work in process is equal to the sum of units in beginning inventory and units started during the current period.

___ 4. In process costing, estimating the degree of completion of units is usually easier for conversion costs than for direct materials.

___ 5. The weighted-average method focuses on the total costs and total equivalent units completed to date, whereas the FIFO method computes unit costs by confining equivalent units to work done in the current period.

___ 6. The weighted-average method uses the stage of completion of the current period's beginning work in process in computing equivalent units.

___ 7. The FIFO method does not use the costs of beginning inventory in computing equivalent unit costs for the current period.

___ 8. In computing equivalent units, transferred-in costs are treated as if they are a separate type of direct material added at the beginning of the process.

___ 9. Transferred-in costs for Process Two in the current period cannot include conversion costs that are incurred in Process One in the current period.

___ 10. The standard-costing method uses "work done during the current period" as the basis for comparing actual costs and standard costs for control purposes.

___ 11. (Appendix) An operation-costing system allocates different amounts of conversion costs to different products that undergo a given operation.

Multiple Choice

Select the best answer to each question. Space is provided for computations after the quantitative questions.

___ 1. (CPA) Kew Co. had 3,000 units in work in process at April 1 of the current fiscal year, which were 60% complete as to conversion costs. During April, 10,000 units are completed. At April 30, 4,000 units remain in work in process and are 40% complete as to conversion costs. Direct materials are added at the beginning of the process. Conversion costs are added evenly during the process. Assuming Kew uses the weighted-average method, how many units were started during April?
   a. 9,000
   b. 9,800
   c. 10,000
   d. 11,000

___ 2. (CPA) Under which of the following conditions will the first-in, first-out method of process costing yield the same equivalent unit costs as the weighted-average method?
   a. If units produced are homogeneous in nature.
   b. If there is no beginning inventory.
   c. If there is no ending inventory.
   d. If beginning and ending inventories are each 50% complete.

___ 3. (CPA) Walton, Incorporated, had 8,000 units of work in process in Department A on October 1 of the current fiscal year. These units were 60% complete as to conversion costs, which are added evenly during the process. Direct materials are added at the beginning of the process. During October, 34,000 units are started and 36,000 units completed. Walton has 6,000 units of work in process on October 31. These units are 80% complete as to conversion costs. For October, how much did the equivalent units under the weighted-average method exceed the equivalent units under the first-in, first-out method?

	Direct Materials	Conversion Costs
a.	0	3,200
b.	0	4,800
c.	8,000	3,200
d.	8,000	4,800

___ 4. (CMA) Kimbeth Manufacturing uses a process-costing system to manufacture Dust Density Sensors for the mining industry. The following information pertains to operations for May 2000:

	Units
Beginning work-in-process inventory, May 1	16,000
Started in production during May	100,000
Completed production during May	92,000
Ending work-in-process inventory, May 31	24,000

The beginning inventory was 60% complete for direct materials and 20% complete for conversion costs. The ending inventory is 90% complete for direct materials and 40% complete for conversion costs.

Costs pertaining to the month of May are as follows:

• Beginning inventory costs are direct materials, $54,560; conversion costs, $35,560.
• Costs incurred during May are direct materials used, $468,000; conversion costs, $574,040.

Using the weighted-average method, the total cost of the units in the ending work-in-process inventory at May 31, 2000, is:
   a. $86,400.
   b. $153,960.
   c. $154,800.
   d. $155,328.
   e. $156,960.

5. Using the data in question 4 and the FIFO method, the total cost of units in the ending work-in-process inventory at May 31, 2000, is:
   a. $153,168.
   b. $154,800.
   c. $155,328.
   d. $156,960.
   e. $159,648.

6. (CPA) The Wiring Department is the second stage of Flem Company's production cycle. On May 1 of the current fiscal year, the beginning work-in-process inventory consisted of 25,000 units that are 60% complete as to conversion costs. During May, 100,000 units are transferred in from the first stage of Flem's production cycle. On May 31, the ending work-in-process inventory consists of 20,000 units that are 80% complete as to conversion costs. Direct materials are added at the end of the process, and conversion costs are added evenly during the process. Using the weighted-average method, the equivalent units are:

	Transferred-in Costs	Direct Materials	Conversion Costs
a.	100,000	125,000	100,000
b.	125,000	105,000	106,000
c.	125,000	105,000	121,000
d.	125,000	125,000	121,000

7. Using the data in question 6 and the FIFO method, the equivalent units are:

	Transferred-in Costs	Direct Materials	Conversion Costs
a.	100,000	100,000	111,000
b.	100,000	105,000	106,000
c.	100,000	105,000	111,000
d.	125,000	125,000	106,000

8. (CPA) An error is made in estimating the percentage of completion of the current month's ending work-in-process inventory. The error results in understating the percentage of completion of conversion costs. What is the resulting effect of this error on:
   1. the equivalent units in total?
   2. the cost per equivalent unit?
   3. costs assigned to work completed during the period?

	1	2	3
a.	Understate	Overstate	Overstate
b.	Understate	Understate	Overstate
c.	Overstate	Understate	Understate
d.	Overstate	Overstate	Understate

9. (CPA) Under the standard-costing method, how (if at all) are equivalent units used in the computations?
   a. Equivalent units are not used.
   b. Actual equivalent units are multiplied by the standard cost per unit.
   c. Standard equivalent units are multiplied by the standard cost per unit.
   d. Standard equivalent units are multiplied by the actual cost per unit.

Exercises

1. Ozark Company uses a process-costing system. **The** following information is for the Testing Department for January of the current year:

	Units
Work in process, January 1, 40% complete	300
Transferred in during January	600
Completed and transferred out of the department during January	700
Work in process, January 31, 50% complete	200

January 1 inventory costs:	
Transferred-in costs	$28,200
Conversion costs	5,560
Current costs in January:	
Transferred-in costs	51,000
Conversion costs	36,040

No direct materials are added in the Testing Department.

a. Using the weighted-average method:
   (1) Compute total physical units accounted for.
   (2) Compute equivalent units of transferred-in costs and conversion costs.
   (3) Compute cost per equivalent unit of transferred-in costs and conversion costs.
   (4) Compute cost of units completed and transferred out of the department.
   (5) Compute cost of work-in-process inventory, January 31.
b. Repeat part (a) using the FIFO method.

2. (Appendix) Fisher Company manufactures two models of aircraft subassemblies, X and Y. The following information is for February 2000:

	Production Orders	
	2,000 Units of Model X	1,000 Units of Model Y
Direct materials	$48,000	$64,000
Conversion costs (allocated on the basis of machine-hours used)		
Operation 1	20,000	10,000
Operation 2	?	?
Operation 3	–	5,000
Total manufacturing costs	$?	$?

For Operation 2, the budgeted costs for the year 2000 are $200,000 for direct manufacturing labor and $880,000 for manufacturing overhead. Budgeted machine-hours are 36,000. Each product unit requires 10 minutes of machine time in Operation 2.

a. Compute the total conversion costs allocated to each model in Operation 2.
b. Compute the total manufacturing costs and the unit cost of each model in finished form.
c. Assume at the end of February 100 units of Model X are in process through Operation 1 only, and 200 units of Model Y are in process through Operation 2 only. Assume no direct materials are added in Operation 2 and that $8,000 (of the $64,000) direct materials are added to the 1,000 units of Model Y in Operation 3. Compute the cost of ending work-in-process inventory for each model.

Answers to Chapter 17 Review Questions and Exercises

Completion Statements

1. completed and transferred out of the process, in ending work in process
2. Equivalent units
3. Finished Goods Control, Work in Process—Painting
4. operation-costing

True-False

1. T
2. T
3. T
4. F   In process costing, estimating the degree of completion of units is usually easier for direct materials than for conversion costs because the quantity of direct materials needed for a completed unit or a partially completed unit can be measured more easily. The degree of completion for conversion costs depends on what proportion of the total effort needed to complete a unit or a batch of production has been devoted to units still in process. This estimate is more difficult to make accurately.
5. T
6. F   Under the weighted-average method, the stage of completion of the current period's beginning work in process *is not used* in computing equivalent units. For example, the 225 units of beginning work in process in Exhibit 17-4, text p. 599, are 40% complete on March 1, but this stage of completion is disregarded in computing equivalent units under the weighted-average method.
7. T
8. T
9. F   Transferred-in costs always include conversion costs incurred in the previous process. Some or all of these conversion costs are incurred in the current period. If none of these conversion costs are incurred in the current period, the transfer took place in the previous period.
10. T
11. F   Under an operation-costing system, *identical* amounts of conversion costs are allocated to all the different products that undergo a given operation.

Multiple Choice

1. d   Total physical units accounted for = 10,000 + 4,000 = 14,000
    Units started during current period = 14,000 − 3,000 = 11,000
    This answer *is not affected* by the process-costing method used.

2. b   Either of two conditions must be met for the two costing methods to produce the same equivalent unit costs: (i) no beginning inventory or (ii) no period-to-period changes in the costs of direct materials and conversion costs. Condition (i) is illustrated in Cases 1 and 2, text p. 594. Condition (ii) rarely exists.

3. d   The differences in equivalent units between the two methods are attributable to work done in the *preceding* period (that is, work done to date minus work done in the current period). The differences can be computed directly by multiplying physical units in October 1 work-in-process inventory by the percentage of work done in September.
    Direct materials: 8,000 × 100% = 8,000
    Conversion costs: 8,000 × 60% = 4,800

Alternative solution: Compare the equivalent units computed under each method. These comparisons are as follows (detailed computations not shown):

	Direct Materials	Conversion Costs
Equivalent units under weighted average	42,000	40,800
Equivalent units under FIFO	34,000	36,000
Difference in equivalent units	8,000	4,800

4. e   Three steps are used to obtain the answer. First, compute equivalent units of work done to date:

Direct materials = 92,000 + 24,000(90%) = 92,000 + 21,600 = 113,600
Conversion costs = 92,000 + 24,000(40%) = 92,000 + 9,600 = 101,600

Second, compute equivalent unit costs of work done to date:

$$\text{Direct materials} = \frac{\$54,560 + \$468,000}{113,600} = \frac{\$522,560}{113,600} = \$4.60$$

$$\text{Conversion costs} = \frac{\$35,560 + \$574,040}{101,600} = \frac{\$609,600}{101,600} = \$6.00$$

Third, compute the total cost of units in ending work in process:

Direct materials = 24,000(90%) × $4.60 = 21,600 × $4.60 = $ 99,360
Conversion costs = 24,000(40%) × $6.00 = 9,600 × $6.00 = $\underline{\quad 57,600}$
Work in process, May 31, 2000 $\underline{\$156,960}$

5. a   Three steps are used to obtain the answer. First, compute equivalent units of work done in the current period:

Direct materials = 92,000 + 24,000(90%) − 16,000(60%)
                 = 92,000 + 21,600 − 9,600 = 104,000
Conversion costs = 92,000 + 24,000(40%) − 16,000(20%)
                 = 92,000 + 9,600 − 3,200 = 98,400

Second, compute equivalent unit costs of work done in the current period:

Direct materials = $468,000 ÷ 104,000 = $4.50
Conversion costs = $574,040 ÷ 98,400 = $5.83

Third, compute the total cost of units in ending work in process:

Direct materials = 24,000(90%) × $4.50 = 21,600 × $4.50 = $ 97,200
Conversion costs = 24,000(40%) × $5.83 = 9,600 × $5.83 = $\underline{\quad 55,968}$
Work in process, May 31, 2000 $\underline{\$153,168}$

6. c

		Equivalent Units		
Flow of Production	Physical Units	Trans.-in Costs	Direct Materials	Conversion Costs
Work in process, May 1	25,000			
Transferred in during May	100,000			
To account for	125,000			
Completed and transferred out during May, 125,000 − 20,000	105,000	105,000	105,000	105,000
Work in process, May 31, 20,000 × 100%; 0%; 80%	20,000	20,000	-0-	16,000
Accounted for	125,000			
Work done to date		125,000	105,000	121,000

The equivalent units of direct materials for the May 31 inventory is zero because materials are added at the *end* of the process.

7. b

Flow of Production	Physical Units	Equivalent Units		
		Trans.-in Costs	Direct Materials	Conversion Costs
Work in process, May 1	25,000			
Transferred in during May	100,000			
To account for	125,000			
Completed and transferred out during May				
From work in process, May 31,	25,000			
25,000 × 0%; 100%; 40%		-0-	25,000	10,000
Started and completed				
100,000 − 20,000	80,000			
80,000 × 100%		80,000	80,000	80,000
Work in process, May 31	20,000			
20,000 × 100%; 0%; 80%		20,000	-0-	16,000
Accounted for	125,000			
Work done to date		100,000	105,000	106,000

8. a Regardless of whether the FIFO or weighted-average method is used, the effects of this error are the same because *both methods treat ending inventory exactly alike*. To illustrate the effects of the error, use assumed figures to satisfy the situation described. For example, assume ending inventory is estimated to be 50% complete as to conversion costs instead of the correct figure of 70%. Using assumed figures, the effect of this error on each of the three items specified in the question is as follows:

(1) Equivalent units are understated:

	Physical Units	Equivalent Units	
		Before Correction	After Correction
Work in process, beginning	-0-		
Started during current period	1,100		
To account for	1,100		
Completed and transferred out during current period, 1,100 − 200	900	900	900
Work in process, ending, 200 × 50%; 200 × 70%	200	100	140
Accounted for	1,100	1,000	1,040

(2) Cost per equivalent unit is overstated:
   Before correction: $2,080 ÷ 1,000 = $2.08 per unit
   After correction: $2,080 ÷ 1,040 = $2.00 per unit

(3) Cost of work completed and transferred out is overstated:
   Before correction: 900 units × $2.08 = $1,872
   After correction: 900 units × $2.00 = $1,800

If this illustration had been based on *direct materials* instead of *conversion costs*, the conclusions would be the same; however, an error in computing the percentage of completion of direct materials is less likely to occur because the quantity of direct materials needed for a completed unit or a partially completed unit can be measured more easily.

9. b Under the standard-costing method, costs are computed by multiplying actual equivalent units for each cost category by the respective standard cost per unit, as shown in Exhibit 17-9, text p. 608.

Exercise 1

a. (1) Total physical units accounted for $= 300 + 600 = 900$

  (2) Equivalent units of work done to date:

    Transferred-in costs $= 700(100\%) + 200(100\%) = 900$

    Conversion costs $= 700(100\%) + 200(50\%) = 800$

  (3) Cost per equivalent unit:

    Transferred-in costs $= (\$28,200 + \$51,000) \div 900$

                     $= \$79,200 \div 900 = \$88$

    Conversion costs $= (\$5,560 + \$36,040) \div 800$

                   $= \$41,600 \div 800 = \$52$

  (4) Costs transferred out $= 700(\$88 + \$52) = \$98,000$

  (5) Cost of ending work in process $= 200(\$88) + 200(50\%)(\$52)$

                                  $= \$17,600 + \$5,200 = \$22,800$

b. (1) Same as a(1) above, 900.

  (2) Equivalent units of work done in current period:

    Transferred-in costs $= (700 - 300)100\% + 200(100\%) = 600$

    Conversion costs $= 300(100\% - 40\%) + (700 - 300)100\% + 200(50\%)$

                       $= 180 + 400 + 100 = 680$

  (3) Cost per equivalent unit:

    Transferred-in costs $= \$51,000 \div 600 = \$85$

    Conversion costs $= \$36,040 \div 680 = \$53$

  (4) Costs transferred out $= (\$28,200 + \$5,560) + 300(100\% - 40\%)\$53 + (700 -$

                       $300(100\%)(\$85 + \$53)$

                       $= \$33,760 + \$9,540 + \$55,200 = \$98,500$

  (5) Cost of ending work in process $= 200(100\%)(\$85) + 200(50\%)(\$53)$

                                    $= \$17,000 + \$5,300 = \$22,300$

Exercise 2

a. Budgeted allocation rate for conversion costs $= \dfrac{\$200,000 + \$880,000}{36,000} = \$30$ per machine-hour

Units produced per hour $= 60$ minutes $\div 10$ minutes per unit $= 6$ units

Conversion costs allocated per unit $= \$30 \div 6 = \$5$

Conversion costs allocated to 2,000 units of Model X $= 2,000 \times \$5 = \$10,000$

Conversion costs allocated to 1,000 units of Model Y $= 1,000 \times \$5 = \$5,000$

b.

	Model X	Model Y
Direct materials	$48,000	$64,000
Conversion costs:		
Operation 1	20,000	10,000
Operation 2	10,000	5,000
Operation 3	-0-	5,000
Total manufacturing costs	$78,000	$84,000
Divide by number of units	÷2,000	÷1,000
Manufacturing cost per unit	$ 39	$ 84

c.

	Model X	Model Y
Direct materials:		
$48,000 × (100 ÷ 2,000)	$2,400	
($64,000 − $8,000) × (200 ÷ 1,000)		$11,200
Conversion costs:		
Operation 1:		
$20,000 × (100 ÷ 2,000)	1,000	
$10,000 × (200 ÷ 1,000)		2,000
Operation 2:		
$5,000 × (200 ÷ 1,000)		1,000
Ending work in process ($17,600)	$3,400	$14,200

Spoilage, Rework, and Scrap

Chapter Overview

This chapter focuses on accounting for the costs of manufacturing outputs that fail to meet established production specifications—called spoilage and rework—and residual materials that result from the production process—called scrap. As companies strive to improve product quality, managers learn that rates of spoilage, rework, and scrap regarded as normal in the past are no longer tolerable. The Appendix to the chapter illustrates the effect of the inspection point being at different stages of the production cycle.

Chapter Highlights

1. **Spoilage** is unacceptable units of production that are discarded or sold at reduced prices. **Rework** is unacceptable units of production that are subsequently repaired and sold as acceptable finished goods. **Scrap** is material left over (such as wood shavings) from making a product(s); it has a low sales value compared with the sales value of the product(s).

2. When accounting for spoilage, it is necessary to distinguish between the costs of **normal spoilage** and **abnormal spoilage**.

- Normal spoilage is an inherent result of the particular production process and arises under efficient operating conditions. The cost of normal spoilage is typically included as a component of the cost of good units manufactured (that is, normal spoilage is an inventoriable cost) because good units cannot be made without simultaneously producing spoiled units.
- Abnormal spoilage is not an inherent result of the particular production process and does not arise under efficient operating conditions. Abnormal spoilage is usually regarded as avoidable and controllable. Abnormal spoilage costs are written off as a loss of the accounting period in which detection of the spoiled units occurs.

3. Spoilage might actually occur at various stages of the production cycle but is typically detected only at one or more inspection points. An **inspection point** is the stage of the production cycle where products are checked to determine whether they are acceptable or unacceptable. There is often a single inspection at the end of the production cycle. The cost of spoiled units is assumed to be all costs incurred by spoiled units prior to inspection. If spoiled goods have a disposal value, the net cost of spoilage is computed by deducting the disposal value from the costs of the spoiled goods accumulated to the inspection point. The unit costs of normal and abnormal spoilage are the same if the two are detected simultaneously. If abnormal spoilage is detected at a different point in the production cycle than normal spoilage, however, the unit cost of abnormal spoilage differs from the unit cost of normal spoilage.

4. In process costing, all spoiled units should be counted and classified as normal and abnormal spoilage. For example, assume a process has 10,000 physical units to account for, 7,000 good units completed and transferred out, 2,000 units in ending inventory, and normal spoilage of 10% of good output. Then:

$$\text{Total spoilage} = 10,000 - 7,000 - 2,000$$
$$\text{Total spoilage} = 1,000 \text{ units}$$
$$\text{Normal spoilage} = 7,000 \times 10\% = 700 \text{ units}$$
$$\text{Abnormal spoilage} = 1,000 - 700 = 300 \text{ units}$$

5. The weighted-average, FIFO, and standard-costing methods of process costing can incorporate both normal and abnormal

spoilage by making only slight modifications to the five-step approach used in Chapter 17. The five steps (with the modifications shown in parenthesis) are as follows:

Step 1: Summarize the flow of physical units of output. (*Identify both normal spoilage and abnormal spoilage.*)

Step 2: Compute output in terms of equivalent units. (Compute equivalent units for spoilage in the same way as for good units.)

Step 3: Compute equivalent unit costs. (None)

Step 4: Summarize total costs to account for. (None)

Step 5: Assign total costs to units completed, to spoiled units, and to units in ending work-in-process inventory. (Compute the cost of each type of spoiled units and the cost of good units.)

6. The weighted-average method of process costing combines costs in beginning inventory with costs in the current period to determine the cost of good units (including a normal spoilage amount) and the cost of abnormal spoilage. EXHIBIT 18-2, text p. 634, illustrates the five-step approach for the weighted-average method. Using dollar amounts from this exhibit, summary journal entries for the completed work of the Processing Department for July are:

Finished Goods	152,075	
Work in Process—Processing		152,075

Loss from Abnormal Spoilage	5,925	
Work in Process—Processing		5,925

7. The FIFO method of process costing keeps costs in beginning inventory separate from the costs in the current period to determine the cost of goods units (including a normal spoilage amount) and the cost of abnormal spoilage. EXHIBIT 18-3, text p. 635, illustrates the five-step approach for the FIFO method.

8. The standard-costing method of process costing uses standard costs to determine the cost of good units (including a normal spoilage amount) and the cost of abnormal spoilage.

EXHIBIT 18-4, text p. 638, illustrates the five-step approach for the standard-costing method.

9. The equivalent units of spoilage computed in EXHIBITS 18-2, 18-3, and 18-4 are based on the fact that the inspection point is at the *completion of the production cycle* in the Processing Department. In this situation, all the cost of normal spoilage is allocated to good units completed and transferred out of the department because none of the units in ending work-in-process inventory passed the inspection point. On the other hand, the cost of normal spoilage is allocated to units in ending inventory (in addition to completed units), if the units in ending inventory did pass the inspection point. For example, if inspection is at the halfway stage of the production cycle, work in process that is at least 50% completed is allocated a full measure of the cost of normal spoilage.

10. The concepts of normal and abnormal spoilage (or rework) also apply to job costing, but job costing requires more detailed classifications of spoilage or rework than those used in process costing. The reason is an item such as normal spoilage or normal rework can be either *attributable to a specific job* or *common to all jobs*. Process costing classifies normal spoilage or normal rework only as common to a process. Job costing uses the following classifications, with journal entries recorded for each "Yes":

	Attributable to a Specific Job	Common to All Jobs
Normal spoilage	Yes	Yes
Abnormal spoilage	Yes	No
Normal rework	Yes	Yes
Abnormal rework	Yes	No

In the example (beginning text p. 637) the journal entries are as follows:

Normal spoilage attributable to a specific job

Materials Control	150	
Work-in-Process Control		150

The $150 is the disposal value of spoiled goods.

Normal spoilage common to all jobs
Materials Control (disposal value)   150
Manuf. OH Control
  (normal spoilage)   350
    Work-in-Process Control
      (gross cost)   500

Here the net cost of spoilage is allocated to production via the budgeted manufacturing overhead rate, which includes a provision for normal spoilage.

Abnormal spoilage
Materials Control (disposal value)   150
Loss from Abnormal Spoilage
  (net cost)   350
    Work-in-Process Control
      (gross cost)   500

Normal rework attributable to a specific job
Work-in-Process Control
  (rework cost)   190
    Materials Control   40
    Wages Payable Control   100
    Manuf. OH Allocated   50

Normal rework common to all jobs
Manuf. OH Control (rework cost)   190
    Materials Control   40
    Wages Payable Control   100
    Manuf. OH Allocated   50

Abnormal rework
Loss from Abnormal Rework
  (rework cost)   190
    Materials Control   40
    Wages Payable Control   100
    Manuf. OH Allocated   50

11. Initial recording of scrap is most often done in physical terms by weighing, counting, or some other expedient means. Scrap records not only help measure efficiency, but also control what is often a tempting source for theft. Scrap reports are prepared as source documents for periodic summaries of the amount of actual scrap compared with the budgeted or standard amount. Scrap is either sold or disposed of quickly, or stored for later sale, disposal, or reuse.

12. Accounting for scrap requires that two questions be answered:

a. When is the disposal value of scrap to be recognized: at the time scrap is *produced* or at the time scrap is *sold*?
b. How is revenue from scrap to be accounted for?

To illustrate, assume the scrap from a job has a disposal value of $45.

- Recognizing Scrap at the Time of Its Sale

  If the disposal value of scrap is *immaterial*, the simplest approach is to make a note of the quantity of scrap returned to the storeroom and to regard scrap sales as other revenues. The only journal entry is:

  Cash or Accounts Receivable   45
      Sales of Scrap   45

  If the disposal value of scrap is *material* and the scrap is sold soon after it is produced, the accounting depends on whether the scrap is attributable to a specific job or is common to all jobs:

  Scrap attributable to a specific job
  Cash or Accounts Receivable   45
      Work-in-Process Control   45

  Unlike spoilage and rework, no cost is attached to scrap and, hence, no distinction is made between normal and abnormal scrap.

  Scrap common to all jobs
  Cash or Accounts Receivable   45
      Manuf. OH Control   45

  If scrap is common to all jobs, the expected sales of scrap are considered in setting the budgeted manufacturing overhead rate. Thus, the budgeted overhead is lower than if the overhead budget had not been reduced for expected sales of scrap.

- Recognizing Scrap at the Time of Its Production

  If the value of scrap is *material* and the time between storing it and selling or reusing it can be quite long, scrap can be inventoried at a conservative estimate of its net realizable value. In this way, production costs and related scrap recovery are recognized in the same accounting period.

Scrap attributable to a specific job

Materials Control	45	
Work-in-Process Control		45

Cash or Accounts Receivable	45	
Materials Control		45

If scrap is reused rather than sold, debit Work-in-Process Control in the preceding journal entry.

Scrap common to all jobs

Materials Control	45	
Manuf. OH Control		45

Cash or Accounts Receivable	45	
Materials Control		45

Accounting for scrap under process costing is like that under job costing if scrap is common to all jobs.

13. The Appendix to this chapter illustrates how the inspection point being at different stages of the production cycle in process costing affects the respective amounts of normal and abnormal spoilage. Regardless of where inspection occurs in the production cycle, normal spoilage is computed on the basis of the number of good units that pass the inspection point during the current period. EXHIBIT 18-5, text p. 646, shows the computation of equivalent units under the weighted-average method when the inspection point is at the 50% stage of the production cycle.

Featured Exercise

Flynn Company uses a process-costing system. Selected information about the Molding Process for July 1999 follows:

	Units
Beginning work in process, 60% complete as of 7/1/99	100
Transferred in	620
Normal spoilage	40
Abnormal spoilage	50
Good units completed and transferred out	550
Ending work in process, 75% complete as of 7/31/99	80
Conversion costs in beginning inventory	$160,000
Current period conversion costs	$960,000

Spoilage is detected when the units are inspected at the end of the process.

a. Using the weighted-average method:
   (1) Compute equivalent units of conversion costs.
   (2) Compute conversion costs per equivalent unit.
   (3) Compute conversion costs component of normal spoilage.
   (4) Compute conversion costs component of abnormal spoilage.
   (5) Compute total conversion costs transferred out to the next process.
   (6) Compute conversion costs component of ending work in process.
b. Using the FIFO method, repeat part (a).

Solution

a. Weighted-average method:

(1) Flow of Production	Physical Units	Equivalent Units of Conversion Costs
Good units completed and transferred out during July	550	550
Normal spoilage	40	
40 × 100%		40
Abnormal spoilage	50	
50 × 100%		50
Work in process, July 31	80	
80 × 75%		60
Accounted for	720	
Work done to date		700

(2) $\dfrac{\text{Conversion costs per}}{\text{equivalent unit}} = \dfrac{\$160,000 + \$960,000}{700} = \dfrac{\$1,120,000}{700} = \$1,600$

(3) Conversion costs component of normal spoilage = 40 × $1,600 = $64,000

(4) Conversion costs component of abnormal spoilage = 50 × $1,600 = $80,000

(5) Conversion costs transferred out to next process

Good units completed, 550 × $1,600	$880,000
Normal spoilage, answer (3) above	64,000
Total	$944,000

(6) Conversion costs component of ending inventory = 60 × $1,600 = $96,000

b. FIFO method:

(1)

Flow of Production	Physical Units	Equivalent Units of Conversion Costs
Good units completed and transferred out during July:		
From work in process, July 1	100	
$100 \times (100\% - 60\%)$		40
Started and completed, $550 - 100$	450	450
Normal spoilage	40	
$40 \times 100\%$		40
Abnormal spoilage	50	
$50 \times 100\%$		50
Work in process, July 31	80	
$80 \times 75\%$		60
Accounted for	720	
Work done in July		640

(2) $\text{Conversion costs per equivalent unit} = \dfrac{\$960,000}{640} = \$1,500$

(3) $\text{Conversion costs component of normal spoilage} = 40 \times \$1,500 = \$60,000$

(4) $\text{Conversion costs component of abnormal spoilage} = 50 \times \$1,500 = \$75,000$

(5) Conversion costs transferred to next process

Good units completed:	
Work in process, July 1	$160,000
Conversion costs added in July	
$40 \times \$1,500$	60,000
Started and completed	
$450 \times \$1,500$	675,000
Normal spoilage, answer (3) above	60,000
Total	$955,000

(6) $\text{Conversion costs component of ending inventory} = 60 \times \$1,500 = \$90,000$

Review Questions and Exercises

Completion Statements

Fill in the blank(s) to complete each statement.

1. Unacceptable units of production that are discarded or sold at reduced prices are called _____.

2. Unacceptable units of production that are subsequently repaired and sold as acceptable finished units are called _____.

3. _____ is material left over from making a product(s); it has a low sales value compared with the sales value of the product(s).

4. _____ is an inherent result of the particular production process and arises under efficient operating conditions.

5. The cost of abnormal spoilage is debited to which account? _____

6. Accounting for spoilage or rework in job-costing systems requires what three distinctions?

_____

_____

_____

True-False

Indicate whether each statement is true (T) or false (F).

___ 1. Normal spoilage is a period cost.

___ 2. In computing equivalent units for process costing, it is more accurate to include normal spoilage and exclude abnormal spoilage.

___ 3. The appropriate base to use in computing normal spoilage is actual units started in production.

___ 4. If a company adheres to a goal of zero defects, all of its spoilage is regarded as abnormal.

___ 5. The cost of normal spoilage should never be allocated to units in ending work-in-process inventory.

___ 6. Unlike spoilage and rework, no cost is attached to scrap and, hence, scrap is not classified as normal or abnormal.

___ 7. (Appendix) Regardless of where in the production cycle inspection occurs, normal spoilage is computed on the basis of the number of good units that pass the inspection point during the current period.

Multiple Choice

Select the best answer to each question. Space is provided for computations after the quantitative questions.

___ 1. (CPA) The Forming Department is the first of a two-stage production process. Spoilage is detected at the end of the Forming Department. Costs of spoiled units are assigned to units completed and transferred to the second department in the period spoilage is detected. The following information concerns Forming's conversion costs in May 2000:

	Units	Conv. Costs
Beginning work in process (50% complete)	2,000	$10,000
Units started during May	8,000	75,500
Spoilage—normal	500	
Units completed and transferred out	7,000	
Ending work in process (80% complete)	2,500	

Using the weighted-average method, how much of Forming's conversion costs were transferred to the second production department?
a. $59,850
b. $64,125
c. $67,500
d. $71,250

2. Using the data in question 1 and the FIFO method, how much of the Forming Department's conversion costs were transferred to the second production department? (Round equivalent unit cost to four decimal places.)
   a. $58,853
   b. $66,618
   c. $67,735
   d. $69,603

3. (CMA) During March of the current fiscal year, Mercer Company completed 50,000 units costing $600,000, exclusive of spoilage allocation. Of these completed units, 25,000 were sold during the month. An additional 10,000 units, costing $80,000, are 50% complete at March 31. The inspection point is at the end of the production cycle. For the month, normal spoilage is $20,000 and abnormal spoilage is $50,000. The portion of total spoilage costs that should be charged against revenues in March is:
   a. $50,000.
   b. $20,000.
   c. $70,000.
   d. $60,000.
   e. $30,000.

4. If spoilage occurs that is normal and common to all jobs, Work-in-Process Control should be credited with:
   a. nothing.
   b. the disposal value of the spoiled goods.
   c. the net spoilage cost.
   d. the gross spoilage cost.

5. In a job-costing system, Work-in-Process Control ordinarily is debited with the cost of rework that is:
   a. abnormal.
   b. normal and common to all jobs.
   c. normal and attributable to a specific job.
   d. discarded.

6. (CPA) Simpson Company manufactures electric drills to the exacting specifications of various customers. During April, Job 403 for the production of 1,100 drills is completed at the following costs per unit:

Direct materials	$10
Direct manufacturing labour	8
Manufacturing overhead allocated	12
Total manufacturing costs	$30

Final inspection of Job 403 discloses 50 defective units and 100 units of normal spoilage attritible to this specific job. The defective drills are reworked at a total cost of $500 and the spoiled drills are sold to a jobber for $1,500. What is the unit cost of the good units produced on Job 403?
   a. $33
   b. $32
   c. $30
   d. $29

7. (CPA) Under Heller Company's job-costing system, the budgeted manufacturing overhead rate includes the estimated costs of defective work (considered normal in the manufacturing process). During March Job No. 210 for 2,000 hand saws is completed at the following costs per unit:

Direct materials	$ 5
Direct manufacturing labour	4
Manufacturing overhead allocated (at 150% of direct manufacturing labour cost)	6
Total manufacturing costs	$15

Final inspection of Job No. 210 discloses 100 defective saws were reworked at a cost of $2 per unit for direct manufacturing labour, plus manufacturing overhead at the budgeted rate. The defective units on Job No. 210 are considered normal. What is the total rework cost and to which account should it be debited?

	Rework cost	Account debited
a.	$200	Work-in-Process Control
b.	$200	Manuf. OH Control
c.	$500	Work-in-Process Control
d.	$500	Manuf. OH Control

8. (CPA adapted) If the disposal value of scrap is material, the scrap is sold soon after its production, and the scrap is common to all jobs in a manufacturing process, the scrap is recorded as a:

a. credit to Manufacturing Overhead Control.
b. debit to Manufacturing Overhead Control.
c. credit to Finished Goods Control.
d. credit to Work-in-Process Control.

Exercises

1. (CMA) JC Company uses a process-costing system. A unit of product passes through three departments — Molding, Assembly, and Finishing — before it is completed. The following activity took place in the Finishing Department during May:

	Units
Work in process, May 1	1,400
Transferred in from the Assembly Department	14,000
Spoilage	700
Completed and transferred out to finished goods inventory	11,200

Direct materials are added at the beginning of the processing in the Finishing Department without changing the number of units processed. Conversion costs are added evenly during the process. The work-in-process inventory was 70% complete as to conversion costs on May 1 and 40% complete as to conversion costs on May 31. All spoilage is detected at the inspection point, which occurs at the end of the production cycle; 560 of the units spoiled are considered normal spoilage.

JC Company uses the weighted-average method. The equivalent unit costs for May are as follows:

	Equivalent Unit Costs
Transferred-in costs	$5.00
Direct materials	1.00
Conversion costs	3.00
Total manufacturing costs	$9.00

a. Compute the equivalent units of transferred-in costs, direct materials, and conversion costs.
b. Compute the cost of units completed and transferred from the Finishing Department to finished goods inventory during May.
c. Compute the cost assigned to the Finishing Department's work-in-process inventory on May 31.
d. Compute the cost of abnormal spoilage.
e. Compute the total transferred-in costs of the Finishing Department during May, assuming the transferred-in costs component of the work-in-process inventory of the Finishing Department on May 1 amounted to $6,300.

2. Boucher Company uses a job-costing system. During November 1999, the following costs are incurred on Job 109 to manufacture 200 motors:

Original costs:
Direct materials	$ 6,600
Direct manufacturing labour	8,000
Manufacturing overhead allocated	
(150% of direct manufacturing labour)	12,000
Total	$26,600

Direct costs of reworking 10 motors:
Direct materials	$1,000
Direct manufacturing labour	1,600
Total	$2,600

a. Prepare the journal entry to record the rework costs, assuming the rework is attributable specifically to Job 109.
b. Compute the cost per finished motor for Job 109, assuming the rework is attributable specifically to this job.
c. Prepare the journal entry to record the rework costs, assuming the rework is common to all jobs.
d. Compute the cost per finished motor for Job 109, assuming the rework is common to all jobs.

Answers to Chapter 18 Review Questions and Exercises

Completion Statements

1. spoilage
2. rework
3. Scrap
4. Normal spoilage
5. Loss from Abnormal Spoilage
6. normal spoilage (rework) attributable to a specific job, normal spoilage (rework) common to all jobs, and abnormal spoilage (rework)

True-False

1. F   Normal spoilage is an inventoriable cost. Abnormal spoilage is a period cost.
2. F   In computing equivalent units for process costing, it is more accurate to include both normal and abnormal spoilage. Panel A of Exhibit 18-2, text p. 634, illustrates this approach.
3. F   The appropriate base to use in computing normal spoilage is *total units of good output*. Actual units started in production is an inappropriate base because it can include both normal and abnormal spoilage.
4. T
5. F   A portion of normal spoilage cost should be allocated to units in ending work-in-process inventory, if these units have passed the inspection point. For example, if the inspection point is at the 50% stage of the production cycle and ending work in process is 70% complete, normal spoilage cost should be allocated to this inventory. The Appendix to this chapter illustrates the effects of the inspection point being at three different stages of the production cycle.
6. T
7. T

Multiple Choice

1. c   Three steps are used to obtain the answer. First, compute equivalent units of conversion costs:

$$7,000 + 500 + 2,500(80\%) = 7,000 + 500 + 2,000 = 9,500$$

Second, compute equivalent unit cost of conversion costs:

$$\frac{\$10,000 + \$75,500}{9,500} = \frac{\$85,500}{9,500} = \$9$$

Third, compute the conversion costs transferred from the Forming Department to the second production department:

$$(7,000 + 500) \times \$9 = 7,500 \times \$9 = \$67,500$$

Alternative solution:

Let X   =   Conversion costs transferred out of Forming
X   =   Total conversion costs to account for in Forming − Ending work in process
X   =   ($10,000 + $75,500) − (2,500 × 80% × $9)
X   = $85,500 − (2,000 × $9)
X   = $85,500 − $18,000 = $67,500

2. c   Three steps are used to obtain the answer. First, compute equivalent units of conversion costs:

Beginning work in process   =   2,000 × 50% = 1,000
Work done in current period   =   7,000 + 500 + 2,500(80%) − 2,000(50%)
                      =   7,500 + 2,000 − 1,000 = 8,500

Second, compute the equivalent unit cost of conversion costs:

$$\text{Beginning work in process} = \$10,000 \div 1,000 = \$10$$
$$\text{Work done in current period} = \$75,500 \div 8,500 = \$8.8824$$

Third, compute the conversion costs transferred from the Forming Department to the second production department:

Beginning work in process:

Previous period costs, $1,000 \times \$10$	$10,000
Current period costs, $(2,000 - 1,000) \times \$8.8824$	8,882
Started and completed	
Good units, $(7,000 - 2,000) \times \$8.8824$	44,412
Normal spoilage units, $500 \times \$8.8824$	4,441
Conversion costs transferred from the Forming Department	$67,735

Alternative solution:

$$\text{Let } X = \text{Conversion costs transferred out of Forming}$$
$$X = \text{Total conversion costs to account for in Forming} - \text{Ending work in process}$$
$$X = (\$10,000 + \$75,500) - (2,500 \times 80\% \times \$8.8824)$$
$$X = \$85,500 - (2,000 \times \$8.8824)$$
$$X = \$85,500 - \$17,765 = \$67,735$$

3. d Normal spoilage included in cost of goods sold

$\$20,000 \times (25,000 \div 50,000)$	$10,000
Abnormal spoilage	50,000
Total spoilage costs charged against revenues	$60,000

4. d This question refers to the second journal entry in paragraph 10 of the Chapter Highlights.

5. c This question refers to the fourth journal entry in paragraph 10 of the Chapter Highlights.

6. b Because the electric drills are manufactured to the exacting specifications of various customers, the rework and normal spoilage are *attributable specifically to Job 403*. Rework costs increase the cost of good units produced, and the disposal value of spoilage decreases the cost of good units produced.

$$\text{Let } X = \text{Unit cost of good units produced}$$
$$X = [(1,100 \times \$30) + \$500 - \$1,500] \div (1,100 - 100)$$
$$X = (\$33,000 - \$1,000) \div 1,000$$
$$X = \$32,000 \div 1,000 = \$32$$

Note that if the rework and normal spoilage are *common to all jobs*, an allowance for these costs is included in the budgeted manufacturing overhead rate. In that case,

$$\text{Let } Y = \text{Unit cost of good units produced}$$
$$Y = [(1,100 \times \$30) - (100 \times \$30)] \div (1,100 - 100)$$
$$Y = (\$33,000 - \$3,000) \div 1,000$$
$$Y = \$30,000 \div 1,000 = \$30$$

7. d Total rework cost $= [\$2 + (\$2 \times 150\%)] \times 100$
$$= (\$2 + \$3) \times 100 = \$500$$

Because normal rework is included in the budgeted overhead rate, this means the normal rework is *common to all jobs*. Thus, debit Manufacturing Overhead Control, as shown in the fifth journal entry in paragraph 10 of the Chapter Highlights.

8. a   If the disposal value of scrap is material, the scrap is sold soon after its production, and the scrap is common to all jobs in a manufacturing process, the scrap is recorded as a credit to Manufacturing Overhead Control. The debit in the journal entry is to Cash or Accounts Receivable. If all of the conditions are the same except the scrap is attributable to a specific job, the debit remains the same and credit Work-in-Process Control.

Exercise 1

a.

Flow of Production	Physical Units	Equivalent Units		
		Trans.-in Costs	Direct Materials	Conversion Costs
Work in process, May 1	1,400			
Transferred in during May	14,000			
To account for	15,400			
Good units completed and transferred out	11,200	11,200	11,200	11,200
Normal spoilage	560	560	560	560
Abnormal spoilage, 700 − 560	140	140	140	140
Work in process, May 1, 15,400 − 140 − 560 − 11,200	3,500			
3,500 × 100%; 100%; 40%		3,500	3,500	1,400
Accounted for	15,400			
Work done to date		15,400	15,400	13,300

b. Because spoilage is detected at the completion of work in the Finishing Department, the cost of all normal spoilage should be allocated to the good units completed and transferred out of the Finishing Department: $(11,200 \times \$9.00) + (560 \times \$9.00) = \$105,840$. This amount is debited to Finished Goods and credited to Work in Process − Finishing Department.

c. Using the equivalent unit amounts for the May 31 work-in-process inventory from the schedule in part (a) above, the costs of this inventory are: $(3,500 \times \$5) + (3,500 \times \$1) + (1,400 \times \$3) = \$17,500 + \$3,500 + \$4,200 = \$25,200$.

d. The cost of abnormal spoilage $= 140 \times \$9.00 = \$1,260$. This amount is debited to Loss from Abnormal Spoilage and credited to Work in Process − Finishing Department.

e. Under the weighted-average method, the equivalent unit cost for each cost category is computed by dividing costs incurred to date by work done to date.

Let X = Transferred-in costs of the Finishing Department during May (that is, costs transferred out of the Assembly Department)

$$(X + \$6,300) \div 15,400 = \$5.00$$
$$X + \$6,300 = \$5.00 \times 15,400$$
$$X = \$77,000 - \$6,300$$
$$X = \$70,700$$

Exercise 2

a. Work-in-Process Control   5,000
      Materials Control   1,000
      Wages Payable Control   1,600
      Manuf. Overhead Allocated
        ($1,600 × 150%)   2,400

b. Cost per finished motor $= \dfrac{\$26,600 + \$5,000}{200} = \dfrac{\$31,600}{200} = \$158$

c. Manuf. Overhead Control   5,000
      Materials Control   1,000
      Wages Payable Control   1,600
      Manuf. Overhead Allocated
        ($1,600 × 150%)   2,400

d. Cost per finished motor = $26,600 ÷ 200 = $133

Cost Management: Quality, Time, and the Theory of Constraints

Chapter Overview

This chapter examines how management accounting helps managers take initiatives that improve quality and reduce delivery times, and make production decisions under conditions of many constraints. Issues relating to quality and timeliness are particularly important because they affect a company's ability to compete in the global marketplace and involve interdependencies across the entire value chain. The chapter uses the relevant-revenues and relevant-cost analysis introduced in Chapter 11.

Chapter Highlights

1. Companies throughout the world view total quality management as one of the most important key success factors of the last decade because it decreases costs, maintains or increases revenues, and increases customer satisfaction. There are several prestigious awards to recognize exceptional quality such as the Malcolm Baldridge Quality Award in the United States. International quality standards also have emerged. For example, ISO 9000, adopted by more than 85 countries, was created to enable companies to effectively document and certify their quality system elements.

2. Two basic aspects of quality are **quality of design** and **conformance quality**.

- Quality of design measures how closely the characteristics of products or services meet the needs and wants of customers. For example, if customers of photocopying machines need copiers that copy and fax, machines that fail to perform both of these functions fail in the quality of their design.
- Conformance quality refers to the performance of a product or service according to design and production specifications. For example, if a photocopying machine mishandles paper, it fails to satisfy conformance quality.

To ensure that actual performance achieves customer satisfaction, companies must design products to satisfy customers through quality of design and meet design specifications through conformance quality.

3. Companies incur the **costs of quality (COQ)** to prevent or rectify the production of low-quality products. These costs focus on conformance quality and occur in all business functions of the value chain. COQ programs use four cost categories:

a. **Prevention costs** are incurred to preclude the production of products that do not conform to specifications.
b. **Appraisal costs** are incurred to detect which of the individual units of products do not conform to specifications.
c. **Internal failure costs** are incurred by a nonconforming product *before* shipping it to customers.
d. **External failure costs** are incurred by a nonconforming product *after* shipping it to customers.

COQ reports give more insight when managers compare trends over time. In successful quality programs, there is a decrease over time in the COQ as a percentage of revenues as well as in the sum of internal and external failure costs as a percentage of the COQ. Many companies believe they should eliminate all failure costs and have zero defects.

4. The COQ for a company can be determined by using an activity-based approach with seven steps:

Step 1: Identify the product whose quality is to be scrutinized.

Step 2: Identify the direct COQ of the product.

Step 3: Select the cost-allocation bases to use for allocating indirect COQ to the product.

Step 4: Identify the indirect COQ associated with each cost-allocation base.

Step 5: Compute the rate per unit of each cost-allocation base used to allocate indirect COQ to products.

Step 6: Compute the indirect COQ allocated to the product.

Step 7: Compute the total COQ of the product by adding all of the direct and indirect costs assigned to it.

The total COQ in Step 7 typically exclude opportunity costs, such as forgone contribution margin from lost sales, lost production, or lower prices resulting from poor quality. While opportunity costs can be important driving forces in quality-improvement programs, they are difficult to estimate.

5.   Three common techniques companies use to identify and analyze quality problems are **control charts, Pareto diagrams,** and **cause-and-effect diagrams** (also called *fishbone diagrams*). A control chart is a key tool of statistical quality control (SOQ) that distinguishes between random and nonrandom variation in an operating process. A control chart is a graph of a series of successive observations of a particular step, procedure, or operation taken at regular time intervals. Each observation is plotted relative to specified ranges that represent the expected statistical distribution. Only those observations outside the control limits are regarded as nonrandom and worth investigating. Observations outside control limits serve as inputs for Pareto diagrams. These diagrams indicate how frequently each type of failure (defect) occurs. The most frequently recurring and costly problems identified by Pareto diagrams are analyzed using cause-and-effect diagrams that pinpoint potential causes of failures or defects—human factors, methods and design factors, machine-related factors, and materials-related factors.

6.   A cause-and-effect diagram can help engineers identify alternative solutions to quality problems. In turn, these alternatives can be analyzed in terms of relevant costs and relevant benefits. The relevant costs of quality improvement are the incremental costs incurred to implement the quality program. The relevant benefits are lower internal and external failure costs and greater contribution margin from higher sales attributable to the quality improvements.

7.   Customer satisfaction is an important element of quality programs. Customer satisfaction is difficult to gauge precisely, but companies track trends in customer satisfaction using both financial and nonfinancial measures. The four COQ are the financial measures. For example, the costs of external failures—such as warranty repair costs and forgone contribution margin on lost sales—are financial measures of poor customer satisfaction. Nonfinancial measures of customer satisfaction include number of customer complaints, number of defective units shipped to customers as a percentage of total units shipped, and on-time delivery rate (percentage of shipments made on or before the scheduled delivery date).

8.   Prevention costs, appraisal costs, and internal failure costs are the financial measures of quality performance inside the company. Examples of nonfinancial measures of internal quality performance are number of defects for each product line and process yield (ratio of good output to total output). For a single reporting period, financial and nonfinancial measures of internal quality have limited meaning. They provide much more information when managers examine trends over time.

9.   Measuring the COQ and the nonfinancial aspects of quality have distinctly different advantages. COQ reports serve as a common denominator for measuring overall quality performance and for evaluating trade-offs among prevention costs and failure costs. Nonfinancial measures of quality are often easy to quantify and understand. These measures direct attention to physical processes and help

focus attention on the precise problem areas that need improvement. Most organizations use both financial and nonfinancial measures to gauge quality performance.

10. Companies increasingly view time as a key success factor. Doing things faster helps to increase revenues and decrease costs. Two common operational measures of time are **customer-response time and on-time performance.**

- Customer-response time is the amount of time it takes to deliver a product or perform a service once a customer places the order. Paragraph 11 discusses customer-response time.
- On-time performance refers to situations in which the product or service is actually delivered by the time it is scheduled to be delivered. On-time performance is an important element of customer satisfaction because customers want and expect on-time deliveries.

Note that there is a trade-off between customer-response time and on-time performance: simply scheduling longer customer-response times makes achieving on-time performance easier.

11. Three components of customer-response time are (a) *order receipt time*, (b) **manufacturing lead time** (also called **manufacturing cycle time**), and (c) *order delivery time*. Order receipt time is the time it takes the Marketing Department to specify a customer's exact requirements to Manufacturing. Manufacturing lead time is the amount of time that transpires once an order is ready to start on the production line (ready to set up) until it becomes a finished good. Manufacturing lead time is the sum of waiting time and manufacturing time for an order. Order delivery time is the time it takes to deliver a completed order to the customer.

12. A **time driver** is any factor where change in the factor causes a change in the speed with which an activity is undertaken. Two important time drivers are (a) uncertainty about when customers will order products or

services and (b) limited capacity and **bottlenecks**. A bottleneck is an operation where the work required to be performed approaches or exceeds the available capacity. For example, a bottleneck is created and delays occur if products that need to be processed at a particular machine arrive while the machine is being used to process other products. **Average waiting time** is the average amount of time that an order waits in line before it is set up and processed. Average waiting time is inversely related to the amount of unused capacity. That is, the more unused capacity, the greater the likelihood that an order arrives when an operation is idle. The formula, text p. 670, computes average waiting time if only one product is manufactured.

13. In some instances, introducing a new product causes delays in the delivery of all of the products. For example, introducing a new product can cause unused capacity to shrink, increasing the probability that new orders will arrive while existing orders are being manufactured or are waiting to be manufactured. Because time is a key factor in competitiveness, the management accountant must identify and analyze the cost of delays in calculating the relevant costs and relevant revenues of introducing a new product.

14. The example, bottom of text p. 670, considers whether or not to introduce a new product, a special type of piston. Interestingly enough, even though the new product has a positive contribution margin of $1,600 per order, the analysis of relevant revenues and relevant costs indicates not to introduce the new product because of the negative effects it has on the existing product—increased inventory carrying costs caused by a higher average manufacturing lead time and decreased revenues caused by customers who are unwilling to pay as high a price for slower delivery. EXHIBIT 19-8, text p. 671, presents the relevant revenues and relevant costs for this decision.

15. When products are made from multiple parts and processed on different machines, interdependencies arise among operations. Some operations cannot be started until parts

from a previous operation are available. In these cases, waiting time occurs for two reasons. First, parts that require processing at a bottleneck machine must wait until the bottleneck machine is free. Second, parts made on nonbottleneck machines subsequent to the bottleneck machine must wait until parts coming from the bottleneck machine arrive.

16. The **theory of constraints (TOC)** describes methods to maximize operating income when both bottleneck and nonbottleneck operations exist. TOC defines three measurements:

- **Throughput contribution** equals revenues minus direct material costs of the goods sold.
- *Investments* equal the sum of material costs in direct materials, work-in-process, and finished goods inventories; R&D costs; and costs of equipment and buildings.
- *Operating costs* equal all manufacturing and nonmanufacturing costs (other than direct materials) incurred to earn throughput contribution. Operating costs include salaries and wages, rent, utilities, and amortization.

The objective of TOC is to increase throughput contribution while decreasing investments and operating costs. TOC considers a short-run time horizon and assumes operating costs are fixed.

17. TOC emphasizes the management of bottleneck operations as the key to improving the performance of the production system as a whole. Managing a bottleneck operation requires four steps:

Step 1: Recognize the bottleneck operation determines throughput contribution of the system as a whole.

Step 2: Find the bottleneck resource by identifying resources with large quantities of inventory waiting to be worked on.

Step 3: Keep the bottleneck operation busy and subordinate all nonbottleneck operations to it. That is, the needs of the bottleneck operation determine the production schedule of nonbottleneck operations.

Step 4: Take actions to increase the efficiency and capacity of the bottleneck operation. The objective is to increase throughput contribution minus the incremental costs of taking such actions.

Featured Exercise

Miller Company expects to spend $100,000 in the year 2000 for appraisal costs if it does not change its inspection method for incoming materials. If Wellington decides to implement a new inspection method, it will save fixed appraisal costs of $10,000 and variable appraisal costs of $0.30 per kilogram of materials inspected. The new method requires annual training costs of $15,000 and equipment rental of $40,000 per year. Each unit of finished product requires two kilograms of materials.

Internal failure costs average $40 per failed unit of finished product. During 1999, 10% of all completed units had to be reworked. External failure costs average $100 per failed unit of finished product. The company's average external failure rate is 2% of units sold. Assume there are no inventories.

a. If the new method is used, how much will appraisal costs change in 2000 if 200,000 kilograms of materials are inspected?

b. Assume the new inspection method reduces failed units of finished product by 20%. How much will internal failure costs change in 2000 if 200,000 kilograms of materials are inspected?

c. Assume the new inspection method reduces external product failures by 50%. How much will external failure costs change in 2000 if 200,000 kilograms of materials are inspected?

Solution

a. Savings in existing appraisal costs:

Fixed portion	$10,000
Variable portion, 200,000 × $0.30	60,000
Total	70,000
Deduct additional appraisal costs:	
Training ($15,000) and equipment rental ($40,000)	55,000
Decrease in appraisal costs	$15,000

b. Production of finished product = 200,000 kilograms ÷ 2 kilograms per unit = 100,000 units
Internally failed units with original inspection method = 100,000 × 0.10 = 10,000 units
Decrease in internal failure costs with new inspection method = 10,000 × 0.20 × $40
= $80,000

c. Production of finished product (including reworked units), from (b) = 100,000 units
Externally failed units with new inspection method = 100,000 × 0.02 = 2,000 units
Decrease in external failure costs with new inspection method = 2,000 × 0.50 × $100
= $100,000

Review Questions and Exercises

Completion Statements

Fill in the blank(s) to complete each statement.

1. _____ measures how closely the characteristics of products or services meet the needs and wants of customers.

2. _____ quality refers to the performance of a product or service according to design and production specifications.

3. Costs of quality (COQ) are classified into which four categories? _____
_____
_____

4. The amount of time it takes to deliver a product or perform a service once a customer places the order is called _____
_____.

5. _____ is the amount of time that transpires once an order is ready to start on the production line (ready to set up) to when it becomes a finished good.

6. An operation where the work required to be performed approaches or exceeds the available capacity is called a _____.

7. Under the theory of constraints, throughput contribution equals _____
_____.

True-False

Indicate whether each statement is true (T) or false (F).

___ 1. Costs of quality incurred in detecting which of the individual products do not conform to specifications are called internal failure costs.

___ 2. All of the costs of quality entail cash outflows.

___ 3. Costs of quality are incurred across the entire value chain.

___ 4. Statistical quality control often uses Pareto diagrams whose basic purpose is to detect operations that are not performing normally.

___ 5. A Pareto diagram helps to identify the potential causes of product failure.

___ 6. Customer-response time is an example of a nonfinancial measure of performance used in quality-improvement programs.

___ 7. Average waiting time is inversely related to the amount of unused capacity.

___ 8. Considering only quantitative factors, it may be undesirable to introduce a new product that has a positive contribution margin, even though machine capacity is available.

___ 9. It is undesirable to have unused capacity at the bottleneck operation in a manufacturing plant.

Multiple Choice

Select the best answer to each question. Space is provided for computations after the quantitative questions.

___ 1. (CMA adapted) The costs of rework in a quality-improvement program are categorized as:
   a. external failure costs.
   b. internal failure costs.
   c. training costs.
   d. prevention costs.
   e. appraisal costs.

___ 2. (CMA) The costs of using statistical quality control in a quality-improvement program are categorized as:
   a. external failure costs.
   b. internal failure costs.
   c. training costs.
   d. prevention costs.
   e. appraisal costs.

___ 3. (CMA) All of the following costs are generally included in a costs of quality report *except*:
   a. warranty claims.
   b. forgone contribution margin on lost sales.
   c. supplier evaluations.
   d. design engineering.
   e. quality training.

4. (CMA) The following selected line items are from the Cost of Quality Report for Watson Company for May.

Cost
Rework	$ 725
Equipment maintenance	1,154
Product testing	786
Product repair	695

Watson's total prevention and appraisal costs for May is:
a. $786.
b. $1,154.
c. $1,849.
d. $1,940.
e. $2,665.

5. John's Custom Shirts has variable demand. Historically, demand has ranged from 20 to 40 shirts a day with an average of 30. John works 8 hours a day, 5 days a week. Each order he receives is to custom print one shirt and each shirt takes 12 minutes to print. The average waiting time (rounded to nearest tenth of a minute) is:
a. 1.8 minutes.
b. 14.1 minutes.
c. 18.0 minutes.
d. 36.0 minutes.

6. Ashmore Company has two production departments, Cutting and Finishing. The Cutting Department is constrained by the speed of the cutting machines. The Finishing Department is constrained by the speed of the workers. The Finishing Department normally waits on work coming from the Cutting Department. Each department works an 8-hour day. If the Cutting Department were to begin work 2 hours earlier than the Finishing Department each day (thereby working a 10-hour day), the two departments would finish their work at about the same time. Not only would this change eliminate the bottleneck, but also it would increase production by 40 finished units per day. The number of units in finished goods inventory would remain the same. It costs $400 to operate the Cutting Department 2 more hours per day. The contribution margin is $15 per unit. If the Cutting Department operates 10 hours per day, the total production per day is:
a. 160 units.
b. 200 units.
c. 220 units.
d. 400 units.

7. Using the data in question 6, and assuming the Cutting Department operates 10 hours per day, the total contribution margin per day:
a. increases by $200.
b. remains the same.
c. decreases by $200.
d. decreases by $400.

8. Which of the following is not one of the steps in managing bottleneck operations under the theory of constraints?
a. Subordinate all nonbottleneck operations to the bottleneck operation.
b. Increase the efficiency and capacity of the bottleneck operation.
c. Identify the bottleneck operation.
d. Increase the efficiency and capacity of nonbottleneck operations.

Exercises

1. Palmateer Company manufactures two products, C and P. Pertinent information is as follows:

	Product C	Product P
Selling price	$90	$100
Market demand per week	100 units	50 units
Direct material costs	$45	$40
Time required to produce one unit:		
Operation 1	18 minutes	10 minutes
Operation 2	15 minutes	30 minutes
Operation 3	10 minutes	5 minutes
Operation 4	12 minutes	10 minutes

Each operation has a capacity of 2,400 minutes per week.

What production schedule for C and P maximizes Palmateer's weekly throughput contribution? Show your computations.

2. Huntington Industries makes an electronic component in two departments, Machining and Assembly. The capacity per month is 30,000 units in the Machining Department and 20,000 units in the Assembly Department. The only variable costs of the product are direct material costs of $100 per unit. All direct material costs are incurred in the Machining Department. All other costs of operating the two departments are fixed costs. Huntington can sell as many of this electronic component as it produces at a selling price of $300 per unit.

Assuming any defective units produced in either department must be scrapped:
a. Compute the loss that occurs if a defective unit is produced in the Machining Department.
b. Compute the loss that occurs if a defective unit is produced in the Assembly Department.
c. Do your answers in parts (a) and (b) relate to the theory of constraints? Explain.

Answers of Chapter 19 Review Questions and Exercises

Completion Statements

1. Quality of design
2. Conformance
3. prevention costs, appraisal costs, internal failure costs, external failure costs
4. customer-response time
5. Manufacturing lead time (Manufacturing cycle time)
6. bottleneck
7. revenues minus direct material costs of the goods sold

True-False

1. F   The statement describes *appraisal costs*, not *internal failure costs*. Internal failure costs are incurred by a nonconforming product before it is shipped to customers.
2. F   The opportunity-cost portion of external failure costs —estimated forgone contribution margin on lost sales (shown in Panel B of Exhibit 19-2, text p. 659)—does not entail cash outflows.
3. T
4. F   Statistical quality control often uses *control charts* whose basic purpose is to detect operations that are not performing normally.
5. F   The statement describes a *cause-and-effect diagram* (also called a *fishbone diagram*), not a *Pareto diagram*. A Pareto diagram indicates how frequently each type of failure (defect)

occurs. Exhibit 19-5, text p. 662, shows a cause-and-effect diagram, and Exhibit 19-4, text p. 662, shows a Pareto diagram.

6. T

7. T

8. T

9. F   If demand uncertainty is high, some unused capacity of the bottleneck operation is desirable. Increasing the capacity of the bottleneck operation can reduce average waiting time and inventories.

Multiple Choice

1. b   The costs incurred by a nonconforming product *before* it is shipped to the customer (such as reworked units) are internal failure costs.

2. e   The costs incurred in detecting which of the individual units of product do not conform to specifications (such as the costs of product testing) are appraisal costs.

3. b   A COQ report generally does not include opportunity costs. Panel A of Exhibit 19-2, text p. 659, illustrates this point.

4. d   Equipment maintenance is a prevention cost and product testing is an appraisal cost: $1,154 + $786 = $1,940. Rework is an internal failure cost. Product repair is an external failure cost, assuming the repair takes place after the product is shipped to customers.

5. c   The formula for average waiting time (AWT) is:

$$AWT = \frac{\left(\begin{matrix}\text{Avg. number of}\\ \text{orders per day}\end{matrix}\right) \times \left(\begin{matrix}\text{Manuf. time}\\ \text{per order}\end{matrix}\right)^2}{2 \times \left[\begin{matrix}\text{Daily capacity}\\ \text{in minutes}\end{matrix} - \left(\begin{matrix}\text{Avg. number of}\\ \text{orders per day}\end{matrix} \times \begin{matrix}\text{Manuf. time}\\ \text{per order}\end{matrix}\right)\right]}$$

$$AWT = \frac{30 \times (12)^2}{2 \times [(8 \times 60) - (30 \times 12)]}$$

$$AWT = \frac{30 \times 144}{2 \times (480 - 360)}$$

$$AWT = \frac{4,320}{240} = 18 \text{ minutes}$$

6. b   The increase of 2 hours per day in the Cutting Department increases the company's production of finished goods by 40 units per day. Thus, the company's production of finished goods per hour of Cutting Department time is 20 units (40 ÷ 2), and the company's total production of finished goods per day is 200 units (20 × 10). *Alternative solution:* If 40 additional finished units are produced in 20% (2 hours ÷ 10 hours) of the Cutting Department's expanded time per day, the company's total production of finished goods per day is 200 units (40 ÷ 0.20).

7. a   Change in total contribution margin per day = (40 × $15) − $400
                                                       = $600 − $400 = $200 increase

8. d   The theory of constraints emphasizes the management of *bottleneck* operations as the key to improving the performance of the production system as a whole. Increasing the efficiency and capacity of *nonbottleneck* operations does not improve that performance.

Exercise 1

Four steps are used to obtain the answer. First, compute the throughput contribution per unit of each product.

	Product C	Product P
Selling price	$90	$100
Deduct direct material costs	45	40
Throughput contribution	$45	$ 60

Second, determine whether there is a bottleneck operation.

Operation	Minutes Required for C	Minutes Required for P	Total Required Minutes
1	$18 \times 100 = 1{,}800$	$10 \times 50 = 500$	$1{,}800 + 500 = 2{,}300$
2	$15 \times 100 = 1{,}500$	$30 \times 50 = 1{,}500$	$1{,}500 + 1{,}500 = 3{,}000$
3	$10 \times 100 = 1{,}000$	$5 \times 50 = 250$	$1{,}000 + 250 = 1{,}250$
4	$12 \times 100 = 1{,}200$	$10 \times 50 = 500$	$1{,}200 + 500 = 1{,}700$

Operation 2 is the only bottleneck operation because its total required minutes exceed its capacity of 2,400 minutes. (Note that if there were no bottleneck operations, the production schedule to meet market demand would be 100 units of C and 50 units of P.)

Third, determine the throughput contribution per unit of the bottleneck operation.

Product C = $45 ÷ 15 minutes = $3 per minute of Operation 2
Product P = $60 ÷ 30 minutes = $2 per minute of Operation 2

Fourth, determine the production schedule of C and P that maximizes throughput contribution.

Given the results in step 3, produce as much C as Operation 2 allows and use the remainder of its capacity to produce P:

Product	Utilization of Operation 2	Production Schedule
C	1,500 minutes (from step 2)	$1{,}500 ÷ 15 = 100$ units
P	$2{,}400 - 1{,}500 = 900$ minutes	$900 ÷ 30 = 30$ units

Therefore, the maximum throughput contribution = (100 × $45) + (30 × $60) = $6,300.

Exercise 2

a.	Direct material costs	$100
	Add forgone contribution margin on lost sale, $0 because Machining has more capacity than Assembly	0
	Loss from producing a defective unit in Machining	$100
b.	Direct material costs	$100
	Add forgone contribution margin on lost sale $300 − $100	200
	Loss from producing a defective unit in Assembly	$300

c. The answers in requirements (a) and (b) are related to the theory of constraints. Under this theory, the objective is to maximize throughput contribution, which is equal to revenues minus direct material costs of the goods sold. In this case, Huntington Industries should focus on improving quality first in the Assembly Department because poor quality (defective units) in that department is more costly. That is, because the Machining Department has more capacity than the Assembly Department, forgone throughput contribution only occurs from poor quality in the Assembly Department.

Inventory Management, Just-in-Time, and Backflush Costing

Chapter Overview

This chapter focuses on **inventory management**, which is the planning, coordinating, and control activities related to the flow of inventory into, through, and from an organization. Many decisions fall under the inventory management umbrella: What is the economic order quantity for an item? When is the best time to order an item? Is it desirable for an organization to use just-in-time purchasing, just-in-time production, and/or backflush costing? In making these decisions, managers use the relevant-cost analysis introduced in Chapter 11.

Chapter Highlights

1. The following cost categories are important when managing goods for sale (or materials):

a. **Purchasing costs** are the costs of goods (or materials) acquired from suppliers including incoming freight or transportation costs.

b. **Ordering costs** are the costs of preparing, issuing, and paying purchase orders, plus receiving and inspecting the items included in the orders.

c. **Carrying costs** arise when an organization holds inventory; these costs include the opportunity cost of the investment tied up in inventory and costs associated with storage, such as space rental, insurance, obsolescence, and breakage or spoilage.

d. *Stockout costs* arise from **stockouts**, which occur if an organization runs out of a particular item for which there is demand. Depending on how managers respond to the stockout, stockout costs are either the costs of expediting an order from a supplier or opportunity costs of forgone contri-

bution margin on current and future lost sales.

e. *Quality costs* are prevention costs, appraisal costs, internal failure costs, and external failure costs (described in paragraph 3 of Chapter 19's Highlights, p. 251).

2. The first major decision in managing goods for sale (or materials) is deciding *how much of a given item to order*. The **economic order quantity (EOQ)** is a decision model that calculates the optimal quantity of inventory to order under a restrictive set of assumptions. The simplest version of this model minimizes the relevant costs of ordering and carrying inventory. The formula is:

$$EOQ = \sqrt{\frac{2DP}{C}}$$

where:

D = Demand in units for a specified time period

P = Relevant ordering costs per purchase order

C = Relevant carrying costs of one unit in stock for the time period of D

Calculate the annual relevant total costs (RTC) for any order quantity, Q (not just the EOQ), as follows:

$$RTC = \frac{DP}{Q} + \frac{QC}{2}$$

3. The second major decision in managing goods for sale (or materials) *is when to order a given item*. The **reorder point** is the quantity level of the inventory on hand that triggers a new order. The reorder point is simplest to compute if both demand and purchase-order lead time are known with certainty. To illustrate, assume 250 units are sold

per week and purchase-order lead time is 2 weeks.

Then,

Reorder point $= 250 \times 2 = 500$ units

In other words, an order should be placed whenever the level of inventory on hand declines to 500 units.

4.　If organizations holding inventory are uncertain about demand, purchase-order lead time, or the quantity that suppliers can provide, they often hold **safety stock**. Safety stock is inventory held at all times regardless of the quantity of inventory ordered on the basis of the EOQ model. Safety stock is a buffer against demand and delivery uncertainty. The optimal safety stock level is the quantity of safety stock that minimizes the sum of the annual relevant stockout costs and carrying costs.

5.　Three main challenges arise in estimating inventory-related costs and their effects. First, only relevant outlay (cash) costs and opportunity costs should be used. Second, the parameters in the EOQ model should recognize the impact of improvements in operations and the advent of new technologies such as placing purchase orders electronically. Third, goal incongruence occurs if there is an inconsistency between the EOQ decision model and performance evaluation of the managers implementing the inventory management decisions. To illustrate goal incongruence, assume opportunity cost of the investment tied up in inventory is included in the EOQ model (as it should be) but is excluded from annual carrying costs in evaluating the manager's performance. Under these conditions, the manager is inclined to purchase a larger order quantity than the EOQ. A likely cause of this inconsistency between the EOQ model and performance evaluation is that opportunity costs are not typically recorded in the conventional accounting system, but this system is the source of information used for performance evaluation.

6.　An important feature of the EOQ model is that the annual relevant total costs are rarely sensitive to sizable variations in cost predictions. Sensitivity is dampened by the effect of the square root in the EOQ model. A three-step approach, text pp. 696-697, determines the cost of a prediction error in ordering costs per purchase order; the prediction error in P is 50%, but the cost of the prediction error is less than 7% of annual relevant total costs.

7.　Some organizations have dramatically reduced their inventories by using **just-in-time (JIT) purchasing**. JIT purchasing is the purchase of goods (or materials) such that a delivery immediately precedes demand (or use). JIT purchasing requires organizations to restructure their relationships with suppliers (that is, have fewer suppliers and establish long-run contracts with them) and place smaller and more frequent purchase orders. Restructuring relationships with suppliers and using computers for order-related activities significantly reduce annual relevant ordering costs, thereby decreasing EOQ. JIT purchasing, however, is not guided solely by the EOQ; in addition to considering the trade-off between carrying costs and ordering costs (which is the scope of the EOQ model), JIT purchasing includes the other costs of inventory management—purchasing costs, stockout costs, and quality costs. EXHIBIT 20-5, text p. 700, compares the annual relevant costs of a company's current purchasing policy with a JIT purchasing policy. EXHIBIT 20-6, text p. 701, compares the annual relevant costs of two suppliers under a JIT purchasing policy.

8.　The level of inventories held by retailers is influenced by demand patterns of their customers and supply relationships with their distributors, and manufacturers. The term *supply chain* describes the flow of goods, services and information, regardless of whether those activities occur in the same organization or in other organizations. There are multiple gains to companies in a supply chain by coordinating activities and sharing information. For example, assume all retailers share daily sales information about a given product. This updated sales information reduces the level of uncertainty manufacturers and suppliers to manufacturers have about retail demand for the product. This reduced uncertainty leads to fewer stockouts at the retail level, lower inventories being held by each company in the supply chain, and fewer expedited orders.

9. Manufacturing companies face the challenging task of producing high-quality products at competitive cost levels. **Materials requirements planning (MRP)** and **just-in-time (JIT) production** (also called **lean production**) are two widely used types of systems developed to help managers plan and implement production and inventory activities.

- MRP is a *push-through* system that manufactures finished goods for inventory on the basis of demand forecasts. Taking into account the lead time required to purchase materials and to manufacture components and finished products, a master production schedule specifies the quantity and timing of each item to be produced. Once scheduled production starts, the output of each department is *pushed through* the production line whether or not it is needed. The result is often an accumulation of inventory at workstations that receive work they are not yet ready to process. The management accountant assists MRP by (a) maintaining accurate and timely information on inventory and (b) providing estimates of the setup costs for each production run (analogous to the ordering costs in the EOQ model), downtime costs, and inventory carrying costs.
- JIT production is a *demand-pull* system in which each component on a production line is produced immediately as needed by the next step in the production line. Demand triggers each step of the production process, starting with customer demand for a finished product at the end of the process and working all the way back to the demand for direct materials at the beginning of the process. JIT production aims to simultaneously (a) meet customer demand in a timely way, (b) with high quality

products, and (c) at the lowest possible total costs.

10. There are five main features in a JIT production system. First, organize production in **manufacturing cells**, a grouping of all the different types of equipment used to make a given product. Second, hire and retain workers who are multi-skilled so they are capable of performing a variety of operations and tasks. Third, aggressively pursue total quality management (TQM) to eliminate the root causes of defects as quickly as possible. Fourth, place emphasis on reducing setup time and manufacturing lead time. Fifth, carefully select suppliers capable of delivering quality materials in a timely manner. Most companies implementing JIT production also implement JIT purchasing.

11. To control and evaluate JIT production, management accountants rely on: (a) personal observation by production line workers and managers, (b) financial performance measures such as inventory turnover ratios, and (c) nonfinancial performance measures of time, inventory, and quality. Rapid, meaningful feedback is critical because the lack of buffer inventories in a demand-pull system creates added urgency to detect and solve problems quickly.

12. Traditional normal and standard costing systems (described in Chapters 4, 7, and 8) use **sequential tracking**, which is a product-costing method that records journal entries in the same order as actual purchases and progress in production. An alternative approach to sequential tracking is **backflush costing**, which delays the recording of some or all the journal entries relating to the cycle from purchase of direct materials to the sale of finished goods; it then uses normal or standard costs to work backward to "flush out" the manufacturing costs in the cycle for which journal entries are not made.

13. There are several versions of backflush costing. They differ with regard to the **trigger points** used. The term trigger point refers to a stage in the production cycle, going from the purchase of direct materials to

the sale of finished goods, at which journal entries are recorded in the accounting system. Regardless of the version of backflush costing used, the period-end location of manufacturing costs in the general-ledger accounts is basically the same as in sequential tracking, except backflush costing bypasses the Work in Process account. Three examples, beginning text p. 707, illustrate different versions of backflush costing; EXHIBIT 20-7, p. 710, shows the related journal entries. In Example 1 the account "Inventory: Raw and In-Process Control" combines materials inventory and materials in work-in-process inventory, and in Example 2 the account "Inventory Control" combines direct materials inventory and any direct materials in work-in-process and finished goods inventories.

14. The financial accounting procedures in backflush costing do not strictly adhere to generally accepted accounting principles (GAAP) and do not provide sufficient information for audit trails. For example, work in process (an asset) exists but is not recognized in the financial statements under backflush costing. Advocates of backflush costing, however, cite the materiality concept in support of their procedures. That is, they maintain that if inventories are low or if total costs are not subject to significant change from one accounting period to the next, operating income reported in a backflush-costing system does not differ materially from operating income reported in a traditional system. If the difference is material, an adjusting entry is recorded to satisfy GAAP.

Review Questions and Exercises

Completion Statements

Fill in the blank(s) to complete each statement.

1. Which five categories of costs pertaining to inventory are distinguished for management purposes? _____ _____ _____ .

2. Which two of the cost categories in the preceding question are considered in the EOQ model? _____ _____ and _____

3. What do each of the letters in the EOQ model stand for?

   D = _____
   _____

   P = _____
   _____

   C = _____
   _____
   _____

4. In purchasing materials or goods, ordering costs are equivalent to _____ costs for a production run.

5. A system of production in which each component on a production line is produced immediately as needed by the next step in the production line is called _____ _____ .

6. A product-costing system in which the recording of journal entries occurs in the same order as actual purchases and progress in production is called _____ _____ .

7. _____ delays recording changes in the status of a product being produced until good finished units appear; it then uses budgeted (or standard) costs to work backward to assign manufacturing costs to units produced and/or sold.

8. A stage in the production cycle, going from the purchase of direct materials to the sale of finished goods, at which journal entries are recorded in the accounting system is called a _____ .

Featured Exercise

Catalina Stores, a retail chain, sells small appliances. Information for one of these appliances is as follows:

Total annual demand in units	3,000
Relevant carrying costs per unit per year	$5
Relevant ordering costs per purchase order	$300
Inventory level when each order arrives	zero
Maximum daily sales	80 units
Average daily sales	70 units
Minimum daily sales	60 units
Purchase-order lead time	22 days

a. Compute EOQ.
b. Compute the total of annual relevant ordering costs and annual relevant carrying costs at the EOQ level.
c. Compute the minimum safety stock needed to be certain a stockout does not occur.
d. Compute the reorder point.

Solution

a. $$EOQ = \sqrt{\frac{2(3,000)(\$300)}{\$5}} = \sqrt{\frac{\$1,800,000}{\$5}} = \sqrt{360,000} = 600 \text{ units}$$

b. Let TRC = Total of annual relevant ordering costs and annual relevant carrying costs at the EOQ level

$$TRC = \frac{DP}{Q} + \frac{QC}{2} = \frac{3,000(\$300)}{600} + \frac{600(\$5)}{2} = \$1,500 + \$1,500 = \$3,000$$

c. Minimum safety stock to prevent a stockout = $(80 - 70) \times 22 = 220$ units
d. Reorder point = $220 + (70 \times 22)$
   = $220 + 1,540 = 1,760$ units
   (*Alternative solution*: $80 \times 22 = 1,760$ units)

Indicate whether each statement true (T) or false (F).

____ 1. Examples of carrying costs of inventory are obsolescence, opportunity cost of inventory investment, and inspection.

____ 2. The EOQ model does not include quantity discounts lost on inventory purchases.

____ 3. EOQ minimizes the annual relevant total carrying costs of inventory.

____ 4. An example of a cost pertaining to inventory that usually is irrelevant to the decision of how much to order is salaries of stockroom workers.

____ 5. The reorder point decreases if the ordering costs per purchase order increase.

____ 6. JIT purchasing should be guided by the EOQ decision model.

____ 7. Adopting JIT purchasing is likely to result in fewer suppliers for each item and more paperwork.

____ 8. JIT production operates as a push-through system.

____ 9. A key feature of backflush costing is that it tracks manufacturing costs sequentially.

____ 10. When a single Inventory Control account is used in backflush costing, this account is restricted solely to raw (direct) materials, whether they are in storerooms, in process, or in finished goods.

____ 11. Although backflush costing may not strictly adhere to generally accepted accounting principles, the accounting principle of materiality works in favour of backflush costing if inventories are low.

Select the best answer to each question. Space is provided for computations after the quantitative questions.

____ 1. (CPA) Barter Corporation has been buying Product A in lots of 1,200 units, a four months' supply. The cost per unit is $100; the ordering costs are $200 per purchase order; and the annual inventory carrying costs for one unit are $25. Assume the units are required evenly throughout the year. The EOQ is:
a. 144 units.
b. 240 units.
c. 600 units.
d. 1,200 units.

____ 2. (CPA) Garmar, Inc., determines the following information for a given year:

EOQ in units	5,000
Total annual ordering costs	$10,000
Ordering costs per purchase order	$50
Costs of carrying one unit for one year	$4

What is Garmar's estimated annual demand in units?
a. 1,000,000
b. 2,000,000
c. 4,000,000
d. Cannot be determined from the information given.

3. (CPA adapted) A manufacturer expects to produce 200,000 widgets during the fiscal year ending June 30, 2000 to supply the demand that is uniform throughout the year. The setup costs for each production run of widgets are $144. The cost of carrying one widget in inventory is $0.20 per year. After a batch of widgets is produced and placed in inventory, it is sold at a uniform rate and inventory is exhausted when the next batch of widgets is completed. The quantity of widgets (rounded to the nearest one hundred widgets) that should be produced in each run in fiscal year 2000 to minimize total annual relevant setup and carrying costs is:
a. 12,000.
b. 12,500.
c. 16,000.
d. 17,000.
e. 19,000.

4. (CPA) For its EOQ model, a company has ordering costs per purchase order of $10, and annual costs of carrying one unit in stock of $2. If the ordering costs per purchase order increase by 20%, and the annual costs of carrying one unit in stock increase by 25%, while all other considerations remain constant, EOQ:
a. remains unchanged.
b. decreases.
c. increases.
d. either increases or decreases depending on the reorder point.

5. (CMA) Canseco Enterprises uses 84,000 units of Part 256 in manufacturing activities over a 300-day work year. The usual purchase-order lead time for the part is six days; occasionally, however, the lead time has been as high as eight days. The company now desires to adjust the size of its safety stock. The size of the safety stock and the likely effect on stockout costs and carrying costs, respectively, are:
a. 560 units, decrease, increase.
b. 560 units, decrease, decrease.
c. 1,680 units, decrease, increase.
d. 1,680 units, increase, no change.
e. 2,240 units, increase, decrease.

6. (CPA adapted) Key Co. changed from a traditional production system with job costing to a just-in-time production system with backflush costing. What are the expected effects of these changes on Key's inspection cost and record-keeping detail of costs tracked to jobs in process?

	Inspection cost	Detail of costs tracked to jobs
a.	Decreases	Decreases
b.	Decreases	Increases
c.	Increases	Decreases
d.	Increases	Increases

7. (CMA) Which one of the following statements best describes material requirements planning (MRP)?
a. A planning system that is used to determine the amount and timing of the optimal inventory level.
b. A software tool that is used to forecast the ordering quantities of inventories that tend to be subject to a variable and continual demand.
c. A planning system that is used to determine the amount and timing of inventories that are dependent on the demand for finished goods.
d. A software tool that is used to forecast the schedule of material purchases that tend to be subject to a variable and continual demand.
e. A formal system of ordering and scheduling finished goods inventories.

Exercises

1. (CMA) Gerstein Company manufactures a line of deluxe office fixtures. The annual demand for its miniature oak file is estimated to be 5,000 units. The annual costs of carrying one unit in inventory are $10, and the setup costs to initiate a production run are $1,000. There are no miniature oak files on hand and Gerstein has scheduled four equal production runs of this file for the coming year, the first of which is to be run immediately. Gerstein operates 250 business days per year. Assume sales occur uniformly throughout the year.

   a. If no safety stock is held, compute the estimated relevant total carrying costs for the miniature oak file for the coming year.

   b. If two equal production runs are scheduled for the coming year rather than four, compute the amount of change in the sum of annual relevant total carrying costs and setup costs.

   c. Compute the number of production runs that minimizes the sum of total relevant carrying costs and setup costs for the coming year.

2. Quinn Electronics manufactures television sets. Quinn implemented a JIT purchasing policy in January 1999. One year later, Sandra Lansing is evaluating the effect of this policy on financial performance. She finds the following information:

   • Average inventory declined from $400,000 to $200,000. Pre-JIT insurance costs of $40,000 per year declined by 40% (due to lower average inventory).

   • Pre-JIT, 5,000 square feet of warehouse space was leased for $10,000 per year. The lower average inventory allowed Quinn to sublet 40% of the space at $2.50 per square foot.

   • The JIT purchasing policy leads to stockouts on 5,000 pieces of direct materials per year. Quinn's policy is to handle stockouts with rush orders at a cost of $4 per piece.

   • Quinn's required rate of return on investment in inventory is 15%.

   Compute the cash savings (loss) from the JIT purchasing policy for 1999.

3. Cumberland Inc. produces video cameras. For November, there were no beginning inventories of raw (direct) materials and no beginning and ending work in process. Cumberland uses a JIT production system and backflush costing. Standard costs per unit for November are: direct materials $52, conversion costs $30. The following data are for November:

Raw materials and components purchased	$21,200,000
Conversion costs incurred	$12,320,000
Number of finished units manufactured	400,000
Number of finished units sold	384,000

Assume there are no variances for materials.

a. Prepare summary journal entries for November (without disposing of under- or overallocated conversion costs), assuming there are two trigger points: (i) purchase of raw (direct) materials and components and (ii) completion of finished goods. The inventory accounts used are Inventory: Raw and In-Process Control, and Finished Goods Control.

General Journal	Debit	Credit

b. Prepare summary journal entries for November, assuming there are two trigger points: (i) purchase of raw (direct) materials and components and (ii) sale of finished goods. The only inventory account, Inventory Control, is restricted solely to raw (direct) materials and components (whether they are in storerooms, in process, or in finished goods). Under- or overallocated conversion costs are written off at the end of each month.

General Journal	Debit	Credit

c. Refer to part (b). Assume conversion costs are regarded as being material in amount. How do your journal entries in part (b) change.

General Journal	Debit	Credit

d. Repeat part (a) with one difference. There is only one trigger point, the completion of good finished units. As a result, there is only one inventory account, Finished Goods Control.

General Journal	Debit	Credit

Answers to Chapter 20 Review Questions and Exercises

Completion Statements

1. purchasing costs, ordering costs, carrying costs, stockout costs, quality costs
2. ordering costs, carrying costs
3. D = Demand in units for a specified time period
   P = Relevant ordering costs per purchase order
   C = Relevant carrying costs of one unit in stock for the time period for D
4. setup
5. just-in-time (JIT) production (lean production)
6. sequential tracking
7. Backflush costing
8. trigger point

True-False

1. F Carrying costs include obsolescence and opportunity cost of inventory investment. Inspection is an ordering cost.
2. T
3. F EOQ minimizes the *annual relevant total costs*, which are the sum of annual relevant ordering costs and annual relevant carrying costs. This minimum occurs where annual relevant ordering costs and annual relevant carrying costs *are equal*.
4. T
5. F Reorder point = $\dfrac{\text{Number of units sold}}{\text{per unit of time}} \times \dfrac{\text{Purchase-order}}{\text{lead time}}$

    A change in the ordering costs per purchase order, therefore, has no effect on the reorder point.

6. F   To understand the full costs and benefits of JIT purchasing, it is necessary to move outside the confines of the EOQ model because that model does not consider three of the five categories of costs pertaining to inventory: purchasing costs, stockout costs, and quality costs.

7. F   Adopting JIT purchasing is likely to result in fewer suppliers for each item and *less* paperwork, such as when purchase orders are placed by means of electronic data interchange (EDI). Other changes associated with JIT purchasing include smaller and more frequent purchase orders, long-term contracts with suppliers, and less inspection of orders received.

8. F   JIT production operates as a *demand-pull* system: demand triggers each step of the production process, starting with customer demand for a finished product at the end of the process and working all the way back to the demand for materials at the beginning of the process.

9. F   Sequential tracking is not used in backflush costing. Instead, some or all journal entries are delayed until the completion of production or the sale of finished goods, and then manufacturing costs are "flushed back" through the accounting system.

10. T

11. T

Multiple Choice

1. b   Demand in units per year = 1,200 × 3 = 3,600;

$$EOQ = \sqrt{\frac{2(3,600)(\$200)}{\$25}} = \sqrt{\frac{\$1,440,000}{\$25}} = \sqrt{57,600} = 240 \text{ units}$$

Note that the cost per unit of $100 is not *explicitly* used in this computation. *Implicitly*, however, the required annual return on the investment of $100 per unit, an opportunity cost, is included in the $25 cost of carrying one unit in stock for one year.

2. a   Let D = Annual demand in units

$$5,000 = \sqrt{\frac{2D(\$50)}{\$4}}$$

$$25,000,000 = \frac{\$100D}{\$4}$$

$$25,000,000 = 25D$$

$$D = 25,000,000 \div 25 = 1,000,000$$

Alternative solution: Relevant total costs are at a minimum (the EOQ level) where annual ordering costs and annual carrying costs are equal:

$$\frac{D(\$50)}{5,000} = \$10,000$$

$$\$50D = \$50,000,000$$

$$D = \$50,000,000 \div \$50 = 1,000,000$$

3. d   Setup costs in production situations are analogous to ordering costs in purchasing situations.

Let EPRQ = Economic production run quantity

$$EPRQ = \sqrt{\frac{2(200,000)(\$144)}{\$0.20}}$$

$$EPRQ = \sqrt{\frac{\$57,600,000}{\$0.20}}$$

$$EPRQ = \sqrt{288,000,000}$$

$EPRQ = 17,000$ widgets (rounded to nearest hundred widgets)

Note that a production run is, in effect, like an *internal* purchase, whereas the two previous questions deal with *external* purchases.

4. b These changes in the variables in the EOQ model can be thought of as an example of sensitivity analysis. Assuming any figure for annual demand (say, 90,000 units), the effect of the changes on EOQ is as follows (rounded to nearest unit):

Before changes:

$$EOQ = \sqrt{\frac{2(90,000)(\$10)}{\$2}}$$

$EOQ = \sqrt{900,000} = 949$ units

After changes:

$$EOQ = \sqrt{\frac{2(90,000)(\$12)}{\$2.50}}$$

$EOQ = \sqrt{864,000} = 930$ units

The changes cause EOQ to decrease. The reorder point, which is mentioned in choice (d), has no bearing on the answer.

5. a Average usage per day = 84,000 ÷ 300 = 280 units
   Safety stock = 280 × (8 − 6) = 560 units
   By having 560 units of safety stock, stockout costs decrease because stockouts are much less likely to occur; carrying costs increase, however, because the buffer of safety stock increases the level of inventory.

6. a One of the main features of JIT production systems is that total quality management is aggressively pursued to eliminate defects, and hence inspection cost is decreased, if not eliminated. Under backflush costing the detail of costs tracked to jobs is decreased, if not eliminated, because typically no record of work-in-process inventory is kept in the accounting system.

7. c Materials requirements planning (MRP)—a push-through system that differs sharply from the demand-pull system of JIT production—takes into account the lead time required to purchase materials and to manufacture components and subassemblies needed to meet forecast demand for finished goods. The resulting master production schedule specifies the quantity and time of each item to be manufactured.

Exercise 1

a. Number of units per production run   = 5,000 ÷ 4 = 1,250 units
    Relevant total carrying costs per year = (1,250 ÷ 2) × $10 = $6,250

b.

Relevant Costs	4 Runs	2 Runs
Annual carrying costs		
[(5,000 ÷ 4) ÷ 2] × $10	$ 6,250	
[(5,000 ÷ 2) ÷ 2] × $10		$12,500
Annual setup costs		
$1,000 × 4; $1,000 × 2	4,000	2,000
Total annual relevant costs	$10,250	$14,500

Cost increase due to fewer runs $4,250

c. Economic production run quantity $= \sqrt{\dfrac{2(5,000)(\$1,000)}{\$10}} = \sqrt{1,000,000} = 1,000$ files

Number of production runs = 5,000 ÷ 1,000 = 5

Exercise 2

Relevant Costs	Previous Policy	JIT Policy
Required return on investment		
15% × $400,000; 15% × $200,000	$ 60,000	$30,000
Insurance costs		
$40,000; $40,000(1 − .40)	40,000	24,000
Warehouse rental		
$10,000; $10,000 − (5,000 × .40 × $2.50)	10,000	5,000
Stockout costs		
5,000 × $4		20,000
Annual total relevant costs	$110,000	$79,000

Difference in favour of JIT purchasing policy $31,000

Exercise 3

a.

Inventory: Raw and In-Process Control	21,200,000	
Accounts Payable Control		21,200,000
Conversion Costs Control	12,320,000	
Various Accounts		12,320,000
Finished Goods Control		
(400,000 × $52) + (400,000 × $30)	32,800,000	
Inventory: Raw and In-Process Control		
(400,000 × $52)		20,800,000
Conversion Costs Allocated		
(400,000 × $30)		12,000,000
Cost of Goods Sold		
384,000 ($52 + $30)	31,488,000	
Finished Goods Control		31,488,000

b.
Inventory Control	21,200,000	
Accounts Payable Control		21,200,000
Conversion Costs Control	12,320,000	
Various Accounts		12,320,000
Cost of Goods Sold		
(384,000 × $52) + (384,000 × $30)	31,488,000	
Inventory Control (384,000 × $52)		19,968,000
Conversion Costs Allocated		
(384,000 × $30)		11,520,000
Conversion Costs Allocated	11,520,000	
Cost of Goods Sold	800,000	
Conversion Costs Control		12,320,000

c. All journal entries in part (b) are the same except the last one. It should now include some conversion costs in Inventory, 16,000 units × $30 = $480,000:

Conversion Costs Allocated	11,520,000	
Inventory Control	480,000	
Cost of Goods Sold	320,000	
Conversion Costs Control		12,320,000

d.
Finished Goods Control		
(400,000 × $52) + (400,000 × $30)	32,800,000	
Accounts Payable Control		
(for materials: 400,000 × $52)		20,800,000
Conversion Costs Allocated		
(400,000 × $30)		12,000,000

Capital Budgeting and Cost Analysis

Chapter Overview

This chapter and the next explain methods for analyzing capital-budgeting projects. These projects typically require large amounts of money, span several years or more, and have uncertain cash flows and income over their lives. To help managers make capital-budgeting decisions, management accountants use the relevant-revenue and relevant-cost analysis introduced in Chapter 11. Income taxes are ignored in, or do not apply to, the examples in this chapter. The next chapter covers income taxes.

Chapter Highlights

1. **Capital budgeting** is the process of making long-run planning decisions for investments in projects. This focus on long-run projects contrasts with the accounting-period focus of the income statement and routine planning and control. This difference is important because of the potential conflict between short-run and long-run performance.

2. Capital budgeting can be thought of as a six-stage process: (a) identification stage, (b) search stage, (c) information-acquisition stage, (d) selection stage, (e) financing stage, and (f) implementation and control stage. *The chapter emphasizes the selection stage.* The purpose of the selection stage is to choose the most desirable projects. Projects are analyzed on the basis of their expected benefits and costs expressed in financial terms. *The analysis for each project includes only relevant items— future cash flow (or income) amounts that differ between the "invest" and "do not invest" alternatives.* The conclusion reached from this analysis is reevaluated in light of qualitative factors.

3. The chapter explains four methods that can be used in the selection stage: **net present value, internal rate of return, payback,** and **accrual accounting rate of return**. *The first three methods use only the expected cash inflows and outflows from a project.* To simplify computations, the textbook assumes that these cash flows occur at the end of the year. *The accrual accounting rate of return method is based on a project's expected average annual income.*

4. Net present value and internal rate of return are **discounted cash-flow (DCF) methods**. DCF methods measure all expected future cash inflows and outflows of a project as if they occurred at a single point in time, thereby comparing them in an appropriate way. *DCF methods are indifferent as to the origin of a project's relevant cash flows—whether they come from operations, purchase or sale of equipment, or investment in or recovery of working capital.*

5. Calculations under DCF methods incorporate the *time value of money*, which takes into account the fact that a dollar (or any other monetary unit) received today is worth more than a dollar received at any time in the future. The time value of money is the opportunity cost (return forgone) from not having the money today. Because the DCF methods incorporate the time value of money, many organizations consider them the best (most comprehensive) methods to use for capital-budgeting decisions.

6. The DCF methods use the **required rate of return (RRR)**, the minimum acceptable rate of return on an investment. The RRR is the return the organization could expect to receive on an investment of comparable risk. The RRR is also called the **discount**

rate, **hurdle rate**, or **(opportunity) cost of capital**.

7. The **net present value (NPV) method** calculates the expected monetary gain or loss from a project by discounting all expected future cash inflows and outflows to the present point in time (referred to as year 0) using the required rate of return. Only projects with a zero or positive NPV are desirable because their returns equal or exceed the required rate of return. Managers prefer projects with higher NPVs to projects with lower NPVs, if other things are equal. EXHIBIT 21-2, text p. 730, shows the computation of NPV; note that the first step in preparing this exhibit is to draw a sketch of relevant cash inflows and outflows.

8. The **internal rate of return (IRR) method** calculates the discount rate at which the present value of a project's expected cash inflows equals the present value of its expected cash outflows. That is, IRR is the discount rate that makes NPV = $0. A project is desirable only if IRR exceeds the required rate of return; in this case, the project has a positive NPV. Managers prefer projects with higher IRRs to projects with lower IRRs, if other things are equal. The IRR can be determined by calculator, computer, or trial and error. The textbook illustrates the trial-and-error approach where interpolation is not required, p. 731, and where interpolation is required, p. 744.

9. The NPV method has two important advantages over the IRR method. First, NPV is expressed in dollars, not a percentage. As a result, the NPVs of individual projects can be summed to see the effect of accepting a combination of projects. The IRRs of individual projects cannot be added or averaged to derive the IRR of a combination of projects. Second, the NPV method can be used in situations where the required rate of return varies over the life of a project. The IRR method cannot be used in such situations.

10. Sensitivity analysis helps managers focus on those capital-budgeting projects that are most sensitive to a failure to achieve the predicted financial outcomes. For example, sensitivity analysis can examine how a project's NPV changes if the expected annual cash flow from operations is not achieved. If a project has a positive NPV, sensitivity analysis can determine how much annual cash flow from operations must fall for NPV = $0. Electronic spreadsheets enable managers to conduct sensitivity analysis in a systematic and efficient way.

11. Four main categories classify the relevant cash flows of capital-budgeting projects. The following table shows these categories in the case of a nonprofit organization that is considering the purchase of a new machine.

Relevant Cash Flow Items for a Capital-Budgeting Project in a Nonprofit Organization

1. Net initial investment
  a. Initial machine investment
  b. Working capital required

2. Current disposal price of old machine
3. Recurring operating cash flows

4. Terminal disposal of investment
  a. Disposal price of new machine
  b. Working capital recovered

- Items 1a, 1b, and 2 occur at the beginning of the new machine's life (year 0).
- The working capital for the new machine (items 1b and 4b) is the incremental investment in current assets minus the incremental amount of current liabilities (for example, the cash outflow to maintain an inventory of supplies and spare parts for the new machine). A project generally requires working capital in year 0 and that investment is recovered in full or in part at the end of its life. A project can *decrease* working capital in year 0, however, such as if a new machine reduces the need for supplies and spare parts; then the working

capital investment *increases* at the end of the machine's life.

- Item 3 can result from either a cash savings in operating costs or producing and selling additional output. *Amortization does not affect annual cash flow from operations in nonprofit organizations.*

- An error in forecasting item 4a is seldom critical for a project with a long life because the present value of the amount to be received in the distant future is usually small.

12. Like the NPV and IRR methods, the **payback method** uses only expected cash inflows and outflows from a project. The payback method measures the time it takes to recover, in the form of annual cash flow, the net initial investment in a project. If the project's cash flow is *the same each year*, the payback period is calculated by dividing net initial investment by the uniform increase in annual cash flow. If the project's annual cash flow is *not uniform*, the payback calculation is cumulative. Cash flow is accumulated year by year until fully recovering the amount of the net initial investment.

13. The payback method highlights liquidity, which is often an important factor in capital-budgeting decisions. Managers prefer projects with shorter paybacks (more liquid) to projects with longer paybacks, if other things are equal. Projects with shorter paybacks give the organization more flexibility because funds for other projects become available sooner. Also, managers are less confident about longer term cash flow predictions.

14. Under the payback method, organizations often choose a cutoff period for projects. The greater a project's risk, the shorter the cutoff period. Only projects with a payback period less than the cutoff period are acceptable.

15. The major strength of the payback method is that it is easy to understand. Advocates of the payback method maintain that it is a useful measure (a) if preliminary screening of many proposals is necessary and (b) if the

predicted cash flows in later years of projects are highly uncertain. Two major weaknesses of the payback method are that it does not (a) incorporate the time value of money and (b) consider a project's cash flows after the payback period.

16. A fourth capital-budgeting method is the **accrual accounting rate of return (AARR) method**. Unlike NPV, IRR, and payback, AARR is based on *operating income* rather than cash flows. Under the AARR method, the increase in expected average annual operating income over the life of a project is divided by net initial investment. AARR is the rate at which an investment generates operating income. Projects whose AARR exceeds the required AARR are considered desirable. Managers prefer projects with higher AARRs to projects with lower AARRs, if other things are equal. The major strengths of the AARR method are it (a) is easy to understand and (b) uses numbers that will be reported in the income statement. Two major weaknesses of AARR are it (a) ignores the time value of money and (b) does not use cash flows.

17. There is an obvious inconsistency between citing the NPV method as being best for capital-budgeting decisions and evaluating performance of managers on the basis of AARR over short time horizons. For example, consider a project that has a positive NPV but entails a large loss from disposing of an old machine in year 0. Despite the positive NPV, the manager's temptation to reject this project is overwhelming because short-run operating (or net) income decreases by the amount of the loss. Resolving this conflict between the decision model and performance evaluation is frequently a baffling problem in practice. The practical difficulty is that accounting systems rarely track each decision separately. Performance evaluation focuses on responsibility centres for a specific time period, not on individual items of equipment for their entire useful lives.

18. A postinvestment audit is an important aspect of the final stage of capital budget-

ing—implementation and control. A post-investment audit compares the actual results for a project to the costs and benefits predicted at the time the project was selected. Post-investment audits not only provide management with feedback about performance, but also discourage managers from making unrealistic forecasts when seeking approval for capital-budgeting projects. Postinvestment audits also can point to areas needing corrective action if there were problems in implementing a project.

Featured Exercise

The City of Kenora, a nonprofit organization, is considering the following capital-budgeting project:

Net initial investment for snow-removal equipment	$125,000
Estimated useful life	7 years
Estimated terminal disposal price	none
Estimated annual cash operating savings	$35,000
Required rate of return	10%
Amortization method: straight-line	

Compute the following items for the project using the interest tables in Appendix B at the back of the textbook or a calculator as needed:
a. Payback
b. Net present value
c. Internal rate of return (to the nearest tenth of a percent)
d. Accrual accounting rate of return on net initial investment (to the nearest tenth of a percent)

Solution

a. $125,000 \div \$35,000 = 3.57$ years
b. Present value of annual cash operating

savings, \$35,000 × 4.868	\$170,380
Net initial investment	(125,000)
NPV	\$ 45,380

NPV via calculator = \$45,395

c.

Let F = Present value factor for 7 years in Table 4 of Appendix B
$35,000F = \$125,000$
F = 3.571, which falls between 3.605 (20%) and 3.416 (22%)

20%	3.605	3.605
IRR		3.571
22%	3.416	
Difference	0.189	0.034

IRR = 20% + (0.034 ÷ 0.189)2%
IRR = 20% + (0.18)2% = 20.4%
IRR via calculator = 20.3%

d. Annual amortization = $125,000 \div 7 = \$17,857$
AARR = ($35,000 - \$17,857) \div \$125,000$
$= \$17,143 \div \$125,000 = 13.7\%$

Review Questions and Exercises

Completion Statements

Fill in the blank(s) to complete each statement.

1. What do each of these sets of initials stand for?

   DCF _____

   NPV _____

   IRR _____

   AARR _____

2. The _____ method of capital budgeting is based on operating income rather than cash flows.

3. The discount rate that makes the net present value of a project equal to zero is called the

   _____.

4. In a capital-budgeting project, the investment required for accounts receivable and inventories is called _____.

5. The technique that examines how a result for a project changes if the original predicted data are not achieved or if an underlying assumption changes is called _____

   _____.

True-False

Indicate whether each statement is true (T) or false (F).

____ 1. The planning and control tools used for year-to-year operating decisions are well suited for capital-budgeting decisions.

____ 2. The present value of $1 million to be received ten years from now is lower if computed at a discount rate of 10% rather than 14%.

____ 3. Assume a required rate of return of 12% is used to compute the NPV of a project. If NPV is negative, IRR is greater than 12%.

____ 4. The payback method does not consider a project's cash flow after the payback period.

_____ 5. An error in forecasting terminal disposal price of new equipment is usually important in capital-budgeting decisions.

_____ 6. The payback method does not consider the profitability of capital-budgeting projects.

_____ 7. It is consistent to cite DCF methods as being best for capital-budgeting decisions and to evaluate subsequent performance on the basis of AARR over short time horizons.

Multiple Choice

Select the best answer to each question. Space is provided for computations after the quantitative questions.

_____ 1. (CMA) Amster Corporation has not yet decided on its required rate of return for use in the evaluation of capital-budgeting projects for the current year. This lack of information prohibits Amster from calculating a project's

	AARR	NPV	IRR
a.	no	no	no
b.	yes	yes	yes
c.	no	yes	yes
d.	no	yes	no
e.	yes	no	yes

_____ 2. (CPA adopted) St. John's Hospital, a nonprofit organization, is reviewing the following data relating to an energy saving investment proposal:

Net initial investment	$50,000
Terminal disposal price at the end of 5 years	10,000
Present value of an annuity of $1 at 12% for 5 years	3.60
Present value of $1 at 12% in 5 years	0.57

What is the amount of annual savings needed to make the investment realize a 12% return?
a. $ 8,189
b. $11,111
c. $12,306
d. $13,889

_____ 3. (CMA) Making the common assumption in capital-budgeting analysis that cash inflows occur in a lump sum at the end of individual years during the life of an investment project when, in fact, they flow more or less continuously during those years:
a. results in increasingly overstated estimates of NPV as the life of the investment project increases.
b. is done because present value tables for continuous flows cannot be constructed.
c. results in understated estimates of NPV of the investment project.
d. results in inconsistent errors being made in estimates of NPV such that projects cannot be evaluated reliably.
e. results in a higher estimate for the IRR of the investment project.

_____ 4. (CPA adapted) The University of Windsor, a nonprofit organization, is considering the purchase of a machine costing $100,000. The machine's expected useful life is five years. The estimated annual cash flow is: $60,000 in year 1, $30,000 in year 2, $20,000 in year 3, $20,000 in year 4, and $20,000 in year 5. Assuming the cash flows will be received evenly during each year, the payback is:
a. 2.50 years.
b. 3.00 years.
c. 3.33 years.
d. none of the above.

____ 5. (CPA adapted) Gravina Hospital, a non-profit organization, is planning to spend $6,000 for a machine that it will depreciate on a straight-line basis over a ten-year period with no terminal disposal price. The machine will generate cash flow from operations of $1,200 per year. What is the AARR based on the net initial investment?

    a. 5%
    b. 10%
    c. 15%
    d. 20%

____ 6. (CMA) Fast Freight Inc. is planning to purchase equipment to make its operations more efficient. This equipment has an estimated life of six years. As part of this acquisition, a $75,000 investment in working capital is required. In a discounted cash-flow analysis, this investment in working capital:

    a. should be amortized over the useful life of the equipment.
    b. should be disregarded because no cash is involved.
    c. should be treated as a recurring annual cash outflow that is recovered at the end of six years.
    d. should be treated as an immediate cash outflow.
    e. should be treated as an immediate cash outflow that is recovered at the end of six years.

____ 7. (CPA adapted) Herman Hospital, a non-profit institution (not subject to income taxes), is considering the purchase of new equipment at a cost of $46,600. The equipment has an estimated life of ten years. There is no terminal disposal price. Annual cash flow from operations is estimated to be $10,000 at the end of each year. The following amounts appear in the interest table for the present value of an annuity of $1 at year-end for ten years:

16%	4.83
18%	4.49
20%	4.19

What is the IRR of the project?

    a. 16%
    b. 17%
    c. 18%
    d. 19%

____ 8. (CMA) If income tax considerations are ignored, how is amortization used in the following capital-budgeting techniques?

	IRR	AARR	Payback
a.	Excluded	Included	Excluded
b.	Included	Excluded	Included
c.	Excluded	Excluded	Included
d.	Included	Included	Included
e.	Excluded	Excluded	Excluded

Exercises

1. Talihina Company is considering the purchase of a machine:

Net initial investment for a machine	$152,000
Estimated useful life	12 years
Estimated terminal disposal price	$10,000
Estimated net annual cash operating savings	$30,000
Required rate of return	16%

Compute NPV of the machine using the interest tables in Appendix B at the back of the textbook or a calculator.

2. Fasken Company is considering the purchase of a machine:

Net initial investment	$180,000
Estimated useful life	15 years
Estimated terminal disposal price	none
Estimated cash flow from operations	$30,000

Compute IRR of the project to the nearest tenth of a percent using the interest tables in Appendix B at the back of the textbook or a calculator.

3. Sisco Industries is considering the purchase of a piece of materials-handling equipment:

Net initial investment	$125,000
Estimated useful life	8 years
Estimated terminal disposal price	$10,000
Estimated annual cash operating savings	$35,000
Required rate of return	10%
Amortization method: straight-line	

a. Compute payback.
b. Compute AARR based on net initial investment.

Answers to Chapter 21 Review Questions and Exercises

Completion Statements

1. discounted cash flow, net present value, internal rate of return, accrual accounting rate of return
2. accrual accounting rate of return
3. internal rate of return
4. working capital
5. Sensitivity analysis

True-False

1. **F** The planning and control tools used for year-to-year (short-run) operating decisions rely on the distinction between variable and fixed costs and generally ignore the time value of money. In contrast, the distinction between variable and fixed costs plays a limited role in capital-budgeting decisions. Capital-budgeting decisions often incorporate the time value of money and use postinvestment audits for control purposes.

2. **F** Using Table 2 in Appendix B at the back of the textbook:
   At 10%, $1,000,000 × 0.386 = $386,000
   At 14%, $1,000,000 × 0.270 = $270,000

3. **T**

4. **T**

5. **F** An error in forecasting the terminal disposal price of new equipment is usually not critical because the combination of a relatively low terminal disposal price and a useful life that tends to be five years or more results in a low present value of this expected cash inflow.

6. **T**

7. **F** It is inconsistent to cite DCF methods as being best for capital-budgeting decisions and to evaluate subsequent performance on the basis of AARR over short time horizons. For example, a manager being evaluated on AARR might reject a project with a positive NPV simply because it lowers AARR in the short run.

Multiple Choice

1. **d** AARR and IRR calculate a rate of return, whereas NPV uses the required rate of return in making its calculations.

2. **c**

Net initial investment	$50,000
Deduct present value of disposal price	
$10,000 × 0.57	5,700
Present value of *total* savings needed	$44,300

   Annual savings needed = $44,300 ÷ 3.60 = $12,306

3. **c** Although present value tables for continuous cash flows are available, they are seldom used. Present value tables for end-of-the-period cash flows are used for convenience. Because *some* cash flows occur only once *sometime during* a period, it is convenient to assume that *all* cash flows occur at the *end* of a period. Under this assumption, cash inflows that occur more or less continuously during a period are discounted at the end of a period. As a result, the true present value of these inflows is *understated*, which in turn understates NPV and IRR. Because the errors introduced by making the end-of-the-period assumption tend to be reasonably consistent, capital-budgeting projects can be evaluated with a satisfactory degree of reliability.

4. **a** Cumulative cash flow from operations:

Year 1	$ 60,000
Year 2	30,000
Subtotal	90,000
Year 3	20,000
Total	$110,000

   Payback = 2 + [($100,000 − $90,000) ÷ $20,000]
   = 2 + ($10,000 ÷ $20,000)
   = 2 + 0.50 = 2.50 years

5. b $\quad \text{AARR} = \dfrac{[\$1,200 - (\$6,000 \div 10)]}{\$6,000} = \dfrac{\$600}{\$6,000} = 10\%$

6. e $\quad$ In Exhibit 21-5, text p. 736, the $10,000 cash outflow for working capital occurs in year 0 and is recovered in year 5.

7. b $\quad\quad$ Let F = Present value factor for 10 years in Table 4 of Appendix B

$10,000F = $46,600

$\quad\quad\quad\quad$ F = 4.66, which falls between 4.83(16%) and 4.49(18%)

16%	4.83	4.83
IRR		4.66
18%	4.49	
Difference	0.34	0.17

IRR = 16% + (0.17 ÷ 0.34)2%

IRR = 16% + (.50)2% = 17%

8. a $\quad$ If income tax considerations are ignored, amortization is excluded under IRR (see Exhibit 21-3, text p. 775), is included under AARR (see the calculations in Exercise 3b below, and is excluded under payback (see the calculations Exercise 3a below).

Exercise 1

Present value of net annual cash operating savings, $30,000 × 5.197	$155,910
Present value of terminal disposal price, $10,000 × 0.168	1,680
Total present value	157,590
Net initial investment	(152,000)
NPV	$ 5,590
NPV via calculator = $5,598	

Exercise 2

$\quad\quad\quad$ Let F = Present value factor for 15 years in Table 4 of Appendix B

$30,000 F = $180,000

$\quad\quad\quad\quad$ F = 6.000, which falls between 6.142 (14%) and 5.575 (16%)

14%	6.142	6.142
IRR		6.000
16%	5.575	
Difference	0.567	0.142

IRR = 14% + (0.142 ÷ 0.567)2%

IRR = 14% + (.25)2% = 14.5%

IRR via calculator = 14.5%

Exercise 3

a. Payback = $125,000 ÷ $35,000 = 3.57 years

b. Annual amortization = ($125,000 − $10,000) ÷ 8 = $14,375;
$\quad$ AARR = ($35,000 − $14,375) ÷ $125,000
$\quad\quad\quad\quad$ = $20,625 ÷ $125,000 = 16.5%

Capital Budgeting: A Closer Look

Chapter Overview

This preceding chapter introduced basic aspects of capital budgeting. This chapter extends that coverage by explaining how managers analyze the effects of three additional factors in capital-budgeting decisions: *income taxes, inflation,* and *risk*. While these economic realities add complexity, they do not change the fundamental ideas underlying discounted cash-flow analysis. Because tax laws are very detailed and frequently change, this chapter focuses only on a general approach to analyzing the effect of income taxes in capital-budgeting analysis.

Chapter Highlights

1. Income taxes are cash disbursements that sizably affect the *amount* and *timing* of cash flows from individual capital-budgeting projects. Income taxes are based on *taxable income,* as distinguished from *accounting income.* Taxable income is computed in accordance with the provisions of the Income Tax Act (ITA). Accounting income is determined in accordance with generally accepted accounting principles.

2. The relevant income tax rate to use in capital-budgeting analysis is the company's **marginal income tax rate.** This is the tax rate paid on incremental amounts of pretax income. Income taxes *directly* affect cash flow from operations as follows:

After tax CI = Before-tax CI × (1 − MTR)
After tax CO = Before-tax CO × (1 − MTR)

where:

$$CI = \text{Cash inflow from operations}$$
$$CO = \text{Cash outflow from operations}$$
$$MTR = \text{Marginal tax rate}$$

3. The preceding chapter explained that amortization is not a cash flow. This chapter explains how the income tax form of amortization, called **capital cost allowance (CCA),** is *a tax shield that indirectly increases cash flow from operations.* Because CCA reduces taxable income, the cash outflow required to pay taxes in any year is reduced:

Tax saving from CCA = CCA × MTR

The Income Tax Act assigns each amortizable asset to a particular pool of assets (called a *class*), depending on the type of asset. The Appendix to this chapter, text pp. 780-781, provides a list of some of the more commonly used CCA classes and their rates.

4. Two concepts relating to CCA are the **half-year rule** and **unamortized capital cost (UCC).** The half-year rule is a tax provision that reduces the CCA on the net additions to a class by 50%. The UCC is the difference between all additions and all disposals to a particular CCA class, reduced by all the CCA claimed for that class. To illustrate, assume a Class 8 asset is purchased during the current year for $12,000 and there is a tradein of $4,000 in the transaction. Given the CCA for a Class 8 asset is 20% and the half-year rule applies in year 1, then for the first three years:

Purchase price	$12,000
Deduct tradein	4,000
Year 1 net addition	8,000
Deduct CCA for year 1	
$8,000 × 0.20 × 0.50	800
UCC at end of year 1	7,200
Deduct CCA for year 2	
$7,200 × 0.20	1,440
UCC at end of year 2	5,760
Deduct CCA for year 3	
$5,760 × 0.20	1,152
UCC at end of year 3	$ 4,608

By making these calculations over time, UCC approaches but never reaches $0.

5. To continue our illustration, assume (a) the company uses the net present value (NPV) method to analyze capital-budgeting projects, (b) the required rate of return is 10%, (c) the marginal tax rate is 40%, and (d) the before-tax cash operating inflows from the asset are expected to be $3,300 per year for 5 years. The first two panels in the box on the next page show how to calculate NPV for the $8,000 net addition.

- Panel A presents the **tax shield formula**. This formula is an efficient way to calculate the present value of the tax savings from CCA.
- Panel B calculates NPV, $1,544. It is desirable to acquire this asset because its NPV is positive.

6. To complete our illustration, assume (a) the before-tax cash operating inflows for 5 years are less than $3,300 per year such that NPV is negative and (b) the existing Class 8 asset is sold now for $4,000. Under these assumptions, a *last tax shield* arises. That is, selling the asset now causes the company to lose the tax shield it would have gotten by keeping the asset. Panel C in the box on the next page calculates the NPV of selling the asset now.

7. Under the NPV method, companies use two approaches that yield the same result: the **total-project approach** and the **differential approach**. The total-project approach calculates the present value of *all* future cash inflows and outflows under each alternative separately. One of the alternatives is "the status quo" (for example, keep the old machine). The differential approach includes *only relevant* cash flows—those future cash inflows and outflows that *differ* between alternatives. The differential approach is generally faster if there are only two alternatives but is unwieldy if the number of alternatives is three or more. In the Potato Supreme example, beginning text p. 765, both approaches use the following seven categories of cash flows:

a. Initial machine investment
b. Tax shield on the initial investment
c. Cash flow from current disposal of old machine
d. Lost tax shield from current disposal of old machine
e. Recurring after-tax cash operating flows
f. Cash flow from terminal disposal of new machine
g. Lost tax shield from terminal disposal of new machine

EXHIBITS 22-4, text p. 767, and 22-5, text p. 769, illustrate the total-project approach in the Potato Supreme example, while EXHIBIT 22-6, text p. 770, illustrates the differential approach.

8. Given that EXHIBITS 22-4 and 22-5, in effect, are combined in EXHIBIT 22-6, the following observations relate to the latter exhibit:

a. The NPV, $88, 711, is the same as the difference between the NPVs in the two alternatives under the total-project approach: EXHIBITS 22-4's NPV is −$551,434 while EXHIBIT 22-5's NPV is −$462,723.
b. Distinguish between cash flow from disposal of the old machine in year 0, an *inflow* of $26,000, and cash flow from terminal disposal of the old machine in year 4, an *outflow* of $6,000 (before calculating present value). The latter amount is regarded as an outflow because it is a *lost cash inflow if the new machine is acquired*.
c. Do not confuse the cash inflow of $26,000 from disposal of the old machine in year 0 with the loss on this asset for accounting purposes of $24,000 ($50,000 book value − $26,000 cash received). Only the $26,000 is relevant to the capital-budgeting decision.
d. When an asset is disposed of, the actual amount received must be removed from its CCA class.

Panel A: Tax shield formula

$$\begin{array}{l}\text{Present value} \\ \text{of tax savings}\end{array} = \left(\begin{array}{c}\text{Investment} \times \\ \text{Marginal} \\ \text{tax rate}\end{array}\right) \left(\dfrac{\text{CCA rate}}{\text{CCA rate} + \text{Required} \atop \text{rate of return}}\right) \dfrac{\left(2 + \text{Required} \atop \text{rate of return}\right)}{\left(2(1 + \text{Required} \atop \text{rate of return})\right)}$$

$$= (\$8,000 \times 0.40) \left(\frac{0.20}{0.20 + 0.10}\right) \left(\frac{2 + 0.10}{2(1 + 0.10)}\right)$$

$$= \$3,200(0.20 \div 0.30)(2.10 \div 2.20)$$

$$= \$3,200(0.667)(0.955) = \$2,038$$

Panel B: NPV of net addition to Class 8 asset

Purchase price	−$12,000
Deduct tradein	4,000
Net addition (year 0)	− 8,000
Present value of after-tax operating inflows (excluding CCA effects) $3,300 × (1 − 0.40) × 3..791*	7,506
Present value of tax shield (from Panel A)	2,038
NPV	$ 1,544

*From Appendix B, Table 4, text p. 879: present value factor for 5-year annuity at 10% required rate of return

Panel C: NPV of selling Class 8 asset

Selling price	$4,000
Deduct lost tax shield ($4,000 × 0.40) [0.20 ÷ (0.20 + 0.10)]	1,067
NPV	$2,933

9. The cash flows used in discounted cash-flow methods need to be adjusted for the effect of **inflation**. Inflation is the decline in the general purchasing power of the monetary unit. Inflation increases the future cash flows from a project above what they would have been had no inflation been expected. These inflated cash flows cause the project to look better than it really is, unless the analyst recognizes the inflated cash flows are measured in dollars that have lesser value than the dollars that were initially invested.

10. In considering inflation, it is important to distinguish between the **real rate of return** and the **nominal rate of return**. The real rate of return is the rate of return required to cover only investment risk. The nominal rate of return is the rate of return required to cover investment risk and inflation risk. The relationship between these rates of return is:

Nominal rate = (1 + Real rate)(1 + Inflation rate) −1

For example, if the real rate is 20% (which includes a risk-free element and a business-risk element) and the inflation rate is 10%, the nominal rate is:

$$
\begin{aligned}
\text{Nominal rate} &= (1 + 0.20)(1 + 0.10) - 1 \\
&= (1.20)(1.10) - 1 \\
&= 1.32 - 1 = 0.32, \text{ or } 32\%
\end{aligned}
$$

11. There are two internally consistent approaches to incorporate inflation in discounted cash-flow analysis. The *nominal approach* predicts cash flows in dollars adjusted for inflation (nominal dollars) and uses a nominal rate as the required rate of return. The *real approach* predicts cash flows in dollars not adjusted for inflation (real dollars) and uses a real rate as the required rate of return. Managers find the nominal approach much easier to understand because it uses the same type of financial numbers (nominal dollars) that will be recorded in the accounting system over time. EXHIBIT 22-7, text p. 772, illustrates the nominal approach. EXHIBIT 22-8, text p. 773, illustrates the real approach. The NPV under either approach is $172,769.

12. The *required rate of return* is a critical variable in discounted cash-flow analysis. It is the rate of return the organization forgoes by investing in a particular project rather than in an alternate project of comparable *risk*. Risk here refers to the business risk of the project. The higher the risk, the higher the required rate of return and the faster management wants to recover the net initial investment. Organizations typically use one or more of the following approaches in dealing with risk in capital-budgeting projects: (a) varying the required payback time, (b) adjusting the required rate of return, (c) adjusting the estimated future cash inflows and outflows, (d) sensitivity analysis, and (e) estimating the probability distribution of future cash inflows and outflows.

13. NPV is generally regarded as the best method for selecting capital-budgeting projects. Conceptually, all projects with positive NPVs should be accepted. In practice, however, there is often a restriction on the total funds available for an organization's capital-budgeting projects. The **excess present value index** (also called the *profitability index*), which is equal to a project's total present value of future net cash inflows divided by its net initial investment, can be a useful tool for selecting projects that maximize NPV when the total funds available are limited. The example, text p. 776, demonstrates, however, optimal decisions do not always result from using this index.

14. NPV and IRR can result in conflicting rankings of mutually exclusive capital-budgeting projects that have unequal lives or that require different net initial investments. The reason is NPV and IRR make different assumptions as to the rate of return on reinvestment of cash proceeds at the end of the shortest-lived project. NPV assumes funds obtainable from competing projects can be reinvested at the company's required rate of return. IRR assumes the reinvestment rate is equal to the IRR on the shortest-lived project.

Featured Exercise

Galen Company Ltd. is considering the purchase of a machine:

Acquisition cost	$100,000
Annual change in revenues	None
Annual before-tax savings in cash operating costs	$30,000
Useful life	5 years
Terminal disposal price	None
CCA rate (Class 8)	20%
Marginal income tax rate	30%
Required rate of return	10%

Compute the following items for the machine using as needed the interest tables in Appendix B at the back of the textbook or a calculator:

a. NPV (Round each component of the tax shield formula to three decimal places and round dollar amounts to the nearest dollar.)
b. Payback (Round up to the nearest year.)
c. IRR (Round each component of the tax shield formula to three decimal places and round your final answer to the nearest tenth of a percent.)

Solution

a. Net initial investment — −$100,000
    Tax shield (see computations below) — 19,110
    Terminal disposal price — none
    Annual after-tax savings in cash operating costs
       $30,000 (1 − 0.30)(3.791) — 79,611
    NPV — −$ 1,279

$$\text{Tax shield} = (\$100,000 \times 0.30) \times \left(\frac{0.20}{0.20 + 0.10} \right) \left(\frac{2 + 0.10}{2\,(1 + 0.10)} \right)$$

$$\text{Tax shield} = \$30,000(0.20 \div 0.30)(2.10 \div 2.20)$$

$$\text{Tax shield} = \$30,000\,(0.667)\,(0.955) = \$19,110$$

b. The annual cash flow from operations, net of income taxes, differs each year because CCA changes.

Year	CCA	Tax Savings
1	$100,000 \times 0.20 \times 0.50 = \$10,000$	$\$10,000 \times 0.30 = \$3,000$
2	$\$90,000 \times 0.20 = \$18,000$	$\$18,000 \times 0.30 = \$5,400$
3	$\$72,000 \times 0.20 = \$14,400$	$\$14,400 \times 0.30 = \$4,320$
4	$\$57,600 \times 0.20 = \$11,520$	$\$11,520 \times 0.30 = \$3,456$
5	$\$46,080 \times 0.20 = \$\ 9,216$	$\$9,216 \times 0.30 = \$2,765$

Annual after-tax savings in cash operating costs = $30,000 (1 − 0.30) = $21,000

Year	Cash Flow from Operations, Net of Income Taxes	Cumulative After-tax Cash Flows
1	$21,000 + $3,000 = $24,000	$ 24,000
2	$21,000 + $5,400 = $26,400	$ 50,400
3	$21,000 + $4,320 = $25,320	$ 75,720
4	$21,000 + $3,456 = $24,456	$100,176*
5	$21,000 + $2,765 = $23,765	$123,941

*The payback is slightly less than 4 years, or 4 years rounded up to the nearest year.

3. Because using a 10% discount rate yielded a small negative NPV in part (a) above, IRR is slightly less than 10%. Find IRR by trial and error. Recompute NPV using an 8% discount rate:

    Net initial investment — −$100,000
        Tax shield (see computations on the next page) — 20,627
        Terminal disposal price — none
        Annual after-tax savings in cash operating costs
           $30,000 (1 − 0.30)(3.993) — 83,853
        NPV — $ 4,480

$$\text{Tax shield} = (\$100{,}000 \times 0.30) \times \left(\frac{0.20}{0.20 + 0.08}\right)\left(\frac{2 + 0.08}{2\,(1 + 0.08)}\right)$$

Tax shield = $30,000 (0.20 ÷ 0.28) (2.08 ÷ 2.16)
Tax shield = $30,000 (0.714) (0.963) = $20,627

Interpolate to find IRR:

NPV at 8%	$4,480	$4,480
NPV at IRR		0
NPV at 10%	−$1,279	
Difference	$5,759	$4,480

IRR = 8% + ($4,480 ÷ $5,759) (2%)
IRR = 8% + (0.778) (2%) = 9.56%, or 9.6%

Review Questions and Exercises

Completion Statements

Fill in the blank(s) to complete each statement.

1. The relevant income tax rate to use in capital-budgeting analysis is the _____ _____.

2. The income tax form of amortization is called _____.

3. _____ is the general decline in the purchasing power of the monetary unit.

4. The rate of return required to cover both investment risk and inflation risk is called the _____ rate of return.

5. The _____ is a project's total present value of future net cash inflows divided by its net initial investment.

True-False

Indicate whether each statement is true (T) or false (F).

___ 1. If the marginal income tax rate for a profitable company is 30%, CCA of $10,000 results in a tax savings of $7,000.

___ 2. The half-year rule means that the normal CCA rate is multiplied by 50% for all additions to the class in a particular year.

___ 3. Unamortized capital cost (UCC) is the difference between all additions and all disposals to a particular class, reduced by all the CCA claimed for that class.

___ 4. Under conditions of inflation, the nominal rate of return is always higher than the real rate of return.

___ 5. Higher risks of individual capital-budgeting projects can be recognized by increasing the required rate of return and/or increasing the required payback time.

___ 6. With no restriction on the total funds available for capital budgeting, all projects that have an excess present value index of more than 100% should be undertaken.

___ 7. If ranking capital-budgeting projects, the internal rate of return method assumes that a project's cash flows are reinvested at the internal rate of return of the shortest-lived project.

___ 8. (Appendix) All CCA rates are based on the declining-balance method, but each class has its own specified rate.

Multiple Choice

Multiple Choice

Select the best answer to each question. Space is provided for computations after each quantitative question.

___ 1. Assume a profitable company pays $10,000 for advertising and has a CCA deduction of $10,000. If the marginal tax rate is 40%, the after-tax effects on cash flow before considering the time value of money are a net outflow of:
   a. $4,000 for advertising and a net inflow of $4,000 for CCA.
   b. $6,000 for advertising and a net inflow of $6,000 for CCA.
   c. $4,000 for advertising and a net inflow of $6,000 for CCA.
   d. $6,000 for advertising and a net inflow of $4,000 for CCA.

___ 2. Ultraviolet Purifiers Ltd. purchased a patent for a new water treatment process for $130,000. The patent has a legal life of 40 years and a terminal disposal price of nil. Patents are Class 14 assets and the CCA is straight-line over the legal life. Assuming the marginal tax rate is 40%, what is the effect on the company's after-tax cash flow from the patent's CCA in the year of acquisition?
   a. $650.
   b. $975.
   c. $1,300.
   d. $1,625.

___ 3. (CMA adapted) Garfield Inc. is considering a 10-year capital investment project with forecasted annual cash revenues of $40,000 and forecasted annual cash operating costs of $29,000. The initial cost of the new equipment is $23,000, and Garfield expects to sell the equipment for $9,000 at the end of the tenth year. The equipment's CCA rate is 20%. The project requires a working capital investment of $7,000 at its inception and another $5,000 at the end of year 5. Assuming a 40% marginal tax rate, the cash flow from operations, net of income taxes, from the project for the second year is:
   a. $4,116.
   b. $520.
   c. $8,256.
   d. $8,440.

4. Waste Management Ltd. (WM) has Class 10 UCC of $9,500 at the beginning of 1999. The company purchased a new automobile (Class 10) for $19,800 in 1999. WM received a trade-in allowance of $5,000 for an old automobile, paying the net amount of $14,800. The company's required rate of return is 10%. Assuming the marginal tax rate is 40%, what is the net present value of the after-tax cash outflow for the new automobile in 1999? (Use three decimal places in each component of the tax shield formula and round dollar amounts to the nearest dollar.)
    a. $4,240.
    b. $5,838.
    c. $9,127.
    d. $10,560.

5. Using the data in question 4 and assuming WM disposed of the old automobile for $5,000 but did not replace it, what is the NPV of the after-tax cash inflow and the amount of CCA?

	NPV	CCA
a.	$1,500	$675
b.	$3,500	$1,350
c.	$3,567	$675
d.	$5,000	$1,350

6. If the nominal rate of interest is 16% and the inflation rate is 5%, the real rate of interest (rounded to the nearest tenth of a percent) is:
    a. 11.0%.
    b. 11.6%.
    c. 10.5%.
    d. none of the above.

7. (CMA adapted) If an investment project has an excess present value index of 115%, then the:
    a. project's internal rate of return is 15%.
    b. required rate of return is greater than the project's internal rate of return.
    c. project's internal rate of return exceeds its net present value.
    d. net present value of the project is positive.
    e. required rate of return used in calculating the index must be less than 15%.

Exercises

1. (CMA adapted) Jasper Company Ltd. has a payback goal of three years on new equipment acquisitions. Jasper is evaluating new equipment that costs $450,000, will have a CCA rate of 20%, an estimated useful life of 8 years, and a zero terminal disposal price. The company's marginal tax rate is 40%.

   Compute the amount of after-tax savings in annual cash operating costs that must be generated by the new equipment in order to meet the company's payback goal.

2. Massey Company's nominal rate of return for capital-budgeting projects is 20%, which includes a 10% inflation rate. The present value of $1 at 20% for one year is 0.833. Assume a 40% marginal tax rate.

   Compute the after-tax present value (expressed in nominal dollars) of:
   a. Expected cash operating savings before taxes of $100,000 (expressed in year 0 dollars) to be received one year from now.
   b. CCA of $70,000 to be deducted one year from now.

Answers to Chapter 22 Questions and Exercises

Completion Statements

1. marginal income tax rate
2. capital cost allowance (CCA)
3. Inflation
4. nominal
5. excess present value index (profitability index)

True-False

1. F   CCA of $10,000 is a tax shield, yielding a tax savings of CCA $\times$ 0.30 = $3,000.
2. F   The half-year rule applies only to *net* additions to the class.
3. T
4. T
5. F   Higher risks on individual projects can be recognized by increasing the required rate of return and/or *decreasing* the required payback period. Other approaches to deal with risk in capital-budgeting projects are decreasing estimated future net cash inflows, using sensitivity analysis, and estimating the profitability distribution of future cash inflows and outflows.
6. T
7. T
8. F   As shown in the Appendix to the chapter, not all classes use the declining-balance method. Classes 14 and 29 use the straight-line method.

Multiple Choice

1. d   Advertising: $-\$10,000 \times (1 - 0.40) = -\$6,000$
        CCA: $\$10,000 \times 0.40 = \$4,000$

2. a   Straight-line CCA = $130,000 \div 40 = \$3,250$ per year
        Under the half-year rule, CCA in year 1 = $\$3,250 \times 0.50 = \$1,625$
        After-tax cash flow of CCA in year 1 = $\$1,625 \times 0.40 = \$650$

3. c   Three steps are used to obtain the answer. First, compute the CCA for year 2:

Year 1 net additions to Class 8	$23,000
Deduct half-year CCA for year 1	
$0.20 \times 0.50 \times \$23,000$	<u>2,300</u>
End of year 1 UCC	<u>$20,700</u>

        Second, compute CCA for year 2: $0.20 \times \$20,700 = \$4,140$
        Third, compute the cash flow from operations, net of income taxes, for year 2:

Tax savings from CCA in year 2	
$\$4,140 \times 0.40$	$1,656
Net cash inflow from cash operating items	
($40,000 − $29,000)(1 − 0.40)	<u>6,600</u>
Total after-tax cash flow from operations	<u>$8,256</u>

4. d   Two steps are used to obtain the answer. First, compute the tax shield:
        The half-year rule applies to net additions only and CCA equals 30%; thus,

$$\text{Tax shield} = (\$14,800 \times 0.40) \times \left(\frac{0.30}{0.30 + 0.10} \right) \left(\frac{2 + 0.10}{2\,(1 + 0.10)} \right)$$

        Tax shield = $5,920 (0.30 $\div$ 0.40) (2.10 $\div$ 2.20)
        Tax shield = $5,920 (0.75) (0.955) = $4,240
        Second, compute net present of the after-tax cash outflow in year 1:
          NPV = $14,800 − $4,240 = $10,560

5. b   Two steps are used to obtain NPV. First, compute the lost tax shield:
        Because there are no net additions, the half-year rule does not apply; thus,

$$\text{Lost tax shield} = (\$5,000 \times 0.40) \left(\frac{0.30}{0.30 + 0.10} \right)$$

        Lost tax shield = $2,000 (0.75) = $1,500

Management Control Systems, Transfer Pricing, and Multinational Considerations

Chapter Overview

This chapter explains the connection between strategy, organization structure, management control systems, and accounting information. These factors influence the degree of decentralization in an organization and the pricing of products or services transferred among its subunits (departments or divisions). Even though this material involves less "number crunching" than most other chapters, the concepts are important because management control systems influence the behaviour of managers and other employees.

Chapter Highlights

1. **A management control system** is a means of gathering and using financial and nonfinancial information to aid and coordinate the process of making planning and control decisions throughout the organization and to guide the behaviour of its managers and other employees. The goal of a management control system is to improve the collective decisions within an organization in an economically feasible way.

2. Management control systems have both *formal* and *informal* components. The formal component includes the explicit rules, procedures, performance measures, and incentive plans that guide the behaviour of managers and other employees. For example, the accounting system is a formal control system that provides information on revenues, costs, and income. The informal component of the systems includes such aspects as shared values, loyalties, and mutual commitments among members of an organization and the unwritten norms about acceptable behaviour for managers and other employees.

3. To be effective, management control systems must have three features. They must (a) be closely aligned with an organization's strategies and goals, (b) be designed to fit the organization's structure and the decision-making responsibility of individual managers, and (c) motivate managers and other employees.

4. **Goal congruence** and **effort** are the dual aspects of **motivation**. Goal congruence exists when individuals and groups, working in their own best interest, take actions that align with the overall goals of top management. Effort is the physical and mental exertion toward a goal. Motivation is the desire to attain a selected goal (the goal-congruence aspect) combined with the resulting drive or pursuit toward that goal (the effort aspect).

5. Top management decides how much **decentralization** is optimal for an organization. The essence of decentralization is the freedom for managers at lower levels of the organization to make decisions. Maximum decentralization means minimum constraints and maximum freedom for managers at lower levels of an organization to make decisions, while maximum centralization means maximum constraints and minimum freedom for managers at lower levels of an organization to make decisions. Conceptually, the degree of decentralization chosen should maximize the excess of benefits over costs. From a practical standpoint, these benefits and costs can seldom be quantified, but the cost-benefit approach helps managers focus on the key issues.

6. A decentralized organization structure has a number of benefits. It (a) creates greater responsiveness to the needs of a subunit's customers, suppliers, and employees, (b) leads to gains from quicker decision making by subunit managers, (c) increases motivation of

subunit managers because they can exercise greater individual initiative, (d) aids management development and learning, and (e) sharpens the focus of subunit managers.

7. A main cost of a decentralized organization structure is **suboptimal decision making** (also called **goal incongruent decision-making**) that arises if a decision's benefit to one subunit is more than offset by its costs (or loss of benefits) to the organization as a whole. *Suboptimal decision making is most likely to occur if the subunits in the organization are highly interdependent;* interdependence exists if the decisions made by one subunit manager will affect the decisions and performance of other subunit managers. Other costs of decentralization are decreased loyalty toward the organization as a whole, increased costs of gathering information, and duplication of activities.

8. Decisions on insourcing or outsourcing (making or buying) products or services are likely to be decentralized, whereas decisions on long-term financing are likely to be centralized. Multinational companies are often decentralized, which enables country managers to make decisions that utilize their knowledge of local business and political conditions.

9. Responsibility centres— such as cost centres, profit centres, and investment centres—are compatible with either decentralization or centralization. For example, profit centres (subunits for which both revenues and costs are reported) normally are associated with high decentralization. A division organized as a profit centre, however, can have a high degree of centralization, as when restrictions are imposed on its out-sourcing.

10. In decentralized organizations, individual subunits act as if they are separate entities, and the management control system often uses **transfer prices**. A transfer price is the price one subunit of an organization charges for a product or service supplied to another subunit of the same organization. The transfer price creates revenues for the selling subunit and purchase costs for the buying subunit, thereby affecting the operating income of both subunits. Operating income can be used to evaluate the performance of individual subunits and to motivate their managers.

11. There are three basic methods for determining transfer prices: *market-based transfer prices, cost-based transfer prices,* and *negotiated transfer prices.* The chosen transfer price(s) should help achieve an organization's strategies and goals, and fit its structure. In particular, transfer price(s) should promote goal congruence and a sustained high level of management effort. Selling divisions should be motivated to hold down their costs of supplying a product or service, and buying divisions should be motivated to acquire and use inputs efficiently.

12. The Northern Petroleum example, beginning text p. 800, illustrates the three transfer-pricing methods. The following table summarizes Horizon's operating incomes for producing, transporting, and refining 100 barrels of crude oil:

	Transfer-Pricing Method		
	Market-Based	Cost-Based	Negoti-ated
Production Division	$500*	$ 80	$200
Transportation Division	100	128	275*
Refining Division	100	492*	225
Total company	$700	$700	$700

*The Division's highest operating income.

Total company income is $700 regardless of the transfer-pricing method used, but division operating incomes differ. The manager of the Production Division prefers the market-based transfer price, the manager of the Transportation Division prefers the negotiated transfer price, and the manager of the Refining Division prefers the cost-based transfer price. Each division manager, therefore, is keenly interested in the setting of transfer prices if his or her compensation is related to division operating income.

13. In the Northern Petroleum example, the choice of the transfer-pricing method *does not affect the size of the company's operating income pie ($700) but does affect how the pie is divided between the three divisions.* The reason is regardless of the transfer price, *the transactions among the divisions are internal to the company.* On the other hand, assume one of the transfer-pricing methods is chosen and the Refining Division, acting in its own best interest, buys crude oil from an *outside supplier.* In this case, the Refining Division's **autonomy** (the manager's degree of freedom to make decisions) is high but could produce suboptimal results. That is, if it is in the best interest of the company as a whole for the Refining Division to buy crude oil internally, the Refining Division's decision to buy from an outside supplier *decreases the size of the company's operating-income pie.*

14. Market-based transfer prices generally lead to optimal decisions by division managers if three conditions are met: (a) the market for the **intermediate product** (a product transferred between subunits of an organization) is perfectly competitive, (b) interdependencies of subunits are minimal, and (c) there are no additional costs or benefits to the organization as a whole from buying or selling in the external market instead of transferring internally. A **perfectly competitive market** exists if there is a homogenous product with equivalent buying and selling prices and no individual buyers or sellers can affect those prices by their own actions. By using market-based transfer prices in perfectly competitive markets, a company can achieve goal congruence, management effort, subunit performance evaluation, and (if desired) subunit autonomy.

15. If supply exceeds demand, market prices may fall well below their historical average. If the decline in prices is expected to be temporary, these low market prices are called *distress prices.* In the short run, the manager of the selling division should meet the distress price as long as it exceeds the incremental costs of supplying the product or service. If the price remains low in the long run, though, the company should use the distress price as the transfer price. Then the manager of the selling division must decide whether to dispose of some manufacturing facilities or shut down and have the buying division purchase the product from an outside supplier.

16. Cost-based transfer prices are helpful if market prices are unavailable, inappropriate, or too costly to obtain. Companies use transfer prices based on full costs even though these prices can lead to suboptimal decisions. Despite this limitation, surveys indicate managers prefer to use full-cost transfer prices because they (a) yield relevant costs for long-run decisions, (b) facilitate external pricing based on variable and fixed costs, and (c) are the least costly to administer.

17. An alternative cost-based approach is to choose a transfer price that splits, on some equitable basis, the difference between the maximum transfer price the buying division is willing to pay and the minimum transfer price the selling division is willing to charge. In the example, text p. 805, this difference is allocated between the Transportation Division and Refining Divisions based on their budgeted variable costs.

18. There is seldom a single cost-based transfer price that simultaneously achieves goal congruence, management effort, subunit performance evaluation, and (if desired) subunit autonomy. As a result, some companies choose **dual pricing**, using two separate transfer-pricing methods to price each interdivisional transaction. Dual pricing is not widely used in practice, however, because it tends to insulate managers from the frictions of the marketplace.

19. Negotiated transfer prices result from a bargaining process between the selling and buying divisions. This type of transfer price preserves division autonomy because the transfer price is the outcome of direct negotiations between division managers. A negotiated transfer price also has the advantage that each division manager is motivated to put forth effort to increase the operating income of his

or her division. The major disadvantage of this transfer price is the time and energy spent on the negotiations.

20. There is no all-pervasive rule for transfer pricing that leads toward optimal decisions for the organization as a whole. A general guideline formula, however, has proven to be a helpful first step in setting a minimum transfer price in many situations: *Minimum transfer price = Incremental costs per unit incurred up to the point of transfer + Opportunity costs per unit to the selling division.* Incremental costs in this context are the additional costs of producing and transferring the products or services. Opportunity costs are the maximum contribution forgone by the selling division if the products or services are transferred internally. If the selling division has idle capacity, these opportunity costs are zero.

21. When multinational companies transfer products between divisions located in different countries, they must consider additional factors in setting transfer prices, including income taxes, customs duties, tariffs, value-added taxes, and dividend payment restrictions. With different income tax rates in various countries, companies want to minimize taxable income reported in the higher-taxed countries. In Canada, Information Circular 87-2 provides guidance to Canadian companies about Revenue Canada's approach to tax issues concerning international transfer prices. The taxpayer in Canada is expected to report taxable income on the basis of having charged a fair price for goods and services provided to non-resident affiliates, and of having paid no more than a fair price for goods and services received from non-resident affiliates.

Featured Exercise

Ajax Division of Carlyle Corporation produces electric motors, 20,000 of which are sold to Bradley Division of Carlyle and the remainder are sold to outside customers. Carlyle treats its divisions as profit centres and allows division managers to choose their sources of supply and to whom they sell. Corporate policy requires variable costs be used as the transfer price for all interdivisional sales and purchases. Ajax Division's estimated revenues and costs for the coming year, based on the full capacity of 100,000 units, are as follows:

	Bradley	Outsiders
Revenues	$ 900,000	$8,000,000
Variable costs	900,000	3,600,000
Contribution margin	-0-	4,400,000
Fixed costs	300,000	1,200,000
Operating income	$(300,000)	$3,200,000
Unit sales	20,000	80,000

Ajax has an opportunity to sell the 20,000 motors to an external customer at a price of $75 per unit on a continuing basis beginning next year. Bradley can purchase its requirement of 20,000 motors from an external supplier at a price of $85 per unit.

a. Compute the increase/decrease in Ajax Division's operating income if Ajax drops the sales to Bradley and adds the new customer for the coming year. Assume Ajax's fixed costs are unavoidable.

b. Instead of using variable costs as the transfer price, assume Carlyle permits the division managers to negotiate the transfer price for next year. The managers agree on a transfer price: $75 per unit minus an equal sharing between the divisions of the additional operating income earned by Ajax from the selling Bradley 20,000 motors at $75 per unit. Compute the transfer price for next year.

Solution

a. In making this decision, the manager of Ajax Division needs to determine the difference between the total relevant operating income of selling externally and of selling internally. The variable manufacturing costs per unit are ($900,000 + $3,600,000) ÷ (20,000 + 80,000) = $45.

Total relevant operating income on external sale	
20,000 × ($75 − $45)	$600,000
Total relevant operating income on internal sale	
20,000 × ($45 − $45)	-0-
Difference in favour of external sale	$600,000

Alternative solution: Compare the financial statement results for the 20,000 units in question:

	Internal Sale (the Present Situation)	External Sale
Revenues, given; 20,000 × $75	$ 900,000	$1,500,000
Variable costs	900,000	900,000
Contribution margin	-0-	600,000
Fixed costs	300,000	300,000
Gross margin	$(300,000)	$ 300,000

Difference in favour of external sale $600,000

b. Two steps are used to obtain the answer. First, determine the amount of additional operating income that results from the internal sale at $75 per unit:

$75 − $45 = $30 per unit

Second, reduce the $75 by a 50%: 50% split between the divisions of the additional operating income:

Transfer price = $75 − 0.50($30) = $75 − $15 = $60 per unit

Review Questions and Exercises

Completion Statements

Fill in the blank(s) to complete each statement.

1. A means of gathering and using information to aid and coordinate the process of making planning and control decisions throughout the organization and to guide the behaviour of its managers and other employees is called a _____.

2. _____ exists when individuals and groups, working in their own perceived best interests, take actions that further the overall goals of top management.

3. The desire to attain a selected goal combined with the resulting drive or pursuit toward that goal is called _____.

4. The essence of _____ is the freedom for managers at lower levels of the organization to make decisions.

5. _____ refers to the degree of freedom to make decisions.

6. _____ arises if the benefit of a decision to a subunit is more than offset by its cost (or loss of benefit) to the organization as a whole.

7. Products transferred between subunits of an organization are called _____ _____.

8. What four criteria help in choosing a transfer price? _____ _____ _____ and _____.

9. In many situations, a general guideline formula has proven to be a helpful first step in setting a minimum transfer price. This minimum transfer price is equal to the sum of which two per-unit costs? _____ _____ and _____ _____.

True-False

Indicate whether each statement is true (T) or false (F).

____ 1. The informal control system in an organization is likely to include a human resources system that provides information on recruiting, training, absenteeism, and accidents.

____ 2. Conceptually, the degree of decentralization in an organization depends primarily on determining the optimal number of profit centres.

____ 3. Suboptimal decisions are often associated with a lack of goal congruence.

____ 4. Decentralization is likely to be most beneficial if an organization's subunits are highly interdependent.

____ 5. One way to limit decentralization is to impose restrictions on the ability of subunits to outsource products that are available from internal subunits.

____ 6. Profit centres are compatible with high centralization.

____ 7. The choice of a transfer-pricing method can sizably affect how a company's operating-income pie is divided among the individual subunits as well as the size of the operating-income pie itself.

____ 8. If top management imposes insourcing on its division managers, total company operating income will be unaffected by the transfer-pricing method used.

____ 9. Full-cost transfer prices are frequently used in practice to help avoid the pitfalls of suboptimal decision making.

____ 10. Compared to domestic companies, multinational companies must consider additional factors in setting their transfer prices, including different income tax rates in various countries and promotion of goal congruence.

Multiple Choice

Select the best answer to each question. Space is provided for computations after the quantitative questions.

____ 1. (CMA adapted) Which of the following is decentralization *least likely* to accomplish?
   a. Provide a pool of management talent.
   b. Shorten decision time.
   c. Heighten goal congruence.
   d. Increase motivation of subunit managers.

____ 2. (CPA) Brent Co. has intracompany service transfers from Division Core, a cost centre, to Division Pro, a profit centre. Under stable economic conditions, which of the following transfer prices is likely to be most conducive to evaluating whether both divisions have met their responsibilities?
   a. Actual cost
   b. Standard variable cost
   c. Actual cost plus mark-up
   d. Negotiated price

____ 3. (CPA) In a decentralized company in which divisions may buy goods from one another, the transfer-pricing system should be designed primarily to:
   a. increase the consolidated inventory costs.
   b. allow division managers to buy from outsider suppliers.
   c. minimize the degree of autonomy of division managers.
   d. aid in the appraisal and motivation of managers' performance.

____ 4. Designing the transfer-pricing system is most difficult in organizations that are:

a. highly decentralized with many inter-dependencies among subunits.

b. highly centralized with many inter-dependencies among subunits.

c. highly decentralized with few inter-dependencies among subunits.

d. highly centralized with few inter-dependencies among subunits.

___ 5. (CMA) Parkside Inc. has several divisions that operate as decentralized profit centres. Parkside's Entertainment Division manufactures video arcade equipment using the products of two of Parkside's other divisions. The Plastics Division manufactures plastic components; one type is made exclusively for the Entertainment Division, while other less complex components are sold to outside markets. The products of the Video Cards Division are sold in a competitive market: however, one video card model is also used by the Entertainment Division. The actual manufacturing costs per unit of the Entertainment Division are as follows:

	Plastics Components	Video Cards
Direct materials used	$1.25	$2.40
Direct manuf. labour	2.35	3.00
Variable overhead	1.00	1.50
Fixed overhead	.40	2.25
Total costs	$5.00	$9.15

The Plastics Division sells its commercial products at full cost plus a 25% markup based on cost and believes the proprietary plastic component made for the Entertainment Division would sell for $6.25 per unit on the open market. The market price of the video card used by the Entertainment Division is $10.98 per unit.

Assuming the Video Cards Division has no unused capacity, a transfer price to the Entertainment Division of $9.15 per unit will:

a. allow evaluation of both divisions on a competitive basis.

b. satisfy the Video Cards Division's profit desire by allowing recovery of opportunity costs.

c. not motivate the Entertainment Division and will cause mediocre performance.

d. provide no incentive for the Video Cards Division to control or reduce costs.

e. encourage the Entertainment Division to purchase video cards from an outside source.

___ 6. Use the data in question 5 but assume the Entertainment Division is able to purchase a large quantity of video cards from an outside supplier at $8.70 per unit. The Video Cards Division, having unused capacity, agrees to lower the transfer price to $8.70 per unit. This action will:

a. optimize the profit goals of the Entertainment Division while subverting the profit goals of Parkside Inc.

b. provide no profit incentive for the Video Cards Division.

c. subvert the profit goals of the Video Cards Division while optimizing the profit goals of the Entertainment Division.

d. cause mediocre behaviour in the Video Cards Division because opportunity costs increase.

e. optimize the overall profit goals of Parkside Inc.

___ 7. Use the data in question 5 and assume the Plastics Division has unused capacity and negotiates a transfer price of $5.60 per plastic component with the Entertainment Division. This price will:

a. cause the Plastics Division to reduce the number of commercial plastic components it manufactures.

b. motivate both divisions.

c. encourage the Entertainment Division to seek an outside source for plastic components.

d. not motivate the Plastics Division, causing mediocre performance.

e. satisfy the Plastics Division's profit desire by allowing recovery of opportunity costs.

___ 8. (CPA adapted) Mar Company has two decentralized divisions, X and Y. Division X has been purchasing certain component parts from Division Y at $75 per unit. Because Division Y plans to raise the price to $100 per unit, Division X desires to purchase these parts from external suppliers for $75 per unit. The following information is available:

Y's variable costs per unit	$70
Y's annual fixed costs	$15,000
Y's annual production of these parts for X	1,000 units

If Division X buys from an external supplier, the facilities Division Y uses to manufacture these parts will be idle. Assuming Division Y's fixed costs cannot be avoided, what is the result if Mar requires Division X to buy from Division Y at a transfer price of $100 per unit?

a. It is suboptimal for the company as a whole because X should buy from outside suppliers at $75 per unit.
b. It is more profitable for the company as a whole than allowing X to buy from outside suppliers at $75 per unit.
c. It provides higher overall company operating income than a transfer price of $75 per unit.
d. It provides lower overall company operating income than a transfer price of $75 per unit.

Exercises

1. During the current year, Division A of Galloway Company incurred the following manufacturing costs for 5,000 units of a component part:

	Total	Per Unit
Variable costs	$200,000	$40
Fixed costs	40,000	8

a. Compute the advantage/disadvantage to the company as a whole (in terms of next year's operating income) if there are no alternative uses for Division A's facilities, and if Division B purchases 5,000 units of this part from an external supplier at a price of (1) $43 per unit (2) $36 per unit.

b. Compute the advantage/disadvantage to the company as a whole (in terms of next year's operating income) if there are alternative uses for Division A's facilities by other Galloway operations that would otherwise require additional outlay costs of $26,000, and if Division B purchases 5,000 units of this part from an external supplier at a price of (1) $43 per unit (2) $36 per unit.

2. Empire Company has two divisions. Division C is located in Canada where the income tax rate is 40%. Division K is located in Korea where the income tax rate is 30%. Division C produces an intermediate product at a variable cost of $100 per unit, and transfers the product to Division K where it is finished and sold for $500 per unit. Variable costs in Division K are $80 per unit. Fixed costs are $75,000 per year in Division C and $90,000 per year in Division K. Assume 1,000 units are transferred annually and the minimum transfer price allowed by the Canadian tax authorities is the variable cost. Also assume operating income in each country is equal to taxable income.

   a. What transfer price should be set for Empire to minimize its total income taxes? Show your computations.

   b. If Empire desires to minimize its total income taxes, compute the amount of tax liability in each country.

Answers to Chapter 23 Review Questions and Exercises

Completion Statements

1. management control system
2. Goal congruence
3. motivation
4. decentralization
5. Autonomy
6. Suboptimal decision making (Goal incongruent decision-making)
7. intermediate products
8. goal congruence, management effort, subunit performance evaluation, (if desired) subunit autonomy
9. incremental cost per unit incurred up to the point of transfer, opportunity costs per unit to the selling division

True-False

1. F A human resources system is part of the *formal control system* in an organization. The *informal control system* includes such aspects as shared values, loyalties, mutual commitments among members of the organization, and unwritten norms about acceptable behaviour for managers and other employees.

2. F To decide how much decentralization is optimal, top management tries conceptually to choose the degree of decentralization that maximizes the excess of benefits over costs From a

practical standpoint, these benefits and costs can seldom be quantified, but the cost-benefit approach helps top management focus on the central issues.

3. T

4. F   Decentralization is likely to be most beneficial if an organization's subunits are *independent*. If the subunits are highly *interdependent*, suboptimal decisions are most likely to occur because the decisions affecting one subunit influence the decisions and performance of one or more other subunits.

5. T

6. T

7. T

8. T

9. F   Although full-cost transfer prices are frequently used in practice, this method can lead to suboptimal decisions, as explained in the Northern Petroleum example, text pp. 803-804. The main rationale for using full-cost transfer prices is they allow divisions to recover their fixed costs.

10. F   All companies (whether multinational or domestic) need to consider the promotion of goal congruence in setting their transfer prices. Compared to domestic companies, however, multinational companies must consider several additional factors in setting their transfer prices: (i) different income tax rates in various countries, (ii) tariffs, custom duties, value-added taxes, and the like, and (iii) restrictions that some countries place on income or dividend payments to parties outside their national borders.

Multiple Choice

1. c   A cost of decentralization is suboptimal decision making (incongruent or dysfunctional decision making). One reason this phenomenon occurs is the goals of subunit managers may not be congruent with top management goals. For example, a division manager, who is acting to maximize his or her division's operating income, might decide to buy a component part from an outside supplier when it is in the company's best interest to buy the part internally. Note that answers (a), (b), and (d) refer to *benefits* of decentralization.

2. b   By using standard variable cost as the transfer price, Division Core is motivated to improve its efficiency in providing services to Division Pro. Under this transfer price, none of Core's cost variances will be allocated to Pro; therefore, Pro's performance could be appropriately measured by its operating income. A negotiated price could not be used in this case because Core is a cost centre, not a profit centre or investment centre.

3. d   In designing a transfer-pricing system, four criteria should be considered: goal congruence, management effort, subunit performance evaluation, and (if desired) subunit autonomy. These criteria are central to the motivation of division managers and appraisal of their performance. Answer (a) is incorrect because, under generally accepted accounting principles, inventory cannot be carried at more than its cost in consolidated financial statements. Therefore, if transfer prices exceed costs, which is often the case, intracompany (interdivisional) operating income must be eliminated from inventory. Answer (b) is incorrect because allowing division managers to buy from outside suppliers should not be the *primary* purpose of designing a transfer-pricing system. In some cases it may be more profitable to outsource, but in other cases it may be more profitable to insource. Answer (c) is incorrect because a transfer-pricing system seeks to optimize (as distinguished from minimize or maximize) the degree of the division managers' autonomy.

4. a   The transfer-pricing problem is the greatest in organizations that are highly decentralized with many interdependencies among subunits. The reason is, under conditions of considerable freedom in decision making, decisions made by one subunit manager affect the decisions and performance of one or more other subunit managers.

5. d The market price of the video card used by the Entertainment Division is $10.98. Because the Video Cards Division has no unused capacity, it obviously has no profit incentive in selling this video card to the Entertainment Division at $9.15 per unit. The Video Cards Division would forgo $1.83 ($10.98 − $9.15) on each unit sold to the Entertainment Division. In contrast, the Entertainment Division would be very pleased to buy the video card internally at $1.83 less than the market price.

6. e Because the Video Cards Division has unused capacity, a selling price of $8.70 contributes $1.80 ($8.70 − $2.40 − $3.00 − $1.50) per unit sold to the recovery of its fixed overhead and then to its operating income. The Entertainment Division is indifferent about buying internally or from an outside supplier at the price of $8.70. Given the benefit to the Video Cards Division and the indifference of the Entertainment Division, the $8.70 transfer price is in the best interest of Parkside Inc. as a whole.

7. b The negotiated transfer price of $5.60 lies between the Plastics Division's variable costs per unit of $4.60 ($1.25 + $2.35 + $1.00) and its regular selling price of $6.25. Because the Plastics Division has unused capacity, the transfer price of $5.60 motivates both divisions. The Plastics Division receives $1.00 ($5.60 − $4.60) more than its variable costs on each unit sold. The Entertainment Division buys the plastic component for $0.65 ($6.25 − $5.60) per unit less than the market price.

8. b If Mar requires transfers be made at $100 per unit, Division X pays Division Y 1,000 × $100 = $100,000. This transaction is intracompany (interdivisional) in nature (that is, money goes out of one corporate pocket into another corporate pocket). *The $100,000, therefore, has no effect on operating income of the company as a whole*. The effect of purchasing internally on the operating income of the company as a whole is:

Total relevant costs of external purchase		
1,000 × $75		$75,000
Deduct total relevant costs of internal purchase:		
Avoidable costs, 1,000 × $70	$70,000	
Opportunity costs to the selling division	-0-	70,000
Difference in favour of buying internally		$ 5,000

This analysis shows operating income of the company as a whole is $5,000 higher if Division X buys from Division Y. Given that transfers are required, *this conclusion holds regardless of the transfer price used*. Of course, performance evaluation of the subunit managers is likely to be affected by the transfer price used.

Exercise 1

a.

	(1)	(2)
Variable costs per unit, $200,000 ÷ 5,000	$ 40	$ 40
External market price per unit	43	36
Advantage (disadvantage) per unit	$ (3)	$ 4
Multiply by number of units	× 5,000	× 5,000
Next year's annual operating income advantage (disadvantage) to the company as a whole	$(15,000)	$20,000

Fixed costs are irrelevant because they remain the same whether Division B buys internally or externally.

b.

	(1)	(2)
Advantage (disadvantage) as above, before considering alternative use of facilities	$(15,000)	$20,000
Advantage from alternative use of facilities	26,000	26,000
Next year's operating income advantage to the company as a whole	$ 11,000	$46,000

As in part (a), fixed costs are irrelevant.

Exercise 2

a. To minimize its total income taxes, the company should report no operating income in Canada, the country with the higher income tax rate. This outcome occurs if the transfer price is set at full cost: $100 + ($75,000 ÷ 1,000) = $175 per unit.

b. Using the $175 transfer price from part (a), the company's tax liability in Canada is $0 and in Korea is $46,500:

Division C (Canada)		Division K (Korea)	
Revenues, 1,000 × $175	$175,000	Revenues, 1,000 × $500	$500,000
		Transferred-in costs,	
Variable costs,		$100,000 + $75,000	(175,000)
1,000 × $100	(100,000)	Variable costs, 1,000 × $80	(80,000)
Fixed costs	(75,000)	Fixed costs	(90,000)
Operating income	0	Operating income	155,000
Income tax	0	Income tax (at 30%)	(46,500)
Net income	$ 0	Net income	$108,500

Performance Measurement, Compensation, and Multinational Considerations

Chapter Overview

This chapter examines issues related to designing performance measures for managers at different levels of the organization. Performance measures are a central component of management control systems, and performance evaluation and rewards (salaries, bonuses, and career advancement) are key elements to motivate managers. Much of the chapter focuses on decentralized companies where the divisions are investment centres.

Chapter Highlights

1. Management control systems use both financial and nonfinancial performance measures. Many common performance measures, such as operating income and return on investment, are based on internal financial information. Increasingly, companies are supplementing internal financial measures with measures based on external financial information (such as stock price), internal nonfinancial information (such as manufacturing lead time), and external nonfinancial information (such as customer satisfaction ratings). Companies often benchmark their financial and nonfinancial measures against the best levels of performance available within the organization or in other organizations.

2. Some organizations present financial and nonfinancial performance measures for their subunits in a single report called the *balanced scorecard* (described in Chapter 13). Although different companies stress different elements in their scorecards, most scorecards include (a) profitability measures, (b) customer-satisfaction measures, (c) internal measures of efficiency, quality, and time, and (d) innovation measures. The balanced scorecard highlights trade-offs among the performance measures and avoids overemphasis on a single measure.

3. Designing an accounting-based performance measures for an organization subunit requires five steps:

Step 1: Choose the variables for performance measures that represent top management's financial goal(s).

Step 2: Define the components of each performance measure in Step 1.

Step 3: Measure the components of each performance measure in Step 1.

Step 4: Choose a target level of performance.

Step 5: Choose the timing of feedback.

Discussion of these steps is keyed to paragraphs 4 through 18.

4. (Step 1) A subunit's operating income should be evaluated by considering the size of the **investment** (assets) used to generate this income. One way to do this evaluation is by computing **return on investment (ROI)**:

$$\text{ROI} = \frac{\text{Income}}{\text{Investment}}$$

ROI has conceptual appeal because it blends all of the ingredients of profitability (revenues, costs, and investment) into a single percentage. ROI can be compared with the rate of return on investment opportunities available elsewhere, inside or outside the company. Like any single performance measure, however, ROI should be used cautiously and in conjunction with other performance measures.

5. (Step 1) Under an approach known as the *DuPont method of profitability analysis*, the

$$\text{EVA} = \begin{array}{c}\text{After-tax}\\ \text{operating}\\ \text{income}\end{array} - [\text{WACC} \times (\text{TA} - \text{CL})]$$

ROI computation is divided into two components:

$$\frac{\text{Revenues}}{\text{Investment}} \times \frac{\text{Income}}{\text{Revenues}} = \text{ROI}$$

also written as:

Investment turnover $\times$ Return on sales = ROI

The DuPont method recognizes that there are two basic ingredients in profit making: (a) using assets to generate more revenues and (b) increasing income per dollar of revenues. ROI increases by improving one or both of these ingredients.

6. (Step 1) ROI highlights to managers the benefits of reducing their subunits' investments in current or long-term assets. Some managers are conscious of the need to boost revenues or to control costs but give less attention to reducing their investment base. Reducing the investment base means decreasing idle cash, managing credit judiciously, determining proper inventory levels, and spending carefully on long-term assets.

7. (Step 1) Another way to consider the size of the investment used to generate income is by computing **residual income (RI)**:

RI = Income − (RRR $\times$ Investment)

where:

RRR = Required rate of return

In this formula, RRR times investment is the **imputed cost** of the investment, which is an opportunity cost—the return forgone as a result of tying up cash in the investment rather than earning returns elsewhere on investments of similar risk.

8. (Step 1) By maximizing RI, managers are induced to expand their subunits as long as the rate of return earned is greater than the required rate of return. In contrast, maximizing ROI may cause managers of highly profitable subunits to reject projects that, from the standpoint of the organization as a whole, should be accepted (that is, the ROI on these

projects exceeds the company's required rate of return). *Goal congruence, therefore, is more likely to be promoted by using RI rather than ROI as a measure of the subunit manager's performance.*

9. (Step 1) Another way to consider the size of the investment used to generate income is by computing **economic value added (EVA)**. This performance measure, a specific type of RI calculation, has recently attracted considerable attention.
where:

WACC = Weighted-average cost of capital on an after-tax basis
 TA = Total assets
 CL = Current liabilities

WACC is the counterpart of "required rate of return" in the computation of RI. To increase EVA, managers must earn more after-tax operating income with the same capital, use less capital to earn the same after-tax operating income, or invest capital in high-return projects. The example, text p. 830, computes EVA.

10. (Step 1) The income-to-revenues ratio—often called *return on sales (ROS)*—is a frequently used financial performance measure. ROS is one component of ROI in the DuPont method of profitability analysis. ROS provides the most meaningful indicator of a subunit manager's performance in markets where revenue growth is limited and investment levels are fixed.

11. (Step 1) Managers could take actions that cause short-run increases in ROI, RI, EVA, and ROS but are in conflict with the long-run interest of the organization. For this reason, many companies evaluate subunit managers on the basis of these measures using a multi-year time horizon. Another reason for evaluating subunit managers over multiple years is the benefits of actions taken in the current period may not show up in short-run performance measures.

12. (Step 1) Using a multi-year time horizon highlights another advantage of RI: the net present value (NPV) of all the cash flows over the life of an investment equals the NPV of the RIs. This relationship means if managers use the NPV method to make capital-budgeting decisions (as advocated in Chapter 21), using multi-year RIs to evaluate managers' performance achieves goal congruence.

13. (Step 1) Another way a company can motivate managers to take a long-run perspective is by compensating them on the basis of changes in the market price of the company's stock (in addition to using accounting-based performance measures over multiple years). This approach helps to extend managers' time horizon because stock prices more rapidly incorporate the expected future period effects of current decisions.

14. (Step 2) Companies that use ROI or RI for performance measures generally define "investment" as *total assets available*. If top management directs a subunit manager to carry extra assets, however, *total assets employed* can be more informative than total assets available. Companies that use EVA define investment as *total assets employed minus current liabilities*. The most common rationale for using this definition of investment is the subunit manager often influences decisions on current liabilities of the subunit.

15. (Step 3) Two alternative ways to measure assets included in the investment base are: *historical cost* or **current cost**. Current cost is the cost of purchasing an asset today identical to the one currently held, or the cost of purchasing the services provided by that asset if an identical one cannot currently be purchased. Adjusting assets to recognize current costs negates differences in the investment base that are caused solely by different levels of historical cost over time. Consequently, compared to historical-cost ROI, current-cost ROI is a better measure of the current economic returns from the investment. A drawback of using current cost, however, is it can be difficult to obtain current-cost esti-

mates for some assets. EXHIBIT 24-3, text p. 836, illustrates a six-step approach to incorporate current-cost estimates of long-term assets into the ROI calculation.

16. (Step 3) Because historical-cost investment measures are often used in practice, there has been much discussion about the relative merits of using *gross book value* (original cost) or *net book value* (original cost minus accumulated amortization). Those who favour using gross book value assert it enables more accurate comparisons across subunits. They point out that if net book value is used, ROI can increase as an asset ages solely because periodic amortization decreases the investment base. Those who favour using net book value maintain it is less confusing because it is consistent with (a) the amount of total assets shown in the conventional balance sheet and (b) income computations that include deductions for amortization. Surveys of company practice report net book value to be the dominant asset measure used by companies in their internal performance evaluations.

17. (Step 4) Despite the fact accounting measures based on historical cost are often inadequate for evaluating economic returns on new investments and sometimes create disincentives for expansion, *historical-cost ROIs can be used to evaluate current performance by establishing target (budgeted) ROIs*. The target ROI should be carefully negotiated with a full knowledge of the accounting pitfalls of historical cost.

18. (Step 5) Performance feedback can be reported daily, weekly, monthly, or at some other time interval. The timing of feedback depends largely on how critical the information is for the success of the organization, the level of management receiving the feedback, and the sophistication of the organization's information technology.

19. Comparing performance of the divisions of a multinational company (that is, a company operating in different countries) is difficult because of legal, political, social, economic, and currency differences. For

example, when divisions of a multinational company record their performance in different currencies, issues of inflation and fluctuations in foreign currency exchange rates become important. The illustration, text p. 839, shows how a Canadian multinational company should compute the ROI of its Mexico division for the current year during which the peso steadily declined in value relative to the dollar.

20. Regardless of whether ROI, RI, EVA, or ROS is used, distinguish between measuring the performance of *a manager* and measuring the performance of *an organization subunit*. For example, the most skillful manager may be put in charge of the division producing the poorest economic returns in an attempt to change its fortunes. In this case, the manager is more appropriately evaluated by comparing his or her performance against a budget rather than against the performance of other divisions. The manager's performance is the basis of his or her compensation, future job assignments, and career advancement, whereas the division's performance is key to allocating resources within the organization.

21. The total compensation of subunit managers usually consists of both a salary and a performance-based incentive (bonus). An important consideration in designing compensation arrangements is the trade-off between creating incentives to get the manager to work hard and imposing risk on the manager. The manager is subject to risk if actual performance depends partially on factors he or she cannot control, such as economic conditions. In this case, the difficulty of monitoring the manager's efforts causes **moral hazard**: situations in which an employee prefers to exert less effort (or report distorted information) compared to the effort (or information) desired by the owner because the employee's effort (or information) cannot be accurately monitored and enforced.

22. The size of the incentive component in a compensation plan relative to the amount of salary should depend on how well the performance measure(s) captures the manager's ability to influence the desired results. *Preferred performance measures are ones that are sensitive to (change significantly with) the manager's performance and do not change much with changes in factors that are beyond the manager's control.* Performance measures that are sensitive to the manager's performance motivate the manager but limit his or her exposure to uncontrollable risk. For example, assume a division manager has no control over revenues and investment but can control costs. Using a cost-based performance measure is desirable because it captures the manager's effort, whereas using ROI as the performance measure is undesirable because it does not capture the manager's effort. If owners have performance measures available to them that are sensitive to the manager's performance, they place greater reliance on incentive compensation.

23. Surveys show that division managers' compensation plans include a mix of salary and long-term compensation tied to the income and stock price of the company. The goal is to balance division and companywide performance, as well as short-term and long-term incentives.

24. It can be cost effective to benchmark a manager's performance against the best levels of performance available within the organization or in other organizations. This approach is called *relative performance evaluation*; it filters out the effects of common uncontrollable factors. Benchmarking the performance of two managers responsible for similar operations within a company, however, can lead to goal incongruence; one manager might improve his or her performance by making the other manager look bad. Managers being unwilling to cooperate and work together is not in the best interest of the organization as a whole.

25. Many manufacturing, marketing, and design problems require managers and other employees with multiple skills and experiences to pool their talents. In these situations, companies often give incentives to individuals

based on team performance. These incentives encourage individuals to help one another as they strive toward a common goal.

26. The principles of performance evaluation described in paragraphs 21 through 25 also apply to executive compensation plans. These plans are based on both financial and nonfinancial performance measures and consist of a mix of (a) base salary, (b) annual incentives such as cash bonuses based on achieving a target annual RI, (c) long-run incentives such as stock options based on achieving a target return by the end of a five-year period, and (d) fringe benefits. Designers of executive compensation plans emphasize three factors: achievement of organization goals, administrative ease, and the likelihood affected executives will perceive the plan to be fair.

27. As they strive to achieve the performance goals of their organizations, managers should be keenly aware of their environmental and ethical responsibilities. Environmental violations (such as water and air pollution) and unethical and illegal practices (such as bribery and corruption) carry heavy fines and are prison offenses under the laws of Canada, the United States, and other countries. Managers' environmental responsibilities and ethical conduct, however, extend beyond legal requirements.

Featured Exercise

The following information is from the financial statements of Duke Company for the fiscal year ending September 30, 1999:

Total assets	$6,000,000
Current liabilities	1,250,000
Operating income	1,140,000

a. Compute return on investment (ROI).

b. Compute residual income (RI), assuming the required rate of return is 18%.

c. Compute economic value added (EVA) assuming (1) Duke has two sources of funds—long-term debt with a market value of $2,500,000 and an interest rate of 10%, and equity capital with a market value of $5,000,000 and a cost of equity of 16%—and (2) Duke's income tax rate is 30%.

Solution

a.   ROI = $1,140,000 \div \$6,000,000 = 19\%$
b.   RI = $1,140,000 - (\$6,000,000 \times 0.18)$
      RI = $1,140,000 - \$1,080,000 = \$60,000$

c.   Three steps are used to obtain the answer. First, compute the after-tax cost of debt financing:

$$\text{After-tax cost of debt financing} = (1.00 - 0.30) \times 10\% = 7\%$$
(The after-tax cost of equity financing, 16%, is given.)

Second, compute the weighted-average cost of capital (WACC) on an after-tax basis:

$$\text{WACC} = \frac{(0.07 \times \$2,500,000) + (0.16 \times \$5,000,000)}{\$2,500,000 + \$5,000,000}$$

$$\text{WACC} = \frac{\$175,000 + \$800,000}{\$7,500,000} = \frac{\$975,000}{\$7,500,000} = 13\%$$

Third, compute EVA:

$$\text{EVA} = (\$1,140,000 \times 0.70) - [0.13 \times (\$6,000,000 - \$1,250,000)]$$
$$\text{EVA} = \$798,000 - (0.13 \times \$4,750,000)$$
$$\text{EVA} = \$798,000 - \$617,500 = \$180,500$$

Review Questions and Exercises

Completion Statements

Fill in the blank(s) to complete each statement.

1. Designing accounting-based performance measure for an organization subunit requires five steps. Step 1 is to choose the variables performance measures that _____ _____ financial goal(s).

2. Using initials, what are the three accounting-based performance measures that relate income to investment? _____, _____ and _____.

3. In the formula to compute residual income, the required rate of return multiplied by investment is called the _____ cost of the investment.

4. _____ cost is the cost of purchasing an asset today identical to the one currently held, or the cost of purchasing the services provided by that asset if an identical one cannot currently be purchased.

5. An important consideration in designing compensation arrangements is the trade-off between creating _____ to get the manager to work hard and imposing _____ on the manager.

6. _____ describes situations in which an employee prefers to exert less effort (or report distorted information) compared to the effort (or information) desired by the owner because the employee's effort (or information) cannot be accurately monitored and enforced.

True-False

Indicate whether each statement is true (T) or false (F).

___ 1. A company's market share is an example of external nonfinancial information.

___ 2. A good reason for using ROI as a performance measure rather than RI is goal congruence is more likely to be promoted by using ROI.

___ 3. The DuPont method of profitability analysis recognizes there are two basic ingredients to profit making: using assets to generate more revenues and increasing income per dollar of revenues.

___ 4. If companies compensate managers on the basis of changes in the market price of the company's stock, this approach tends to shorten managers' time horizon because stock prices more rapidly incorporate the expected future period effects of current decisions.

___ 5. Companies using EVA define investment as total assets employed minus current liabilities.

___ 6. Those who favour using net book value as the investment base in ROI calculations claim this approach enables more accurate comparisons across subunits.

___ 7. Comparing performance of the divisions of a multinational company is difficult because of legal, political, social, economic, and currency differences.

___ 8. A necessary and sufficient condition for moral hazard to exist in a company is the employee's interest differs from the owner's interest.

___ 9. Performance measures that are sensitive to the manager's performance motivate the manager but limit his or her exposure to uncontrollable risk.

___ 10. It can be cost effective to benchmark a manager's performance against the best levels of performance available within the organization or in other organizations.

___ 11. Managers' environmental responsibilities and ethical conduct extend beyond legal requirements.

Multiple Choice

Select the best answer to each question. Space is provided for computations after the quantitative questions.

___ 1. Roma Bottling Co. has an investment of $3,000,000, an income-to-revenues ratio of 4%, and an ROI of 12%. Its revenues are:
a. $360,000.
b. $9,000,000.
c. $1,440,000.
d. $12,000,000.

___ 2. Using the data in question 1, the revenues-to-investment ratio is:
a. 5 times.
b. 4 times.
c. 3 times.
d. 2 times.

___ 3. (CMA adapted) A company's ROI increases if:
a. revenues increase by the same dollar amount that costs and total assets increase.
b. revenues remain the same, and costs are reduced by the same dollar amount that total assets increase.
c. revenues decrease by the same dollar amount that costs increase.
d. revenues and costs increase by the same percentage that total assets increase.
e. none of the above.

___ 4. Fletcher, Inc. has an RI of $180,000 and operating income of $500,000. If the required rate of return is 16%, the amount of investment is:
a. $320,000.
b. $3,125,000.
c. $8,000,000.
d. $2,000,000.
e. none of the above.

___ 5. Using the data in question 4, ROI is:
a. 5%.
b. 10%.
c. 15%.
d. 20%.
e. none of the above.

___ 6. (CPA) Marsh Inc. has an incentive compensation plan under which its president is paid a bonus equal to 10% of Marsh's income after deducting the bonus but before deducting income taxes. For the fiscal year ended December 1999. Marsh's income was $110,000 before deducting the bonus and income taxes. Marsh had income taxes of $40,000 in 1999. How much bonus should Marsh pay its president for 1999?
a. $0
b. $7,000
c. $10,000
d. $11,000

Exercises

1. Rochelle Company has just purchased a milling machine at a cost of $200,000. The machine is expected to generate operating income of $18,000 per year during its 10-year useful life. Rochelle uses the straight-line method of amortization with a zero terminal disposal price.

Compute ROI in the following situations:
a. First year using gross book value as the investment base.
b. Sixth year using gross book value as the investment base.
c. First year using net book value at the end of the year as the investment base.
d. Sixth year using net book value at the beginning of the year as the investment base.

2. The Kline Corporation manufactures pharmaceutical products in Canada and China. The operations are organized as decentralized divisions. The following information is available for 1999:

	Canada Division	China Division
Operating income	$2,400,000	11,400,000 yuan
Total assets	$16,000,000	75,000,000 yuan

The exchange rate at the time of Kline's investment in China on December 31, 1999 was 7.5 Chinese yuan = $1 U.S. During 2000, the yuan declined steadily in value and the exchange rate on December 31, 2000, was 8.5 yuan = $1. The average exchange rate during 2000 was 8 yuan = $1.

a. Compute the Canada Division's ROI for 2000 based on dollars.
b. Compute the China Division's ROI for 2000 based on yuan.
c. Which of Kline's two division's earned the better ROI in 2000? Explain your answer, complete with supporting computations.

3. Endicott Inc. has four divisions. Each division produces and sells a variety of industrial products. The company is developing a compensation plan for the division managers. Three options are being considered: (a) salary, (b) a performance-based incentive using RI, (c) mix of salary and a performance-based incentive using RI. What factors should be considered in designing this plan?

_____
_____
_____
_____
_____
_____
_____
_____

Answers to Chapter 24 Review Questions and Exercises

Completion Statements

1. represent top management's
2. ROI, RI, EVA
3. imputed
4. Current
5. incentives, risk
6. Moral hazard

True-False

1. T
2. F   ROI and RI are reversed in the statement. The correct statement is: A good reason for using RI as a performance measure rather than ROI is goal congruence is more likely to be promoted by using RI.
3. T
4. F   The statement is true except for one point. The approach described helps to *extend* managers' time horizon, not *shorten* it.
5. T
6. F   The argument cited is put forth by those who favour using *gross book value*, not *net book value*.
7. T
8. F   The statement accurately describes one of the two necessary conditions for moral hazard to exist. The other condition is the employee's effort cannot be accurately monitored and enforced.
9. T
10. T
11. T

Multiple Choice

1. b   Income $= 12\% \times \$3,000,000 = \$360,000$
   Revenues $= \$360,000 \div 0.04 = \$9,000,000$
2. c $\$9,000,000 \div \$3,000,000 = 3$ times
3. b   To answer this question, use assumed amounts. Assume the present ROI is 20% as follows:

$$\frac{\text{Revenues}}{\text{Investment}} \times \frac{\text{Income}}{\text{Revenues}} = \text{ROI}$$

$$\frac{\$100,000}{\$50,000} \times \frac{\$100,000 - \$90,000}{\$100,000} = 20\%$$

Using assumed amounts for the changes specified in the question, the effect on ROI in each of the answers is as follows:

a. Revenues increase by $30,000, which is the amount that costs and total assets increase:

$$\frac{\$130,000}{\$80,000} \times \frac{\$130,000 - \$120,000}{\$130,000} = 12.5\%$$

b. Revenues remain the same, costs decrease by $6,000, and total assets increase by $6,000:

$$\frac{\$100,000}{\$56,000} \times \frac{\$100,000 - \$84,000}{\$100,000} = 28.6\%$$

c. Revenues decrease by $5,000, costs increase by $5,000, and total assets remain the same:

$$\frac{\$95,000}{\$50,000} \times \frac{\$95,000 - \$95,000}{\$95,000} = 0\%$$

d. Revenues and costs increase by 15% and total assets increase by 15%:

$$\frac{\$100,000(1.15)}{\$50,000(1.15)} \times \frac{\$100,000(1.15) - \$90,000(1.15)}{\$100,000(1.15)} = \frac{\$115,000}{\$57,500} \times \frac{\$115,000 - \$103,500}{\$115,000} = 20\%$$

ROI increases in answer (b).

4. d Imputed interest cost = $500,000 − $180,000 = $320,000
      Investment = $320,000 ÷ 0.16 = $2,000,000

5. e $500,000 ÷ $2,000,000 = 25%

6. c Let B = Bonus
         B = ($110,000 − B) × 0.10
         B = $11,000 − 0.10B
     1.10B = $11,000
         B = $11,000 ÷ 1.10 = $10,000
   The income taxes of $40,000 should not be used in computing the bonus.

Exercise 1

a. ROI based on gross book value in the first year = $18,000 ÷ $200,000 = 9%
b. ROI based on gross book value in the sixth year = $18,000 ÷ $200,000 = 9%
c. ROI based on net book value at the end of the first year:

   Net book value at end of first year = $200,000 − [($200,000 − $0) ÷ 10]
                                        = $200,000 − $20,000 = $180,000

   ROI = $18,000 ÷ $180,000 = 10%

d. ROI based on net book value at the beginning of the sixth year:

   ROI = $18,000 ÷ (0.50 × $200,000)
       = $18,000 ÷ $100,000 = 18%

Exercise 2

a. Canada Division's ROI for 2000 = $\dfrac{\$2,400,000}{\$16,000,000}$ = 15%

b. China Division's ROI for 2000 = $\dfrac{11,400,000 \text{ yuan}}{75,000,000 \text{ yuan}}$ = 15.2%

c. Three steps are used to determine the answer. First, convert total assets in the China Division into dollars at the December 31, 1999, exchange rate, the rate prevailing when these assets were acquired (7.5 yuan = \$1):

$$\text{Total assets} = \frac{75,000,000 \text{ yuan}}{7.5 \text{ yuan per dollar}} = \$10,000,000$$

Second, convert operating income in the China Division into dollars at the average exchange rate prevailing during 2000 when the operating income was earned;

$$\frac{11,400,000 \text{ yuan}}{8 \text{ yuan per dollar}} = \$1,425,000$$

Third, compute the China Division's comparable ROI for 2000 $= \dfrac{\$1,425,000}{\$10,000,000} = 14.25\%$

The China Division's ROI measured in yuan is helped by the inflation that occurred in China during 2000 because inflation boosted the China Division's operating income. Given that the assets were acquired on December 31, 1999, the asset values should not be increased to reflect the inflation that occurred during 2000. The net effect of inflation on ROI computed in yuan is to use an inflated value in the numerator relative to the denominator. Adjusting for inflation using currency differences that represent differential inflation negates the effects of any differences in inflation rates between the two countries on the computation of ROI. After these adjustments, the Canada Division shows a higher ROI (15% from part (a) above) than the China Division (14.25%).

Exercise 3

The basic trade-off to consider in designing a compensation plan for the division managers is between creating incentives to get the managers to work hard and imposing risk on them. Compensation based on RI creates incentives for the managers to work hard, but they also bear risk because RI is affected by some factors outside their control. For example, a division manager may work hard but uncontrollable factors (such as economic conditions) may cause RI to be reduced, thereby reducing the manager's compensation. A salary, independent of RI performance, does not impose any risk on the managers but it also creates no incentives for them. For this reason, many companies use a mix of salary and a performance-based incentive—the salary component reduces risk while the performance-based component creates incentives.

Check Figures for Exercises

Chapter 1
1. No check figure
2. No check figure
3. No check figure

Chapter 2
1. (a) $7.20 (b) $747,000
2. 50,000 units
3. (a) $198,000 (b) $224,000 (c) $589,000

Chapter 3
1. (a) $135,000 (b) 3,000 tonnes
2. 2,025 units of T; 10,125 units of U
3. 833,334 units
4. (a) 10,200 units (b) 0.40

Chapter 4
1. (a) $11,000 underallocated (b) $91,700 (c) $205,800 (d) $12,600
2. No check figure
3. $4,250

Chapter 5
1. $59.57 per case
2. (a) Jason $7 undercosted
3. (b) Fuentes audit $36,000
4. (b) $0.849 per box (c) $1.362 per box

Chapter 6
1. (a) 665,720 (b) $3,034,320
2. Budgeted operating income $3,516,000
3. $161,280

Chapter 7
1. (a) Price variance $800 F, Efficiency variance $1,000 U
2. (a) $1,460 U (b) $10,660 F (c) 50,700 (d) $4.985 (e) $252,000 (f) $309,960

Chapter 8
1. (a) $2 (b) 600 (c) Spending variance $50 F
2. (a) $6 (b) Production-volume variance $120 U
3. (a) 121,000 (b) 115,000

Chapter 9
1. (a) $1,200,000 (b) $2,600,000 (c) $1,000,000 (d) $700,000 U (e) $2,400,000 (f) $1,400,000
   (g) $122,000 increase (h) $157,000 increase
2. (a1) $60 per machine-hour (a2) $780,000 (a3) Overallocated $40,000 (a4) $60,000 F
   (b) $135,000 U (c) $252,000 U

Chapter 10

1. $2 per unit
2. (a) $896,000 (b) 84% (c) $1,022,480
3. No check figure

Chapter 11

1. $14,000 decrease per month
2. 1,440 machine-hours used for T
3. (a) $900 increase (b) $1,250 decrease (c) $1,515 decrease
4. X=2; Y=3

Chapter 12

1. (a) $240 (b) 25%
2. (a) Operating income of Quick Tax $700,000

Chapter 13

1. (a) Industry-market-size factor $48,600 F
2. (a) Change in partial productivity for direct materials −2.0% (b) Change in total factor productivity +1.9%

Chapter 14

1. (a) $86,000 allocated to A (b) $91,000 allocated to A
2. (a) $10,800 decrease (b) $1,400 decrease (c) $1,200 decrease
3. (a) Adams $41,250 (b) Adams $48,000

Chapter 15

1. (a) T $750 (b) T $3,450 (c) T $1,898 (d) T $2,120
2. Gross margin $33,900

Chapter 16

1. (a) Bus tour $163 (b) Air travel $209
2. (a) $15,000 F (b) $13,000 U (c) $28,000 F
3. (a) Langley $89,280 (b) Langley $269,200

Chapter 17

1. (a4) $98,000 (b4) $98,500
2. (a) Model X $10,000 (b) Model X $39 per unit (c) Model X $3,400

Chapter 18

1. (a) 13,300 equivalent units of conversion costs (b) $105,840 (c) $25,200 (d) $1,260 (e) $70,700
2. (b) $158 (d) $133

Chapter 19

1. Produce 100 units of C and 30 units of P
2. (a) $100 (b) $300

Chapter 20

1. (a) $6,250 (b) $4,250 increase (c) 5 production runs
2. JIT saves $31,000
3. (a) credit Finished Goods Control $31,488,000 (b) debit Cost of Goods Sold twice: $31,488,000 and $800,000 (c) debit Inventory Control $480,000 (d) debit Finished Goods Control $32,800,000

Chapter 21

1. $5,590
2. 14.5%
3. (a) 3.57 years (b) 16.5%

Chapter 22

1. $124,560
2. (a) $54,978 (b) $23,324

Chapter 23

1. (a1) $15,000 disadvantage (a2) $20,000 advantage (b1) $11,000 advantage (b2) $46,000 advantage
2. (a) $175 per unit (b) Canada $0; Koren $46,500

Chapter 24

1. (a) 9% (b) 9% (c) 10% (d) 18%
2. (a) 15% (b) 15.2% (c) Canada Division 15% versus China Division 14.25%
3. No check figure